THE NEW Age OF Adventure

TEN YEARS *of* GREAT WRITING

THE
NEW
Age
OF
Adventure

TEN YEARS *of* GREAT WRITING

THE BEST OF  MAGAZINE

 NATIONAL GEOGRAPHIC

WASHINGTON, D.C.

Published by the National Geographic Society

1145 17th Street N.W., Washington, D.C. 20036

ISBN: 978-1-4262-0546-0

Library of Congress Cataloging-in-Publication Data

The new age of adventure : 10 years of great writing / edited by John Rasmus.
   p. cm.
 ISBN 978-1-4262-0546-0
 1. Voyages and travels. 2. Travelers' writings. I. Rasmus, John, 1954-
 G465.N485 2009
 808.8'0355--dc22

               2009018455

The National Geographic Society is one of the world's largest nonprofit scientific and educational organizations. Founded in 1888 to "increase and diffuse geographic knowledge," the Society works to inspire people to care about the planet. It reaches more than 325 million people worldwide each month through its official journal, *National Geographic,* and other magazines; National Geographic Channel; television documentaries; music; radio; films; books; DVDs; maps; exhibitions; school publishing programs; interactive media; and merchandise. National Geographic has funded more than 9,000 scientific research, conservation and exploration projects and supports an education program combating geographic illiteracy.

For more information, please call 1-800-NGS LINE (647-5463) or write to the following address:

National Geographic Society
1145 17th Street N.W.
Washington, D.C. 20036-4688 U.S.A.

Visit us online at www.nationalgeographic.com

For information about special discounts for bulk purchases, please contact
National Geographic Books Special Sales: ngspecsales@ngs.org

For rights or permissions inquiries, please contact National Geographic Books
Subsidiary Rights: ngbookrights@ngs.org

Printed in the United States of America

Interior design: Cameron Zotter

09/WOR/1

INTRODUCTION

By John Rasmus

———

WHAT IS ADVENTURE? First of all, it's a big idea: On some level, everybody wants their lives to be one. The spirit of adventure makes us want to explore the world, take some risks, and have rich, surprising, memorable experiences. It's driven generations of National Geographic writers, photographers, and researchers, and, for the past ten years, a new generation for National Geographic ADVENTURE magazine. For us as editors it's meant a steady stream of great stories—and now this collection of the best of them.

What is the "new age" of adventure? Ten years ago, at the end of the 20th century, we still had one foot in the classic age of exploration. In our first issue, we paid tribute to geographers Brad and Barbara Washburn, then in their 80s, who literally filled in some of the last blank spaces on the map, from Everest to the Alaska Range. We recognized Ian Baker, who rediscovered the hidden falls of Tibet's Tsangpo River Gorge, and profiled Robert Ballard, the great underwater explorer who found the wreckage of the *Titanic*.

Since then, however, we have been making a subtle transition. Here in the 21st century, as the futurist (and National Geographic Emerging Explorer) Andrew Zolli puts it, we are moving from "the age of exploration to the age of conservation." We know that there aren't many more blank spots on the map. We understand that we live on a small planet with a thin layer of atmosphere surrounding it, with more people making ever greater use of its resources. The last rain forests are being cut down for timber and agriculture, species large and small are threatened or reduced to small, protected populations. The climate has changed. And so has the mission of the National Geographic Society. Over the past 121 years our mission statement has evolved from promoting "the increase and diffusion of geographic knowledge"—very much in the spirit of exploration, circa 1888—to "inspiring people to care about the planet." It's a recognition that if we aren't careful, the things we have discovered and valued during the age of exploration can be lost forever. Our stories reflect that reality too.

As you read these pieces, keep that in mind. Some of them, like David Roberts's account of the life, death, and rediscovery of George Mallory, are pure old-fashioned adventures—men and women with big dreams trying to reach the ends of the Earth. Others, like his story about Everett Ruess, a mystery he helped solve after 75 years, have a second dimension—and sometimes a third and a fourth. Sebastian Junger's moving profile of Ahmad Shah Massoud, the great Afghan resistance fighter, reminds us that we don't simply live in a world of heroic causes and ideals, but also of the great costs that come with war. Paul Kvinta's "Stomping Grounds," on the intrusion of elephants into the human communities of India (or vice versa), examines the enormous challenges of population growth and habitat destruction. Gretel Ehrlich's story of a lost tribe of Siberian reindeer herders is a glimpse of a people whose existence was all but forgotten—until they were about to disappear. Peter Matthiessen's "Emperors at the End of the Earth," on the astoundingly harsh lives of Antarctica's emperor penguins, is also a haunting meditation on the hardiness and fragility of life. Laurence Gonzales's stories about people in harrowing survival situations teach us how to tackle big problems, not only when we are lost in the wild, but when life takes unexpected and threatening turns. The survivor's secret, he says, is to face the reality of the situation and never give up, even if you know you may not succeed. Good advice as we move from the last great era to the next.

If the subtexts are serious, don't let that fool you: The writers enjoy (almost) every minute of it, and so do we. Often, on their way home from their adventures, they come back through our offices in New York to tell us about them. Sometimes I'll be in my office with the door closed, talking on the phone about three-year plans or looking at layouts, and hear the sounds of incoming writers. Anything from boisterous greetings to muffled howls. Then loud knocking on my door. Deputy editor Steve Byers—who assigned, edited, and selected many of these stories—will be there with somebody who's just back from somewhere, with stuff they can't wait to tell. They come in, and they're into it. Scott Anderson's eyes narrow as he talks about a bar brawl in Lhasa, patting his shirt pocket for a cigarette he can't smoke. Tim Cahill chuckles happily at his own jokes, trying out some of the material we'll read . . . whenever he turns in his manuscript. Kira Salak matter-of-factly lays out the most extreme stories of man's inhumanity to man and beast, then smiles serenely. As they unspool the tales they've brought back, sometimes at crazy risk to themselves, they never, ever say they wish they hadn't gone through the hassle of having a great adventure and sharing it with the world. Or more specifically with you, again, right now.

I.

REPORTING FROM THE EDGE

THE LION IN WINTER

By Sebastian Junger

———

*In November 2000, Afghanistan was way off the geopolitical radar and
falling under the control of Islamic fundamentalists called the Taliban.
One man, the warrior Ahmad Shah Massoud, stood tall against this violent
group's grip on the nation. For his profile of Massoud, the author of*
The Perfect Storm *spent a month with the "Lion of Panjshir" as he waged
his guerrilla war, finding a character and a story that would prove prophetic.*

THE FIGHTERS WERE DOWN BY THE RIVER, getting ready to cross over, and we drove out there in the late afternoon to see them off. We parked our truck behind a mud wall, where it was out of sight, and then walked one by one down to the position. In an hour or so, it would be dark, and they'd go over. Some were loading up an old Soviet truck with crates of ammunition, and some were cleaning their rifles, and some were just standing in loose bunches behind the trees, where the enemy couldn't see them. They were wearing old snow parkas and blankets thrown over their shoulders, and some had old Soviet Army pants, and others didn't have any shoes. They drew themselves into an uneven line when we walked up, and they stood there with their Kalashnikovs and their RPGs cradled in their arms, smiling shyly.

ACROSS THE FLOODPLAIN, low, grassy hills turned purple as the sun sank behind them, and those were the hills these men were going to attack. They were fighting for Ahmad Shah Massoud—genius guerrilla leader, last hope of the shattered Afghan government—and all along those hills were trenches filled with Taliban soldiers. The Taliban had grown out of the *madrasahs,* or religious schools, that had sprung up in Pakistan during the Soviet invasion, and they had emerged in 1994 as Afghanistan sank into anarchy following the

Soviet withdrawal. Armed and trained by Pakistan and driven by moral principles so extreme that many Muslims feel they can only be described as a perversion of Islam, the Taliban quickly overran most of the country and imposed their iron-fisted version of koranic law. Adulterers faced stoning; women's rights became nonexistent. Only Pakistan, Saudi Arabia, and the United Arab Emirates recognize their government as legitimate, but it is generally thought that the rest of the world will have to follow suit if the Taliban complete their takeover of the country. The only thing that still stands in their way are the last-ditch defenses of Ahmad Shah Massoud.

The sun set, and the valley edged into darkness. It was a clear, cold November night, and we could see artillery rounds flashing against the ridgeline in the distance. Hundreds of Taliban soldiers were dug in up there, waiting to be attacked, and hundreds of Massoud's soldiers were down here along the Kowkcheh River, waiting to attack them. In a few hours, they would cross the river by truck and make their way through the fields and destroyed villages of no-man's-land. Then it would begin.

We wished Massoud's men well and walked back to the truck. The stars had come out, and the only sound was of dogs baying in the distance. Then the whole front line, from the Tajik border to Farkhar Gorge, rumbled to life.

I'D WANTED TO MEET MASSOUD FOR YEARS, ever since I'd first heard of his remarkable defense of Afghanistan against the Soviets in the 1980s. A brilliant strategist and an uncompromising fighter, Massoud had been the bane of the Soviet army's existence and had been largely responsible for finally driving them out of the country. He was fiercely independent, accepting little, if any, direction from Pakistan, which controlled the flow of American arms to the *mujahidin*. His independence made it impossible for the CIA to trust him, but agency officials grudgingly admitted that he was an almost mythological figure among many Afghans. He was a native of the Panjshir Valley, north of Kabul, the third of six sons born to an ethnic Tajik army officer. In 1974, he went to college to study engineering, but he dropped out in his first year to join a student resistance movement. After a crackdown on dissidents, Massoud fled to Pakistan, where he underwent military training. By 1979, when the Soviet Union invaded Afghanistan to prop up the teetering communist government, Massoud had already collected a small band of resistance fighters in the Panjshir Valley.

As a guerrilla base, the Panjshir couldn't have been better. Protected by the mountain ranges of the Hindu Kush and blocked at the entrance by a narrow gorge named Dalan Sang, the 70-mile-long valley was the perfect staging area for raids against a highway that supplied the Soviet bases around Kabul, Afghanistan's capital. Massoud quickly organized his Panjshiri fighters—rumored to number as few as 3,000 men—into defense groups comprising four or five villages each. The groups were self-sufficient and could call in mobile units if they were threatened with being overrun. Whenever a Soviet convoy rumbled up the highway, the mujahidin would mine the road, then wait in ambush. Most of the fighters would provide covering fire while a few insanely brave men worked their way in close to the convoy and tried to take out the first and last vehicles with rocket-propelled grenades. With the convoy pinned down, the rest of the unit would pepper it with gunfire and then retreat. They rarely stood and fought, and the Soviets rarely pursued them beyond the protection of their armored vehicles. It was classic guerrilla warfare, and, if anything, Massoud was amazed at how easy it was. For his defense of the valley, Massoud became known as the "Lion of Panjshir."

Very quickly, the Soviets understood that there was no way to control Afghanistan without controlling the Panjshir Valley, and they started attacking it with forces of up to 15,000 men, backed by tanks, artillery, and massive air support. Massoud knew that he couldn't stop them, and he didn't even try. He would evacuate as many civilians as possible and then retreat to the surrounding peaks of the Hindu Kush; when the Soviets entered the Panjshir, they would find it completely deserted. That was when the real fighting began. Massoud and his men slept in caves and prayed to Allah and lived on nothing but bread and dried mulberries; they killed Russians with guns taken from other dead Russians; and they kept fighting, until the Soviets simply couldn't afford to fight anymore. Then the Soviets would pull back, and the whole cycle would start all over again.

Between 1979 and their withdrawal ten years later, the Soviets launched nine major offensives into the Panjshir Valley. They never took it. They tried assassinating Massoud, but his intelligence network always warned him in time. They made local peace deals, but he used the respite to organize resistance elsewhere in the country. The ultimate Soviet humiliation came in the mid-eighties, after the Red Army had lost hundreds of soldiers trying to take the Panjshir. The mujahidin had shot down a Soviet helicopter, and some resourceful Panjshiri mechanic patched it up, put a truck engine in it, and started running it up and down the valley as a bus. The Soviets got wind of this, and the next time their troops invaded, the commanders decided to remove the helicopter. The last thing they must have seen was a flash; Massoud's men had packed it with explosives.

THE NIGHT ATTACK ON THE TALIBAN positions began with waves of Kat-yusha rockets streaming from Massoud's positions and arcing across the valley. The rockets were fired in volleys of ten or twelve, and we could see the red glare of their engines wobble through the darkness and then wink out one by one as they found their trajectories and headed for their targets. Occasionally an incoming round would explode somewhere down the line with a sound like a huge oak door being slammed shut. The artillery exchange lasted an hour, and then the ground assault started, Massoud's men moving under the cover of darkness through minefields and machine gun fire toward the Taliban trenches. The fighting was three or four miles away and came to us only as a soft, frantic *pap-pap-pap* across the valley.

We had driven to a hilltop command post to watch the attack. The position had a code name, *Darya*, which means "river" in Dari, the Persian dialect that's Afghanistan's lingua franca, and on the radio we could hear field commanders yelling "Darya! Darya! Darya!" as they called in reports or shouted for artillery. The commander of the position, a gentle-looking man in his 30s named Harun, was dressed for war in corduroy pants and a cardigan. He was responsible for all the artillery on the front line; we found him in a bunker, studying maps by the light of a kerosene lantern. He was using a schoolboy's plastic protractor to figure out trajectory angles for his tanks.

Harun was working three radios and consulting the map continually. After a while, a soldier brought in tea, and we sat cross-legged on the floor and drank it. Calls kept streaming in on the radios. "We've just captured another position—it's got a big ammo depot," one commander shouted. Another reported, "The enemy has no morale at all; they're just running away. We've just taken ten more prisoners."

Harun showed us on the map what was happening. As we spoke, Massoud's men were taking small positions around the ridgeline and moving into the hills on either side of a town called Khvajeh Ghar, which was at a critical part of the front line. Khvajeh Ghar was held by Pakistani and Arab volunteers, part of an odd assortment of foreigners—Burmese, Chinese, Chechens, Arabs, Algerians—who are fighting alongside the Taliban to spread fundamentalist Islam throughout Central Asia. Their presence here is partly due to Saudi extremist Osama bin Laden, who has been harbored by the Taliban since 1997 and is said to repay his hosts with millions of dollars and thousands of holy warriors. The biggest supporter of the Taliban, however, is Pakistan, which has sent commando teams, military advisers, and regular-army troops. More than a hundred Pakistani prisoners of war sit in Massoud's jails; most of them—like the Taliban—are ethnic Pashtuns who trained in the madrasahs.

None of the help was doing the Taliban fighters much good at the moment, though. Harun switched his radio to a Taliban frequency and tilted it toward us. They were being overrun, and the panic in their voices was unmistakable. One commander screamed that he was almost out of ammunition; another started insulting the fighters at a neighboring position. "Are you crazy are you crazy are you crazy?" he demanded. "They've already taken a hundred prisoners! Do you want to be taken prisoner as well?" He went on to accuse them all of sodomy.

Harun shook his head incredulously. "They are supposed to represent true Islam," he said. "Do you see how they talk?"

I WENT INTO AFGHANISTAN WITH IRANIAN-BORN photographer Reza Deghati, who knew Massoud well from several long trips he'd taken into the country during the Soviet occupation. Back then, the only way in was to take a one- to three-month trek over the Hindu Kush on foot, avoiding minefields and Russian helicopters, and every time Reza did it he lost 20 or 30 pounds. The conditions are vastly easier now but still unpredictable. Last summer, in a desperate effort to force international recognition for their regime, the Taliban launched a six-month offensive that was supposed to be the coup de grâce for Massoud. Some 15,000 Taliban fighters—heavily reinforced, according to Massoud's intelligence network, by Pakistani Army units—bypassed the impregnable Panjshir Valley and drove straight north toward the border of Tajikistan. Their goal was to move eastward along the border until Massoud was completely surrounded, and then starve him out. They almost succeeded. Waiting to go into Afghanistan that September and October, Reza and I watched one town after another fall into Taliban hands, until even Massoud's old friends began to wonder if he wasn't through. "It may be his last season hunting," as one journalist put it.

Massoud finally stopped the Taliban at the Kowkcheh River, but by then the season was so far advanced that the mountain roads were snowbound, and the only way for Reza and me to get in was by helicopter from the Tajik capital of Dushanbe. Massoud's forces owned half a dozen aging Russian military helicopters, and the Afghan Embassy in Dushanbe could put you on a flight that left at a moment's notice, whenever the weather cleared over the mountains. On November 15, late in the afternoon, Reza and I got the word. We raced to the airfield, and two hours later we were in Afghanistan.

The helicopters flew to a small town just across the border called Khvajeh Baha od Din, and we were provided a floor to sleep on in the home of a former mujahidin commander who was now a local judge. Each night, anywhere from ten to twenty fighters stayed there, sleeping in rows on the floor next to us. The electricity was supplied by a homemade waterwheel that had been geared to a generator through an old truck transmission. Some fuel came in by truck over the mountains—a five-day trip—but farther north it all came in by donkey and cost $20 a gallon. (The locals jokingly refer to donkeys as "Afghan motorcycles.") We washed at an outdoor spring and subsisted on rice and mutton and kept warm at night around a woodstove; we lived comfortably enough. The situation around us, though, was unspeakable.

Eighty thousand civilians had fled the recent fighting—adding to the 100,000 or so who were already displaced in the north—and thousands of them were subsisting in a makeshift refugee camp along the Kowkcheh River half a mile away. They slept under tattered blue UN tarps and had so little food that some were reduced to eating grass. Tribal politics have long dominated Afghanistan; many observers, in fact, say that Massoud, a Tajik, will never be able to unite the country. These refugees were mostly ethnic Tajik and Uzbeks, and they claimed that when the Taliban—who are Pashtun—took over a town, they raped the women, killed the men, and sold the young into servitude. One old man at a refugee camp pulled back his quilted coat to show me a six-inch scar on his stomach. A Taliban soldier, he said, had stabbed him with a bayonet and left him for dead.

A WEEK OR SO AFTER WE ARRIVED INSIDE AFGHANISTAN, Reza and I were told that Massoud was coming in—he'd been in Tajikistan negotiating support from the government—and we rushed down to the river to meet him. A lopsided boat made of sheet metal, powered by a tractor engine that had paddle wheels instead of tires, churned across the Kowkcheh with Massoud in the bow. He wore khaki pants and Czech army boots and a smart camouflage jacket over a V-neck sweater. He looked to be in his late 40s and was as lean and spare as the photographs of him from the Soviet days. He was not tall, but he stood as if he were. The great man stepped onto the riverbank along with a dozen bodyguards and greeted us, then we all drove off to the judge's compound in Khvajeh Baha od Din.

There, he met with his commanders, listened to their preparations for the coming offensive, then hurried off. We later found out that he'd been forced to return to Tajikistan because of a chronically bad back; apparently the problem was so severe that it had put him in the hospital.

Finding ourselves once again waiting for Massoud, Reza and I decided to go out to the front line to see a position that had just been taken from the Taliban.

We drove south along the Kowkcheh, past miles of trenches and bunkers, and stopped at an old Soviet base that had been gutted by artillery fire. The local commander was there, housed in the shell of the building. The wind whistled through the gaping windows, and his soldiers crouched in the shadows, preparing their weapons. The commander said that the position they'd taken was code-named Joy and that the bodies of the dead Taliban were still lying in the trenches.

He made a call on his radio and arranged for some men and pack horses to meet us on the other side of the river. Then he directed us to the crossing point; it was in a canyon a few miles away, just below a town called Laleh Meydan. When we stopped there to sort our gear, a Taliban MiG jet appeared and made a pass over the town, completely ignoring the antiaircraft fire that was directed at it. The townsmen scattered but drifted back within minutes to help us carry our gear down to the river. The raft that was to ferry us across was made from a design that must have been around since Alexander the Great: eight cowhides sewn shut and inflated like tires, each stoppered by a wood plug in one leg and lashed to a frame made of tree limbs. Four old men paddled it across the river and then tied our gear to some horses. Three soldiers with Kalashnikovs were waiting to take us to the front.

It took us all afternoon to get there, walking and riding through mud hills, bare and smooth as velvet, that undulated southward toward the Hindu Kush. There was no sound but the wind—not even any fighting—and nothing to look at but the hills and the great, empty sky. When we turned the last ridgeline, we saw Massoud's men silhouetted on a hilltop, waving us on.

Maybe the Taliban spotted our horses, or maybe they'd overheard the radio communications, but we were halfway up the last slope when I found myself facedown in the dirt as a Taliban rocket slammed into the hillside behind us. Then we were up and running, and the next rocket hit just as we got to the top, and they continued to come in, slightly off target, as we crouched in the safety of the trenches.

There was nothing exciting about it, nothing even abstractly interesting. It was purely, exclusively bad. Whenever the Taliban fired off another salvo, a spotter on a nearby hilltop would radio our position to say that more were on the way. The commander would shout a warning, and the fighters would pull us down into the foxholes, and then we'd wait five or ten seconds until we heard the last, awful whistling sound right before they hit. In a foxhole, you're safe unless the shell drops right in there with you, in which case you'd never know it—you'd simply cease to exist. No matter how small the odds were, the idea that I could go straight from life to nonexistence was almost unbearable;

it turned each ten-second wait into a bizarre exercise in existentialism. Bravery—the usual alternative to fear—also held no appeal, because bravery could get you killed. It had become very simple: It was their war, their problem, and I didn't want any part of it. I just wanted off the hill.

The problem was, "off" meant rising up out of this good Afghan dirt we'd become part of and running back the way we'd come. Four hundred yards away was a hilltop that they weren't shelling; over there, it was just another normal, sunny day. After we'd spent half an hour ducking the shells, the commander said he'd just received word that Taliban troops were preparing to attack the position, and it might be better if we weren't around for it. Like it or not, we had to leave. Reza and I waited for a quiet spell and then climbed out of the trenches, took a deep breath, and started off down the hill.

Mainly there was the sound of my breathing: a deep, desperate rasp that ruled out any chance of hearing the rockets come in. The commander stood on the hilltop as we left, shouting good-bye and waving us away from a minefield that lay on one side of the slope. Ten minutes later, it was over: We sat behind the next ridge and watched Taliban rockets continue to pound the hill, each one raising a little puff of smoke, followed by a muffled explosion. From that distance, they didn't look like much—they almost looked like the kind of explosions you could imagine yourself acting bravely in.

The Taliban kept up the shelling for the next 12 hours and then attacked at dawn. Massoud's men fought them off with no casualties.

MASSOUD RETURNED ONE WEEK LATER, flying in by helicopter to Harun's command post to start planning a heavy offensive across the entire northern front. The post was at the top of a steep, grassy hill in some broken country south of a frontline town called Dasht-e Qaleh. It was late afternoon by the time we arrived, and Massoud was studying the Taliban positions through a pair of massive military binoculars on a tripod. The deposed Afghan government's foreign minister, a slight, serious man named Dr. Abdullah, walked up to greet us as we got out of the truck. Reza wished him a good evening.

"Good morning," Dr. Abdullah corrected, nodding toward the Taliban positions across the valley. "Our day is just beginning."

The shelling had started again, an arrhythmic thumping in the distance that suggested nothing of the terror it can produce up close. That morning, I'd awakened from a dream in which an airplane was dropping bombs on me, and in the dream I'd thrown myself on the ground and watched one of the bombs bounce past me toward a picnicking family. Good, I'd thought; it will kill them and not me. It was an ugly, ungenerous dream that left me unsettled all day.

Massoud knew where the Taliban positions were, and they obviously knew where his were, and the upshot was that you were never entirely safe. A guy in town had just had both legs torn off by a single, random shell. You couldn't let yourself start thinking about it or you'd never stop.

Massoud was still at the binoculars. He had a face like a hatchet. Four deep lines cut across his forehead, and his almond-shaped eyes were so thickly lashed that it almost looked as if he were wearing eyeliner. When someone spoke, he swiveled his head around and affixed the speaker with a gaze so penetrating it occasionally made the recipient stutter. When he asked a question, it was very specific, and he listened to every word of the answer. He stood out not so much because he was handsome but simply because he was hard to stop looking at.

I asked Dr. Abdullah how Massoud's back was doing. Dr. Abdullah spoke low so that Massoud couldn't hear him. "He says it's better, but I know it's not," he said. "I can see by the way he walks. He needs at least a month's rest . . . but, of course, that won't be possible."

The shelling got heavier, and the sun set, and Massoud and his bodyguards and generals lined up on top of the bunker to pray. The prayer went on for a long time, the men standing, kneeling, prostrating themselves, standing again, their hands spread toward the sky to accept Allah. Islam is an extraordinarily tolerant religion—more so than Christianity, in some ways—but it is also strangely pragmatic. Turning the other cheek is not a virtue. The prophet Muhammad, after receiving the first revelations of the Koran in A.D. 610, was forced into war against the corrupt Quraysh rulers of Mecca, who persecuted him for trying to make Arab society more egalitarian and to unite it under one god. Outnumbered three to one, his fighters defeated the Quraysh in 627 at the Battle of the Trench, outside Medina. Three years later, he marched 10,000 men into Mecca and established the reign of Islam. Muhammad was born during an era of brutal tribal warfare, and he would have been useless to humanity as a visionary and a man of peace if he had not also known how to fight.

It was cold and almost completely dark when the prayers were finished. Massoud abruptly stood, folded his prayer cloth, and strode into the bunker, attended by Dr. Abdullah and a few commanders. We followed and joined them on the floor. A soldier brought in a pot for us to wash our hands, then spread platters of rice and mutton on a blanket. Massoud asked Dr. Abdullah for a pen, and Dr. Abdullah drew one out of his tailored cashmere jacket.

"I recognize that pen—it's mine," Massoud said. He was joking.

"Well, in a sense everything we have is yours," Dr. Abdullah replied.

"Don't change the topic—right now I'm talking about this pen." Massoud wagged his finger at Dr. Abdullah, then turned to the serious business of preparing the offensive.

Massoud's strategy was simple and exploited the fact that—no matter how one looked at it—he was losing the war. After five years of fighting, the Taliban had fractured his alliance and cut its territory in half. Massoud was confined to the mountainous northeast, which, although easily defensible, depended on long, tortuous supply lines to Tajikistan. The Russians, ironically, had begun supplying Massoud with arms—with the Taliban near their borders, they couldn't afford to hold a grudge—and India and Iran were helping as well. It all had to go through Tajikistan. The most serious threat to Massoud's supply lines came last fall when he lost a strategically important town called Taloqan, just west of the Kowkcheh River. The Taliban, convinced that recapturing Taloqan was of supreme importance to Massoud, shipped the bulk of their forces over to the Taloqan front. Massoud arrayed his forces in a huge V around the town and began a series of focused, stabbing attacks, usually at night, that guaranteed that the Taliban would remain convinced that he would do anything to retake the town.

In the meantime, he was thinking on a completely different scale. Massoud had been fighting for 21 years, longer than most of the Taliban conscripts had been alive. In that context, Taloqan didn't matter, the next six months didn't matter—all that mattered was that the Afghan resistance survive long enough for the Taliban to implode on their own. The trump card of any resistance movement is that it doesn't have to win; the guerrillas just have to stay in the hills until the invaders lose their will to fight. The Afghans fought off the British three times and the Soviets once, and now Massoud was five years into a war that Pakistan could not support forever. Moreover, the civilian population in Taliban-controlled areas had started to bridle under the conscription of soldiers and the harshness of Taliban law. Last summer, in fact, a full-fledged revolt boiled over in a town called Musa Qaleh, and the Taliban had to send in 600 troops to crush it. "Every day, I bathe in the river without my pistol," the local Taliban governor later told a reporter, with no apparent irony. "What better proof is there that the people love us?" The end of the Taliban, it seemed, was only a matter of time.

The Dari word for war is *jang*, and as Massoud ate his mutton, he explained to his commanders that within weeks he would start a *jang-e-gerilla-yee*. Here in the north he was locked into a frontline war that neither side could win, but he had groups of fighters everywhere—even deep in areas the Taliban thought they controlled. "In the coming days, we will engage the Taliban all over

Afghanistan," he announced. "Pakistan brought us conventional war; I'm preparing a guerrilla war. It will start in a few weeks from now, even a few days."

Massoud had done the same thing to the Soviets. In 1985, he had disappeared into the mountains for three months to train 120 commandos and had sent each of them out across Afghanistan to train a hundred more. These 12,000 men would attack the vital supply routes of the cumbersome Soviet Army. They used an operations map that had been found in a downed Soviet helicopter, and they took their orders from Massoud, who had informers throughout the Soviet military, even up to staff general. All across Afghanistan, Russian soldiers traded their weapons for drugs and food. Morale was so bad that there were gun battles breaking out among the Soviet soldiers themselves.

Dinner finished, Massoud spread the map out on the floor and bent over it, plotting routes and firing questions at his commanders. He wanted to know how many tanks they had, how many missile launchers, how much artillery. He wanted to know where the weapons were and whether their positions had been changed according to his orders. He occasionally interrupted his planning to deliver impromptu lectures, his elegant hands slicing the air for emphasis or a single finger shaking in the harsh light of the kerosene lantern. His commanders—many of them older than he, most veterans of the Soviet war—listened in slightly chastised silence, like schoolboys who hadn't done their homework.

"The type of operation you have planned for tonight might not be so successful, but that's OK—it should continue," he said. "This is not our main target. We're just trying to get them to bring reinforcements so they take casualties. The main thrust will be elsewhere."

Massoud was so far ahead of his commanders that at times he seemed unable to decide whether to explain his thinking or to just give them orders and hope for the best. The Soviets—having lost as many as 15,000 men in Afghanistan—reportedly now study his tactics in the military academies. And here he was, two decades later, still waging war from some bunker, still trying to get his commanders to grasp the logic of what he was doing.

It was getting late, but Massoud wasn't even close to being finished. He has been known to work for 36 hours straight, sleeping for two or three minutes at a time. There was work to do, and his men might die if it wasn't done well, and so he sat poring over an old Soviet map, coaxing secrets from it that the Taliban might have missed. At one point, he turned to one of the young commanders and asked him whether he could fix the hulk of a tank that sat rusting on a nearby hill.

"I have already been up there to see it," the young man said. "I have fixed tanks much worse than that."

There were a total of three destroyed tanks; Massoud thought they could all be salvaged. One was stuck in an alleyway between two houses, and the young commander said the passageway was too narrow for them to drag it out. "Buy the houses, destroy them, and get it out," Massoud said. "Get two more tanks from Rostaq; that's five. Paint them like new and show them on the streets so people will see them. Then the Taliban will think we're getting help from another country."

On and on it went, commander by commander, detail by detail. *Don't shell from Ay Khanom hill; you're just wasting your ammunition. Don't shell any positions near houses or towns; the Taliban are too deeply dug in in those spots and you'll just hurt civilians. Send your men forward in jeeps to save the heavy machinery and shell heavily beforehand to raise a lot of dust. That way, the Taliban won't see the attack.*

When Massoud was growing up in Kabul, he was part of a neighborhood gang that had regular battles with other gangs. One particularly large gang would occupy a hilltop near his house, and he and his friends would go out and challenge them. Naturally enough, Massoud was the leader. He would split his force, sending one half straight up the hill while the other half circled around and attacked from the rear. It always worked. It still worked.

Massoud sat cross-legged on the floor, bent forward at the waist, methodically opening and eating pistachios. His head hung low and swung from side to side as he spoke. He had a slight tic that ran like a shiver up his back and into his shoulders. "Get me your best guys," he said, looking around. "I don't want hundreds. I want 60 of your best. Sixty from each commander. Tomorrow I want to launch the best possible war."

LIKE SO MANY FUNDAMENTALIST MOVEMENTS, the Taliban were born of war. After the Soviet Union invaded Afghanistan on December 27, 1979, it ultimately sent in eight armored divisions, two enhanced parachute battalions, hundreds of attack helicopters, and well over 100,000 men. What should have been the quick crushing of a backward country, however, turned into the worst Soviet defeat of the Cold War. The very weaknesses of the fledgling resistance movement—its lack of military bases, its paucity of weapons, its utterly fractured command structure—meant that the Soviets had no fixed military objectives to destroy. Fighting Afghans was like nailing jelly to a wall; in the end, there was just a wall full of bent nails. Initially using nothing but old shotguns, flintlock rifles, and Lee-Enfield .303s left over from British colonial days, the mujahidin started attacking Soviet convoys and military bases all across Afghanistan. According to a CIA report at the time, the typical life span of a mujahidin RPG operator—rocket-propelled grenades were the anti-tank weapon of choice—was three weeks. It's not unreasonable to assume that every Afghan who took up arms against the Soviets fully expected to die.

Without the support of the villagers, however, the mujahidin would never have been able to defeat the Soviets. They would have had nothing to eat, nowhere to hide, no information network—none of the things a guerrilla army depends on. The Soviets knew this, of course, and by the end of the first year—increasingly frustrated by the stubborn mujahidin resistance—they turned the dim Cyclops eye of their military on the people themselves. They destroyed any village the mujahidin were spotted in. They carpet bombed the Panjshir Valley. They cut down fruit trees, disrupted harvests, tortured villagers. They did whatever they could to drive a wedge between the people and the resistance. And still, it didn't work. After ten years of war, the Soviets finally pulled out of Afghanistan, leaving behind a country full of land mines and more than one million Afghan dead.

A country can't sustain that kind of damage and return to normal overnight. The same fierce tribalism that had defeated the Soviets—"radical local democracy," as the CIA termed it—made it extremely hard for the various mujahidin factions to get along. (It would be three years before they would be able to take Kabul from the communist regime that the Soviets had left.) Moreover, the mujahidin were armed to the teeth, thanks to a CIA program that had pumped three billion dollars' worth of weapons into the country during the war. Had the United States continued its support—building roads, repatriating the refugees, clearing the minefields—Afghanistan might have stood a chance of overcoming its natural ethnic factionalism. But the U.S. didn't. No sooner had the Soviet-backed government crumbled away than America's Cold War-born interest in Afghanistan virtually ceased. Inevitably, the Afghans fell out among themselves. And when they did, it was almost worse than the war that had just ended.

The weapons supplied by the U.S. to fight the Soviets had been distributed through Pakistan's infamous Inter-Services Intelligence branch. The ISI, as it is known, had chosen a rabidly anti-Western ideologue named Gulbuddin Hekmatyar to protect its strategic interests in Afghanistan, so of course the bulk of the weapons went to him. Now, using Hekmatyar to reach deep into Afghan politics, Pakistan systematically crippled any chance of a successful coalition government. As fighting flared around Kabul, Hekmatyar positioned himself in the hills south of the city and started raining rockets down on the rooftops. His strategy was to pound the various mujahidin factions into submission and gain control of the capital, but he succeeded merely in killing tens of thousands of civilians. Finally, in exchange for peace, he was given the post of prime minister. But his troops remained where they were, the barrels of their tanks still pointed down at the city they had largely destroyed.

While the commanders fought on, life in Afghanistan sank into a lawless hell. Warlords controlled the highways, opium and weapons smuggling became the mainstay of the economy, private armies battled one another for control of a completely ruined land. This was one of the few times that Massoud's forces are thought to have committed outright atrocities, massacring several hundred to several thousand people in the Afshar district of Kabul. There is no evidence, however, that Massoud gave the orders or knew about it beforehand. As early as 1994, Pakistan—dismayed by the fighting and increasingly convinced that Hekmatyar was a losing proposition—began to look elsewhere for allies. Its attention fell on the Taliban, who had been slowly gaining power in the madrasahs while Afghanistan tore itself apart. The Taliban were religious students, many of them Afghan refugees in Pakistan, who were trained in an extremely conservative interpretation of the Koran called Deobandism. Here, in the tens of thousands of teenage boys who had been orphaned or displaced by the war, Pakistan found its new champions.

Armed and directed by Pakistan and facing a completely fractured alliance, the Taliban rapidly fought their way across western Afghanistan. The population was sick of war and looked to the Taliban as saviors—which, in a sense, they were, but their brand of salvation came at a tremendous price. They quickly imposed a form of Islam that was so archaic and cruel that it shocked even the ultratraditional Muslims of the countryside. With the Taliban closing in on Kabul, Massoud found himself forced into alliances with men—such as Hekmatyar and former communist Abdul Rashid Dostum—who until recently had been his mortal enemies. The coalition was a shaky one and didn't stand a chance against the highly motivated Taliban forces. After heavy fighting, Kabul finally fell to the Taliban in early September 1996, and Massoud pulled his forces back to the Panjshir Valley. With him were Burhanuddin Rabbani, who was the acting president of the coalition government, and a shifty assortment of mujahidin commanders who became known as the Northern Alliance. Technically, Rabbani and his ministers were the recognized government of Afghanistan—they still held a seat at the UN—but in reality, all they controlled was the northern third of one of the poorest countries in the world.

Worse still, there was a growing movement from a variety of Western countries—particularly the United States—to overlook the Taliban's flaws and recognize them as the legitimate government of the country. There was thought to be as much as 200 billion barrels of untapped oil reserves in Central Asia and similar amounts of natural gas. That made it one of the largest fossil fuel reserves in the world, and the easiest way to get it out was to build a pipeline across Afghanistan to Pakistan. However appalling Taliban rule might be, their cooperation was needed to build the pipeline. Within days of the Taliban takeover of Kabul, a U.S. State Department spokesman said that he could see "nothing objectionable" about the Taliban's version of Islamic law.

While Massoud and the Taliban fought each other to a standstill at the mouth of the Panjshir Valley, the American oil company Unocal hosted a Taliban delegation to explore the possibility of an oil deal.

THE DAY BEFORE THE OFFENSIVE, Massoud decided to go to the front line for a close look at the Taliban. He couldn't tell if the attack, as planned, would succeed in taking their ridge-top positions; he was worried that his men would die in a frontal assault when they could just as easily slip around back. He had been watching the Taliban supply trucks through the binoculars and had determined that there was only one road leading to their forward positions. If his men could take that, the Taliban would have to withdraw.

Massoud goes everywhere quickly, and this time was no exception. He jumped up from a morning meeting with his commanders, stormed out to his white Land Cruiser, and drove off. His commanders and bodyguards scrambled into their own trucks to follow him.

The convoy drove through town raising great plumes of dust and then turned down toward the river and plowed through the braiding channels, muddy water up to their door handles. One truck stalled in midstream, but they got it going again and tore through no-man's-land while their tanks on Ay Khanom hill shelled the Taliban to provide cover. They drove up to the forward positions and then got out of the trucks and continued on foot, creeping to within 500 yards of the Taliban front line. This was the dead zone: Anything that moves gets shot. Dead zones are invariably quiet—there's no fighting, no human noise, just an absolute stillness that can be more frightening than the heaviest gunfire. Into this stillness, as Massoud studied the Taliban positions, a single gunshot rang out.

The bullet barely missed one of his commanders—he felt its wind as it passed—and came to a stop in the dirt between Massoud's feet. Massoud called in more artillery fire, and then he and his men quickly retraced their route to the trucks. The trip had served its purpose, though. Massoud had identified two dirt roads that split in front of the Taliban positions and circled around behind them. And he had let himself be seen on the front line, which would reinforce the Taliban assumption that this was the focus of his attack.

Late that afternoon, Massoud and his commanders went back up to the command post. The artillery exchanges had started up again, and a new Ramadan moon hung delicately in the sunset over the Taliban positions. That night, in the bunker, Massoud gave his commanders their final instructions. The offensive was to be carried out by eight groups of 60 men each, in successive waves. They must not be married or have children; they must not be their family's only son. They were to take the two roads Massoud had spotted and encircle the Taliban positions on the hill. He told them to cut the supply road and hold their positions while offering the Taliban a way to escape. The idea was not to force the Taliban to fight to the last man. The idea was just to overtake their positions with as few casualties as possible.

The commanders filed out, and Reza and Dr. Abdullah were left alone with Massoud. He was exhausted, and he lay down on his side with his coat over him and his hands folded under his cheek. He fell asleep, woke up, asked Reza a question, then fell asleep, over and over again for the next hour. Occasionally a commander would walk in, and Massoud would ask if he'd repositioned those mortars, or distributed the 50,000 rounds of ammunition to the front. At one point, he asked Reza which country he liked best of all the ones he'd worked in.

"Afghanistan, of course," Reza said.

"Have you been to Africa?"

"Yes."

"Have you been to Rwanda?"

"Yes."

"What happened there? Why those massacres?"

Reza tried to explain. After a few minutes, Massoud sat up. "A few years ago in Kabul, I thought the war was finished, and I started building a home in Panjshir," he said. "A room for my children, a room for me and my wife, and a big library for all my books. I've kept all my books. I've put them in boxes, hoping one day I'll be able to put them on the shelves and I'll be able to read them. But the house is still unfinished, and the books are still in their boxes. I don't know when I'll be able to read my books."

Finally Massoud bid Reza and Dr. Abdullah good night and then lay back down and went to sleep for good. Though he holds the post of vice president in Rabbani's deposed government, Massoud is a man with few aspirations as a political leader, no apparent desire for power. Over and over he has rejected appeals from his friends and allies to take a more active role in the politics of his country. The Koran says that war is such a catastrophe, it must be brought to an end as quickly as possible and by any means necessary. That, perhaps, is why Massoud has devoted himself exclusively to waging war.

I WOKE UP AT DAWN. The sky was pale blue and promised a warm, clear day, which meant that the offensive was on. Reza and I ate some bread and drank tea and then went outside with the fighters. There seemed to be more of them milling around, and they were talking less than usual. They stood in tense little groups in the morning sun, waiting for Commander Massoud to emerge from his quarters.

The artillery fire started up in late morning, a dull smattering of explosions on the front line and the occasional heavy boom of a nearby tank. The plan was for Massoud's forces to attack at dusk along the ridge, drawing attention to that part of the front, and then around midnight other attacks would be launched farther south. That was where the front passed close to Taloqan. As the afternoon went by, the artillery fire became more and more regular, and then suddenly at 5:15 a spate of radio calls came into the bunker. Massoud stood up and went outside.

It had begun. Explosions flashed continually against the Taliban positions on the ridge, and rockets started streaking back and forth across the dark valley. We could see the lights from three Taliban tanks that were making their way along the ridgeline to reinforce positions that were getting overrun. A local cameraman named Yusuf had shown me footage of seasoned mujahidin attacking a hill, and I was surprised by how calm and purposeful the process was. In his video, the men moved forward at a crouch, stopping to shoot from time to time and then moving forward again until they had reached the top of the hill. They never stopped advancing, and they never went faster than a walk.

Unfortunately, I doubted that the battle I was watching was being conducted with such grace. They were just kids up there, mostly, on the hill in the dark with the land mines and the machine gun fire and the Taliban tanks. Massoud was yelling on the radio a lot, long bursts of Dari and then short silences while whoever he was talking to tried to explain himself. Things were not going well, it seemed. Some of the commanders weren't on the front line, where they belonged, and their men had gone straight up the hill instead of circling around. As a result, they had attacked through a minefield. Massoud was in a cold fury.

"I never told you to attack from below—I knew it would be mined," he told one commander in the bunker. The man's head tipped backward with the force of Massoud's words. "The plan was not to attack directly. That's why you hit the mines. You made the same mistake last time."

The commander suggested that the mistake might have been made by the fighters on the ground.

"I don't care—these are my children, your children," Massoud shot back. "When I look at these fighters, they are like lions. The real problem is the commanders. You attacked from below and lost men to land mines. For me, even if you took the position, you lost the war."

THE OFFENSIVE WAS SUPPOSED TO CONTINUE all night. Reza and I ate dinner with Massoud, then packed up our truck and set out on the long drive back to Khvajeh Baha od Din. We were leaving the front for good, and on the way out of town we decided to check in at the field hospital. It was just a big canvas tent set up in a mud-walled courtyard, lit inside by kerosene lanterns that glowed softly through the fabric. We stopped the truck and walked inside, and we were just wrapping up our conversation with the doctor when an old Soviet flatbed pulled up.

It was the first truckload of wounded, the guys who had stepped on mines. They were stunned and quiet, each face blackened by the force of a land mine blast, and their eyes cast around in confusion at the sudden activity surrounding them. The medics lifted the men off the back of the truck, carried them inside, and laid them on metal cots. A soldier standing next to me clucked his disapproval when he saw the wounds. The effect of a land mine on a person is so devastating that it is almost disorienting. It takes several minutes to understand that the sack of bones and blood and shredded cloth that you're looking at used to be a man's leg. One man lost a leg at the ankle, another man lost a leg at the shin, a third lost an entire leg to the waist. This man didn't seem to be in pain, and he didn't seem to have any understanding of what had happened to him. Both would come later. "My back hurts," he kept saying. "There's something wrong with my back."

The medics worked quickly and wordlessly in the lamplight, wrapping the stumps of the legs with gauze. The wounded men would be flown out by helicopter the next day and would eventually wind up in a hospital in Tajikistan. "*This* is the war," Reza hissed over and over again as he shot photos. "*This* is what war means."

Reza had covered a lot of wars and seen plenty of this in his life, but I hadn't. I ducked out of the tent and stood in the cold darkness, leaning against a wall. Dogs were barking in the distance, and a soldier shouted into his radio that the wounded were coming in and they needed more medicine, *now*. I thought about what Reza had said, and after a while I went back inside. This is the war, too, and you have to look straight at it, I told myself. You have to look straight at all of it or you have no business being here at all.

One month after Reza and I left Afghanistan, Massoud's forces unexpectedly seized large areas in Bamian and Ghowr Provinces, hundreds of miles west of his front lines. These were areas that the Taliban had controlled since 1995. "Our bases there are three times the size they were when you were here," Dr. Abdullah told me by phone in early January. "Despite the very cold weather, those districts have been liberated."

Massoud's jang-e-gerilla-yee *had begun.*

MARCH/APRIL 2001

Postscript: On September 9, 2001, just two days before the 9/11 attacks, the Taliban assassinated Massoud by inviting the warlord to an interview and posing as a television crew.

DANGEROUS MEDICINE: ON THE FRONT LINE OF THE EBOLA EPIDEMIC

By Tom Clynes

Following an outbreak of what is arguably the world's deadliest disease, a team of doctors, researchers, and the author converge in a small Ugandan village, scrambling to assemble a plan to fight an invisible killer virus.

AFTER THE SUN SETS, A DISTANT CLANGING BEGINS. It starts faintly, a rhythmic din that gets closer and louder. Soon it's joined by deeper drumbeats. At the beginning of the outbreak, the drumming—on pots and pans as well as drums—became a nightly ritual to chase away the Ebola demon. After a few weeks it diminished as the local population began to feel more secure. Now the drumming is back.

DR. ANTHONY SANCHEZ got the news on a Sunday afternoon in mid-October when he stopped by his lab at the Centers for Disease Control and Prevention (CDC), in Atlanta. Sanchez was surprised to find his boss, Pierre Rollin, in the office.

Rollin began by telling Sanchez that he could decline the assignment. After all, Sanchez had a four-month-old daughter at home.

"Feel free to say no, Tony," Rollin said. "But I'm putting together a team to go over and set up a lab; we could use you." This was the first Sanchez had heard that Ebola, after a four-year respite, had resurfaced, this time in northern Uganda.

Sanchez, 47, had spent much of his career researching the Ebola virus, often in the CDC's maximum-containment lab, protected by a space suit. But he had never seen it operate in a human epidemic. Once, a few years ago, he wondered if he had missed his chance, if it would ever come again.

Now the agency was spread thin, with a team in Saudi Arabia trying to contain an epidemic of Rift Valley fever. And an on-site laboratory could give the Ebola containment operation a tremendous advantage. Sanchez walked to his office and picked up the phone. He dialed his home number and told his wife that there was something he needed to talk about when he got home, something important. The line was silent for several long seconds, and then:

"I'm not going to be happy about this, am I?"

THE OLD CZECH PROP PLANE lurches to a halt at the side of the military airstrip; the doctors unfurl their stiff legs, disembark, and begin unloading. They shift 47 boxes—a metric ton of laboratory gear—onto a truck and drive toward town, trailing a spiral of orange dust as they pass army checkpoints and outsize churches, roadside vendors, and crowds of people listening to radios, talking, and singing.

The most surprising thing is how ordinary it all looks, at first. Set in the middle of a fertile, if unrelieved, savanna, the town of Gulu, Uganda, could be any other East African provincial center. Everywhere, people are on the move, some pedaling bikes, others riding on the fringed rear seats of bicycle taxis, most just walking. They walk upright, with stone-straight posture, some carrying babies on their backs, some balancing loads on their heads, some barefoot, others in sandals. They walk—and the doctors drive—past the field where the pope once spoke; past the turnoff that leads to the witch doctor's house; past another road that leads to a small village near the forest, where, maybe, it all started.

It takes a few minutes, as if their eyes were getting used to a new light, before hints begin to emerge that life here is far from normal: There are none of the usual swarms of schoolchildren in uniform. White trucks drive through town, emblazoned with the red crosses and acronyms—UN, WHO, MSF—that portend crisis. The hospital building, where the doctors pull up, is wrapped in white plastic sheeting; a hand-lettered sign warns "No entrance without permission." The sign is illustrated with a crude human figure with an X drawn over it.

FIVE WEEKS INTO THE CRISIS, a crowd of foreigners occupies a government office room in a yellow concrete-block building on the north side of Gulu. Doctors and scientists hunch over notebook computers and speak into walkie-talkies. Amid the babble of languages and accents, an American woman's voice talks into a satellite telephone: "We've got more Ebola-positives in Pabo now—we've got to get on top of this."

Whenever a serious epidemic is confirmed anywhere in the world, an alert goes out to members of the Global Outbreak Alert and Response Network, and scores of doctors, scientists, and humanitarian workers start packing bags and booking flights. The international disease-fighting team assembled to combat the Ebola outbreak in Uganda ultimately numbers more than a hundred professionals from a dozen countries, plus more than a thousand Ugandans. Among them are epidemiologists and virologists, physicians and nurses, laboratory workers, logistics specialists, and educators. Later, they'll be joined by researchers eager to take advantage of a rare opportunity to learn more about a virus that has baffled scientists for 25 years.

The Ebola virus is named after the river in Zaire (now called the Democratic Republic of the Congo) where it was first identified in 1976, during an outbreak that killed 280. Since that epidemic, and a concurrent outbreak in Sudan, the disease has struck in Côte d'Ivoire, again in Sudan and Congo, and three times in Gabon. Ebola is one of the deadliest, most infectious pathogens known to man; once in the bloodstream, it wipes out the immune system within a matter of days, causing high fever, vomiting, diarrhea, and, in a small but well-publicized number of cases, uncontrolled bleeding. There is no cure and no effective treatment. No one knows its natural host—the organism it usually infects—and no one knows why or how it sometimes leaps into the human realm.

Right now, though, the focus is not on solving Ebola's mysteries. Right now, everyone in this room has only one goal: to stop the epidemic.

The woman on the satellite phone, Cathy Roth, a 47-year-old physician with the World Health Organization (WHO), is currently coordinating the containment operation. She hangs up, and I walk over to introduce myself. When I extend my hand, she throws both of hers over her head in a "Don't shoot!" gesture.

"Uh, we're not actually doing that anymore," Roth says, smiling down at my retreating hand. Ebola is spread through contact with bodily fluids, including sweat. And although it's unlikely that either of us is carrying the virus, people are avoiding handshakes like . . . well, like the plague.

A dozen or so exhausted-looking professionals trudge in for Roth's afternoon update meeting. "Everyone's getting really tired now," she tells me. "We were thinking we had it under control, and I was thinking about giving the mobile teams a Sunday off. After five weeks of 24-7, they're at risk of making mistakes, and they need rest." But now Roth is worried that the illness is flaring up again, threatening to break through the containment operation.

In the past, Ebola has struck only in rural areas, and the disease's rapid death sequence has actually worked in favor of containment, since infected people couldn't travel far before they succumbed. But the Gulu area is densely populated, with transport links to East Africa's major cities—and, from there, to anywhere in the world. No one in this room is interested in finding out what might happen if they were to give the virus a chance to take advantage of these more favorable conditions.

CDC medical epidemiologist Scott Harper begins the meeting with bad news from Pabo, a refugee camp north of Gulu. "A woman came into the clinic last Sunday and miscarried, and there was a lot of hemorrhaging," he says. "No one knew she was Ebola-positive, and she spent at least two days in the maternity ward, bleeding."

His colleague Marta Guerra picks up the story: "She had five women in the maternity ward with her, plus at least 15 visitors. Eleven nurses and other workers were exposed before they got her isolated. So far, we've taken blood from all but one."

Roth tucks her hair behind her ears. "This thing has the potential to blow up into a huge problem," she says.

A FEW BLOCKS FROM the international team's headquarters, a teenage boy motions for me to follow him. "Miracle," he says, and he leads me into a crowd gathered at a gate, peering into a brown-dirt courtyard. In the shade of a sprawling tree, a woman sits in a plastic chair, her head arched backward. Eyes wide and teary, she stares into the branches while another woman cuts her hair, felling the thin braids with slow, deliberate snips of the scissors.

A preacher stands in front of her, aiming a video camera with his outstretched left hand, rocking back and forth as he calls out a surreal narration: "She was mentally deranged for 12 years," he says. "She was possessed by evil powers. The family took her to many witch doctors, but the demon inside would not relent."

He turns toward the crowd. "We prayed and we urged her to surrender her witch doctor gadgets. And now, look at her!" The woman smiles and sobs silently as her braids fall. "Look at her!" the preacher says, his voice rising. "The Lord has rescued her from demonic oppression!"

Watching the faces in the crowd, I have no doubt that everyone wants to believe that a miracle—be it religion, witchcraft, or science—could defeat a demon. But the woman's gaze remains unsettled, and her eyes dart tentatively, searching among the branches.

DR. SIMON MARDEL ENTERS the dressing room outside the isolation ward at St. Mary's Lacor Hospital and pulls a full-length surgical smock over his head. He stretches a first layer of gloves over the top of the smock's tight elastic cuffs, then he pulls knee-high gum boots over his feet and tucks in his pants. He puts on a paper shower cap and a thick plastic surgical apron, then a second pair of gloves and a mask. Just before he walks through the first of two disinfectant boot baths, he places the final protective barrier—goggles—over his eyes.

An expert in emergency and refugee health care, Mardel had taken a leave of absence from his duties as an emergency room physician in England's Lake District to assist at a recent epidemic of another highly contagious hemorrhagic fever—Marburg—in Congo. He was on his way home in October when he was diverted to Gulu. A few years earlier, during the war in Bosnia, Mardel hiked into Srebrenica to treat wounded civilians while the city was under siege—a heroic action that earned him the Order of the British Empire for humanitarianism.

Mardel arrived in Gulu with the first WHO team and took charge of the isolation wards, calmly demonstrating barrier-nursing techniques to terrified hospital workers. "Remember," the clear-eyed 43-year-old told a group of nurses and nuns, "the system is only as strong as its weakest moment."

Mardel enters the suspect ward, set aside for people who are symptomatic but unconfirmed as Ebola-positive. In one corner of the room, a male patient lies sideways on a bed, coughing and moaning. He holds a wad of tissues to his nose, which streams with black blood. He seems utterly indifferent to the doctor's presence.

"We'll get some blood from him," Mardel says, and the patient offers his arm weakly to the needle.

The Lacor hospital is well endowed and well equipped by African standards, and its wood-trimmed wards and array of diagnostic equipment stand in contrast to the bare concrete of the government-run Gulu Hospital, across town, where doctors scrounge for basic supplies. In the mission-hospital tradition, Lacor's care is intensive and hands-on. Because of the vomiting, diarrhea, and hemorrhaging, Ebola patients need massive care; at Lacor, nurses and nuns are responsible for everything from mopping up to helping patients die with as much dignity as possible.

Inside the isolation ward, health workers are fully enveloped in protective gear; their goggled eyes are their only semirecognizable features. To aid identification, many have scrawled their names with markers on the fronts of their white plastic surgical aprons.

Mardel spots an apron across the room labeled "Dr. Matthew" and heads over to a corner where Matthew Lukwiya is treating an Ebola-stricken nurse. Lukwiya, 42, Lacor's medical superintendent, had been on leave in Kampala, 200 miles south of Gulu, when he received word of "a strange new illness" making its way through the hospital's wards. He immediately left his wife and five children in the capital and drove up to Gulu. Within two days of his arrival, 17 people— including three nurses—were dead or dying with the same dire symptoms.

"At first it looked like some sort of super-malaria," he says. "But the patients did not respond to quinine treatment, and it was killing people very quickly." He began flirting with the possibility that one of the rare diseases of the filovirus family, Ebola or the somewhat less deadly Marburg, might have come in from Sudan or Congo. However unlikely this diagnosis—Ebola had never been seen in Uganda—he sent samples off to a laboratory in Johannesburg. Three days before the results were due, Lukwiya concluded that all signs were pointing to the worst possible scenario—Ebola—and that he needed to act immediately. He stayed up all night reading a manual titled "Infection Control for Viral Hemorrhagic Fevers in the African Health Care Setting," downloaded from the Internet. In the morning, he and his staff started setting up a barrier-nursing environment, using whatever resources were on hand. They built hands-free boot removers from scrap wood and constructed an incinerator out of a 55-gallon drum. They fashioned aprons from duct tape and plastic sheeting and converted a hospital pavilion into an isolation ward. Then, from behind these crude protective layers, they began nursing Ebola patients.

Through the goggles, Mardel's eyes meet Lukwiya's, which are heavy with concern. The nurse he is treating is in critical condition.

"If she dies," Lukwiya says, "she will be our seventh."

IN THE MORNING, volunteer James Kidega reports to the Red Cross office, where a map hangs on one wall, dotted with pushpins: green for refugee camps, red for land mine sites, pink for recent ambushes. Since the mid-1980s, a nebulous guerrilla force known as the Lord's Resistance Army (LRA), whose stated objective is to carve a Christian state out of Uganda, has terrorized the region's civilian population. To protect their children at night, when the rebels usually operate, most of the rural population has moved into refugee camps near Ugandan army barracks. Every day since the containment operation began, scores of Red Cross volunteers have fanned out to these "protected villages" to follow up on Ebola rumors, call for ambulances, educate the populace, and relay information about hospitalized relatives and neighbors.

Before the epidemic hit, the 25-year-old Kidega had worked at a charitable agency that helps children who have escaped from the rebels. Because of his extensive contacts in the villages and his polished demeanor—he is rarely seen without a clean shirt and necktie—Kidega was recruited as a volunteer leader.

Today, he will lead a team that will visit two villages north of Gulu. With red-and-white flags flying, two trucks set out. As Kidega guides the trucks north, he recalls the first few days of the epidemic. At Gulu's two hospitals, he says, many nurses and orderlies stopped coming to work, fearing that they might be assigned to the isolation wards, and some international agencies based in Gulu left town. In the villages surrounding Gulu, rumors of sorcery circulated as entire families were wiped out. In Rwot Obilo village, the virus moved through one family so quickly that a dying woman told her young grandson, moments after his mother's death, "Suck your mother's last milk so you, too, can die—there is no one here to look after you now."

"It felt like being on a sinking ship," Kidega says. "You can't believe the fear." Some victims swarmed the hospitals; others ran away in panic as nurses fell ill all around them. Even the rebels were spooked; the LRA released 40 prisoners, fearing that they might be carrying the virus.

When the trucks pull into Akwayugi, villagers look up from their work of sifting maize and wheat. This isn't as bad as sub-Saharan Africa gets, but there's serious squalor here. About a fifth of the children have the bulging bellies that indicate severe malnutrition.

The Red Cross volunteers divide into four-person teams and move through the village, asking questions of the small crowds that gather wherever they go: Has anyone had a fever? Has anyone had bloody diarrhea or vomit? Was there a sudden death?

The team has a "reintegration kit" for two girls who survived Ebola after they lost their mother to the disease. They find them with their father, Charles Odongo, outside the family's round, mud-brick hut. Two weeks earlier, Odongo returned from the fields to find his wife in the hut with a headache and a high fever. "It took six hours for the ambulance to get here," he says. "By the time they arrived, she had died." When he sees the kit—cooking pots, blankets, soap, salt, and clothing—he smiles gratefully. "Immediately after we left for the hospital with my wife's body, our things were burned by the neighbors," he says.

Although the Ebola-Zaire strain can kill nearly 90 percent of its victims, the Gulu virus is similar to the less lethal Sudan strain, which has a mortality rate of about 50 percent. Odongo's three-year-old daughter, Skovia, survived the disease that killed her mother. "You should not fear her," a volunteer says to a circle of onlookers. "This is not a contagious little girl." The motherless girl seems to brighten when she sees the dress the team has brought for her, but her nine-month-old sister, Geoffrey, clings to her father listlessly. She's severely malnourished, weakened by the disease, and silent except for an occasional phlegmy cough. It's hard to imagine her making it to her first birthday.

ON THE WAY BACK TO TOWN, Kidega stops by his mother's house for a cup of tea. "James," his mother asks him, putting the kettle on the stove, "why so many coffins passing by here today?"

"It's going up again," Kidega says. "We were beginning to think it was nearly over, that they would reopen the schools, but I think now they will wait. People are hiding the facts. They think they will be shunned."

"Why don't they put the coffins inside when they transport them?" she asks. "This is making people very nervous." As she pours the tea, her 20-year-old niece, Sarah, walks in.

"This Ebola, I wish we could see it," Sarah says, clucking her tongue. "If we could see it, then we could beat it to death, with a stick."

Later, Kidega's radio crackles. A teenage girl has run into the clinic in Pabo, terrified of bleeding that would turn out to be nothing more than her first menstrual period. There's gunfire on the road near the Lacor hospital. And north of Gulu, a soldier in an armored personnel carrier has broken out in a fever and is vomiting red inside the vehicle. The other soldiers have run away.

"Can you send an isolation ambulance?" the military commander pleads.

SATURDAY MORNING AT THE HOSPITAL guest house, Tony Sanchez and Pierre Rollin are finishing breakfast in the dining room, getting ready to suit up for the lab. Since arriving in Gulu, they've been occupied controlling the outbreak; they're hoping to soon shift their focus to research.

"You can't do productive field research on Ebola when it vanishes," says Rollin. "So you need to get the information when you can."

Researchers at the National Institutes of Health recently announced progress in developing an Ebola vaccine that works in monkeys, but the virus's underlying logic is still beyond the reach of science. Since coming to the world's attention in 1976, the disease has baffled a generation of researchers, who have collected hundreds of thousands of specimens from plants, animals, and insects. Humans are what research virologists like Sanchez and Rollin call "accidental hosts" for the Ebola virus. "We don't know where it hides," Rollin says. "It may turn out to be something right under our noses. There are different schools of thought. Some say it is carried by rodents, or insects, or bats. . . ."

At that moment, as if summoned, Bob Swanepoel strides into the dining room, decked out in a khaki bush-hunter outfit. Swanepoel is a bat man. The director of the Special Pathogens Unit of the South African Institute for Virology, in Johannesburg, the goateed, 64-year-old veterinarian has made a career out of tramping into Africa's remote jungles, looking for the natural reservoirs of Ebola and other hemorrhagic fevers.

"He's at every outbreak," says Rollin. Over the past 20 years, the 47-year-old Rollin and Swanepoel have developed a bond that's fed by a shared fascination for viral diseases. When they're not working together at an outbreak, they communicate over the phone, from Atlanta to Johannesburg, at least once a week.

Swanepoel was in Saudi Arabia at the Rift Valley-fever epidemic when the first samples of Ebola-infected blood, sent by Lukwiya, arrived at his Johannesburg lab. Now he has finally made it to Gulu, along with two assistants and several bundles of nets and poles. "Pierre told me not to come," he says, settling in at Rollin's table. "He said there is nothing here, that we're too far downstream in the epidemic. But what do you do when you hear that? Do you stay home? No, you have to see for yourself."

Swanepoel is eager to do some reservoir hunting, but his bat-nabbing nets remain bundled outside his room. "Right now," he says, "there are several hurdles. First, I need to know the focal point before I start trapping. Did one person get it first, or were there a lot of people who separately picked up this thing from nature? It's the Sudan strain of Ebola, but was it brought in by a rebel from Sudan, or did it start near here? Northern Uganda and southern Sudan have roughly the same terrain and ecology, and the entire region is like a Bermuda Triangle of filoviruses. We're close to the Ebola River, to Durba, Mount Elgon, Kitum Cave—all the hotbeds of Marburg and Ebola.

"The second hurdle is, I need approval. You go out in a place like this without approval, and the next thing you know you're into ten kinds of shit. We got arrested in Congo, and it took half a day before they tracked down the colonel to vouch for us. He was at a brothel.

"Third, there are security issues. It's best to work at night, but . . ."

Rollin finishes Swanepoel's sentence: "But if you put a net up at night, you're more likely to catch a rebel than a reservoir."

Rollin often raises an eyebrow when he talks, which gives him a wryly comical look. "What I would like to know," Rollin says, "is did somebody do something in the bush that people don't normally do? Something seemed to be happening in September, before Matthew arrived. There was a lot of diarrhea, and rumors about some unusual malaria in a certain village. What you want to find is, was there a village where it started? But because of stigma, and because so much time has passed and so many people are dead, you don't get the straight story."

As Rollin talks, a dark spot forms above his left eyebrow. No one says anything, but in a minute Rollin feels the liquid as it starts to run down his forehead. He wipes it with his index finger.

"Hmm. It's blood. Very strange. I don't think I cut myself here. And I haven't shaved my forehead lately."

He wipes it away. When it keeps coming, he gets up and grabs a tissue. He succeeds in stanching the flow and sits back down. All conversation has stopped.

"Maybe I have started to bleed with Ebola a new way," he says, smiling as he raises an eyebrow. And everyone laughs.

Nervously.

AFTER BREAKFAST, Tony Sanchez walks out of the Lacor guest house, toward the lab. An ambulance pulls around the corner, and Sanchez averts his eyes as an Ebola suspect is led into the ward.

"What we don't experience up in Atlanta is the wards, the bleeding," he says. "I talked to Pierre about what to expect, but to tell you the truth, I've never seen large numbers of people dead and dying before—and the way they suffer. . . . During the day, you're doing your job, and you don't think about it. But at night, you see their faces. Your subconscious comes up with questions you can't answer."

Brother Elio Croce calls Sanchez's name and trots over. A Verona missionary who runs Lacor's technical and transportation services, Brother Elio, 54, is a plump Sean Connery look-alike with a compassionate demeanor that's balanced by a cranky sanctimoniousness.

"Tony, I need to take you out to Bardege Village," Elio says, "to get blood and a skin sample for a biopsy from a little girl who just died. We need to get there before they bury her."

I introduce myself to Elio and extend my hand—it's amazing just how reflexive the custom is. Before I realize my mistake, Elio reaches out, grabs my hand, and looks me straight in the eye. "We're not shaking hands here anymore," he says, shaking my hand. "There's an Ebola epidemic going on here you know."

Actually, the Gulu epidemic was initially spread more by contact with the dead than with the living. According to local ritual, a dead body stays in the house for a day or two while extended family and friends wash the corpse, eat and drink, and wash hands in a communal basin. Then they bury the body next to the house. ("For you, the dead take care of themselves," James Kidega says. "For us, we take care of the dead.")

The viral count is at its peak in a just expired body, but despite the risk and despite an aggressive education campaign, it's been extremely difficult to get people to stop customs that have been entrenched for generations. For that reason, health workers have encouraged residents to report deaths in neighboring families.

Sanchez grabs his gear, and we jump into a truck with Elio. As the clergyman drives, he talks nonstop in a singsongy Italian accent that seems incongruous with the content of his monologue: "The nurse, Grace Akulu, died. She was conscious until the very end—it's not true that everyone is demented in the final stages. She died singing; she never feared to encounter our Lord. We buried her behind the hospital in a beautiful ceremony. I have tape-recorded the singing. I will play it for you later."

"I thought it was supposed to be slowing down," Sanchez says.

"I do not think it is slowing down now," Elio says. "Tomorrow, we have to dig more graves."

With the isolation ambulance trailing, Elio turns off the road and drives through the elephant grass, following a single-track trail that terminates in a tidy dirt courtyard surrounded by a half dozen round mud-brick huts with thatched roofs.

The deceased girl's name is Sunday Onen; she was two years old. Her mother sits next to two other women, who are nursing young children; her grandfather, Peter Ola, talks to Sanchez and Elio.

"The child was healthy," Ola says incredulously. "She ate breakfast around nine, then she had a fever and began vomiting. When her diarrhea became bloody, my daughter began to carry her to the hospital. But midway, she did not cry out any longer, so she brought her back here."

Ebola doesn't usually work that quickly, but there are enough Ebola symptoms that it must be treated as a suspect case. The villagers watch in silence as Sanchez suits up; the three ambulance crew members stand in the sun, sweating inside their protective clothing.

As Sanchez bends down and leans into the hut, Brother Elio pulls out his tape recorder and begins a peculiar commentary.

"He's down on one knee, entering the hut. Yes, that's it, careful."

Encumbered by the hut's darkness and his layers of protective gear, Sanchez draws blood and cuts a skin sample from the tiny corpse. It takes longer than it should, because the lab has run out of biopsy punches, devices that work like high-tech cookie cutters to neatly remove a small patch of skin. He has to tug the girl's skin up, then make the cut with surgical scissors, working slowly, with full awareness of the consequences of even the smallest nick to his hands.

"He's down on both knees now," Elio continues. "Respect. Respect."

Sanchez backs out of the hut and straightens up, breathing hard through his surgical mask. He walks to the center of the clearing and lays out a sheet of white cloth, then he kneels down to pack the specimens. An ambulance crew member comes over with a garden-pump dispenser of disinfectant and sprays the bottoms of Sanchez's feet. Then the sprayer follows the other two crew members into the hut. Sanchez stands up just as the crew emerges, carrying a small white bundle.

"My God," Sanchez says. "I thought this was going to be an easy day." His right hand is twitching.

As the body is brought to the ambulance, the villagers suddenly become agitated. They gather around Brother Elio, talking to him in the Acholi language. Elio approaches Sanchez.

"See the problem now, Tony," he says, "there's been a misunderstanding. They thought that we would come out and test the girl, and if it wasn't Ebola, we would leave her here for them to bury her according to tradition."

Sanchez does his best to explain that he needs to bring the blood back to the lab to test for the Ebola antibody. The test takes several hours, and it may not be conclusive. They need to send the skin samples away for testing in Atlanta. In the meantime, the whole village may be vulnerable to infection until the body is taken away and buried at the isolation graveyard.

After a few minutes, the villagers stop talking; they just stare at Sanchez, the white man in the white suit insisting that their loved one be sent off to the afterlife unprepared, buried as if she had never lived at all. There is no actual threat—apart from the threat of having to remember these faces for the rest of a lifetime.

Sanchez takes Elio aside, and the two men's roles flip-flop. Sanchez, the scientist, wants to compromise, to humanize the rules. The body was in good condition, he says. It may not have been Ebola. Maybe it was a snakebite. . . .

"But the grandfather said she did not cry out," Elio says sharply. Sanchez's hand twitches again.

"What are we going to do?" he asks.

"We're not going to do anything," Elio snaps. His face is pinched, and the words come out that way, in a clipped staccato. "We can't let them bury her here. They will not do it the way we want."

Sanchez and Elio move toward the truck, and the villagers follow, forming a crescent around the front of the vehicle, continuing to stare as the two men get in.

It feels as if the air had been sucked out of the sky.

Elio starts the truck and shifts it into reverse. He begins to let out the clutch—then he stops.

"Hey," he says, looking at Sanchez. "What do you think? We let them bury her here. We stay, we supervise, they dig the grave very fast. It's more human, no?"

In an instant, they're out of the truck. Elio makes the announcement, and the dirt starts flying, with Sunday's father, who can't be more than 17 years old, leading the dig. A half hour later, the hole is completed, six feet deep. The ambulance crew lowers Sunday Onen's body gently into the ground.

SATURDAY EVENING, THE TEAM GATHERS in the courtyard at the Acholi Inn, tucked behind the roofless carcass of a burned-out building on the northern edge of town. Under a canopy of trees thick enough to block a light rain, a waitress runs back and forth with food and rounds of the local beer, Nile Special, politely requesting that the foreigners not lean back on the rear legs of the fragile plastic chairs. As the shadows lengthen, monkeys and an occasional rat scurry around the garden's perimeter; after sunset, bats swoop among the overhead branches.

Even the Nobel Peace Prize-winning Doctors Without Borders (Médecins Sans Frontières) is perennially short of recruits who are willing to turn their backs on comfortable, lucrative careers to come to needy places like Gulu, where the patient-to-doctor ratio approaches 18,000 to 1. (In the United States, it's around 400 to 1.) Yet despite the high stress and low comfort, despite the sound of machine gun fire in the night, everyone seems to feel privileged to be here.

"I had been wanting to do something like this since I was a teenager," says Patricia Campbell, an American physician with Doctors Without Borders. "I saw medicine as a passport to the world. But then I got married and had children, so I had to put it off until my kids were older." Now in her mid-60s, Campbell says she's "addicted."

"I go home to Scarsdale [New York], and I wonder how anyone can stand it, treating rich kids for tonsillitis. After a few weeks, I'm saying, 'Get me out of here!'"

The obvious question: Are you afraid?

"No," Campbell says flatly. "You follow protocol. Unless you're in direct contact with body fluids, you won't get Ebola."

Murmurs of agreement wash over the table. "If there was that high of a risk," says Simon Mardel, "I wouldn't be here."

Of course, playing down the risks is a coping mechanism, a way of keeping panic at bay. Like cigarette smoking or gallows humor, denial keeps you functioning effectively in the presence of danger and death—whether you're a doctor in a plague zone or a soldier in a battle zone.

For all the talk about managing risk, though, the odds don't look very good for medical people in their ongoing battle with the Ebola virus. In the 1995 Ebola outbreak in Congo, 80 medical workers became infected; 63 died. Hospitals—especially deprived African hospitals—provide an ideal environment for the virus to prosper, and health workers are vulnerable targets because of their close contact with bodily fluids. Ebola does not forgive even the smallest mistake.

On Sunday morning, grief takes a holiday. James Kidega walks through the double doors of Christ Church and joins the congregation in the throes of a full-blown dance party. At the front of the low altar, a band of musicians strum on stringed gourd instruments; they're nearly drowned out by a platoon of drummers, whacking away in a polyrhythmic fury. Around the musicians and into the back pews, people of all ages pogo up and down, driven in a raucous call-and-response by a young woman croaking through a distorted sound system.

"The love of Jesus has taken away the sins of the people," she sings.

"Evil can't touch us!" the dancers cry.

OUTSIDE HIS GUEST ROOM in a wooded corner of the Lacor hospital compound, Bob Swanepoel slouches in a chair, flinging pebbles into the trees with a wrist-rocket slingshot. Nearby, Pierre Rollin sits on the concrete floor of the patio, his back against the door, his legs stretched in front of him. Someone brings over a straw-colored fruit bat killed by a local boy, and Swanepoel perks up.

"These things are vicious," Swanepoel says, spreading the bat's wings. "Look at these teeth, and these claws—they're like razors. They'll go after you like a dog." He asks one of his researchers to put it in the refrigerator, along with a cobra that was killed on the Lacor grounds yesterday after menacing some nurses.

Swanepoel's bat-trapping expedition has been approved, but he's pessimistic about what the fieldwork might turn up. If you don't know where the epidemic started, he says, "it's a shot in the dark."

"Also," he says, "we've learned that the caves in the Kalak Hills aren't what we thought they were. Apparently, there are lots of very narrow caves that are difficult and dangerous to navigate. Maybe we can go up to the top and drop the nets—I don't know."

Elio rides up on his bike. He wants Rollin to test him for Ebola.

"That will be the third time you've been tested," says Rollin. "You keep thinking you're infected."

"We lost another nurse today," Elio says. "That makes eight, plus a nurse's boyfriend. We can't figure out how the boyfriend was exposed, since the nurse did not get Ebola. He was a young man, and strong. At the end, he told me he wanted to get married before he died, so I got the priest and sent for the girl. But as she was on her way here, we realized that we had time only to give him his last sacraments. When she arrived, the father went out to meet her." Elio pauses.

"He told her that he had already left for the long safari."

AT HEADQUARTERS, Cathy Roth comes outside and announces that she's "canceled the cancellation of this afternoon's meeting." Everyone troops inside.

There have been five deaths today so far. The CDC's Scott Harper reports that six people were admitted yesterday, and they aren't on any contact lists. "People seem to be hiding family members," he says. "The system seems to be breaking down. In Atiak, a suspect was buried, and no one got a specimen."

In Pabo, some recovering patients have been lost. At Gulu Hospital, an Ebola-positive patient "escaped" last night. (He later turned up at Lacor.) As for the infected woman who miscarried, there are now 32 contacts, including 11 health-care workers. After her procedure, two deliveries were performed on the same table.

Dr. Paul Onek, the district health director, gives voice to everyone's frustration. "If we have escaped patients, if we are not even able to take specimens from deceased people, then we are back to square one." He is silent for half a minute, then he speaks. "Yesterday, we breathed a sigh of relief. But now . . ." He purses his lips and sighs. There's no relief in it.

AFTER THE CHURCH SERVICE, James Kidega travels past the field where the pope spoke. He approaches a cluster of huts. The witch doctor, Abodtu, is in, although the authorities ordered him to remove his "traditional African healing" banner after a witch doctor in Rwot Obilo treated—and possibly infected—up to 30 people before dying of Ebola.

But Abodtu doesn't claim to cure Ebola—at least, not yet.

"Right now, I have no medicine for this," he says, lighting a candle inside his hut. "I cure people who are lame or berserk. I make the leg stop swelling and the brain start working. Or I send death to someone who has done wrong to your family.

"As for the white man's medicine and the white man's religion, I do not cross there. *This* is what I know." He sweeps his eyes over his altar—a clutter of beads and bones, snake skins and rattles, jugs and strings of shells.

Where does Ebola come from?

"I have asked my bad-thing where it came from. The spirit tells me to wait for instructions, then to go to the forest and look up to a special big tree. This tree has the answer; it will tell me where it comes from." He inhales deeply. "I will look up to the tree, and I will learn from the tree how to stop it."

DR. MIKE RYAN ARRIVES FROM LONDON, and three-quarters of the international team and seemingly half the town converge in the headquarters' parking lot within minutes to welcome him. A WHO medical officer, Ryan, 36, led the first team to hit the ground in Gulu, and he spent the next four weeks coordinating the operation before being summoned to London to represent the WHO at an infectious-disease conference. Now he's back, and with his long red sideburns bursting out from under his baseball cap he jumps from a rented van and immediately starts greeting people with big handshakes and bear hugs.

Suddenly, the energy seems cranked up.

"We managed to convince ourselves that it was under control," Ryan says, torching a cigarette as he addresses a group of mobile-team members. "Everyone's getting lethargic and exhausted. But we've got 17 people in the hospital now, and four new ones already today. We've got 45,000 people living in Pabo, and we can't afford to let it go. We can't take our eyes off the ball."

Waving his arms and bellowing, Ryan manages to get his audience guffawing, then he springs onto the porch. Just before dashing into the room, he turns and yells back at the group, loud enough for the entire parking lot to hear: "Let's keep our boots down on the neck of this bastard!"

AT NOON, BOB SWANEPOEL'S TEAM finally rolls out of Gulu for the Kalak Hills, escorted by 13 soldiers and an armored personnel carrier. They drive along the dirt roads, between walls of eight-foot-tall elephant grass, dodging bicyclists and pedestrians. Arriving at the refugee camp of Guruguru, Swanepoel negotiates with the villagers—two of whom say they dined on bats earlier that day—and sets out with a team of bat hunters and porters. In a scene that's vaguely reminiscent of some Great White Hunter epic, Swanepoel's party—soldiers, hunters, porters, and scientists—trudges over the hills toward the Kalak caves, trailed by an enthusiastic swarm of village children.

"It's very unlikely that we'll turn anything up," Swanepoel says, wiping sweat off his forehead as he walks. "You could test 100,000 bats for a virus before you find it; that's the sort of job we face."

Swanepoel decided a few years ago to shift his gaze upward, to arboreal virus carriers such as bats and canopy-dwelling insects, after exhaustive tests on ground-dwelling animals failed to reveal anything conclusive.

"At several points," he says, "bats have figured prominently in outbreaks of Ebola and Marburg. In some of those incidents, so have monkeys and chimps—but they died just like humans, so they can't be the reservoir. It has to be something that can carry Ebola without coming to harm. In the lab, when we injected Ebola into bats, we found that it could grow to a very high concentration, but it did not kill them. In fact, some of them excreted virus in their feces."

Arriving at the caves, Swanepoel assembles the lab on a large rock. The caves are narrow and steep, and the locals have been climbing in on rope ladders and using thorny branches to hook bats. But it's dangerous work; in the past year, more than ten residents of Guruguru have died in the caves, most by falling off the ladders. It's agreed that the bat hunters will work only in the most accessible caves to lessen the chance of anyone getting hurt. They head into the caverns, outfitted with nets and instructions to bring the animals back alive.

In Congo, Swanepoel used huge nets mounted on bamboo poles; in Gabon, he hunted with slingshots and live traps; in Côte d'Ivoire, he ascended elaborate walkways built in the treetops. He has used UV-light traps and fogging machines to collect insects. But today the expedition is decidedly low-tech, with teenage hunters wielding simple nets. As they bring in the bats, Swanepoel extracts vials of blood and puts the bodies in a freezer box for later dissection.

After four hours, the sun is moving toward the horizon, and the army commander indicates that it's time to go. The hunters have collected only nine bats, and Swanepoel is clearly disappointed. "To do this properly, you need hundreds, and you should really work at night. Like I said, it's a shot in the dark. I doubt we'll find anything—but we'll be back."

When the convoy pulls into town at dusk, Ryan and Kidega come out to the office parking lot, looking relieved. All afternoon, they've monitored radio reports of an ambush near where the expedition was working. The rebels attacked a vehicle, blowing it up with a rocket-propelled grenade, killing three people.

JUST PAST SUNSET, MOST OF THE TEAM gathers in the Acholi Inn courtyard. After dinner, they linger under the trees, drinking Nile Specials and occasionally getting scolded for leaning on the hind legs of the chairs. The talk gets around to the first few days of the epidemic.

"This is the one that could have gotten away," Ryan says. "And it still might. But if we manage to contain it, we've got Matthew [Lukwiya] to thank. By the time we got here, he was already mobilizing the community and building a containment operation, and that gave us a head start we haven't had in other outbreaks."

Looking back, Ryan says he's amazed by Lukwiya's instincts: "Ebola isn't the first thing you'd think about here; it's not even the tenth thing. But Matthew put two and two together—and he got *shite* for an answer. Had he not taken action when he did, I don't know what would have happened."

By all accounts, though, the first few days were shambolic. When Ryan arrived, he found Gulu in the grip of panic. Immediately, he began coordinating the multi-agency, multilingual war against the virus, cracking jokes and chain-smoking cigarettes, winning the confidence and support of local health officials and military personnel. "We needed to train, to get equipment, to get people off 24-hour shifts," he says. "We stopped all IV interventions and cut down admissions to only the most life threatening. We needed to get simple things right, like standardizing disinfectant mixes and training people to use the protective gear."

Ryan orders another round. "When we arrived," he says, "there were bodies piling up at the morgue. It's an old brick building that sits in the middle of a field on the outskirts of town, like something out of a 19th-century horror story."

Once an isolation graveyard was established, several military personnel were assigned the grim, dangerous task of burying the highly contagious bodies.

"The first guys," says Simon Mardel, "when they saw us coming with the bodies, they ran away. We were yelling, 'Hey, at least leave your shovels!'"

"They were terrified," says Ryan. "They were convinced they'd get Ebola if they got anywhere within an arse's roar of the virus. Simon and I realized that we couldn't expect them to do it if we weren't willing to do it ourselves. So we suited up and jumped in with the shovels. We were trying to joke with the fellows—saying things like, 'Hey, you just volunteered for the graveyard shift'—but they were pretty grim at first. In the end, though, they became the Olympic burial team; we wouldn't have had a prayer without them."

THE NEXT DAY, MARDEL JOINS Lukwiya for rounds in the Lacor isolation ward. The two play a "good cop, bad cop" routine as they urge the more coherent patients to drink their rehydrating fluid. The majority of Ebola victims die of shock due to fluid loss; aggressive hydration is the only real treatment available for the disease.

Among the most serious cases on the ward are several nurses. Despite efforts to improve staff safety procedures and reduce fatigue, Lacor's nurses continue to get infected. But Mardel has a plan, and he tries to convince Lukwiya to buy into it.

"From now on, how about if we have the mobile teams bring all the new cases from the community to Gulu Hospital, to give your people a rest? We could still treat existing patients at Lacor, until they die or recover, and let self-referrals choose their hospital. That way, we keep all avenues of admission open."

Lukwiya says he'll consider it, but the following morning dawns with more bad news. Two nurses and a nun have died during the night, and the surviving medical-ward nurses walk out in frustration, grief, and terror. They assemble in a meeting hall and send for Lukwiya.

Lukwiya is calm and resolute as he walks into the room. For the past 17 years, he has been the stabilizing force at Lacor, the gentle but unyielding leader who has refused to let a civil war, a lack of resources, or anything else get in the way of helping his patients. A few years ago, on Good Friday, a band of rebels came to the hospital to take nurses as hostages. Lukwiya stepped forward and persuaded the guerrillas to take him instead. He spent a week on the move with them, treating their wounded soldiers, before they let him go.

Lukwiya tells the nurses of the plan to shift the bulk of the isolation work to Gulu Hospital and of his efforts to convince the government to provide hardship pay and compensation to the families of fallen nurses. He reemphasizes the need for full vigilance and adherence to the barrier-nursing techniques, especially at night, when tired workers are more likely to let down their guard. "Those who want to leave, can leave," he finally says. "As for me, I will not betray my profession."

Lukwiya's words and the afternoon funerals, which take place in a downpour with lots of singing and praying, have a calming effect. The nurses return to work.

LUKWIYA HAS SEEN MORE THAN A HUNDRED Ebola patients, but none have developed the relatively rare severe hemorrhagic form of Ebola. Unfortunately, one of his nurses, 32-year-old Simon Ojok, is the first. Sanchez, who had begun to think that the stories of spectacular bleeding were "a bunch of crap," now sees it with his own eyes.

Ojok's condition deteriorates quickly, and in the middle of the night he starts thrashing in his bed, pulling off his oxygen mask and spraying bright-red, oxygen-saturated blood all around him. He stumbles out of bed, and, as night-shift nurse Stanley Babu pleads with him to stay put, Ojok walks out of the room, tearing away from his IV tube. Agitated and mumbling, Ojok stands in the hallway, coughing infectious blood and mucus onto the walls and floor. Terrified, Babu runs to Lukwiya's quarters and wakes him.

"Blood is pouring from his eyes and nose like tap water," Babu tells Lukwiya. "He is confused, fighting death. We are afraid to take him back to bed because he seems violent."

Lukwiya sprints across the compound and hurries into the dressing room. He can hear the commotion through the wall as he pulls on his gown, his boots, his apron. Then his mask, his cap, his two pairs of gloves. He does not put on his goggles.

When Lukwiya enters the room, Ojok has stumbled back into bed and is gasping for breath, wrapped in his blood-soaked gown and sheets. Lukwiya props him up to help him breathe and changes his gown and bedding. Just past dawn, as Lukwiya is mopping the floor, Ojok dies.

A FEW DAYS LATER, Lukwiya sends for Rollin and Sanchez. Could they please come to his office—and could they bring their blood-sampling gear?

When they arrive, Lukwiya is calm. "I've developed a fever," he says. Rollin tells him that it's probably just the flu or malaria, nothing to worry about.

Rollin draws Lukwiya's blood, then heads to the lab, where he changes into a respirator suit with a battery-powered filter unit. He centrifuges the blood and generates a master plate, then dispenses a measured amount of the sample into the dimpled well of the plate. Pausing often to wipe the sweat from his face with the inside of his cloth hood, he deposits and rinses the various agents—among them are mouse and rabbit antibodies, horseradish peroxidase, and skim milk—in a strict order. Finally, some five hours after he began, he positions the pipette tip over the sample well and adds the final reagent, the telltale chemical that will turn green if the sample contains Ebola. The mixture doesn't turn green.

"Tony, he's negative," Rollin says. There's no sign of Ebola.

That night, Lukwiya vomits and develops a headache. When Rollin draws blood the next morning, Lukwiya's eyes are a ghostly gray. This time, the reagent turns a weak green.

OK, Rollin thinks, there's a 50 percent chance that he'll make it. The viral count is still low. Maybe he'll develop a mild case.

But the next day, the test goes a solid green, and Lukwiya asks to be taken to the isolation ward. "If I die," he tells the hospital's administrator, Dr. Bruno Corrado, "I only pray that I am the last."

He requests that his wife, Margaret, be told just that he has a fever and that she should not come up from Kampala. She comes anyway, of course, not letting herself imagine where she will be led when she walks through the hospital's front gate. Then it's as if she had practiced walking toward the building covered in plastic, practiced suiting up, practiced being strong and cheerful as she enters the ward to see her husband, dying of Ebola.

"Look here, Margaret," Lukwiya says when he sees her. "It is dangerous in here. Don't even come in." Then: "If you must come in, please stay for just one minute."

Wearing protective clothing, Margaret sees him twice a day for the next two days, unable to embrace or even touch him. Once, she breaks down.

"If you cry," Lukwiya says, "you'll rub your face, which won't be safe. Cool down, Margaret—and stand firm. Keep praying."

Simon Mardel and a Lacor doctor, Yoti Zabulon, team up to treat him, experimenting with aggressive interventions. As Lukwiya's breathing becomes more and more labored, they decide to artificially ventilate him.

His pulse returns to near normal, and his fever comes down. A second round of chest X-rays looks better, and the hospital announces that his condition has begun to improve. But later that night, he hemorrhages into his airway, and the doctors realize that what is happening to their friend is beyond their power to arrest, or even influence.

"There's nothing more anyone can do," Mike Ryan says. "Except say good-bye."

On December 5, at 1:20 a.m., Matthew Lukwiya, who fought so hard to keep the statistics down, joins the numbers himself, the 156th recorded victim of the outbreak.

The next afternoon, he is buried—in a tightly sealed coffin, with pallbearers wearing head-to-toe protective gear—in the shade beneath a mango tree in the Lacor hospital courtyard.

"I don't think he would regret this," Margaret Lukwiya says at the memorial service. "He knew the risk. He saw what was needed for his patients and he did it. That was him. Matthew was not for worldly desires."

Bruno Corrado says he sees Lukwiya's death as a symbol of defeat—a defeat made more painful by the hospital's initial success in containing the outbreak's first wave. "We all wanted Matthew to survive, not only because he was our colleague and friend but as living proof that this disease could be defeated," Corrado says. "We wanted to be able to declare that we fought against this thing together, and we won. But this is not the case. We did not defeat it."

YET, BY THE TIME OF LUKWIYA'S DEATH, the epidemic was on the wane, largely due to his efforts during the first days of the outbreak. After a brief flare-up, admissions slowed to just a handful each day, all of whom were now directed to Gulu Hospital. And although several workers temporarily left as a result of Lukwiya's death, the majority stayed on, inspired by his dedication. True to his hopes, Lukwiya was the last of the hospital staff to die.

On January 23, Uganda's last known Ebola patient was discharged, and the virus retreated back to nature, taking its secrets—including when it will come again—along with it. The international team scattered back to families and routines, in Geneva, Tokyo, Johannesburg.

In Atlanta, months later, Gulu already seems to Tony Sanchez like another life in another universe, a place that exists in flashes of memory and unaccountable longings—for that place where he dealt with things as they were, not as he wished they were; where he felt at once close to death and unimaginably alive. Sometimes, the place comes back in dreams, images piled one atop the other. In one, he is in the isolation ward, treating a terrified little girl not much older than his own daughter, whom he was afraid to touch for a few days after he returned. In the dream, sometimes, one girl becomes the other, and he's helpless—he can't soothe her with his touch, and he can't save her life.

But there are good memories, too. One night at the Acholi Inn, as bats swooped overhead, Mike Ryan held forth on one subject after another, a font of vinegar and piss. The waitress came out and scolded him for leaning back in his chair, and he apologized. Then he settled back squarely on the chair and requested another round of Nile Specials.

"Ah, the source of the Nile," he said when she returned. And he smiled mischievously and rocked back in the chair again, unthinkingly. And she smiled back, and said nothing.

A few minutes later, Simon Mardel and Cathy Roth said good night, and Ryan leaned back with his hands clasped behind his neck and let out a big sigh. "What a bloody ride this is," he said, looking up into the dark foliage overhead.

Like the woman and her exorcist, like the witch doctors in the villages and all the churchgoers in Gulu, like the doctors and nurses and virus hunters, Ryan imagined that there might be answers up there in the trees. But until someone manages to coax those answers out of the darkness, he and the others will be there to stanch the blood.

The truth is, you can't always slay the dragon. But sometimes, if you manage to keep your boot down on its neck long enough, you can quiet it.

MAY/JUNE 2001

LAND OF THE LOST

By Laurence Gonzales

---

*Anyone can get lost (even the author, an award-winning writer on
wilderness survival), but the key to staying alive isn't enduring
cold or hunger—it's defeating the enemy inside your head.*

W HEN KEN KILLIP SET OUT ON THE TRAIL in Colorado's Rocky Mountain National Park at dawn on August 8, 1998, he had the nagging sense that he should not have come. A group of friends had planned the three-day fishing trip, but the others had gradually dropped out until only Killip and his friend John York were left. Killip wondered if he should drop out himself but decided to go ahead with the trip. From the trailhead at Milner Pass, their route would follow the Continental Divide south for four miles, climbing 2,000 feet to the top of Mount Ida. There, at an altitude of 12,889 feet, they'd turn east, descend into the Gorge Lakes drainage, and hike two miles to Rock Lake. While six miles doesn't sound like much, the tiny lake sits at the edge of Forest Canyon, a densely wooded wilderness in the Big Thompson River valley. "It's one of the most remote areas in the park," district ranger Doug Ridley would later say. "It's pretty unforgiving."

At 48, Killip had plenty of outdoor experience. He had been with the Parker Fire Protection District just south of Denver for 24 years. He'd even had some survival training in the military. But he'd never been in a place quite so rugged, and before long the altitude and pace began to wear him down. He fell behind, and York had to keep stopping. After five or six hours, York told Killip to meet him at Rock Lake and then went on alone. Splitting up is never a good idea, but Killip didn't want to slow down his friend.

Both men had maps, but Killip's compass was in the pocket of a shirt that York now carried.

Soon a lightning storm came rolling in, and Killip descended from the exposed ridge to wait it out. By the time the lightning had passed, it was late afternoon. It continued to rain, but Killip shouldered his pack and started up the steep slope, convinced he was climbing Mount Ida.

When Killip at last reached the top and turned east, his first glance into the drainage told him that something was wrong: The Gorge Lakes should have appeared as a string of pearls far below, but there were no lakes. And the large rock shelf that York had told him to expect was not there. In fact, Killip had not reached the summit of Mount Ida. He was looking down a parallel drainage about a mile to the north. It was after 5 p.m., and the sun was getting low behind him. The temperature had begun to drop. He'd been in motion for more than ten hours and had drunk the last of his water three hours earlier.

It was a crucial moment. Killip was now teetering on the invisible dividing line between two worlds: He was in a state of only minor geographical confusion, for he could still turn back. But by the simple act of putting one foot in front of the other, he could very quickly cross over into the state of being genuinely lost.

The late William G. Syrotuck was one of the first search-and-rescue (SAR) experts to conduct systematic research on the behavior of people who become lost in the wilderness. In his pioneering monograph, "Analysis of Lost Person Behavior" (Barkleigh Productions, 1976), he wrote:

> Panic usually implies tearing around or thrashing through the brush, but in its earlier stages it is less frantic. . . . It all starts when they look about and find that a supposedly familiar location now appears totally strange, or when they start to realize that it seems to be taking longer to reach a particular place than they had expected. There is a tendency to hurry to "find the right place." "Maybe it's just over that little ridge."

As darkness and rain fell around him, Killip started down the unfamiliar drainage. In a short while, he found himself blundering through dense timber in total darkness. A chance flicker of lightning ignited reflections on a pond. Parched with thirst, Killip headed for it. He used his pump to filter some water and prepared to spend the night.

Killip had food, but York had the tent. Killip carried garbage bags in his pack but didn't use them for shelter. Although he needed a fire, he knew that open fires weren't permitted in that part of the park. And, as a firefighter, he reasoned, he of all people should follow the rules. Still, he was able to rest, rehydrate, and even heat a meal on his camp stove.

When he awoke on the second day, Killip felt somewhat refreshed. At that point, he still had the option of retracing his steps to his car. But he was determined to find his way to Rock Lake. He began bushwhacking through forest so dense that he sometimes had to remove his backpack to squeeze between the trees.

If things get progressively more unfamiliar and mixed up, [the victims] may then develop a feeling of vertigo, the trees and slopes seem to be closing in and a feeling of claustrophobia compels them to try to "break out." This is the point at which running or frantic scrambling may occur. . . . —*Syrotuck, 1976*

By afternoon, Killip's circle of confusion had expanded to such an extent that he had no means of finding his way to any known location. He was now profoundly lost. Convinced that he was getting close to Rock Lake, he began scrambling up a steep scree slope to get a better view. About halfway up, he lost his footing and began to tumble down the long grade, arresting himself only by chance. His injuries were sobering: severely pulled muscles in his shoulder, ligament and cartilage damage in his knees, and two sprained ankles. Killip dragged himself a short distance to a small pond, where he had no choice but to remain through another rainy night. Again he made no shelter or fire.

If they do not totally exhaust or injure themselves during outright panic, they may eventually get a grip on themselves and decide on some plan of action. What they decide to do may appear irrational to a calm observer, but does not seem nearly so unreasonable to the lost person who is now totally disoriented. Generally, they would be wiser and safer to stay put and get as comfortable and warm as possible, but many feel compelled to push on, urged by subconscious feelings. —*Syrotuck, 1976*

Killip awoke sore and frustrated. Although he had no idea in what direction he was going, he told himself that he could still return to his car. He began limping through the forest. Though he didn't know it, he passed within a quarter mile of Rock Lake. Eventually, he began struggling up another rocky slope, which later analysis showed to be 12,718-foot Terra Tomah Mountain. But an approaching storm forced him back down to the tree line, where he took shelter among the rocks and passed out with one arm wrapped around a tree trunk. It was past midnight when he awoke, wet and shivering, to find hailstones covering the ground to a depth of 12 inches. His fatigue was so severe that he had slept through a driving hailstorm.

When he'd set out on August 8, Killip had been a healthy, competent, well-equipped hiker. His pack contained everything he needed to survive at least a week in the wild. Now, just over two days after taking his wrong turn off the Continental Divide, he was huddled on an icy mountainside, exhausted, hungry, injured, and slipping dangerously toward hypothermia. What had begun as a small error in navigation had progressed, step-by-step, to a full-blown battle for survival.

Into the Wild

Anyone can get lost. I know; I've done it myself. But surprisingly few of us are genuinely prepared to live through the experience. Syrotuck analyzed a group of 229 search-and-rescue cases (of which 11 percent had ended in fatalities) and concluded that almost three-quarters of those who died perished (generally from hypothermia) within the first 48 hours of becoming lost. As sketchy as these figures may be, they suggest that those who die do so surprisingly quickly. But no one knows what the odds are that a particular individual will survive an episode of being lost.

In fact, the more I investigated the subject of survival, the more I was struck by how little research has been done on the topic. The few statistics that do exist show that growing numbers of people are finding themselves in Killip's situation. In 1995, SAR teams responded to 3,725 incidents in the National Park System. By the year 2000, that number had risen 31 percent, to 4,869. One reason is the boom in outdoor recreation. Between 1994 and 2000, the number of American adults who participated in adventure activities (including hiking, backpacking, rock climbing, and off-road driving) increased by 55 percent. In 1999, some 44 million people went mountain biking; 23 million went backpacking. Almost 71 million people visited wilderness or primitive areas.

Another reason for the increase in the number of SAR incidents is technology: ATVs, snowmobiles, mountain bikes, and fat skis are carrying relatively inexperienced people deeper into the wilderness than ever before. All it takes is the malfunction of a minor part to turn a 30-minute ride into a three-day walk.

In Rocky Mountain National Park alone there were one hundred SAR operations last year, and six involved fatalities. So Killip's case is hardly unusual. In fact, the first time I heard Killip's story, it felt eerily familiar. Like him, I had once made a series of seemingly reasonable decisions that ultimately put me in a life-threatening situation.

I was staying at Many Glacier Hotel in Montana's Glacier National Park and had decided to hike the half-hour nature trail with a friend before breakfast. But the woods and the light and the piney smell were all so intoxicating that we left the little loop trail and headed up into the wilderness, following a sign for Grinnell Lake. We took one fork, then another, then another. When the first drops of rain started falling, we slipped into our cheap gift-shop ponchos and hurried on with a growing sense of urgency.

When we finally stood on the lakeshore, trying to remember why it had seemed so important to get there, the soft hissing of rain was suddenly replaced by the clattering of hailstones. I looked over at my companion and saw that her face was pale and blotchy. Her teeth had begun to chatter. I felt a cold dread set like plaster in my stomach as the realization hit me that we were standing in a hailstorm, dressed in cotton T-shirts and garbage bags, at least two hours from home with no map or compass. What had we been thinking?

We took off down the trail at a dead run, but when we reached a fork, she went one way, and I went the other. We turned back to look at each other in horrified amazement. We had no idea which way we'd come. We finally chose one of the paths and had just set foot on it when we heard a human voice. We crashed toward it through a few meters of dense forest and found ourselves on a dock at another lake, where a tourist boat had just pulled up. As we clambered aboard, we were told that it was the last boat of the day.

I still sometimes wake up at night wondering what it would have been like if we had stayed on that path (which led deeper into the wilderness, we later learned) with no water, no fire, and no warm clothing in what turned out to be a two-day storm.

In just a few hours, we'd gone from being carefree day hikers to panicked victims, saved only by dumb luck. I've hiked, paddled, flown airplanes, and ridden dirt bikes everywhere from the Sonoran Desert to the Arctic Circle, but until that day in Glacier, I would not have believed you if you had told me how easily I could get lost or how quickly I could lose my ability to reason. If I was going to understand survival, I realized, I'd first have to learn how capable outdoorspeople can so quickly become their own worst enemies.

The Science of Losing It

Kenneth Hill, a professor of psychology at St. Mary's University in Halifax, Nova Scotia, has spent the past 15 years analyzing how people get lost and how to find them once they do. One of his experiments involves taking a group of students into a small forest. "It's about the size of a large city park," he says, "and notorious for its maze of poorly marked trails." He leads the students in and then asks them to lead him out. Only one person has ever succeeded.

Hill cites cases to further demonstrate how easy it is to get lost: the farmer who got lost on his own property and then wandered nearly 12 miles from home; a construction worker who became lost between two tees while clearing brush for a golf course. "If you ask hikers on a trail to point out where they are on a map at any given moment," Hill says, "they are usually wrong."

To be sure, "lost" is a relative term; the only time when most people are not lost to some degree is when they are home. It's quite possible to know the route from one place to another without knowing precisely where you are at a given moment along the way. "It rarely occurs to us," Hill writes in his book, *Lost Person Behaviour* (National Search and Rescue Secretariat, 1999), that "we lack 'real' spatial orientation, such as knowing . . . the layout of the land. Rather, we may have the illusion of being oriented."

In daily life, that illusion is necessary. While our senses are capable of perceiving the world around us, the human mind is not capable of processing it in all its complexity. Instead, we create simplified models of our environment. "We are constantly maintaining a model in terms of our position," Hill says, "and most of the time it's wrong." Nevertheless, that simplified model is normally good enough to get us where we're going. When it's not, we get lost.

Here's how it works: Suppose you're searching the house for your copy of *Moby Dick,* and you remember it being a red paperback edition. When you search, you don't examine every item in the house to see if it's *Moby Dick.* In fact, your mental model of the red paperback allows you to screen out nearly everything you see until, at last, a red book blossoms in your field of vision. If, on the other hand, your memory is imperfect and the book is actually a blue hardback copy of *Moby Dick,* chances are you won't find it even if the title comes into view. Everyone is familiar with finding something "right under my nose." A faulty mental model is the explanation. It's the reason card tricks and magic acts work: You see what you expect to see.

When it comes to our perception of where we are, the mental model can be unbelievably strong. "I saw a man I was hiking with smash his compass with a rock," Hill says, "because he thought it was broken. He didn't believe we were heading in the right direction."

Bending the Map

The first step in becoming lost is to persist in following your mental model even when the landscape tries to tell you that your model is wrong. Edward Cornell, a psychology professor at the University of Alberta in Edmonton, also specializes in studying the behavior of people who become lost. "Whenever you start looking at your map and saying something like 'Well, that lake could have dried up' or 'That boulder could have moved,' a red light should go off," he says. "You're trying to make reality conform to your expectations rather than seeing what's there. In the sport of orienteering, they call that bending the map." Ken Killip was bending the map when he headed down the wrong drainage despite ample evidence that he was starting from the wrong place.

Once the map is bent, it can be extremely difficult to get it straight again. And so we proceed until we come to a point at which we can no longer deny the evidence of our senses. "It's not something that happens immediately," Hill says. "First, it's a sense of disorientation: 'Uh-oh, I'm not in Kansas anymore.' Then the woods start to become strange; landmarks are no longer familiar."

The mind's functioning—indeed, our very sanity—depends on a reasonable match between our mental models and the world around us. (It could be argued that insanity amounts to the conviction that the world, not the model, is faulty.) As the mental model becomes more and more sharply at odds with the environment, many people will experience the vertigo, claustrophobia, and panic that Syrotuck described. But since most of us are not conscious of the process, we have no way to reflect on what's happening to us. All we know is that it feels as if we're going mad. When at last the full weight of the incongruity hits us, the impact can be staggering.

"'Woods shock' is a term for the fear associated with complete loss of spatial orientation," Hill says. "It is unique. It has very little similarity to any other kind of fear. None of the rational abilities the victim had before being lost are useful to him anymore." In severe cases, the actions of even the most experienced outdoorspeople seem inexplicable. Hikers have abandoned full backpacks; hunters have left their guns behind.

The simple truth is, everyone who dies out there dies of confusion. But woods shock is seldom the sole cause of wilderness deaths. In most cases, there is a destructive synergy among various factors, including exhaustion, dehydration, hypothermia, anxiety, hunger, and perhaps even injury. First, woods shock leads to frantic, poorly planned actions that expose the victim to fatigue, thirst, and cold; these stresses then incapacitate the victim further. People in the last stages of hypothermia, for example, sometimes disrobe completely. One man, lost for five days in Colorado's San Juan Wilderness, was rescued wearing nothing but his wristwatch. In the worst cases, the impaired mind and the impaired body drag each other down until, like two drowning swimmers, they pull each other under.

Going Through Stages

Being lost, then, is not a location; it is a transformation. Though there is no standard model for describing this mental and physical metamorphosis, the research of Hill, Syrotuck, and others suggests five general stages. In the first, you deny that you're disoriented and press on with growing urgency. In the next stage, as you admit that you're lost, you begin to panic. In the third stage, you calm down and form a strategy. In the fourth stage, you deteriorate both mentally and physically as your strategy fails to get you out. And in the final stage, you become resigned to your plight as you run out of options.

Of course, these stages might be reordered, occur almost simultaneously, or, in some cases, be repeated. But the overall direction of events appears to be all too common. It is perhaps no surprise that this pattern closely resembles the now widely accepted stages of dying described by psychologist Elizabeth Kübler-Ross: denial, anger, bargaining, depression, and acceptance. And the end result is often the same. "Once the stage of psychological disintegration is reached, death is often not far away," observes John Leach, a professor of psychology at Britain's Lancaster University, in his book *Survival Psychology* (New York University Press, 1994). "The ability people possess to die gently, and often suddenly, through no organic cause, is a very real one."

This is a lesson Hill knows well. "I have photos of a man who settled into a cozy bed of pine needles after removing his shoes, pants, and jacket and setting his wallet on a nearby rock," Hill says. "In the photos, he seems so peaceful; it's hard to believe he's dead. The photos have special significance for me, because I helped coordinate the search. Whenever I start to believe I'm some hot-shit SAR expert, I pull the photos out and I'm over it."

By his third night lost in the wild, when Killip awoke amid the hailstones at the foot of Terra Tomah Mountain, he had arguably passed through denial (descending the wrong drainage), panic (climbing up the dangerous scree slope), and strategic planning (attempting to backtrack) and was well into the penultimate stage of deterioration. But he did not succumb to resignation.

Instead, he pulled himself together. He put on his fishing waders and started walking around to get warm, made a fire, and built a makeshift shelter using his garbage bags. For the next two days, he stayed put and attended to the business of living. Killip had entered the final stage that separates the quick from the dead: not helpless resignation but pragmatic acceptance. As Killip would prove, that final stage in the process can be either a beginning or an end. For some, it's when they give up and die. For others, it's when they stop denying and begin surviving. If the disorientation of woods shock is the first transformation the lost person goes through, Killip had now gone through a second, and that second transformation is the secret to survival.

"You get into some really crazy thinking," Killip says now, three years after his rescue. "You don't realize that you've started talking to yourself." He began feeding his rations to marmots just to get them to come close. Then he talked to them as well. But having faced the reality of his situation, he was now able to concentrate on keeping himself alive. On his fifth and final day of being lost, Killip watched in horror as a helicopter passed right over him, so close that "I felt like I could throw a rock at him. Then he turned and flew away. It was almost breaking my spirit." But the pilot had seen Killip's blue parka hanging on a branch and directed the searchers to his location.

"I lost 30 pounds in five days," Killip says. His knee injuries required two operations. Today, he gives talks to Boy Scouts and other groups on wilderness safety. "Now I carry a survival pack and a map and compass everywhere," he says. "And I'm very careful about who I go out with. If I have a bad feeling about something, I don't go."

Who Makes It—And Why

One of the great riddles in the study of survival is why some people live while others, often facing less difficult conditions, die. "It's not who you'd predict, either," says Hill, who has studied the survival rates of different demographic groups. "Sometimes the one who survives is an inexperienced female hiker, while the experienced hunter gives up and dies in one night, even when it's not that cold."

Among healthy people, he says, "the category that has one of the highest survival rates is children six and under—the very people we're most concerned about." Despite the fact that small children lose body heat much faster than adults, they often survive in the same conditions better than experienced hunters, better than physically fit hikers, better than former members of the military. And one of the groups with the poorest survival rates is children seven to twelve. Clearly, those youngest children possess some secret that trumps knowledge and experience.

Scientists do not know exactly what the secret is, but the answer may lie in some very basic childhood traits: Small children do not create complex mental maps. They don't understand traveling to a particular place, so they don't run to get somewhere beyond their field of vision. They also follow their instincts. If it gets cold, they'll crawl into a hollow tree to get warm. If they're tired, they rest, so they don't fatigue. If they're thirsty, they drink. They try to make themselves comfortable. And staying comfortable helps keep them alive.

Children ages seven to twelve, on the other hand, behave much like adults: They panic and run. They look for shortcuts. If the trail peters out, they keep going, ignoring thirst, hunger, and cold, until they fall over. In learning to think more like adults, it seems, they have suppressed the very instincts that might have helped them survive.

I set out for survival school troubled by this deep puzzle. We like to think that education and experience make us more competent, more capable. Yet it seemed the opposite might sometimes be true in life-or-death situations. I wondered if there was a way to learn the skills of survival while keeping the instincts of a small child. I couldn't help thinking of the Zen concept of the "beginner's mind," the mind that remains open and ready despite years of training. "In the beginner's mind there are many possibilities," said Zen master Shunryu Suzuki. "In the expert's mind there are few."

Learning to Live

Byron Kerns is a big, macho-looking guy with 14 years of military experience, including four years as an Air Force survival instructor. He now runs the Mountain Shepherd Wilderness Survival School in Lynchburg, Virginia, in the foothills of the Blue Ridge Mountains, where the woods are dense and rugged. It's a perfect place to get lost. On my first day, we hiked up a rocky river drainage and into the wilderness, where we practiced navigation, fire craft, making shelter, and finding water—the basics of survival that anyone who enters the woods ought to know. But the skills and tools are only the beginning, he told me. What's in your heart and head is far more important than what's in your pack.

The first time I saw him, Kerns was sauntering across a parking lot, wearing a 16-inch Panamanian machete. I had the definite impression that I was about to meet a hardball military type who was going to make things rough on me. But Kerns is soft-spoken, polite, earnest, and gentle to a fault. Even after a life spent in the wilderness, each time he enters the woods he approaches it with a deep sense of respect and humility, like a man approaching a magnificent and unpredictable creature.

He wasn't always that way. Early in his Air Force days, Kerns told me as we walked, he took a group of pilots into the mountains near Spokane, Washington, for survival-training maneuvers. He was trying to be the hard-driving drill instructor: Go, go, go; push, push, push. They were crossing a vast field of slushy snow, and the pilots began to fatigue, but Kerns kept driving them. "I now realize that was a mistake," he said. As darkness came down like a curtain, the temperature dropped. "Suddenly everybody wanted to give up. They just sat down and lost all their will." Apathy is a common reaction to any sort of disaster. After the bombing of Hiroshima, the Japanese who observed that reaction among survivors called it *burabura,* or do-nothing sickness. If not countered, it can rapidly lead to complete physical deterioration.

"All at once it hit me that those million-dollar pilots could die," Kerns said. "I fell to my knees, and I prayed." Which turned out to be exactly the right thing to do. Having mustered his inner resources, he was then able to rise from his knees and take charge. He pulled a cedar fence post out of the snow, carved off shavings for tinder, and built a fire. "It's amazing to see what fire can do," he said. "The minute you light that fire, you're home, the lights are on, and supper's cooking. It just turned everybody around."

Kerns learned many lessons that night: "That experience taught me to carry everything in my pack, have everything ready to make that fire," he said. But, more than that, he saw how his own mastery of the situation inspired the pilots. That lesson was driven home to me again and again: Helping someone else is the best way to ensure your own survival; it gives you a mission and lets you rise above your fears. You're now a leader, not a victim.

"Lack of leadership in a survival situation can be fatal," Leach writes in *Survival Psychology.* He tells of the fishing boat *West I,* which sank in the Pacific, leaving eight members of its crew floating in two life rafts, which were tethered together by a 30-meter line. In one raft, the third mate quickly took charge, setting watches and assigning the men chores. In the second raft, which included the captain, no leader emerged. "Instead of discipline, there was disintegration," Leach writes. When the crew was rescued two weeks later, the men in the first raft climbed aboard the rescue ship under their own power. Those in the second, who'd been only 30 meters away, were helpless and had to be carried aboard. The captain had already succumbed to the elements.

"Establishing a definite purpose to one's existence strengthens survival," Leach concludes. "But . . . it must be coupled with . . . the breaking down of the person's aim or purpose into simple tasks so that life can be handled one step at a time."

Taking things one step at a time is the essence of modern survival technique. A survival situation is a ticking clock, Kerns told me. You have only so much water, so much energy, so much emotion stored inside you. Every time you exert yourself, you're using them up. The heart of his teaching is learning to be stingy with those scarce resources. To help reinforce this idea, he recited the seven-point survival checklist used by the Air Force and other groups: (1) positive mental attitude, (2) first aid, (3) shelter, (4) fire, (5) signaling, (6) water, (7) food.

"The first thing you do is STOP," Kerns said. "It's an acronym: stop, think, observe, plan. That's your first order of business." In other words, first organize your mind.

Next, Kerns said, "you check the physical condition of your people: Is someone sick? Is someone hurt?" Stabilizing the injured or sick takes precedence over all other needs.

Since hypothermia can kill so quickly, shelter is next on the list. "Shelter begins with your clothes," Kerns said. With the right clothing, you don't always need additional shelter, but he advises carrying a plastic drop sheet and large garbage bags for conserving body heat.

"After that, you can think about your fire craft." While you may not need fire to survive, he said, "seeing that light as the sun goes down sure is nice." A fire is also useful for signaling, the next item on the list.

In most cases, water and, especially, food are less urgent. ("We've never found somebody starved to death," says Steve Foster, of the National Association for Search and Rescue, or NASAR.) You don't want to be crashing through the woods, trying to find a stream, when a helicopter happens to fly over.

I noticed that Kerns didn't talk much about "positive mental attitude." But on my last day of training, we were hiking in dense timber when Kerns suddenly began shivering and refused to go on. "Help me," he moaned. "I'm freezing. I can't walk any farther."

Earlier he had shown me how to assemble a ready pack that contained everything I'd need to survive for three days. I opened it and whipped out a large orange plastic garbage bag, one with a face hole already cut in it, and put it over him. I had him kneel on a bit of foam rubber to insulate him from the ground. "You're going to be just fine," I said. When you're working to save someone else, it's amazing how the tricks of survival come tumbling out. Pulling my tarp and cord from my ready pack, I erected an emergency shelter. Then, using Vaseline-coated cotton balls and a small chunk of a fake fireplace log, I was able to get a roaring fire going in minutes. And when he asked for a cup of tea, I had my canteen cup ready to boil water. From there, I felt as if we could do anything.

"The most terrifying thing in the world to me," Kerns said after our simulated emergency, "is to be in the woods and not be able to help someone who needs my help." And as we sat relaxing under our makeshift shelter, I realized that Kerns had taught me about the first item on the checklist, positive mental attitude, while barely mentioning it.

One point of survival training, of course, is to prevent you from becoming lost in the first place. But what if you are lost for a reason beyond your control, such as a plane crash? I asked Kerns. How do you find yourself? "You don't," Kerns said. "It's extremely difficult to get your bearings once you are really lost, even if you have a map and compass and can see mountains." You cannot solve an equation in which all the variables are unknown. If you do not know your present location, you cannot readily navigate to any other point in space. So Kerns, like most survival experts, advises staying put and waiting for help to come. My training and the ready pack were designed to keep me alive for 72 hours, which, he said, was generally the maximum time it would take for SAR to find me and have me sitting down to a hot meal. The problem was, I'd come across some rare, but chilling, exceptions to that rule.

The Long, Long Wait

In June 1990, David Boomhower set out on a ten-day hike on New York's Northville–Lake Placid Trail. He was traveling alone, and although he had done a lot of planning, he started running low on food after about five days. So he looked at his map and decided that Sucker Brook Trail would take him to a road, which he could take to the nearest town.

He was not in trouble yet, but he had begun putting together a plan that would end his life. He'd left a copy of his route with the authorities, but now that he had altered his course, they would have no way of knowing where he was. All he needed was one surprise, and he'd be in big trouble.

He got more than one. The trail was far more rugged than he'd expected. It crossed a stream 14 times before it petered out. Then the weather arrived. Although he was only two miles from the road, he could not figure out how to reach it. Even so, when he admitted to himself that he was lost, he did things by the book. He made camp and awaited rescue.

The search for Boomhower wasn't begun until he'd been gone thirteen days and was three days overdue. More than once, he saw the airplane that was ferrying state troopers and search volunteers, but it didn't occur to him that they were looking for him, so he didn't signal. At dark he would light his lantern, but the plane didn't fly at night. There is an annual Fourth of July fireworks display at a nearby campsite, and Boomhower reasoned that he'd hear it and be able to walk in that direction. But for the first time in ten years, the fireworks were canceled.

Boomhower kept a diary, and it is heartbreaking to read. By the time he realized that he might not be rescued, he'd grown too weak to travel. In one of his journal entries, he wrote: "I wonder if anyone has died out here, waiting, believing in that 'stay calm and help will arrive' bullshit." David Boomhower set out on June 5; his body was found by accident on October 20. According to his journal, he had lasted 55 days.

The truth is that if you do get lost, it's not a foregone conclusion that anyone will even search for you, let alone find you. In some states—Washington and New Mexico, for example—the search-and-rescue operations are well organized and scientific. In many other regions in the U.S., however, searches are haphazardly organized by local sheriffs, state police, and fire departments. Many rely on well-intentioned but poorly supervised volunteers. "It's the posse method," Kenneth Hill says. "Send some people west and some people east, and tell them to bring 'em back if you find 'em, boys."

So the question of whether to stay put or go back is not a trivial one. And the answer might depend on a number of other questions: Have you left your route with the authorities? Are you close to where you said you'd be? Are you able to retrace your steps?

That life-and-death decision could be the most difficult one you might ever face, and you would be forced to make it at a time when your own mind is deeply unreliable. Think about it: If your predicament begins with an inability to interpret information correctly, how can you trust yourself? Therein lies the Zen paradox of survival.

If I was ever faced with that decision, I like to think I would remember first to sit down and quiet my mind. I would make sure that I was rested, fed, and hydrated. I would go back over my actions to see if they fit the pattern of denial, panic, strategy, and so on. And only then, I hope, would I consider trying to backtrack. (Those who do attempt to backtrack should remember to mark their trail as visibly as possible.)

The mind is the ultimate survival kit. But the mind that gets us into trouble is not the same mind that will save us. Part of the process of survival is to move through those stages with as little trauma as possible, coming out the other side with a new kind of rationalism. With the rationalism that comes from acceptance. I needed to know if it was possible to train my mind to recognize its own shortcomings.

Beginner's Mind

The morning I arrived at the Vermont Wilderness Survival School near the Green Mountains, a group of children about eight years old were moving through the forest, pretending to be deer. They had their hands cupped to their ears to amplify sounds. A twig snapped, and they scattered and vanished.

The school's co-founder, Mark Morey, and I watched them silently. Morey, who has studied at Tom Brown, Jr.'s famous Tracker School, teaches what some term "primitive" survival skills, though he likes to call them "the ancient ways of adaptation." The children were taking part in a youth program affiliated with his school. When Morey and I caught up with the kids, he sat them down and told them a tale loosely based on Jack London's short story "To Build a Fire." As he recounted how the main character froze to death, their eyes grew wide. Then Morey said, "Now, I've just fallen in a stream, and I'm freezing. We have only one match. You have five minutes to build me a fire. Go!" The children rushed around without talking, gathering wood. As Morey counted off the minutes, they expertly laid the fire and had it going in four minutes and fifteen seconds.

The exercise wasn't about fire craft. "What we're doing," Morey explained, "is loss-proofing these kids by building empathy and observational skills. In that last exercise, we demonstrated something we've discussed with them: The fight for survival can require a burst of energy. Those kids just saved my life. One day they may save a life for real."

We moved to a group of older children working with bow-drill sets. I was amazed to see a ten-year-old boy use his crude wooden bow drill to twirl a thin spindle until it generated a spark. He had a roaring fire going in under ten minutes. It had taken him two years to learn that skill.

That afternoon, I began work on my own fire, first by collecting the materials to make a bow drill. By evening, I was dirty and drenched in sweat and glad my life didn't depend on that fire.

The second day, with Morey coaching me every step, I did manage to make fire. It took hours, and I almost blew it at the end when my spindle slipped, sending the fragile coal flying. But Morey salvaged it and transferred it to a tinder bundle he'd fashioned (an art in itself). He gave me the honor of cupping it in my hands and blowing it to life. Within seconds, I could feel the heat searing through the tinder. Its power was immediate and magnificent. The burning bush had spoken. I was a believer.

But, again, fire was not the point. What Morey really teaches is a path to seeing and knowing the world. And to see and know the world is to survive in it. Not that Morey would disagree with the modern survival techniques I learned from Kerns. By all means, carry matches, a compass, and a tarp, he said. But learning ancient skills means learning a deeper level of awareness, which in turn might save you from becoming your own worst enemy in the woods. None of Morey's students would have ignored a big storm cloud, as I'd done in Glacier. They would have smelled it, seen it, felt it, long before it came. "We come from cities and learn to expect things to stay the same," he said. "But they don't. And it kills us, quickly or slowly."

When Morey said that he could teach me to navigate without a compass or map, I was skeptical. Then, as we hiked through the dense forest, he stopped every 20 or 30 yards to examine and discuss things we found there. After a while, he asked me to close my eyes and point the way back to where we'd started. It was a humbling experience to find that I couldn't. We hadn't even gone that far, and I was, technically, lost.

Morey directed my attention to the last place we'd stopped. "Remember? We talked about the bittersweet vine there." We'd taken a sample of a type of vine that's good for cordage. So we walked back to that spot. Then he pointed to another place where he'd shown me ways of seeing and walking that were used by native peoples. We returned to that spot. From there, we could see the place where we'd found the entrance to a vole tunnel. Thus we carried on our conversations in reverse and were able to retrace our steps exactly. The lesson was not just about finding your way in the woods, of course. It was about navigating the human mind.

Morey compared our walk to the ancient navigational techniques, often called songlines, used by Australian Aborigines. Aborigine culture includes detailed songs that recount the journeys of ancestors. Knowing these songs means knowing the geography of the Aborigine world. Morey's running commentary during our walk allowed us to find our way back. "If you do that whenever you go into the woods," he told me, "you'll never be lost."

Three weeks later, Morey was still able to recite in detail the steps of our journey. "It's not like I tried to remember that," he said. "It's an ancient instinct. And it's still alive." Here was a strategy for making our mental map match the world; a map and compass are just another method for doing the same thing.

Each child in Morey's school selects a secret spot in the woods. Every day, the students spend time at their secret spots. "They do this through all the seasons," Morey said. "They learn to stop and think. They learn to be calm and alone. They will never feel that the woods are alien. So if they ever get lost or otherwise stranded, they won't panic." Research has shown that people revert to automatic behavior in emergencies. Morey was teaching his children to behave automatically like survivors.

Deep Survival

Morey told me that children from farms and from the inner city do well in his courses, while suburban kids tend to give up. "They have no survival instinct," he said, "because they have no predators." Perhaps the illusion of safety and comfort in our lives today is eroding our will to survive. I couldn't help thinking of one of the strangest survival cases I'd come across: In August 1999, Raffi Kodikian, age 25, and his friend David Coughlin, 26, got lost while camping in New Mexico's Carlsbad Caverns National Park. For four days, they wandered with no food (save a can of beans) and no water. Then, according to Kodikian, Coughlin couldn't stand it any longer and begged to be put out of his misery. Kodikian obliged him, stabbing his best friend twice in the chest. Kodikian was rescued that same day, having never gone more than 1.5 miles from the road. (He is now serving a two-year prison term in New Mexico for second-degree murder.)

"The behavior of people suddenly caught in the eye of a catastrophe varies from individual to individual, but across the spectrum, there does appear to be an identifiable pattern of responses," Leach writes in *Survival Psychology*. About 10 to 20 percent of people will stay calm during the initial crisis. "These people will be able to collect their thoughts quickly," he writes. "They will be able to assess the situation, make a plan, and act upon it." A second group, comprising about 75 percent of the population, is simply "stunned and bewildered. . . . They will behave in a reflexive, almost automatic or mechanical manner." A third group, 10 to 15 percent, will exhibit inappropriate behavior—confusion, screaming, weeping, or paralyzing anxiety.

Even the military, which invests huge resources in survival training, can't predict who will and will not fold under extreme conditions. But the accounts of those who've made it through the worst situations hold some clues to the heart of the true survivor. In 1982, Debbie Kiley, an accomplished ocean racer, was delivering a yacht to Florida when it sank in a storm, stranding her and four others in an inflatable Zodiac boat. As she recounts in her book, *Untamed Seas* (Mariner Books, 1994), they drifted for five days. Passenger Meg Mooney slowly died of injuries she'd sustained when the yacht sank; Captain John Lippoth and crew member Mark Adams drank seawater, became delirious, and went over the side, where they were eaten by sharks. Only Kiley and her friend and fellow crew member Brad Cavanaugh survived. Her analysis of why they lived is telling: "I felt like it was my job to keep him alive," she says. "And I think he thought the same about me." When the sharks attacked, Kiley and Cavanaugh could only sit and listen helplessly to the frenzied battle beneath the boat. "That is the only time in my life I felt like I was just walking down that fine line of sanity," she says. "Here's Mark, he's overboard, the sharks are eating him, Meg's dying, it's in the middle of the night, and it's the first night that the stars are out. It was just very haunting."

Yet she never doubted herself. "When I was out there and people started to die, I knew that I wasn't going to die," she says. "It was just a matter of figuring out how [to stay alive]." Kiley and Cavanaugh took turns keeping watch, and she endlessly recited the Lord's Prayer. But mostly they hunkered down, trying to stay warm and conserve energy. "You have to take responsibility for your own survival," she says. "You can't just sit back and let someone else do it for you."

One SAR worker told me the possibly apocryphal story of a man who had survived six days in the desert with no water, in temperatures above 100 degrees. When his rescuers asked him how he did it, he told them he was in the middle of a divorce and "just didn't want to let the bitch get everything." Anger, focus, determination, prayer, faith—whatever keeps the boat afloat. But what seems to set deep survivors apart is their ability to tap into it when they need it. Leach puts it this way: "When the personality is ripped away, there has to be a core remaining to carry the person through. This inner character is self-supporting and if a person can carry all his support within him then it matters little what the external environment comprises."

In some ancient cultures, young men (and a few women) were sent into the wilderness to fast for days in search of a vision. The vision quest was a rite of passage, a religious custom; but underneath, it was survival school, too, a test of those inexplicable reserves that separate the living from the dead. It was a way of simulating that split state of mind that survivors describe, a state that grants us peace at the very moment when panic is closest.

Kiley and others describe an eerie sort of calm that settles over people when they have accepted the brutal reality of their situation. "Be still," Kiley says. "If you can't make a decision, just be still." Leach calls this state "active-passiveness." It is the ability to accept one's plight without giving in to it.

At the ultimate stage of a survival situation, we are faced with two paths: Taking one, we perish. Taking the other, we accept the new world in which we've found ourselves. Leach calls this final transformation "survival by surrender." It sounds almost Zen.

Ken Killip's transformation took place when he settled down to use the materials he had with him instead of trying to thrash his way back to a world he could no longer reach. Even his befriending the marmots could be seen as an acceptance of his new environment.

Having to fight in order to live another day is among the most fundamental transforming experiences a human being can have. And yet so few of us ever have to face that struggle. Rarely do we take true responsibility for our actions. We live in a culture of lifeguards, of insurance and lawsuits, where someone else is always responsible and someone else is always to blame. But take one wrong turn in the woods (or, more aptly, in the mind), and we go directly to the Stone Age. With our survival at stake, we're suddenly called to account for the long arrears of our inattention. Then it's up to us to find our place in that new world.

NOVEMBER/DECEMBER 2001

FINDING EVERETT RUESS

By David Roberts

A young vagabond's 1934 disappearance in Utah canyon country spawned an enduring legend. Seven decades later, the discovery of a burial site on sacred Navajo ground, followed by a battery of genetic and forensic analyses, finally lays the mystery to rest.

IT WAS A CHILLY DAY IN NOVEMBER 1934. The country had been mired in the Great Depression for morethan five years, and no town felt the pinch of poverty more acutely than Escalante. Founded by Mormon pioneers 59 years earlier, the small settlement in southern Utah—then one of the most remote towns in the United States—had been stricken in successive summers by a plague of grasshoppers that ruined the crops and by the worst drought in nearly eight decades. In late autumn, the arrival of any visitor in Escalante was a rare occurrence. It was all the more surprising, then, when the thin, sandy-haired stranger rode into town from the west, saddled on one under-sized burro, leading another that was packed with camping gear. His name, he told the locals, was Everett Ruess. He was from California. And although he was only 20, he had been wandering all over the Southwest for the better part of the previous four years.

The young boys of Escalante took an instant liking to the vagabond. During the next several days, they rode horseback with him along the nearby ridges, hunted for arrowheads, and shared his campfire dinner of venison and pota-toes. On his last night in town, Ruess (pronounced ROO-ess) treated a couple of the boys to the local movie theater. They watched *Death Takes a Holiday*.

Then Ruess rode alone out of town, headed southeast down the Hole in the Rock Trail toward the barren plateau the locals called the Desert. The day before, he had mailed a last letter to his brother in California. "It may be a month or two before I have a post office," he wrote, "for I am exploring southward to the Colorado [River], where no one lives."

Ruess was launched on the next leg of his quest for beauty and adventure. A week later, 50 miles out, he sat around a campfire with a couple of Escalante sheepherders.

And then, Everett Ruess disappeared from the face of the Earth.

IT WAS A WARM DAY IN MAY 2008. Daisy Johnson had come from her home in Farmington, New Mexico, to Shiprock to visit her younger brother, Denny Bellson. And to tell him a story he had never heard before—a story about their grandfather, Aneth Nez, that took place back in the 1930s.

Fifty-six years old last May, Johnson was a troubled woman. A year before, she had been diagnosed with ovarian cancer. She underwent a round of chemotherapy that nauseated her and caused her hair to fall out, but the cancer had gone away. Now, just in the past few weeks, it had come back. This time Johnson, a traditional Navajo, went to a medicine man.

"He told me this all came about because of our grandpa," Johnson said to her brother. She knew in a heartbeat that the medicine man must be right. How else had he known about her grandfather?

Bellson lives on the Navajo Reservation, just off U.S. Highway 191, not far from where he and his sister had grown up, and where their grandfather, Aneth Nez, had lived. Last May he listened to his sister's story in electrified silence.

"A long time ago," she said, "Grandpa was sitting up there on the rim of Comb Ridge [a sandstone uplift that crosses the Utah-Arizona border]. For several days he watched this guy—he was a real young Anglo dude—riding up and down the canyon below him. The guy had two mules, one that he rode and one that was packed with things dangling off the side. It was like he was looking for something."

One day, according to Johnson, Nez saw the young man down in the riverbed, only this time he was yelling and riding fast. Nez scanned the wash below and saw three Utes chasing the boy. "They caught up with him and hit him on the head and knocked him off his mule," she recounted. "They left him there and took off with the mules and whatever else the guy had."

As he watched the scene unfold, Nez stayed out of view. For centuries Utes living north of the San Juan River had been fierce enemies of the Navajo, whose homeland lay south of the river. As late as the 1930s, tensions between the groups occasionally broke out in violence. Nez's perch was only a few miles from that ethnic frontier.

When the Utes had gone, Nez descended some 300 feet from Comb Ridge to the bed of Chinle Wash. The young man was dead by the time Nez got to him. Rather than looking for a burial site in the open wash, the Navajo hauled the body up to the rocky folds of the ridge, in all likelihood on the back of his horse. "Grandpa got a lot of blood on him," Johnson said. "That's what made him get sick later. Then he buried the young guy up there on the rim."

For more than three decades, Aneth Nez had told no one about this dark episode in his past. Then, in 1971, at the age of 72, he also had fallen ill with cancer. Nez paid a medicine man to diagnose his trouble. "He said," Daisy Johnson recalled, "'You had no business messing around with that body.'"

The medicine man told Nez that the only way he could cure his cancer would be to retrieve a lock of hair from the head of the young man he had buried decades earlier, then use it in a five-day curing ceremony. "I was 19," Johnson said. "I was home for the summer. That was the first time I ever heard anything about the young dude the Utes had killed down there in Chinle Wash."

Johnson drove Nez out toward the Comb in a pickup. She waited in the cab for two hours, guessing that her grandfather was reconnoitering the land or perhaps even praying to prepare himself. He returned to the pickup empty-handed.

Later, Nez traveled back to the Comb with a medicine man. This time he retrieved a lock of hair from the grave. In the curing ceremony, Johnson said, the medicine man dusted the hair with ashes—"so it will never bother the patient again." At the end of the five days, the medicine man shot the lock with a gun, to destroy it completely.

"And then Grandpa got better," Daisy Johnson said. "He lived another ten years."

As he listened to her story, Bellson realized that the grave must lie not far from the house he had built in 1993. Thirteen years younger than his sister, Bellson has kept a close bond with the land on which he grew up. Now he was seized with a passion to find the grave where Nez had buried the "young dude" back in the 1930s.

Several weeks later, Bellson drove to Farmington to see his sister. He brought with him a USGS topo map. "I tried to get her to show me where she'd parked the pickup with our grandpa," Bellson told me later. "When I showed her the map, she recognized a Y in the road near Colored Rock Woman's house. She gave me real good directions."

During the next few weeks, Bellson, a carpenter and craftsman, spent his free time out hiking Comb Ridge, looking into every corner and crack along the rim. Then, one day, in an obscure crevice just under the crest of the Comb, he found a grave. Bellson saw at once that the person whose bones lay in that unlikely tomb had been buried in haste, and perhaps in great fear. A traditional Navajo himself, Bellson did not touch a thing.

When he got home, he called Johnson. "I found the grave," he told her.

AFTER EVERETT RUESS DISAPPEARED in November 1934, nearly four months passed before anyone organized a search. The alarm went out only after Ruess's parents in California received a packet of their letters to their son, returned as unclaimed.

On horseback, a band of Escalante men started looking out on the Desert, where the sheepherders had sat beside Ruess's campfire back in November. After several tries, they entered Davis Gulch by an old livestock trail and hit pay dirt.

According to Utah historian W. L. Rusho, author of *Everett Ruess: A Vagabond for Beauty,* the searchers discovered a makeshift brushwork corral that confined Everett's two burros, still fat and healthy. On the brush fence the men found a bridle, halter, and rope. In a nearby alcove in the sandstone cliff they discovered empty cans, the impression of a bedroll in the dirt, and numerous footprints. But after intensive searching up and down Davis Gulch, the ranchers never came across Ruess's camping gear, cook set, or supplies of food—nor his beloved painting kit or the journal he scrupulously kept on every trip.

For decades, scores of wanderers in the convoluted Southwest have disappeared, and their remains have seldom been found. The mystery posed by their vanishing usually lasts for a few weeks in the newspapers. But Ruess's disappearance launched what can only be called a cult. In bars from California to Colorado, the mere mention of his story could be counted on to provoke a heated debate over the possible ways he met his fate.

In 1940 a small California press published *On Desert Trails With Everett Ruess,* a handsome collage of excerpts from the young man's letters home, his poems and essays, and his watercolor paintings and woodblock engravings. It was the first of seven books, along with two documentary films, to chronicle the explorer's life and vanishing. Then, in 1996, Jon Krakauer devoted ten pages of *Into the Wild* to Ruess. Krakauer saw in the vagabond a kindred soul to Chris McCandless, the doomed young wanderer who had starved to death in the wilderness north of Denali. After *Into the Wild* Ruess's cult status skyrocketed. By now, Ruess has emerged as the subject of pop song lyrics, as a T-shirt icon for adventure, and as the patron saint of an arts festival held every September in Escalante.

Ruess "lives" while other lost wanderers have faded from memory for several reasons, chief among them the fact that his intense passion for wilderness resonates deeply with every romantic idealist who longs to escape. In his flight from all things safe, familiar, and domestic, Ruess stands as the real-life counterpart to Jack London's sourdoughs or Mark Twain's Huck Finn. He disappeared, moreover, with his dream intact but his pursuit of it poignantly unfulfilled.

In the dozens of letters he sent home, Ruess's writing soars with rhapsodic, even grandiose, evocations of the wilderness: "I have seen almost more beauty than I can bear." But his aesthetic flights are balanced by a sense of despair and often a premonition of impending doom. "I must pack my short life full of interesting events," he wrote to his brother from an Arizona outpost at the age of only 17. "I shall go on some last wilderness trip, to a place I have known and loved. I shall not return."

Like many teenagers, Ruess was convinced that he was destined to be a lifelong loner. "My friends have been few," he wrote to one confidant in 1931, "because I'm a freakish person." Only days before his arrival in Escalante, he wrote to his brother: "I stopped a few days in a little Mormon town and indulged myself in family life, church-going, and dances. If I had stayed any longer I would have fallen in love with a Mormon girl, but I think it's a good thing I didn't. I've become a little too different from most of the rest of the world."

In contrast to his writing, Ruess's woodcuts and paintings are strikingly simple and vivid, condensing the landscape into a few bold elements with a Japanese economy: a pair of cypress trees tossed by the wind, a sandstone buttress thrusting into the sky. (The logo of the Escalante arts festival adapts Ruess's vignette of a silhouetted youth leading burros off toward the unknown.)

In 1942 author Wallace Stegner took the measure of Ruess, offering a final word on his enduring legacy: *What Everett was after was beauty, and he conceived beauty in pretty romantic terms. We might be inclined to laugh at the extravagance of his beauty-worship if there was not something almost magnificent in his single-minded dedication to it. . . . If we laugh at Everett Ruess we shall have to laugh at John Muir, because there was little difference between them except age.*

IN MAY 2008 NEITHER Daisy Johnson nor Denny Bellson had ever heard of Everett Ruess. After listening to his sister's remarkable story about Aneth Nez, Bellson Googled "Missing persons + Arizona/Utah + 1930s." It was only then that he came across the story of the romantic vagabond who had disappeared near Escalante in 1934. The similarities with Aneth Nez's sinister tale were too striking to ignore.

A few days after his discovery Bellson took his friend Vaughn Hadenfeldt out to the gravesite. A wilderness guide based in Bluff, Utah, and my longtime hiking companion, Hadenfeldt knew the Ruess story backward and forward. The next day he called me. "It could be a Navajo crevice burial," he reported. "But there's something pretty weird about it." (Hadenfeldt is well versed in the common Navajo practice of burying a body, along with certain precious possessions, in a natural fissure in the bedrock.) Then Hadenfeldt relayed the details of the Aneth Nez story, as Johnson had recounted it to Bellson.

By the time he had finished, the hook was set. I'd never met Bellson, but Hadenfeldt had spoken highly of his friend's sagacity about local lore. I decided I ought to head out myself and see what was going on along Comb Ridge.

Before I could get to Utah, however, Bellson called the FBI in Monticello. If by some remote chance the grave was that of Everett Ruess—or of some other Anglo who had been killed by Utes—it was thus a crime scene. Fearful of sidestepping the law, Bellson felt it his duty to notify the authorities.

I called up special agent Rachel Boisselle, who worked in the Monticello office. Over the phone, she seemed friendly. She, too, had never heard of Everett Ruess, so I filled her in on the 75-year-old saga. Boisselle was planning to head out to the site with Bellson in a few days. But she was plainly skeptical. "Denny's already dragged us out to another place down near Poncho House where he found bones coming out of the ground," she told me. "When we got there, we could see right away that it was an Anasazi mother and child. We covered the bones back up."

The Ruess story clearly intrigued Boisselle, however. "You can be sure we'll treat this new burial with the utmost respect," she told me just before we hung up. "We won't disturb a thing."

I phoned another friend, Greg Child, who lives in Castle Valley, Utah. In 2004 Child, Hadenfeldt, and I had hiked the full length of Comb Ridge. As we later realized, we had come within a hundred yards of the gravesite without having the faintest notion that there was anything interesting just above us, on the rim to our right.

Child drove down to Bluff and found Bellson, who took him out on the Comb. "At the grave, Denny didn't touch a thing," Child told me later. "And on the way out, he made me wash my hands in a spring. I had to wash them over and over again before Denny would let me get back in his truck."

At the site Child spent an hour photographing the burial. Outside the crevice Bellson had found a wooden stirrup, tattered strips of leather, and the frame of a saddle with a rusted iron pommel. Just inside the crevice, lying on the ground, was a black leather belt decorated with metal studs. Curiously, the belt was buckled, so it lay in a closed but empty loop.

Of the partially buried body itself, the most striking feature was the top of the skull, intact but fragile, protruding from the dirt, almost as if the victim were in a sitting position. Bellson and Child both observed a dent in the back of the cranium, suggestive of a mortal blow.

Child's photos, it turned out, would provide the only careful documentation of the burial site before the FBI team came in and trashed it completely.

IN BLUFF LAST SUMMER I MET DENNY BELLSON. Forty-three years old, he had a quiet demeanor but, I sensed at once, an alertness that took in every nuance of his surroundings. Of medium build, with dark hair flecked with gray and a mustache drooping past the corners of his mouth, he squinted through the rimless spectacles of a professor.

With Hadenfeldt we drove south on Highway 191, then turned west on a gravel road. Bellson took one fork after another as the branching trails petered out in vestigial slickrock tracks. "When I was a kid," he said, "I asked my dad, 'Do people live out there?'" He pointed through the windshield at the stark plateau ahead of us. "Dad said, 'Nope. You go out there and it just drops off into a big canyon.' I thought it was like the end of the world."

Finally we parked the truck and started hiking. It was 96 degrees and windless, and within minutes my face and chest were covered in sweat.

We came to the rim. Now Bellson dropped one level, scuttled around a few corners, then stopped before a cranny so nondescript I wouldn't even have bothered to search it for potsherds.

"Who piled up those rocks?" Hadenfeldt asked, pointing at an assemblage that covered some six feet of crevice.

"FBI," Bellson answered.

As we pulled the camouflaging stones away from the grave, Hadenfeldt groaned, and I cursed out loud, having seen Child's photos of the site before the Feds had gotten here. "What the hell did they do?" I asked.

In a deadpan voice, Bellson described his outing a week before with the FBI. The team had consisted of Boisselle, two Navajo criminal investigators, and the San Juan county sheriff, who had invited his three teenage sons along. "One of the CIs tried to lift the skull," Bellson recounted, "and it broke into pieces. The FBI lady decided right off that it was a Navajo burial. They acted like I was wasting their time."

I was staring at the desecrated grave. The saddle frame, the stirrup, and other odds and ends that Bellson had originally found on the ledge in front of the crevice had been jammed into the tight space, further damaging the skeleton. When they were done, the team, including the teenagers, had piled up stones to hide the grave.

"Sounds like they thought they were out on a goddamned picnic," I muttered.

Bellson smiled. "It kinda was."

"You just sat there and let them do it?"

"Wasn't up to me. They're the FBI."

The three of us sat on boulders, surveying the wreckage. I wiped my brow with a bandanna. "I can smell those bones," Bellson said. I couldn't, but Hadenfeldt nodded. "I could smell 'em when I got here the first time," Bellson added.

"How did you find the grave?" I asked.

"Came around that corner there." Bellson pointed north. "I saw part of the saddle. That led me to the crevice."

"Was it exciting?"

"No. Spooky."

From the rim we could see Chinle Wash stretching north into the distance. Bellson pointed to a pair of tall cottonwood trees 300 feet below and a half mile away. "I think that's where the kid was killed by the Utes."

I asked Bellson, "You think the saddle was Aneth's?"

He nodded. "It would've been contaminated."

I hesitated before asking what felt like an intrusive question. "Denny, is it dangerous for you to come here?"

"It is," he answered right away. "Doesn't matter if this guy is white, Mexican, or Navajo. It will probably affect me later."

I thought about that. "Why are you willing to take Vaughn and me here?"

"I want to find out who this guy is." Bellson stared at the crevice. "Well, he sure picked the loneliest place to die."

I was impressed. Bellson had been doing his homework. On July 12, 1932, Everett Ruess had written to his brother, Waldo, "And when the time comes to die, I'll find the wildest, loneliest, most desolate spot there is."

THE NEXT DAY I DROVE TO FARMINGTON to talk to Daisy Johnson. We met for lunch at the International House of Pancakes. She had dressed up for the occasion, wearing a bright red blouse and a brooch made of concentric rings of turquoise stones. Her face bore a frown of anguish—the residue, I guessed, of her months of suffering from a cancer that would not go away.

Johnson recounted Nez's story in great detail. Since I'd first heard it, I had wondered why the medicine man thought that Johnson's own illness was connected to her grandfather's burial of the white man so long ago. Was it simply because in 1971 she had driven Nez out toward the Comb in the pickup?

"When Grandpa brought the lock of hair back, it was in a plastic bag," Johnson explained. "I saw it later for just a second. Maybe I wasn't supposed to see it. Maybe I wasn't supposed to know what Grandpa did with that white man."

But there was another, and more grievous, cause for Johnson's trouble. "Ten years later—it was 1981," she told me, "Grandpa got sick again. I went to Cortez to drop in on him in the hospital. There was a nurse coming out of his room. She said, 'I just took his temperature. You can visit him, but he's not talking much.'

"I went in, but Grandpa had already passed. His mouth was open. I started shaking him. He was already gone, but I kept shaking him, and saying, 'Grandpa! Grandpa!' He didn't answer."

Johnson sighed deeply. "This year, when I went to the medicine man, I told him about shaking Grandpa in the hospital and calling out to him. He said, 'That would have done it. You don't ever touch the dead or talk to the dead. You don't mess with death.'"

There was a long silence. Johnson hadn't eaten her dessert. "How do you feel about the possibility this could be Everett Ruess?" I asked. By now, Johnson knew the story of the vagabond who had disappeared in 1934.

"I hope it is," she answered. "He was such a young guy. What was he doing out here all alone? I hope they take him back to wherever he came from. He's got family there."

TEN YEARS AGO, on assignment for the premiere issue of ADVENTURE, I spent months pursuing my own search for clues to the Everett Ruess mystery. At one point, I thought I had solved the puzzle, even discovering a mound of earth that I thought might have been the Ruess grave. But with time and distance, I had to concede, as W. L. Rusho had in 1983, that Ruess's fate remained unsolved, and perhaps unsolvable.

For the burial site on Comb Ridge to be that of Everett Ruess, a couple of logical problems would have to be resolved. The most troublesome has to do with the burros themselves. As Rusho reported, the searchers in March 1935 claimed to have found Ruess's pack animals in Davis Gulch. Why would the Utes have stolen the two burros in Chinle Wash, only to ditch them 60 miles away in a side canyon near the Escalante River?

If the animals found in Davis Gulch were not Ruess's, however, that problem vanishes. Indeed, in 1999, I had unearthed some odd contradictions that made Rusho's whole story about the burros unreliable. According to the historian, after the search team recovered the pack animals, one man, Gail Bailey, had led them back to Escalante and pastured them on a nearby mountain. But when I talked to old-timers in Escalante 16 years after Rusho had done his research, I was told again and again that Bailey had found the burros on his own, before the search had even been organized. Bailey, who died in 1997, had evidently lied to Rusho. No one I talked to could verify that anyone except Gail Bailey had ever seen the burros, and so no one could be certain that those pack animals (if they existed) had belonged to Ruess.

This helps resolve the second puzzle: the fact that Ruess would have had to cover more than 60 miles as the crow flies between Davis Gulch and Comb Ridge, maybe 90 miles as a hiker might wend his way. In four years of exploring the Southwest, Ruess had never been known to stray far from his pack animals. But if he took his burros with him, there's nothing improbable about that final trip eastward. The young man had once ventured 400 miles by burro in just six weeks.

A string of graffiti left by Ruess may furnish a startling corroboration of that last journey. Like Chris McCandless, who in his final years gave himself the alias Alexander Supertramp, Ruess toyed with pseudonyms. For a while in 1931, he signed his letters "Lan Rameau," while he transferred the name "Everett" to one of his burros. Later that year, he became "Evert Rulan." Downstream from the burro corral in Davis Gulch, the searchers in 1935 found two inscriptions, one on the sill of an Anasazi granary, the other below a pictograph panel. They read: NEMO 1934.

Ruess's father interpreted the alias as a joint allusion to Odysseus's ruse of calling himself Nemo (Latin for "no man") when trapped in the Cyclops's cave, and to Captain Nemo of Jules Verne's *Twenty Thousand Leagues Under the Sea,* one of Ruess's favorite books. (The inscriptions are gone today, lost beneath the waters of Lake Powell.)

More than three decades later, horse packer Ken Sleight, who was fascinated by the Ruess mystery, discovered another NEMO inscription carved in the mud wall of an Anasazi granary in Grand Gulch, 45 miles east of Davis Gulch. As far as anyone knew, Ruess had never explored Grand Gulch.

Hadenfeldt and I hiked into the granary to look at the inscription ourselves in 1999. By then it had faded almost to illegibility, but Hadenfeldt, an expert in reading historic signatures, saw the four block capitals in the mud. The splayed out "N" and the shallow-troughed "M" were identical to those in the photos from Davis Gulch—which were first published a decade after Sleight's discovery. Sleight's NEMO was clearly no copycat graffito.

Since Ruess had only started signing himself NEMO in late 1934, did the Grand Gulch inscription prove that he had wandered there after carving his name in Davis Gulch? And if so, was he on the way to his demise in Chinle Wash? A comment in Ruess's last letter to his parents, written on November 11, 1934, dovetails strikingly with this itinerary: "I am going south toward the [Colorado] river now, through some rather wild country. I am not sure yet whether I will go across Smokey Mountain to Lee's Ferry and south, or whether I will try and cross the river above the San Juan. The water is very low this year." Either route would have launched Ruess straight on the trail to Grand Gulch and Chinle Wash.

By now I was captivated. I got in touch with Brian Ruess in Oregon—Everett's nephew, born too late to have met the vagabond. Everett's older brother, Waldo, had pursued a relentless quest to solve the great mystery. Even before Waldo's death in 2007, his son Brian and Brian's three siblings had redoubled the search. Over the decades, the family had fielded scores of leads and hints and theories, none of which had panned out. They had become jaded and skeptical that any new evidence would ever surface.

After my long phone conversation with Brian, however, he immediately emailed his siblings. "How is this for weird?" his missive began. He deftly summarized the story of Bellson, Johnson, and Aneth Nez, and signed off, "Pretty fascinating!"

Was there any way to prove or disprove whether the bones Bellson had discovered in the Comb Ridge crevice could possibly be those of Everett Ruess? What about DNA?

I contacted Bennett Greenspan, president of Family Tree DNA, a Texas-based firm that has collaborated with the National Geographic Society. Once more I related the bizarre story Daisy Johnson had told me. After a pause, Greenspan gave me an answer. It was a long shot—a very long shot. But with the right pair of samples and the most sophisticated sort of lab work, Family Tree just might be able to demonstrate a match. Or prove a mismatch.

IF WE WERE EVER TO PROBE THE MYSTERY DEEPER—by retrieving a DNA sample from the Comb Ridge skeleton, for instance—that was a business that had to be done with the utmost delicacy and through the proper channels. On our various visits to the site, Hadenfeldt, Bellson, and I had not so much as touched a single bone. If "messing with death" was a dire Navajo taboo, it would be flagrant desecration for us to disturb what might well be a Native American burial.

Before heading out to Utah, I had gotten in touch with Ron Maldonado, the supervisory archaeologist in the Cultural Resource Compliance Section of the Navajo Nation, based in Window Rock, Arizona. Maldonado was instantly intrigued—and instantly cautious. He agreed, however, to go out to the site with us and have a look around. Maldonado, I learned, was married to a Navajo, and he had vast experience with crevice burials on the reservation.

Hadenfeldt, Bellson, and I met Maldonado at the café cum convenience store that amounts to the town of Mexican Water, Arizona. With Bellson leading the way, we once again drove the maze of roads out onto the slickrock plateau, then hiked to the rim. The day was as hot as on our previous foray, and my mouth was parched long before we arrived.

FBI agent Boisselle had called Maldonado before heading out to the Comb, and I had forwarded him Child's photos of the grave as it looked when Bellson found it. Now, as Maldonado peered into the crevice, he drew in his breath. "Rachel promised me they wouldn't move anything," he said. "I'm really ticked off." Gently he removed the saddle and the other artifacts from the crevice. "In a crime scene," he said, "you don't just shove the goods into the grave."

For the next hour, lying awkwardly on his side, sweating profusely, Maldonado reached into the crevice and expertly wielded a trowel to pick the dirt away from the bones. He too avoided touching any part of the skeleton. Instead, he studied its layout. As he had two days before, Bellson sat ten yards away, watching and saying little.

After a while, Maldonado commented, "It's definitely a full-size skull. But it's still growing. It looks like a guy in his 20s." Many minutes later: "He's not facing east. As far as I can tell, he's facing to the southwest. If it was a Navajo burial, he'd be facing east."

Later still: "It just doesn't look like a Navajo burial. They would have put the saddle in the crevice with him."

Bellson spoke up. "They would have killed the horse too. Hit it with an ax, and left the ax handle in the grave.

"Smell the bones?" Bellson asked.

Maldonado sat up, trowel in hand. "Yeah. You can smell them even when they're a thousand years old. It gets into the dirt. It's a smell I can never forget. This guy I used to work with calls it 'people grease.'"

We took a break to sit in the shade and eat lunch. Maldonado mused: "Look at that crevice. It's not a likely place to bury somebody. You could make a much better burial right over there, or there." He pointed to a pair of ample slots in the rimrock cliff just behind us. "He may have been trying to hide the body in a hurry," Maldonado went on. "Just stuff him in there, then maneuver him around. He had to get him in the ground before sunset.

"It all makes sense. The 1930s were a really volatile time on the reservation. The government had started wholesale livestock reduction, killing thousands of Navajo sheep and cattle. They were hauling the kids off to boarding schools. Here's a Navajo guy who witnesses a murder. Your grandpa," Maldonado nodded at Bellson, "doesn't want the remains just lying out on the ground. In the '30s, if a white guy gets killed on the rez, they call out the cavalry. Round up a bunch of Navajos, pick a suspect, and lock him in jail. I can see why your grandpa would have tried to hide the guy. And then I can see why he wouldn't tell anybody about it for 37 years."

After lunch, Maldonado went back to work. Finally, toward late afternoon, we sat in the shade again. The archaeologist lowered his head and wiped his brow as he pondered, silent for so long that he seemed to be meditating. Finally he spoke: "It just doesn't look like a Navajo burial. Who else lives in this area?"

"Nobody," said Bellson.

"Who else could be buried out here?"

Bellson shook his head. He had asked his neighbors. There were no stories of gravesites on this part of the Comb. "Mom and Dad," Bellson added, "always told us to stay away from here. They never told us why."

"According to Navajo Nation policy," Maldonado said, "we're supposed to protect graves, whether Native American or not. But we're also supposed to try to find the lineal descendants if there's an unidentified body." He turned to me. "Who's the relative you talked to?"

"Brian Ruess. He's Everett's nephew," I replied.

"Ask him to request a DNA sample." It was obvious that Maldonado's decision had not come easily to him. He stood up and hoisted his fanny pack. "Out here," he said, "Navajo oral tradition is pretty accurate. Based on that tradition, I think there's a good chance this is Everett Ruess."

BRIAN RUESS CONFERRED WITH HIS THREE SIBLINGS. They agreed to request the DNA sample. According to Greenspan of Family Tree, Everett's nieces and nephews (his closest living relatives) were genetically too distant to yield good results for a mitochondrial DNA test. The only useful source was Waldo—but Everett's older brother had died the previous year. In the end, Brian's sister Michele carefully wrapped and sent Waldo's favorite hairbrush, which his widow had kept after his death. Still caught in the bristles were some strands of Waldo's hair.

On July 22 Ron Maldonado went back out to the site with Bellson and Child. Maldonado started excavating as gingerly as he could. Meanwhile, Child discovered an artifact we had previously overlooked. Lying loose in a cranny in front of the crevice was a 1912 dime that had been converted into a button. The thing struck all three men as a very Navajo kind of relic (antique Navajo belts made of silver dollars fetch high prices). But we also knew that Ruess loved to wear Indian jewelry. In any event, the button gave us a terminus ad quem: the burial could not have taken place before 1912.

Almost at once, to his relief, just inches below the surface Maldonado came across two loose molar teeth. With great care, he removed and packaged them. There would be no more digging that day.

As soon as he got back to Window Rock, Maldonado emailed me about a bizarre event that had occurred as the men returned to their truck: *A dust devil (whirlwind) started at or near me, violently sending dust into the area. It seemed that it visited each of us individually and slowly meandered down the road, lingering, appearing to die out, then starting again. It is all very strange and definitely associated with the burial. Bellson stated that it was Mister Ruess. Such things are associated with the dead and should be avoided at all costs. It has been a strange day.*

It took weeks for the results of the DNA testing to come back. Finally, on September 30, Greenspan reported that the molar DNA was "European in origin and not Native American." Maldonado's intuition was validated—the gravesite on the Comb was not a Navajo crevice burial.

But Greenspan went on to explain in an email that the DNA from the hairbrush did not match that from the molars. A white guy, but not Everett Ruess? Who else would have been out there in the 1930s?

Later, over the phone, Greenspan admitted to me that he was not at all happy with the hairbrush sample. A mitochondrial DNA test required an exact match, but the DNA from Waldo's hair was "degraded," and it might have been contaminated by being handled by others. The mitochondrial reading from the molar was reliable, but the test using the hairbrush was far from conclusive.

As far as Maldonado, Hadenfeldt, Bellson, and I were concerned, the answer was still out there.

NOW THAT GREENSPAN HAD PROVED the bones Bellson had discovered were Caucasian, Maldonado had decided to complete the excavation in hopes of coming up with further clues to the young man's identity.

In November I was in Boulder, Colorado, having dinner with my friend Steve Lekson, the most brilliant Southwestern archaeologist I have met. I told

Lekson about our Comb Ridge quest. He didn't know much about Ruess, but his eyes lit up. "You can do a lot more than just DNA," he said. "A forensic anthropologist can tell all kinds of things from bones. What kind of bones have you got?" At the end of the evening, Lekson gave me the email address of a colleague at the University of Colorado.

Dennis Van Gerven ignored my first two messages. Later he admitted he was doing his best to stiff-arm my inquiries, since he tended to get bombarded with pleas from nutcases who had watched too many episodes of *CSI*. His first communiqué had annoyance written all over it: "In short a study of the [bones] from my point of view would be quite pointless," he signed off.

I persisted. "Would there not be some chance you might see something the DNA test couldn't tell us?"

Meanwhile, on the Internet I had found the report of one of Van Gerven's cardinal triumphs. In 2007 the professor led a team that exhumed a body in Kansas that had been at the center of a legal dispute stretching back to 1879. When the excavation failed to turn up sufficient DNA material, Van Gerven used 47 bone fragments and a technique called facial superimposition to ID the corpse, which was long considered unidentifiable. Reading the report, I realized that Van Gerven was something of a forensic genius.

I hammered away, emailing a detailed account of Everett Ruess and our efforts so far on Comb Ridge. Slowly, Van Gerven warmed to the challenge. By the end of the month, he and his grad-student assistant, Paul Sandberg, were fully on board. On January 24, having driven from Boulder to Bluff, they joined Ron Maldonado and Vaughn Hadenfeldt at the site, where they excavated the crevice completely.

Piece by piece, the anthropologists retrieved one rib and vertebra and toe bone and tooth after another; they also salvaged many fragments of the young man's skull. Each bone was gently handled and wrapped for transport to a university lab. The only artifacts the men found were scores of beads—yellow, orange, white, and blue, made apparently of coral or shell—and a metal button, embossed with the word "mountaineer" curving around the rim above an "X." We later learned that the button could have been produced only by one of three manufacturers, all of which were out of business by 1936.

BACK IN BOULDER, Van Gerven and Sandberg's first task was to stabilize the very fragile pieces of bone—especially the skull fragments. Many of the bones were sun-bleached and eroded after decades of exposure to the elements. But the anthropologists were heartened to find, as Sandberg wrote me in late

February, that "three fragments of the face, two of them with teeth still in place, were tightly embedded and protected in the dirt, and we had a nearly complete mandible. It seems as though a previous attempt to force the skull out of the dirt [by the FBI] had left much of the face intact under the surface."

From the very start, Van Gerven and Sandberg were able to make what they called a "biological profile" of the victim. "The shape of the pelvis told us that the individual was male," Sandberg explained. "The degree of developmental maturity of the bones told us that he was between the ages of 19 and 22, and measurement of the femur gave us a stature estimate of approximately five feet eight inches."

The facial fragments were critical to reconstructing the dead man's physiognomy. Joining the stabilized bones with clay, the scientists painstakingly rebuilt pieces of the skull. For comparison, they had two of the splendid portraits of Ruess that his friend, the famed photographer Dorothea Lange, had shot in 1933, one face-on, one in profile. As Sandberg explained, "Using Adobe Photoshop CS, we blended images of Ruess and the bones together. This technique is good at excluding people, almost too good because it can easily exclude the right person due to distortions that arise in photography."

When the two men had started their work, Van Gerven warned me, "I'd be just as happy to disprove the match as I would to prove it." But day by day, he grew more animated. "I have a really good feeling about this," he said in early February. A few days later: "So far, there's nothing exclusionary."

Finally, at the end of February, Van Gerven phoned me with his verdict. "All the lines of evidence converge," he said. "This guy was male. Everett was male. This guy was about 20 years old. Everett was 20 years old. This guy was about five foot eight. Everett was five eight.

"Everett had unique facial features, including a really large, jutting chin. This guy had the same features. And the bones match the photos in every last detail, even down to the spacing between the teeth. The odds are astronomically small that this could be a coincidence."

Van Gerven paused. "I'd take it to court. This is Everett Ruess."

As THIS ISSUE WENT TO PRESS, a second DNA test, comparing yet another molar from the grave with saliva samples from Ruess's two nieces and two nephews, was under way. If there is even a 25 percent overlap in the genetic makeup of the tooth and the saliva, Van Gerven explained, that would absolutely clinch the case.

Meanwhile, thanks to the brilliant sleuthing of Denny Bellson, a 75-year-old mystery, which hundreds of investigators have set out to untangle, seems at last to have been solved. Only a handful of lost American adventurers in the 20th century—Amelia Earhart among them—have stirred so much passion and speculation. And from beyond the grave, Aneth Nez's haunting story, which he kept secret most of his life, stunningly confirms the veracity of Navajo oral tradition.

Yet even now, Ruess's final days pose further mysteries. What happened after Davis Gulch? How did the vagabond, exploring through the winter, make his way to Chinle Wash? What went wrong that day, when the Utes hunted him down and took away his dream?

What was Ruess looking for? And what did he find before he died?

In the last letter he ever sent, from Escalante on November 11, 1934, Everett wrote Waldo, "As to when I shall visit civilization, it will not be soon, I think. I have not tired of the wilderness. . . ."

Pending DNA confirmation, Brian, Michele, and their two siblings have planned the final disposition of their lost uncle's bones. They will not be returned to the crevice on Comb Ridge, for if they were, the site would inevitably become a pilgrimage shrine—like the bus rusting away in the Alaska tundra in which Chris McCandless died.

Instead, Ruess will be cremated, his ashes strewn across the waters of the Pacific Ocean near the Ruess home, just as Waldo's were in 2007, and just as his parents' were after their earlier deaths. In the end, Daisy Johnson's plaintive wish for the young wanderer may come to pass. Ruess could be going back to where he came from. He's got family there.

APRIL/MAY 2009

Postscript: Soon after this story appeared on magazine newsstands, DNA results confirmed that the remains found on Comb Ridge were, indeed, Everett Ruess.

OFF THE FACE OF THE EARTH

By Peter Lane Taylor

―――――――

In 1942, as the Nazis intensified their hold on Eastern Europe,
a Jewish family disappeared into a vast underground labyrinth in western Ukraine.
Six decades later, a curious reporter stumbled across the remnants of their
subterranean asylum and set out to find the survivors.

THE NIGHT OF OCTOBER 12, 1942, when the Stermers finally ran for good, was moonless and unseasonably cold. The roads in and out of the town of Korolówka, deep in the farm country of western Ukraine, were empty of the cart traffic that had peaked during the fall harvest days. After a month of backbreaking work, most residents had already drifted off to sleep.

Zaida Stermer, his wife, Esther, and their six children dug up their last remaining possessions from behind their house, loaded their wagons with food and fuel, and, just before midnight, quietly fled into the darkness. Traveling with them were nearly two dozen neighbors and relatives, all fellow Jews who, like the Stermers, had so far survived a year under the German occupation of their homeland. Their destination, a large cave about five miles to the north, was their last hope of finding refuge from the Nazis' intensifying roundups and mass executions of Ukrainian Jews.

The dirt track they rode on ended by a shallow sinkhole, where the Stermers and their neighbors unloaded their carts, descended the slope, and squeezed through the cave's narrow entrance. In their first hours underground, the darkness around them must have seemed limitless. Navigating with only candles and lanterns, they would have had little depth perception and been able to see no more than a few feet. They made their way to a natural alcove not far from the entrance and huddled in the darkness. As the Stermers and the other families settled in for that first night beneath the cold, damp earth, there was little in their past to suggest that they were prepared for the ordeal ahead.

AT THE SURFACE, Priest's Grotto is little more than a weedy hole in the ground amid the endless wheat fields stretching across western Ukraine. A short distance away, a low stand of hardwoods withers in the heat and is the only sign of cover for miles around. With the exception of a shallow, 90-foot-wide depression in the flat ground, there's nothing to indicate that one of the longest horizontal labyrinths in the world lies just underfoot.

On the afternoon of July 18, 2003, I am standing with Chris Nicola, a leading American caver, at the bottom of the sinkhole, sorting our gear. It has taken us four days, traveling by jet, train, and finally ox cart, to get here from New York City. It's tornado season on the Ukrainian plateau, and overhead, the blue sky is rimmed with cumulus clouds sheared off at the top. Our guides, 46-year-old Sergey Yepephanov and 24-year-old Sasha Zimels, are standing next to the rusting, three-foot-wide metal entrance pipe that leads underground. They've been ready to go for an hour.

I've come here to explore Priest's Grotto for the first time. For Nicola, a 20-year veteran of major cave systems in the U.S. and Mexico, our expedition is the culmination of a journey that began in 1993, soon after the fall of the Soviet Union, when he became one of the first Americans to explore Ukraine's famous Gypsum Giant cave systems. On that trip he met dozens of local cavers eager to share news about their recent discoveries. His last excursion was here, to the cave known locally as Popowa Yama, or Priest's Grotto, because of its location on land once owned by a parish priest.

At 77 miles, Priest's Grotto is the second longest of the Gypsum Giants and currently ranks as the tenth longest cave in the world. Yet what Nicola found fascinating about the cave was located just minutes inside the entrance: Soon after they'd set out, his group passed two partially intact stone walls and other signs of habitation including several old shoes, buttons, and a hand-chiseled millstone. Nicola's guides from the local caving association told him the campsite had already been there when their group first explored that portion of the cave in the early 1960s.

"My guides called the site Khatki, or 'cottage,'" Nicola, now 53, recalls. "They told me that it was settled by a group of local Jews who had fled to the cave during the Holocaust. But that's where the story ended. No one else could remember what had actually happened there, or even if the Jews had survived the war at all."

Intrigued, Nicola began asking questions in the nearby towns. Western Ukraine is a region where the Gypsum Giants have long been revered as national landmarks and where uncomfortable memories of the Holocaust still linger. Some local villagers told him that, after the Russian troops pushed back the Germans in 1944, the survivors were seen stumbling back to town, covered in thick, yellow mud. Others said the Jews never saw daylight again.

On a later trip, Nicola learned more. "Rumors kept developing that at least three families did survive," he says. But how had they lived in such an inhospitable environment, Nicola wondered, and where were they today? As a caver, he was awed by the courage and resourcefulness that such long-term survival underground must have demanded. And he was amazed that the story wasn't better known, even among Holocaust experts.

Back home in Queens, New York, Nicola intensified his efforts to locate a Priest's Grotto survivor. He added information about the story to his Web site on Ukrainian caves (*www.uaycef.org*), hoping that anyone searching the Internet for the topic would contact him. For four years he got no response. Then, one evening in December 2002, Nicola received an e-mail from a man who said that his father-in-law was one of the original Priest's Grotto survivors and was, in fact, living just a few miles away in the Bronx. "I couldn't believe what I was seeing," Nicola says. "I was afraid to even touch the print key in case I were to accidentally erase it."

Seven months later we are standing outside the cave itself. It's 4:30 p.m. by the time Nicola and I are finished suiting up for entry. Our two dozen duffels contain over 200 pounds of photographic and survey gear and enough supplies to remain underground for three days.

As current president of the Ternopil Speleo Club, the local group that has been pushing the exploration of this cave for 40 years, Sergey Yepephanov is eager to show us his domain. He sticks his arm through the steel plate at the top of the pipe, swings open the trapdoor as if he's removing a manhole cover, and ushers us inside. (The club installed the pipe several years ago to keep seasonal mudflows from clogging the cave's entrance.) Two dozen rickety metal rungs spot-welded to the inside of the pipe disappear straight down into the darkness. There is just enough room for each of us and our gear bags to squeeze down the rusty 30-foot shaft. When I reach the bottom, I can still make out Sergey's silhouette at the top of the ladder, rimmed by bright, white light. The rush of wind across the prairie is the last sound I hear before he reaches through the small access port and slams the door shut and everything goes black.

"MY MOTHER ALWAYS SAID, 'We are not going to go to the slaughterhouse.' She said to my brother Nissel, 'Go to the forest, find a hole, anything.' Thanks to him, we survived."

Shulim Stermer leaned forward across the dining room table as he spoke, his eyes wide through heavy prescription glasses. His brother Shlomo, their sister Yetta Katz, and his niece Pepkale Blitzer sat respectfully on either side of him, surrounded by Shulim and Shlomo's wives and several children and grandchildren. At 84, Shulim is the oldest living survivor from Priest's Grotto.

After Chris Nicola met that first Priest's Grotto survivor, Solomon Wexler, in the Bronx, Wexler had introduced him to his Canadian cousins and fellow survivors, the Stermers. Throughout 2003, Chris and I made five trips to Montreal to interview the Stermer family. Over the course of several long conversations we learned that the facts of their story were even more extraordinary than the rumors. The Stermers and several other families had escaped the Holocaust by living in two separate caves for close to two years. The first was a tourist cave known as Verteba. Only later did their group—which eventually swelled to 38 people—discover and inhabit the then unexplored Priest's Grotto, where they lived for 344 days. Though some of the survivors lost touch with each other in the years after the war, the Stermers, their in-laws the Dodyks, and Sol Wexler remained close. In all, we were able to make contact with six living survivors: the two Stermer brothers (Shulim, 84, and Shlomo, 74); their sister, Yetta, 78; their cousin, Sol Wexler, 74; and their nieces Shunkale, 70, and Pepkale, 65.

Shulim Stermer's ninth-floor apartment was spacious and airy, with high ceilings and eight-foot plate glass windows running the length of the western wall. Hung on one wall was a large, striking photograph of the six Stermer children with their parents, Esther and Zaida, taken a few years before World War II. On the dining room table lay one of their most precious family treasures: a memoir of their survival, originally written in Yiddish by their mother Esther and then privately published in English in 1975.

"My mother never trusted authority," Shulim told us. "The Germans, the Russians, the Ukrainians. It didn't matter. She taught us early on that no matter who it was, if they told you to do one thing, you always did the opposite. If the Germans said, 'Go to the ghettos, you'll be safe there,' you went to the forest or the mountains. You went as far away from the ghettos as you could go."

In the early 1930s, Esther Stermer was the proud matriarch of one of the most well-regarded families in Korolówka. Her husband was a successful merchant. It was a rare time of opportunity for many Jews in western Ukraine; Jewish cultural life and Zionist and socialist movements were thriving.

But with the rise of Nazi power in Germany, and increasing anti-Semitic violence at home, all that soon came to an end. In 1939 the Germans seized Czechoslovakia and then invaded Poland. Threatened by Hitler's eastward advance, the Russians countered by invading western—or Polish—Ukraine. For a short time, a cynical non-aggression pact between the Germans and the Russians kept the region quiet even as the rest of Europe erupted in war. That shaky peace collapsed in June 1941, when Hitler's armies stormed the border from Poland and rolled across Ukraine's open plains toward Stalingrad and the oil fields of the Caspian Sea. Almost immediately, German Einsatzgruppen paramilitary units began roaming the country, executing Jews and others at will.

The Stermers' town of Korolówka was officially declared *judenfrei*—"free of Jews"—in the summer of 1942, and the Germans stepped up their efforts to eliminate the Jewish population. During the holiday of Sukkoth, the Gestapo encircled the town, forced the Jews to dig mass graves, and executed them dozens at a time. Though the Stermers and a few other families managed to escape, their fate seemed inevitable: No Jew would get out alive.

"Death stalked each step," Esther wrote of that autumn. "But we were not surrendering to this fate. . . . Our family in particular would not let the Germans have their way easily. We had vigor, ingenuity, and determination to survive. . . . But where can we survive? Clearly, there was no place on the Earth for us."

IT'S ALREADY PAST DINNERTIME WHEN CHRIS NICOLA, Sergey Yepephanov, Sasha Zimels, and I reach our underground camp 400 yards from the entrance to Priest's Grotto. Although unimpressive in terms of distance, a sixth of a mile is considerable when you're hauling 12 man-days' worth of supplies through the cave's tortuous passageways. The tunnels are low and uneven, forcing us to crouch down and drag our duffels through the mud on our hands and knees. Despite the cave's constant temperature of a chilly 50°F, we've been sweating beneath our coveralls for hours.

Our bivouac is a large diamond-shaped chamber that has been used for more than a decade by teams making deep pushes into the cave. There are a dozen smaller bivouacs scattered strategically throughout the cave's 77 miles. For cavers, these encampments serve the same purpose as high alpine camps on mountaineering expeditions: to keep food and water in constant supply and to maintain lines of communication with the surface.

To put our current location in context with the rest of the cave, Sergey uses his finger to draw a rough map of our surroundings in the mud floor.

"We're right here," he explains, pressing his finger into the dense clay. "And this is the entrance to the cave," he says, sticking his finger in the mud again, four inches away. Next he draws a zigzagging line leading three inches straight up to another dot. "This is Khatki"—the cottage—"where the Jews were during the war."

Sergey then gets up and takes one large step backward to a spot on the floor about three feet away.

"Right here," he says, smiling, "is the farthest point we've reached in the cave. That was last year."

Seeing Sergey's pride in the extent of their explorations, one can understand why the cavers who found the survivors' encampment didn't linger over their discovery. In Khatki, the explorers saw little more than a place that humans had already been; as cavers, they were seeking virgin passage, not old shoes and stone walls.

The longest period of time a human is recorded to have survived underground is 205 days. The record was set in Texas' Midnight Cave in 1972 by Frenchman Michel Siffre, as part of a NASA-sponsored experiment studying the effects of long-duration spaceflight. Yet, in listening to the survivors, Chris Nicola and I had realized that the true record was set by the women and children of Priest's Grotto, who never ventured out of the cave during their entire 344-day ordeal. Modern cavers require special clothing to ward off hypothermia, advanced technology for lighting and travel, and intensive instruction in ropes and navigation to survive underground for just a few days. How did 38 untrained, ill-equipped people survive for so long in such a hostile environment during history's darkest era? That was the question our expedition had come some 7,000 miles to answer.

THE STERMERS' FIRST UNDERGROUND HOME, the tourist cave of Verteba, was a temporary refuge at best. At worst, it was a death trap. The cave had poor ventilation and no dependable water source. And the families would almost certainly be discovered when the snows melted in April and the local peasants (many of whom had welcomed the invading Germans) returned to their fields near the mouth of the cave.

"Our situation at that time was really, really bad," recalled Shlomo Stermer, the youngest brother. "We didn't have any water, and we had to catch the drips that came off the walls in cups. We also couldn't cook inside without choking on the smoke. We had no idea how we were going to survive."

Much of the heavy labor fell to the Stermer men: the father, Shabsy—whom everyone called Zaida, or Grandpa—and his three sons, Nissel, age 25,

Shulim, 22, and Shlomo, 13. Esther Stermer and her adult daughters Chana and Henia took charge of domestic chores with the help of Yetta, 17, the family's youngest girl.

Before fleeing with their families to the cave, Zaida, Nissel, and Henia's husband, Fishel Dodyk, had received special permission to collect scrap metal under official protection from the local police. It was perilous, humiliating labor. But their ability to return to their houses, move freely in public, and buy supplies on the black market represented their families' only lifeline. Week after week, they drove their wagons to the cave under cover of darkness through the deep snow. At the edge of the sinkhole, they descended the icy slopes carrying hundred-pound sacks of flour, potatoes, kerosene, and water on their backs, and then dragged them through the mud inside the cave. Through the winter of 1942–43, the families' survival hung in a precarious balance between the secrecy of their location and the security of their supply lines.

The men warned their families that the Germans were intensifying their hunt for Jews, and in February 1943, the group decided to move even deeper into the cave. They sealed themselves in a low, sickle-shaped room more than a thousand feet from daylight and began to search for a second, secret exit in case the Gestapo attempted to blockade them inside. The Stermer brothers discovered a small fracture in the ceiling of a nearby passage and feverishly began digging with picks and axes. Day after day, the men tunneled upward, finally breaking through to the surface after four weeks. It was the first time many of them had seen the sky in months.

Before returning underground, Shulim concealed their exit with earth and logs and suspended a long chain down to the cave's floor below. If the Nazis discovered their refuge, his family could escape by climbing up the chain using small kick steps in the walls for support. After roughly 150 days of living in perpetual terror of being discovered, the Stermers and their neighbors finally began to feel they might have a chance of surviving.

FOUR WEEKS LATER, THE JEWS' OPTIMISM was shattered by the sound of bootsteps and rattling guns. "The Germans are here!" someone suddenly yelled in Yiddish. "They've discovered us!"

Young Shlomo was sleeping closest to the entrance of the chamber and was caught helpless before he had the chance to run. In the glare of the Gestapo's flashlights he could see that others had been captured, too. At the entrance to their refuge, Shlomo's mother, Esther, was standing toe-to-toe with the Gestapo's commanding officer. Shlomo could hear her speaking in German.

"Very well, so you have found us. What do you think?" Esther said. "Do you think that unless you kill us the Führer will lose the war? Look at how we live here, like rats. All we want is to live, to survive the war years. Leave us here."

Sixty years later, Shlomo rose out of his chair to imitate his mother as he quoted her. "I couldn't believe what I was hearing!" he continued. "Here was my mother, in the middle of the war, standing up to the Germans!"

As Esther confronted the soldiers, stalling for time, the rest of her children and the other survivors slipped away into the dark maze of passageways branching off from the campsite. In the end, the Germans managed to seize just eight of the Jews and began to march them back to the cave's entrance at gunpoint. Miraculously, six of the prisoners, including Esther, were able to escape and eventually return to their families. But Sol Wexler would soon learn that his mother and nine-year-old brother had been forced into an open grave and shot.

For those who remained inside the cave, the next three hours were spent in a state of terror and confusion. Few of the survivors had kept track of how far they had fled in the dark, and many ended up out of earshot of one another, lost without matches, candles, water, or any idea of how to find their way back to camp.

For the middle son, Shulim, in particular, the shock of being discovered was cataclysmic. When Esther finally found her way back to the encampment, she was horrified to see her middle son lying paralyzed at the bottom of the exit shaft he had dug just weeks earlier.

"I saw that all had climbed through the exit except Shulim, who was sitting on the ground trembling, head thrown back," she wrote. "I ran to him, spoke to him, but he did not reply. His eyes were glazed, his teeth clenched and he was drooling at the mouth."

Back in Montreal, Shulim grew quiet when we raised the topic of his breakdown.

"I was almost destroyed in the first cave," he finally offered. "I had a complete shock. I couldn't talk, I couldn't walk, I couldn't take a spoon and pick it up to my mouth. It was a miracle that I even survived."

It was the worst possible time for Shulim to break down. No one else knew how to open the trap door at the top of the exit shaft. Shulim's sister Chana and Sol Wexler were the first to reach the top, but they were unable to move the logs that locked the door in place. As the other survivors began to bottleneck near the surface, panic set in.

Finally, with one last effort, Sol and Chana succeeded in breaking through to the surface, and everyone rushed from the exit. Outside, the air was cold and wet, and many of the survivors began to shiver uncontrollably. To the north, they could see the Gestapo and their dogs running search grids around the sinkhole looking for a secret exit. Shulim was the last to leave, carried up the shaft on his brothers' shoulders. Then the survivors slipped away through the grass and fled into the darkness.

My wristwatch tells me it's just past eight in the morning when Chris and I wake up from our first night underground. After less than 18 hours in the cave, I can already feel the sense of suspended reality that the Stermers told me about in Montreal: With nothing to mark the passing hours, everything seems like it's happening in slow motion. The French caver Siffre called his experience of sensory deprivation in Midnight Cave "living beyond time." After only a few weeks he couldn't remember simple names and dates, and had difficulty managing basic tasks like cooking and shaving.

Sergey leads Chris and me on the most direct course to Khatki, navigating the entire way from memory. Unlike most vertical caves, where the greatest dangers are falling or being struck by rocks, it's randomness and repetition that kill in caves like Priest's Grotto. Passages propagate in all directions, like the cracks across a shattered car windshield, and every passageway looks the same. Our route redirects itself—left, right, and backward—exactly 16 times before we finally arrive at a round, natural archway into Khatki, the historic encampment. To make sure we can find our way back to camp later in the day, Sergey flags our route every 10 to 15 feet with pink survey tape.

"In caves like Priest's Grotto, you don't need to pay a guide to get you in," Sergey jokes. "You pay me to show you the way back out."

Throughout the month of April 1943, the Jews lived like outlaws in their own community. The Stermers moved along the back roads at night between the boarded-up remains of their house in Korolówka and a hidden bunker in a barn.

Desperate to find a permanent refuge, the Stermers' eldest son, Nissel, sought the counsel of his friend Munko Lubudzin, a forester who lived in the woods near Korolówka. Though many Ukrainian Christians willingly participated in the Holocaust—and the Ukrainian police actively collaborated with the Nazis—Munko Lubudzin faithfully assisted the Stermers throughout the war. Munko told Nissel about a sinkhole a few miles outside of town, located in the fields of a local parish priest. At the surface, there was nothing remarkable about the place. Unlike at Verteba, there was little indication that the sinkhole might contain an entrance to a sizable cave. It was only a hole in the ground where farmers threw their dead livestock to rot.

Nissel knew there were several caves in the area that had a history of ancient human habitation. Based on this slim hope, Nissel and his brother Shulim left Korolówka at first light on May 1, 1943, along with their friend Karl Kurz and two of the Dodyk brothers. The young men raced through the fields north of town to the edge of the sinkhole. "When we came there, there was some nice, nice grass, like a golf course," Shulim remembered, his voice rising excitedly. "And then you have a big ravine about 40 feet deep and water used to drip in."

The men descended the loose dirt at the top using an old rope, then clambered down the last 20 feet using logs as a makeshift ladder. At the bottom, the mud came up to their knees, and the stench of the rotting livestock made the men gag, but they could see a small opening, about the size of a fireplace. Nissel was the first to squeeze through. Inside, it was completely black, but by the dim light of their candles, the men could see that they were in a small room surrounded by large boulders. "After that," Shulim said, "the cave just kept on going."

Seventy-five feet farther on, the men crawled into a chamber so large that their candles could scarcely light the walls or the ceiling overhead. After their six months in Verteba, they were now experienced cave explorers. They pulled out a coil of rope, tied one end to a boulder, and began searching the network of passages for a suitable place for camp. Three hours later, disoriented and fatigued, Shulim dragged his foot over a small ledge, dislodging a stone, which rolled downhill and splashed into a clear underground lake. The men laughed for the first time in months: They had found a water source.

"By the time we went into the second cave, I think there was truly no place else that we could go," Pepkale said. "It was judenfrei. Any Jew who was seen anywhere could have been shot by anybody. It was just a godsend that they found this place."

Five days later, on May 5, the Stermers, their in-laws the Dodyks, and various other relatives and friends packed up their last supplies and fled to Priest's Grotto. The group now numbered 38 in all. The oldest was a 75-year-old grandmother; the youngest included Esther's four-year-old granddaughter Pepkale and a toddler. They descended the sinkhole one by one in silence, climbing hand over hand down the rocky faces and stepping on the slippery, wet logs for support. At the bottom, the complete darkness inside the narrow entrance was terrifying, and the youngest children started to cry as they crawled through the opening. It would be the last time many of them would see the sky for nearly a year.

FOR THEIR NEW HOME, the survivors chose a series of four interconnected rooms far to the left of the cave's main passageways. Compared with the world they had left above them, the initial security of their new refuge must have seemed like heaven. For the smallest children, Priest's Grotto was the first taste of real freedom they had ever experienced. "We would sing and play in the grotto," Pepkale recalled back in Montreal. "It was the only place I had ever felt safe."

"Long ago," Esther wrote of their refuge, "people believed that spirits and ghosts lived in ruins and in caves. Now we could see that there were none here. The devils and the evil spirits were on the outside, not in the grotto."

It wasn't long, however, before the Jews' initial relief was overshadowed by the question of how they were going to survive. Drawing on the lessons of Verteba, the families found a ventilated chamber for their cooking fire, isolated their water sources, and constructed beds of wooden planks. Reestablishing their supply lines was their next urgent priority. The men had lost their scrap-metal exemption, and there was only enough kerosene, flour, and other supplies to last two weeks.

The three Stermer brothers made their first foray out of the cave accompanied by several other men. At the top of the sinkhole, they sprinted through the high grass to the edge of the woods a thousand feet away, where they crouched down and waited. Overhead, a thin crescent moon lay hidden behind a dark skin of low clouds, and the wind blew across the plains with a persistent moan. From behind the trees, Nissel scanned the horizon to see if anyone had seen them come out of the sinkhole. But the landscape was quiet, a few smoldering buildings the only signs of life.

On Nissel's cue, the men scattered into the woods and began to dismember 20 large trees, working frantically with axes and saws in almost total darkness. Half the men chopped off the branches and cut the trunks into five-foot lengths, while the others carried the logs back to the cave across the open fields.

"This was terrible danger," Shulim exclaimed. "You hear . . . you listen. And you hear the cutting with the ax: 'Pow! Boom! Ba!' So much noise!" As he spoke, Shulim cut his hands through the air, a sense of defiance still lingering in his voice.

Their second covert mission took place a few days later. The men left the cave as a group and then split up at the edge of the sinkhole to secure food and other vital reserves for their own individual families. Nissel and Shulim sprinted west through the fields, staying near the trees for cover. It was a three-mile round-trip journey from Priest's Grotto to their friend Munko Lubudzin's house, where the brothers traded a few remaining valuables for cooking oil, detergent, matches, and flour.

"When we got out, there was the Big Dipper," Shulim told us when we asked how they kept time without watches. "The Big Dipper was like that"—in the empty space in front of him, he circumscribed a wide arc with his arms across the table. "It was turning, turning, and when it was almost horizontal we knew it would soon be morning. We knew that we had to get back."

When Nissel, Shulim, and the other men finally returned to the cave, they whispered a password to one of the younger boys, posted just inside of the entrance, who quickly dislodged a large boulder to let them back in.

The next day, the men slept for 20 uninterrupted hours, while Esther and her daughters piled the Stermers' rations neatly on shelves they'd built under their wooden bunks. In all, the men had secured enough supplies for another six weeks.

As Shulim finished his story, Yetta turned to face him. She had been watching her older brother intently while he spoke, "We wouldn't be alive today if it weren't for them!" she finally burst out through a surge of tears. "Every time we needed something, they brought the flour and potatoes so I could make the soup."

Shulim smiled at his sister.

"Yetta made the best soup in the world," he said softly.

CHRIS NICOLA IS IN THE LEAD as we enter the first of Khatki's four primary rooms. "The stone walls are still here!" he shouts back over his shoulder. In the months preceding our expedition, we often worried about whether Khatki might have been ransacked by vandals or washed clean by the floods that periodically sweep the cave. Instead, our team has encountered a near virgin archaeological site. Each of Khatki's main rooms is approximately 8 feet wide, between 30 and 80 feet long, and linked to the others by a network of narrow, body-width tunnels at either end. The rock ceiling curves down to the floor like the canopy of a covered wagon.

At the back of the entry room, Chris kneels in the weak orange glow spilling from his carbide headlamp. "The walls are leveled at the bottom with rocks," he says. "And there's smoke on the ceiling," he adds, tracing the dark smudge from a cooking fire across the tunnel's roof with his headlamp.

In the next room, Sergey examines the 150-pound millstone that Nissel carried on his back from a farmer's barn more than three miles away. Placed atop a solid rock base hand-chiseled by Shulim with a six-inch railroad spike, the millstone was the Jews' most important tool in the cave, allowing them to grind flour from grain. Lit by the beams of our headlamps, the millstone looks like a museum display. Impulsively, Sergey steps forward to pick it up. He puts his hands on the cold sides of the stone and jerks his small, powerful body upward. The millstone barely moves from its base.

Past the remains of another man-made wall, we crawl on our hands and knees into the survivors' sleeping quarters. The passage is almost 80 feet long and in many places less than 4 feet high. On the left near the entrance, there's a trench dug down into the earth that allows us to walk half the distance standing almost upright. On the right, the floor is scattered with artifacts, including more than a dozen leather shoes, porcelain buttons, broken ceramics, and a red metal cup. Chris and I photograph each object and map its location. Toward the rear of the passage, Chris discovers several rows of small, round posts driven straight down into the mud: bedposts, used to elevate the sleeping platforms off the cold cave floor.

As we follow the bright strips of tape back to our camp for dinner, Chris explains why Priest's Grotto was such an ideal hiding place. Not only was there ample fresh water, he notes, but there were no bats to spread disease. Most importantly, while many caves flood annually, Priest's Grotto is known to flood roughly once every two decades. "This cave is one in a million," he says.

As summer 1943 arrived, World War II raged across Europe more fiercely than ever. Poland's remaining ghettos were liquidated and Jewish resistance crushed. All the while, the Stermers and their neighbors lived in a state of near-hibernation under the fields of Ukraine. The combination of the cave's naturally high humidity and the moisture from their own respiration kept their tattered clothes constantly damp; even the slightest breeze could induce hypothermia. They slept for up to 22 hours at a time, lying side by side on their plank beds and rising only to eat, relieve themselves, or attend to other rudiments of staying alive.

Survival expert Kenneth Kamler, M.D., author of *Surviving the Extremes*, believes the combination of stress and sensory deprivation the Jews endured was almost without parallel. "Their experience was analogous to long-duration spaceflight. They had no day-night rhythm, and because of the lack of light, slept for extensive periods, but they could never relax."

During their waking hours, the Stermers worked on improving their home, digging stairs and trenches to make walking easier. They limited their use of candles and lanterns to two or three brief periods each day, often working in complete darkness. The family obeyed a chain of command that began with Esther and extended down through her eldest sons with military precision. In explorer Ernest Shackleton's account of his ship's long imprisonment in the Antarctic sea ice, he stressed the importance of maintaining shipboard routines and adhering to a strict code of responsibilities. Esther's memoir reveals a similar attitude toward discipline. "Inside our cave, each one of us did his assigned duties," she writes. "We cooked, we washed, we made needed repairs. Cleanliness was of the utmost importance. Life in our grotto went on with its own normality."

In early July, however, the survivors' rising confidence was shattered by the sound of one of the Dodyk men screaming.

"The entrance to the cave is blocked!" he shouted, scrambling into Khatki. "We will all die here of starvation!"

The other men jumped from their beds and crawled quickly to the entrance, discovering a wall of earth and boulders trapping them inside. From underground, it was impossible to know if some of the men had been spotted in the woods, or if a Gestapo patrol had followed their tracks to the entrance. Instead of storming the entrance, whoever it was had simply sealed them in.

The men found a narrow gap between two rocks a few feet from the blocked entrance and frantically started to dig for daylight. For the next three nights they tunneled upward, chiseling away at the stones as the loose fracture gradually turned toward the ceiling. On the fourth day, Nissel pried a large rock from the top of the shaft and felt the wind rush in from outside, carrying with it the warm, tangy aroma of a passing thunderstorm.

The survivors later learned that a group of Ukrainian villagers had worked with picks and shovels until they filled the ravine and blocked the entrance to the cave. "Some of the Ukrainians helped us to survive," Shulim said simply. "But some of them were very bad."

With their refuge no longer a secret, the Jews stood steady guard with sickles and axes at the bottom of the entrance shaft and listened constantly for the sound of strange voices. It was impossible to know whether the Nazis or local police were planning to ambush the cave or if they had given its inhabitants up for dead.

Nissel and Shulim ventured even deeper into the cave's labyrinths, looking desperately for a breach where they could begin digging a secret exit. By this time the two older brothers were finely attuned to the state of sensory deprivation underground. They could walk for hours without retracing their steps, recognizing each passageway merely by feel. It took two weeks to find a suitable spot, and more weeks to tunnel through layers of rock, gravel, and clay. As they reached the 50-foot mark, however, the shaft started to collapse, showering the men with rock and debris. After two serious cave-ins, they gave up for good.

Though exhausted from their failed effort, the Jews could no longer put off restocking their supplies for another long winter. The plains of Ukraine yield an unimaginable bounty every September and October. Yet the risk of being caught above ground had never been greater. The lack of food over the summer had made the men weak, and during harvest the nearby fields were crowded with farmers and prowled by Nazi patrols.

"In the fall the farmers harvested potatoes and made big piles," Shulim said. "Twelve of us went out with sacks and carried potatoes all night long. We would come up to a pile and say, 'Good evening. Is anyone there?' And if no one answered, we would get to work." The men collected enough potatoes to last through the winter and hauled them to Priest's Grotto, where the younger boys and women were waiting to drag them back to Khatki.

ON NOVEMBER 10, 1943, the older Stermer men went to their friend Semen Sawkie, who, like Munko Lubudzin, faithfully sold them food and fuel throughout the war. Sawkie sold them 250 pounds of desperately needed grain and helped them transport it to the woods near Priest's Grotto in his wagon. Nissel then ventured to the cave entrance, where his youngest brother Shlomo was waiting, to make sure all was clear. Soon the men were lugging the heavy sacks to the cave.

Unknown to them, the Ukrainian police had watched them approach and were preparing for an ambush. When Nissel and Shulim reached the edge of the sinkhole, they slipped down the entrance shaft and, with Shlomo's help, began pulling the sacks into the cave from below. "But one of the sacks got stuck," Shulim said suddenly, shoving his shoulder against an imaginary obstacle in front of him. "And the entrance was blocked. No one could get in or out."

Then the men heard footsteps above them. "We're all here," the men in the cave said to themselves. "So who's outside?"

The next thing Shulim and Shlomo remember hearing was a barrage of bullets ricocheting into the cave's narrow opening. The men took cover behind the boulders that had been used to blockade the entrance. Other than barring entry to the bottom of the shaft, the men were helpless against a full-scale assault.

But after the initial round of gunfire, the survivors never heard another shot. Local peasants who gathered around the grotto after the attack told the Ukrainian police that the Jews were armed and had secret exits all over the place, information that they believed to be true. Scared of what might await them at the bottom of the sinkhole, the officers didn't attempt to enter but instead swept the fields looking for another way in. They found nothing.

"If that sack didn't get stuck, we wouldn't be here," Shulim finally said. "It was one of many miracles."

AS THE FIRST SNOWS BEGAN TO FALL across western Ukraine, the sinkhole drifted over, leaving no trace of the entrance. Underground, with enough food and fuel for more than two months, the men moved a massive boulder in front of the entry shaft and barricaded it with logs.

After seven months underground, the Jews' fight for survival was becoming a war of attrition. Their meager diet of grain and soup lacked protein, calcium, and crucial vitamins, leaving them vulnerable to jaundice and scurvy. "I remember that I was always hungry" the Stermers' granddaughter, Pepkale, said. "I knew I mustn't ask for more, but I used to say to my mother, 'Couldn't I have just a little bit more bread?' But that was the ration for the day." Many of the survivors would eventually dwindle to two-thirds their normal weight.

Yet, surrounded by family, the Stermers were able to draw on more than just physical courage and endurance to keep themselves alive. "We knew that our family would always be loyal to one another," Pepkale said. "Even when things were at their worst, you could always look around and see your sister, your mother, and the rest of your family. It helped us to remember what we were fighting for."

Survival expert Kamler suggests that Pepkale's view is more than sentiment. "The one thing that's common to every survival story is the belief in something greater than yourself," he says. "For the Jews hiding in the cave, it was their need to save their families. There's no doubt that family was the number one factor in their survival."

WITH ONLY A FEW HOURS REMAINING until our planned rendezvous with our surface support team, Sergey appears in the entry room. During a two-hour solo, he's rediscovered a chamber a half mile from Khatki that has graffiti written on the walls. Chris, Sasha, and I reach the room a few minutes later and find Sergey kneeling under a large crack between two sheets of bedrock. He rolls his face skyward, sending a curtain of soft orange light across the ceiling, where there are at least ten different inscriptions scrawled into the stone.

The first words Chris and I see are written in Ukrainian, some as recently as 2000. The others are the names of various local cavers who first explored this region of the cave some 40 years ago. When Chris first saw this chamber on one of his early trips, led by legendary Ukrainian caver Valery Rogozhnikov, these names were just graffiti. Now he sees something different. "My God," I hear him whisper.

Directly above him, written in charcoal on the ceiling, are the words: "Stermer," "Dodyk," "K. Kurz," "Salomon," and "Wekselblad"—a name we knew was later anglicized to "Wexler." Two feet farther down on the ceiling is the date "1943."

The unique thing about caves, as compared with other environments, is the way history survives underground, almost as if in a vacuum. Aboveground, buildings decay, memories fade, the past is gradually lost. But over our heads the five names look as bold as the day they'd been written; only a faint encrustation of tiny gypsum crystals—which grow continually on the cave walls—betrays the intervening six decades. Chris gazes at the names for a long while. After ten years of searching for the survivors, months of interviews, and three days of reconstructing the smallest details of their lives here in the cave, his mission is nearly complete. The only sound is the hissing of our carbide headlamps.

As THE WINTER OF 1944 TURNED TO SPRING, their friend Munko told the Stermer men that he could see bright, orange explosions over the eastern hills at night. Though it would be another year until the final collapse of Hitler's Third Reich, the Russian front was quickly advancing west.

The survivors greeted the news of their potential liberation with a mixture of elation and dread. Overhead, the front passed back and forth over the entrance to the sinkhole in a volley of artillery and small-arms fire, but beneath dozens of feet of solid bedrock, the Jews had no way of knowing when it was safe to come out. One morning in early April, Shlomo approached the bottom of the entrance shaft and saw a small bottle in the mud. The message in the bottle, dropped by a peasant friend, read simply: "The Germans are already gone."

For ten more days the Stermers and their neighbors waited for the chaos to subside; then, on April 12, 1944, they stashed their tools and supplies deep inside the cave and squeezed one by one through Priest's Grotto's narrow entrance. Heavy snow had fallen over the previous week, and ice-cold water flowed into the shaft from above, covering them with mud. Outside the entrance, the Jews scaled the steep banks of the sinkhole and rose to stand in the blinding sunshine for the first time in 344 days.

At first, they stood motionless, barely able to recognize one another in the brilliant light reflecting off the snow. Their faces were jaundiced and drawn, their clothes were tattered, and they were caked with thick, yellow mud. In the distance, the road to Korolówka was littered with burnt-out German tanks and machinery, but for Esther and her family, the sight of their war-torn homeland was one of the most beautiful things they had ever seen.

Sixty years later, in the soft afternoon light of the Stermers' living room in Montreal, the survivors recounted their memories of their liberation with quiet awe. Shulim was silent for the first time all afternoon, and Shlomo said repeatedly, "It was a beautiful, beautiful day."

"When we came out the sun must have been shining," Pepkale said. At five years old, she had spent nearly a third of her life underground. "I told my mother, I said, 'Close the candle! Turn out the light!' I couldn't believe it. I had forgotten completely what the sun was."

Their town of Korolówka had been almost completely destroyed. Of the more than 14,000 Jews that lived in the region before World War II, barely 300 had survived. Even with the Germans gone, Ukraine remained a dangerous place. After surviving the Nazi Holocaust, both Zaida Stermer and Fishel Dodyk were killed that summer by local Ukrainians.

The Stermers told no one about their underground refuge; who knew when they might need to take to it again? They abandoned Korolówka forever in June 1945, finally arriving at a displaced-persons camp in Fernwald, Germany, in November. They spent the next few weeks eating, showering, and sleeping securely for the first time in more than half a decade. Family photos from that period show the survivors dressed in tailored shirts and jackets and posing defiantly, as if nothing in the world could defeat them.

In 1947 the Stermers arrived in Canada. Nissel took up work as a butcher. Shulim found a factory job. Esther and her daughters became homemakers. The three brothers eventually found success in the construction business, drawing on many of the skills they had learned underground. Yet even among their closest friends, they talked little of their experiences.

Today, the Stermers' survival saga continues to shape virtually everything about their lives. Some, like Pepkale, travel with small stashes of food to safeguard against the possibility of going hungry. Many of the survivors remain devoutly religious, both in spite of and because of their time underground. When Chris and I asked if the Stermers felt they were blessed to survive, however, Shulim and Shlomo were dismissive of the notion that divine intervention had played a role in their triumph. God remains a controversial protagonist for almost every Holocaust survivor. But in the Stermers' case specifically, attributing their survival to a higher power risks understating the resolve and the courage it took to fight for every day they stayed alive.

"We were . . . masters of our own fate in the cave," Esther wrote at the end of her memoir. "There was no one to whom we owed our safety or upon whom we depended. . . . After our men came in from the outside and scraped off the mud which would cling to their clothing as they slid through the entrance, and they had washed, they were free men."

As Chris and I prepared to leave, the Montreal skyline was going dark. Most of Shulim's relatives were gone, and his apartment was still and quiet.

"When we get together like this and I see the grandchildren, and it's an affair," he said at the door, "I see the family and I see nice kids. And I say to myself, It was worth the fight to survive."

By THE END OF OUR THIRD AND LAST DAY underground, Chris and I have been working for almost 40 straight hours, barring short intermittent naps. Thanks in large part to Sergey and Sasha's agility moving in small spaces, we've mapped and inventoried all four of Khatki's main rooms and carefully photographed each one of the artifacts to show to the Stermers back in Montreal.

While the sun is setting above ground, we hastily disassemble our camp and celebrate the success of our expedition with a ceremonial shot of local vodka. Then comes the long chore of dragging all of our equipment back to the entrance through the mud. Even after just 72 hours underground, the anticipation of feeling the wind and smelling the earth is overpowering. Sergey throws open the steel door at the top of the entrance shaft, and the passageway where Chris and I are waiting fills instantly with warm, fresh air.

June/July 2004

THE LEGEND OF
HEAVY D & THE BOYS

(or, how the Green Berets learned to
stop worrying and love the warlord)

By Robert Young Pelton

---

*Heavy D is General Dostum, Afghanistan's most feared commander. The boys
are the elite U.S. Special Forces who rode (on horseback when necessary), lived,
and fought alongside his troops as they liberated the north from the Taliban.
How an odd-couple alliance routed the extremists, quashed a bloody prison uprising,
and discovered the American Talib John Walker Lindh.*

THE REGULATORS FLEW IN from Uzbekistan at night on a blacked-out Chinook helicopter and landed near a mud-walled compound in a remote valley in northern Afghanistan. As they began unloading their gear, they were met by Afghans in turbans, their faces wrapped. "It was like that scene in *Close Encounters* where the aliens meet humans for the first time," one soldier says later. "Or maybe that scene in *Star Wars*: These sand people started jabbering in a language we had never heard." The Americans shouldered their hundred-pound rucksacks while the Afghans hefted the rest of the equipment. The gear seemed to float from the landing site under a procession of brown blankets and turbans.

The next morning, about 60 Afghan cavalry came thundering into the compound. Ten minutes later, another 40 riders galloped up. General Abdul Rashid Dostum had arrived.

"Our mission was simple," another soldier says. "Support Dostum. They told us, 'If Dostum wants to go to Kabul, you are going with him. If he wants to take over the whole country, do it. If he goes off the deep end and starts whacking people, advise higher up and maybe pull out.' This was the most incredibly open mission we have ever done."

Before heading in-country, the soldiers had been briefed only vaguely about Dostum. They'd heard rumors that he was 80 years old, that he didn't have use of his right arm. And they'd been told that he was the most power-ful anti-Taliban leader in northern Afghanistan. "I thought the guy was this ruthless warlord," one soldier says. "I assumed he was fricking mean, hard. You know: You better not show any weakness. Then he rides up on horseback with one pant leg untucked, looking like Bluto."

Dostum dismounted and shook everyone's hand, then sat on a mound covered with carpets. He talked for half an hour. Dostum's strategy was now their strategy: to ride roughshod over Taliban positions up the Darra-e Suf Valley, roll over the Tingi Pass in the Alborz Range, then sweep north across the plains and liberate Mazar-e Sharif, Afghanistan's second largest city. When the council broke up, Dostum stood and motioned toward the horses. America's finest were about to fight their first war on horseback in more than a hundred years.

THE ROCKET HOWLS OVER THE ROOF of General Dostum's house in Khoda Barq at about 10 p.m. It's November 26, my second day in Afghanistan, and already I'm in the middle of a hellacious firefight. Although nighttime gunfire is normal in Afghanistan, there is an urgency to the sound of the deep explosions that come from the 19th-century fortress of Qala Jangi, just over a mile east from Khoda Barq, a Soviet-era apartment complex west of Mazar. The heavy shooting, the worried soldiers, the rapid radio chatter—all signal that something ugly is going on over there.

Meanwhile, I'm hunkered down, waiting for Dostum. I've arranged through intermediaries to spend a month with the general, but for the past week, he has been a hundred miles east, trying to subdue Taliban forces that control the city of Kunduz. General Abdul Rashid Dostum is a man who has rarely been interviewed but has often been typecast as a brutal warlord—usually because of his reputation for winning. He is a man who is said by some journalists to define violence and treachery. (In *Taliban*, author Ahmed Rashid reports a tale he heard that Dostum once ordered his men to drag a thief behind a tank until all that was left was a bloody pulp of gore.) Beyond that, all I know is that Dostum, born a poor peasant, grew up to be a bril-liant commander, a general, and a warlord—one of the many regional leaders across Afghanistan whose power derives both from ethnic loyalties and from military strength. That he is known to be a deft alliance maker—and breaker. And that he became the first Afghan commander to take over a major city when he entered Mazar-e Sharif on November 10. It's an irresistible story, made all the more so by a convincing rumor I've been hearing since my arrival:

that Dostum triumphed with a little help from his friends—specifically, the Green Berets.

As I wait for Dostum to return, though, the constant chatter of machine guns and the *badoom badoom* of cannons from an American gunship bombarding the fort—Dostum's military headquarters—suggest that I might be a bit premature in offering any congratulations on winning the war. I soon learn that yesterday some 400 foreign Taliban prisoners overpowered their guards, broke into arsenals, and took over part of the fortress.

At 3:30 a.m., I go to bed. Three hours later, I am awakened by a massive explosion a few yards from the house—another near miss by a rocket fired from inside the fort. The sound of bombing continues without a break but at a slower pace. Villagers come out in the crisp, golden light of morning, shivering and tired. Some huddle together to watch the gray pillars of smoke from the bombing runs. Others begin the work of the day without even paying attention to the nearby fighting.

In the afternoon, when I visit Qala Jangi, bullets sing over my head. Up on the parapets, Dostum's troops stream toward a gap in the ramparts created yesterday by what I've heard was an errant American bomb. Soldiers run up to the bite in the wall, shoot into the fort, and then scurry back down. I watch a fighter go up to the top, then crumple into a black pile of rags. Astoundingly, after two days of bombardment, the prisoners still control the fort.

Late in the afternoon, a convoy of mud-spattered off-road vehicles pulls up, and a dozen dusty Americans in tan camo climb out. They have Beretta pistols strapped to their thighs like gunslingers and short M-4 rifles slung across their chests. They're polite but wary about having their pictures taken as they set up their night-vision scopes. After a final check of their gear, they head into the fortress. Later, I find out that they've come hoping to retrieve the body of Central Intelligence Agency officer Johnny Micheal Spann, who was killed by Taliban prisoners—the first American combat casualty in Afghanistan.

DOSTUM ARRIVES THAT NIGHT, DUCKING TO AVOID banging his head as he strides through the guest-house door. He takes my hand in a meaty grip and apologizes for being dirty and tired; he has just driven eight hours on a shattered road from Kunduz. He has two weeks of beard, beetling eyebrows, and a graying brush cut. When Dostum frowns, his features gather into a dark, Stalin-like scowl—his usual expression for formal portraits. But when he smiles, he looks like a naughty 12-year-old.

He sits and makes small talk, then excuses himself to take a shower. When he returns, the dark weariness has lifted. Over *chai* (tea), he announces good news. He has ended the bloody battle for Kunduz by negotiating with Mullah Faizal and Mullah Nuri, the two most senior Taliban leaders in the north. It seems that the "brutal warlord" has engineered the biggest peaceful surrender in recent Afghan history—more than 5,000 Afghan Taliban fighters and foreign volunteers laid down their arms. He waves the accomplishment aside with a shy smile even as he promises to introduce me to his new trophies—the mullahs. It turns out they're staying next door, guests in Dostum's house.

Dostum proves to be significantly more expansive in conversation than his scant press clippings would suggest, and he's happy to fill me in on his background. (Over the next few weeks, as these conversations work to humanize the warlord, I privately coin for him a nickname: Heavy D, after the 1980s rapper.) He was born Abdul Rashid in 1954 in the desolate village of Khvajeh Do Kuh, about 90 miles west of Mazar. The most significant tidbit I glean about his childhood is that he was adept at the game of *buzkashi*, in which teams of horsemen attempt to toss the headless carcass of a calf into a circle. Dating at least to the days of Genghis Khan, the violent game is not so much about scoring as it is about using every dirty trick possible—beating, whipping, kicking—to prevent the opposing team from scoring. Buzkashi is the way Afghan boys learn to ride—and it's the way Afghan politics is played: The toughest, meanest, and most brutal player takes the prize.

After the seventh grade, Dostum left school to help his father on the family farm. At 16, he started working as a laborer in the government-owned gas refinery in nearby Sheberghan, where he dabbled in union politics. When a Marxist government came to power in a bloody coup in 1978, the new regime's radical reforms ignited a guerrilla war with the *mujahidin* who based themselves in the country's remote mountain ranges. Dostum enlisted in the Afghan military—one of the few ways for poor men to escape lives of labor and hardship in rural Afghanistan.

The people of Dostum's village were so impressed with his leadership that they recruited 600 men for him to command. It was about this time that Abdul Rashid became "Dostum." In Uzbek, *dost* means "friend"; *dostum* means "my friend." It was a nickname that the young soldier was given for his habitual way of addressing people. When a local singer wrote a song about "Dostum," the name stuck.

In the bewildering matrix of Afghan politics, Dostum has frequently—and nimbly—switched allegiances. In the 1980s, as a young army officer in the Soviet-backed government, he fought against the mujahidin. When the regime fell in 1992, three years after the Soviets departed, Dostum fought alongside the mujahidin and helped the Northern Alliance's legendary Ahmad Shah Massoud battle the fundamentalist Pashtun forces of Gulbuddin Hekmatyar and gain control of the capital. The shelling, raping, pillaging, looting, and house-to-house fighting that then befell Kabul stained the name of every mujahidin commander, including Dostum's, and fueled his reputation for brutality. I show Dostum the chapter in Rashid's book that includes the account of the gruesome execution of the thief. Dostum chuckles and denies the allegation. He freely admits that in two decades of war, abuses have been committed by the troops of every commander. "What else do you expect my enemies to say?" he asks. "That I am kind and gentle? I will let what you see be the truth."

In 1996, when the Taliban rolled into Kabul, Dostum was forced to retreat to his stronghold in Mazar as the mullahs instituted their version of a pure Islamic state. "At first I thought, Why not let them rule?" he says. "Power is not given to anyone forever. If the Taliban can rule successfully, let them." A year later, betrayed by his second in command, who had defected to the Taliban, Dostum fled to Turkey.

Those among Dostum's men who had remained in Afghanistan now became guerrilla fighters, holed up in the mountains, attacking the troops of the latest regime. Dostum's lieutenants would call him in Turkey and tell him how difficult life had become. They had to kill their horses for food. They didn't have enough cloth for shrouds, so they had to bury dead comrades in burqas. "People demanded that I do something," says Dostum. "Commanders, clergymen, women—they would all tell me very bitter stories. I was full of emotions. My friends were struggling against the Taliban, and I was sitting there."

Dostum says that to help him get back into the fray, the former president of Afghanistan, Burhanuddin Rabbani, raised about $40,000. The Turks, long staunch enemies of Islamic extremism, contributed a small sum as well, and, on April 22, 2001, General Dostum and 30 men were ferried into northern Afghanistan on Massoud's aging Soviet helicopters. "That," says Dostum, "was when the war against terror began."

Living in caves and raiding Taliban positions, Dostum's men slowly began to harass the well-entrenched Taliban along the Darra-e Suf. They moved and attacked mostly at night, riding small, wiry Afghan horses that are well suited to steep slopes and long desert walks. "The money was hardly enough for feeding my horses," Dostum says. "They had tanks, air force, and artillery. We fought with nothing but hope."

Then came September 11. Using a United Nations envoy as an intermediary, Dostum suggested that the United States might want to give him some help.

THE MORNING AFTER HEAVY D'S return from Kunduz, he greets me with a deep, booming "Howareyou?" Today, he tells me, he is eager for me to meet his trophy mullahs.

Next door, in Dostum's pink house, Mullah Faizal and Mullah Nuri sit on pillows in a small room. These are two of the Taliban who chased Dostum out of Mazar in May 1997, but still he treats them more like honored guests than prisoners of war. Faizal has his prosthetic leg off. He is a thick man with a pug nose, bad skin, tiny teeth, and a cruel stare. Nuri has the black look of a Pashtun who has endured a lifetime of war. Wrapped in blankets, members of the mullahs' entourage fix me with soulless stares. Nuri is chatty, although he often looks to the silent Faizal before answering my questions. During the Taliban's reign, thousands of Hazara Shias were murdered in northern Afghanistan; the mullahs are unrepentant. "We fought for an idea," says Nuri. "We did all that we could. Now we hope that America will not be cruel to the Afghan people."

That afternoon, Dostum and I set off for the fort, where the uprising has been all but quelled. He brings the mullahs along, to show them the havoc incited by their foreign volunteers. Perhaps they'll convince any surviving prisoners to surrender.

After four days of bombardment, the interior of the fort is a scene of utter devastation. Blackened, twisted vehicles are perforated with thousands of jagged holes. The crumpled bodies of prisoners, frozen in agony, are scattered everywhere. Most of the fallen look as if they were killed instantly. Some are in pieces; others have been flattened by tank treads. More than 400 prisoners are said to have died; I count only about 50 bodies in the courtyard. The estimated 30 Alliance soldiers who died have already been taken away by their friends. When an American team finally recovered Spann's body, they discovered it had been booby-trapped with a live grenade (which they removed without incident).

It is also rumored that there are many dead and at least two live prisoners holed up in the subterranean bomb shelter. The entrance to the bunker was pierced by cannon shots and is blackened from explosions. Dostum's men have been throwing down grenades and pouring in gasoline and lighting it, but the foreign Taliban refuse to come up. Dostum implores the mullahs to call down to the bunker and tell the remaining men to surrender. Mullah Faizal and Mullah Nuri refuse: They claim they don't know these people.

The trapped Taliban volunteers, it seems, remain hungry for martyrdom. A day later—Thursday, five days since the uprising broke out—they are still firing sporadically at soldiers removing bodies from the courtyard of the fortress. At least two Red Cross workers who descend into the bunker are shot and wounded.

LATER THAT WEEK, DOSTUM CASUALLY mentions that 3,000 other foreign fighters from the surrender at Kunduz are in a Soviet-era prison in the city of Sheberghan, 80 miles west. Anticipating more fireworks, I head there with him and move into another of his residences, a huge, high-walled compound that includes a mosque and, improbably, an unfinished health-club complex.

Some American soldiers are billeted upstairs in the guest houses; men in camo pants run up and down the stairs. Their rooms are filled with green Army cots, dirty brown packs, and green flight bags. Rifles, night-vision gear, and boots are strewn everywhere. I head downstairs and discover a group of soldiers bantering cheerfully, mostly in southern accents. They've just finished installing a satellite TV. When the television begins to blare, the men stare at the screen. "We haven't seen a TV or news in two months," one soldier says apologetically. Transfixed, they watch the Christmas tree being lit in Rockefeller Center.

These are the soldiers I saw back at Qala Jangi preparing to go in and retrieve the body of the dead CIA agent, Mike Spann. "Don't I know you?" one of them says. "Aren't you the guy who goes to all those dangerous places?"

It feels more than a bit odd to be recognized for my books and TV show—as someone who specializes in traveling to the world's hot spots—while poking around a war in Afghanistan. It feels even more odd when I discover that these are Green Berets—soldiers who truly specialize in the world's hot spots. But I never travel without a few "Mr. DP" hats, so I dig them out of my bag and pass them around.

Over the ensuing days, I take every opportunity to spend time in these makeshift barracks, particularly once I discover that this is the very unit of Green Berets that I'd been hearing rumors about—this is Dostum's covert support team. At night we sit around talking over stainless steel cups of coffee. Some details of their mission they can't discuss. Some are provided by Dostum and others. But the story gradually emerges.

There are twelve Green Berets here and two Air Force forward air controllers. Green Berets work in secrecy, so only their first names can be used: There's Andy, the slow-talking weapons expert who is never without his grenade launcher; back home, he keeps the guns in his collections loaded "so they are ready when I am." Both he and Paul, a quiet, bespectacled warrant officer, have been in the unit 11 years. Then there's Steve, a well-mannered southern medic; Pete, the burly chaw spitter; Mark, their blond, midwestern captain; and so on. It's like a casting call for *The Dirty Dozen*. Their motto is "To Free the Oppressed"—something they have done so far in this war with no civilian casualties, no blowback, and no regrets.

These soldiers, I soon realize, come from much the same background as Dostum's: sons of miners, farmers, and factory workers; men whose only way out of poverty is the military. They range in age from mid-20s to late 30s. They are men with wives, children, mortgages, bills. Men who are the Army's elite, who are college educated and fluent in several languages, yet who are paid little more than a manager at McDonald's. They spend every day training for war, teaching other armies about war, and waiting for the call to fight in the next war.

They are direct military descendants of the Devil's Brigade, a joint Canadian-American unit that fought in Italy during the Second World War. That group was disbanded and then re-formed in the early 1950s as Special Forces, which John F. Kennedy later nicknamed the Green Berets. The men I'm staying with have dubbed their unit the Regulators, after the 19th-century cowboys who were hired by cattle barons to guard their herds from rustlers. The Regulators have served in the gulf war, Somalia, Saudi Arabia, the United Arab Emirates, and in other places they can't talk about. Their home base is Fort Campbell, Kentucky, but they spend only a few months of the year there. The rest of the time they travel.

On the morning of September 11, the team was returning to base after an all-night training exercise. "The post was in an uproar," says Paul. No one knew just when or where the team would be sent. They cleaned and stowed their gear and awaited the order. And waited. There was talk that the team might be split up—rumors of differences with a commanding officer who didn't appreciate the traditional independence of the Green Berets. But toward the end of September, the word came down: "Pack your shit."

Fifteen days later, the team boarded a C-5 Galaxy with a secret flight plan. The Regulators' final destination turned out to be Uzbekistan, where they spent a week building a tent city and waiting for a mission. "We were at the right place at the right time," says Steve. "Fifty tents later, they told us to pack our shit again."

"We had two days to plan," another Regulator says. "The CIA gave us a briefing." Although the Regulators were among the first, other small teams of

U.S. forces would soon be airlifted in for similar missions, a response to Dostum's request for American assistance to be sent to other Northern Alliance commanders. Atta Mohammed, for example, would get his own Green Beret escort several weeks later as he raced Dostum to claim Mazar. Once they hit the ground, the Regulators would be writing their own game plan. "Our commanders said they didn't know what to expect, but at least they were honest enough to admit it," the Green Beret continues. "They said, 'You guys will be on the ground; you figure it out.' "

WITHIN HALF AN HOUR OF MEETING Dostum at the mud-walled compound in the Darra-e Suf, the Regulators swung into action. Some stayed behind to handle logistics and supplies. The rest mounted up and rode north. "It was pretty painful," Paul says. "They use simple wooden saddles covered with a piece of carpet, and short stirrups that put our knees up by our heads. The first words I wanted to learn in Dari were, 'How do you make him stop?'"

Their most important immediate order of business was to establish themselves in Dostum's eyes. "The first thing we wanted to do was to say to Dostum, 'The Americans are here,' " Paul explains, "and to make it a fearsome prospect to mess with us." The Americans set up their gear at Dostum's command post—which overlooked Taliban positions about six miles away—and immediately began the process of calling in close air support, or CAS. "You see the village; you see the bunkers," says a second Steve, one of the two Air Force men attached to the team to help coordinate air strikes. "You call in an airplane; you say, 'Can you see that place? There are tanks. You see this grid? Drop a bomb on that grid.' Pretty straightforward stuff."

It took a few hours for bombers to arrive from their carriers. At first, the planes wouldn't fly below 15,000 feet—the brass was worried about surface-to-air missiles—so targeting was sketchy. But coordination soon improved, and the improbable allies fell into a rhythm: The Americans would bomb; Dostum's men would attack.

A crude videotape made by one of Dostum's men shows a battle in the rolling hills of the Darra-e Suf, where the yellow grass contrasts with the deep blue sky. The Americans, up on the ridge, are using GPS units to finalize coordinates. Down below, small Afghan horses are nipping the dry grass on the safe side of the hill, their riders chatting while awaiting the order to charge. The horses cast long shadows in the late afternoon. The only sign that something is about to happen is a white contrail high in the sky. The radio crackles with call signs and traffic broadcast between bombardiers and the

American soldiers. First, a soft gray cloud of smoke rises in a lazy ring. Then the concussion: *ka-RUMPH!*

The tape now shows Dostum, leaning against a mud wall, watching through large binoculars. The dirty gray mushroom cloud slowly bends in the wind. Dostum stays in contact with the Americans by radio, working to help focus the bombing: a man with a seventh-grade education directing the fire of the world's most powerful military.

Ka-RUMPH! More hits: Tall, fat smoke plumes cast moving shadows on the grass. The riders mount their horses, check their weapons, and begin the one-kilometer sprint to the Taliban front lines. There's the erratic chatter of AK-47s and the deep *dut dut dut dut* of Taliban machine guns. Then the radios are jammed with Dostum's men shouting and celebrating. The Taliban are running.

The videotape cuts to the next morning. Dostum's men are touring the battle scene. The twisted rag doll bodies of dead Taliban fighters lie heads back, fingers clutched, legs sprawled as if they fell running. Dostum's men kick the corpses into the trenches and cover them with the tan dirt, not bothering to count the dead.

The Regulators were joined by at least three CIA officers kitted in full combat gear, including a 32-year-old ex-Marine named Mike Spann. "We were surprised at how good they were," says Captain Mark. "What we are doing now has not occurred since Vietnam. Up until now the CIA has been hog-tied. Now the CIA and spec ops have been let loose."

Each night, Dostum would sit down with the Americans and lay out the battle plan for the next day. "He would say he is going to attack at about 2 p.m.," says Air Force Steve. "So we would put in for priority for the planes." The team's primary weapons were not pistols or rifles; they were the most fearsome tools in the American arsenal: F-18s, F-16s, F-14s, and B-52s. They chose not bullets or grenades but ordnance that ranged from Maverick missiles to laser-guided bombs.

In contrast to the Americans' high-tech warfare, some of Dostum's tactics would have seemed familiar to the British troops who tried and failed to pacify this region in the 19th century. Before the arrival of the Americans, Dostum fought mostly at night. "He couldn't expose his small force to Taliban missile strikes," explains Captain Mark, "so they would hit and retreat. He never sac-rificed his men. He would take a village by getting the mounted guys up close. When it looked like they would break the back of the position, he would ride through as fast as he could and keep the Taliban on the run."

With their knowledge of military history, the Regulators appreciated the ironies of this strange war: "The Taliban had gone from the 'muj' style of fighting—in the mountains, on horseback—to working in mechanized columns," says Will, another Green Beret. That heavy reliance on tanks and trucks meant the Taliban wound up fighting a defensive, Russian-style war. "Then, here is Dostum," continues Will, "a guy trained in tanks who's using tactics developed in Genghis Khan's time."

The Regulators' job was to invent a new form of warfare: coordinating lightly armed horseback attacks with massive applications of American air power—all without hitting civilians or friendly forces.

"In an air attack," says Air Force Steve, "you do one of two things. You can bomb it until there is no resistance, or you bomb and, as soon as the bomb goes off, you charge. By the time they come up and look, you are on them." The latter approach was well suited to Dostum's style of attack. "A cavalry charge is an amazing thing," Will says. "At a full gallop, it's a smooth ride. The Afghans shoot from horseback, but there is no aiming in this country. It's more like, 'I am coming to get you—whether I hit you is another story.' It's Old World combat at its finest.

"There's one time I'll never forget," he says. "The Taliban had dug-in, trench-line bunkers shooting machine guns, heavy machine guns, and RPGs [rocket-propelled grenades]. We had an entire 250-man cavalry ready to charge." The Regulators wanted Dostum's right-hand man, Commander Lahl Mohammed, to hold off while they got their aircraft in position, but Lahl had already given the order. In seconds, 250 men on horseback were thundering toward the Taliban position a mere 1,500 meters away.

"We only had the time it takes 250 horses to travel 1,500 meters, so I told the pilot to step on it," Will says. "I looked at Lahl and said, 'Bombs away.' We had 30 seconds till impact; meanwhile, the Afghan horde is screaming down this ridgeline. It was right at dark. You could see machine gun fire from both positions. You could see horses falling." An outcrop obscured views of the last 250 meters to the target. The lead horsemen disappeared behind the rocks, and the Regulators all held their breath, praying the bombs would reach the bunkers before the cavalry did. "Three or four bombs hit right in the middle of the enemy position," says Will. "Almost immediately after the bombs exploded, the horses swept across the objective—the enemy was so shell-shocked. I could see the horses blasting out the other side. It was the finest sight I ever saw. The men were thrilled; they were so happy. It wasn't done perfectly, but it will never be forgotten."

AROUND EIGHT O'CLOCK ON SATURDAY NIGHT, while I'm talking with the Green Berets, one of Dostum's men comes into the house and asks us to follow him outside. Beyond the high steel gates is a confusion of trucks, headlights, and guns, and the sound of men moaning in pain. Lined up against a wall is the most pathetic display of humanity I have ever seen: the survivors of the bunker at Qala Jangi fortress. Dostum's men had finally flooded them out by sluicing frigid water into the subterranean room. Instead of the expected handful of holdouts, no fewer than 86 foreign Taliban emerged after a week in the agonizing dark and cold—starved, deaf, hypothermic, wounded, and exhausted. Their captors brought them here en route to the Sheberghan prison.

They send off steam in the cold night, their brown skin white with dust. Some hide their faces, others convulse and shiver. I talk to an Iraqi, as well as to Pakistanis and Saudis—all of whom speak English. On another truck are the seriously wounded. Some cry out in pain, some are weeping, and others lie still, their faces frozen in deathly grimaces.

They put the prisoners back on the truck. A few minutes later, one of Dostum's men runs up breathlessly, saying there is an American in the hospital. I grab my cameras and ask Bill, a pensive Green Beret medic, to come with me.

The scene at the hospital is ugly. The warm smell of gangrene and human waste hits me as I open the door to the triage room. Shattered, bearded men lie everywhere on stretchers, covered by thin blue sheets. The doctors huddle around a steel-drum stove, smiling and talking, oblivious to the pain and suffering around them. In the back, a doctor leans over a man with a smoke-blackened face, wild black hair, and an unkempt beard. He lies staring at the ceiling. The doctor yells in halting English, "What your name?" He jabs at the half-conscious man's face. "Open your eyes! What your name? Where you from?" The man finally answers. "John," he says. "Washington, D.C."

The man is terribly thin and severely hypothermic. At first he is hostile, like a kitten baring its claws. He won't tell me who to contact, or provide any information that would get him out of the crudely equipped hospital. I convince the staff to move him to an upstairs bed, where Bill inserts an IV of Hespan into the man's dehydrated body to increase blood circulation. As Bill checks for wounds, he talks to the young man briefly in Arabic. I tell the prisoner where he is and who he's talking to. Bill finds a shrapnel wound in the emaciated man's right upper thigh and wounds from grenade shrapnel in his back; he also finds that part of the second toe on his left foot has been shot away.

As the Hespan drips into his veins, I fire up the video camera, and the man begins to tell his story. His name, he says, is John Walker. He studied Arabic in Yemen and then enrolled in a *madrasah,* or religious school, in northern Pakistan. He says it was an area sympathetic to the Taliban and that his heart went out to them.

Six months ago, he traveled to Kabul with some Pakistanis to join the Taliban. Since he can't speak Urdu, he was assigned to the Arab-speaking branch of Ansar ("the helpers"), a faction that Walker claims is sponsored by Osama bin Laden—whom Walker says he saw many times in the training camps and on the front lines.

He ended up in the Takhar Province, in the northeastern part of the country. Then the war began. After the American bombing campaign decimated their forces, Walker and members of his unit fled on foot nearly a hundred miles west to Kunduz—all for nothing, as it turned out. Mullah Faizal and Mullah Nuri soon surrendered Kunduz to Dostum, and Walker was imprisoned with the other foreign volunteers in the bunker at Qala Jangi.

When I look at the terrible conditions and the predicament that Walker is in, I have to ask him if this is what he expected.

"Definitely."

Was it his goal to become a martyr?

"It is the goal of every Muslim."

Then the morphine begins to kick in. I suggest to Bill that we remove Walker from the hospital, where he might be killed by other patients, many of whom were fighting against him at the fortress. We transfer him to Dostum's house, and the next day he's spirited away at the same time that his story is being broadcast around the world.

When the videotape of my interview with Walker hits the airwaves back in the U.S., the country focuses its white-hot anger on him, and some of that anger spills over onto me. In the conservative press I am criticized for being too gentle in my questioning of an obvious traitor, on the left for cold-bloodedly tricking a helpless boy into incriminating himself.

IF YOU DRIVE WEST FROM MAZAR, past Qala Jangi, past Khoda Barq, past the ancient, crumbling city of Balkh, and head south toward a ridge of snow-dusted mountains called the Alborz Range, you will see a gap—the Tingi Pass. This is where the Taliban made their last stand. The Green Berets call it the Gap of Doom.

Two of the Green Berets I've been chatting with—Andy and Paul, the pair with the longest tenure in the company—have decided that I need to see this place for myself, or maybe simply that they need to go see it again one last time. We jump in an off-road vehicle and set off. Soon we're winding past an ancient brick bridge that crosses a roaring gorge; on the west side are large caves that shepherds have scooped out of the soft rock over the centuries.

As we drive, Paul tells me that, back in the U.S., even the Regulators are subject to a military culture of rules and red tape. Planning a one-day live-ammo training exercise can require six months of paperwork. "If there is no enemy, then bureaucracy is the enemy," he says. But on the ground in Afghanistan, they're on their own. The greatest restrictions they face have been placed on them by Dostum himself. "Dostum was very concerned about us getting too close to the battlefield," Captain Mark had told me back at the barracks. "In the last two semi-wars we have been in, every time American soldiers get killed we pull out. That is one of the premises Osama bin Laden operates under." Dostum wasn't about to let an American casualty put a premature end to his battle plan.

Their closest call came toward the end of the campaign, before they'd reached the Tingi Pass; I'd gotten an account of it last night from Mike, a big, bearded, soft-spoken soldier. The conflict began with several hundred Taliban troops moving into positions on an adjacent hill. Outmanned, the Green Berets decided to move out on horseback. They had gone only about 600 meters when they started taking fire. "I figured I could whip my horse and run across an open area," Mike said. "I whip my horse, it takes three steps, and stops. The rounds are zinging over my head. Somehow I make it across the open area. I get off the horse and say, 'Screw this; I'm walking.'

"We set up in a bomb crater and used it as our bunker. We were receiving more fire. It was somewhere between harassing and accurate—enough to keep our heads down. We called in a couple of bomb strikes. We could see a bunch of Taliban come out of another bunker complex off to the south and disappear behind a hill. It took about an hour to get the aircraft. All the while, we could see troops moving and disappearing. I'm looking through the optics while rounds are zinging all around us." At this point in the tale, Mike nodded toward Paul, who was sitting next to him on the couch at Dostum's guest house. "Paul here is busy shooting at guys. What we didn't realize was that the Taliban who we saw coming out of the bunker had gone into the low ground and were sprinting up the hills at us in a flanking maneuver.

"Our Afghans are running out of ammo. Their subcommander has told us at least six times over the radio to get out of there. You have to understand: Dostum had told them, 'If an American gets hurt . . . you die.' We were focused on calling in an air strike to take out this truck that had rumbled into view, and now RPG rounds are flying over our heads. We're not about to stand up and watch what's going on. The pilot asked us, 'What's the effect [of the bomb attack on the truck]?' We yell over the radio, 'We don't know! We're not lifting our heads up!'

"When we turn around and notice what's going on, we see our Afghans have split."

The team decided to call in a B-52 strike practically on their own position—a drastic move considering the planes were flying above 15,000 feet. The enemy was 700 meters out and moving quickly. "Matt yelled, 'Duck your head and get down!' And that pilot dropped a shitload of bombs," Mike said. "You felt the air leave. After the bombs hit, I peeked over the side of the bunker; our horses were gone. We grabbed our stuff and ran."

PAUL, ANDY, AND I DRIVE PAST villages of round, domed huts, past a checkpoint manned by Dostum's men, and up along the winding road to the Tingi Pass. Three years of drought have broken: A cold rain pours down in gray sheets. We pass the twisted, stripped wrecks of trucks. Afghans in a blue truck are scavenging for parts. The two Green Berets are solemn; they insist on driving through the gap so they can tell their story from the right perspective.

We wind through the tight pass alongside a swollen mountain river, go over the pass, then head a kilometer down the south side of the divide and stop at a freshly mudded house. We get out of the jeep and stand in the rain and slick mud. Paul picks up the story, raindrops dotting his gold-rimmed, government-issue glasses.

"We kept moving north on horseback, but at that point, no one could tell where the front line was anymore. Once we hit Keshendeh-ye Bala, we picked up a road and followed it north in a truck Dostum's men had captured from the Taliban. At eight that night, we pulled into Shulgareh, which is the biggest town in the valley. We were ready to throw down the mattress and settle in for the night when one of the security guards came up with a radio and said that Dostum needed someone to go up to the front to call in aircraft. We jumped in the back of a truck and drove up to Dostum's HQ here in this house."

In the courtyard, a soft-eyed cow tries to eat spilled oats just beyond its reach. A hundred yards away, villagers stand against a long compound. They huddle in brown blankets, trying to avoid the soaking rain. Paul points to a misty, triangular peak that forms one side of the gap. It served as Paul's command post.

"When we climbed up to the top of that hill, we could see the Taliban on the other side, regrouping for the final attempt to stop us. They were setting up fixed positions—bunkers with Y-shaped fighting trenches—on the northern side of the gap. It works against tanks, but it's plain stupid in this terrain. We had unrestricted movement into the gap, which gave us the high ground."

Andy chimes in. "Whoever gets the high ground first wins the wars here." From their perch on the east side of the gorge, the Green Berets could shoot directly into the trenches of the Taliban.

"Once the plane got there, it circled about six times," Paul says. "Every time the plane would circle, the Taliban would run behind their bunker. After four times or so, they didn't get bombed, so they just stayed there. I targeted a spot right next to this guy's head. I was sick of this guy running back and forth getting ammo. Then the bombs are dropped, and I look through the scope and see body parts flying everywhere. We moved our targeting up along the ridgeline to the second bunker. Same thing: We identity it and *boom!* No more Taliban. I target the third bunker. They just can't figure it out. The bomb lands and hits and *bam!* After that hit, all of them took off on foot to Mazar. And that ended the resistance." As the three of us climb back into our vehicle, I glance back at the battlefield. All I see is grass growing beside abandoned trenches. Only Paul and Andy are able to appreciate what happened here.

EARLY IN THE AFTERNOON ON NOVEMBER 10, Dostum reached Mazar. His men rounded up vehicles that the Taliban had left behind, and Heavy D entered the city as a conquering hero, standing through the sunroof of a 4x4. The crowds quickly grew; people threw money in the air for good luck. Dostum's first stop was the blue mosque at the tomb of Hazrat Ali, the revered son-in-law of the Prophet. Men wept as the imam prayed and thanked Dostum for deliverance.

The joy was short-lived. It turned out that 900 Pakistani Taliban had been left behind in a madrasah in the center of a compound about the size of a city block, and they were ready to fight to the death. Dostum and his commanders wanted to negotiate, but the foreign Taliban shot and killed their peace envoys, which left Alliance leaders with little choice. "We had hardened fighters holed up in the middle of an urban area who wanted to die," says Will. "And we were going to oblige them."

The team set up on the roof of a building about 400 meters from the madrasah and called in a strike. When the two aircraft were on location, the Green Berets radioed Alliance commanders to evacuate civilians from the area. The pilots, however, could not lock in on the laser-sighting device that the team was using to identify the target. The madrasah was surrounded for about a mile on each side by identical buildings, which made it difficult for the pilots to pick out the school. "Finally, the pilot says he has the target in sight. I asked him to describe it, just to be sure," says Will. "He described the building we were sitting on to a T." Finally, Air Force Steve guided the pilot to the correct building, and he dropped the ordnance: direct hit.

The team cleared him for immediate re-attack, but the pilot radioed back that he had "hung a bomb"—a bomb had not released. When the pilot radioed that he needed to return to base, the other pilot swung into action. On the next pass, three more bombs went through the hole in the roof made by the first bomb, killing most of the holdouts inside.

Under intense pressure, the Regulators had called in a perfect surgical strike—a bomb drop in a crowded urban area without a single civilian casualty. "This is the first close-air-support strike in years in an urban area," says Air Force Steve. "It was old-fashioned professionalism. The whole team jelled."

THE STEEL GATE TO THE GUEST HOUSE OPENS, and Dostum strolls out, hands in pockets, and is ushered into a black sedan with tinted windows. Dozens of dark-eyed men in turbans scramble into battered pickup trucks and assorted four-wheel-drive vehicles. Armored personnel carriers jerk to life in clouds of black diesel exhaust. It's three weeks after the madrasah bombing, and word has come down that 3,000 Taliban are still occupying the city and environs of Balkh, Alexander the Great's old walled capital, a few miles west of Mazar. Dostum has decided to clean up the region's last remaining pocket of Taliban himself.

I ride in the warlord's communications truck. The Regulators rush to catch up in two mud-covered cars. We roll past weathered villages unchanged in two millennia. Abandoned Soviet-era tanks are scattered about the flat countryside like dinosaur skeletons.

This part of Afghanistan is ancient, arid, windblown—and is the real cradle of its history and wealth. This is where Alexander ruled, where Zoroaster was born, where Buddhists came on pilgrimages, a center of art, poetry, and study where lions were hunted and where Genghis Khan came to conquer. Now, in a scene that has been repeated over and over for the past 2,000 years, a warlord is arriving.

In a village on the outskirts of Balkh, the convoy rumbles to a halt near an ancient castle that is now a rounded mound of tan mud. The truck-mounted ZU antiaircraft guns are cranked down to eye level. Twenty Urgan missiles point toward the village. Dostum's men load RPGs and check their ammo drums. About 200 men have taken up positions around the village, eyeing ragged locals, who stare back from a careful distance. It feels like a scene out of a bad Mexican movie.

After a cinematic pause to allow the implications of his arrival to sink in, Dostum phones the village leadership from the car: Send out your weapons and any fighters or we're going in. The deadline is noon.

The general climbs out of the tiny black car and tucks his hands into his belt. He rolls in a John Wayne walk to Commander Lahl, who's in charge of the standoff. The two Afghan leaders study a map with Captain Mark, just in case air strikes are needed. When noon comes and goes, I expect the order to fire. I am surprised, then, to see Dostum wrap his blue turban around his head and chin and stride into the village . . . to talk.

Ironically, it was this sort of diplomatic triumph—the surrender at Kunduz just before my arrival—and not a battle that gave the Regulators their most bitter experience of the war. "We thought Kunduz was [going to be] a full-scale attack," says Captain Mark. "When we got there, we were sitting on our asses." It was while they watched the drawn-out surrender that Mike Spann was attacked at Qala Jangi and the uprising began. "This was a guy we considered part of our unit," says Mark. "If we had been there, Mike's death would not have happened."

When they got word of the incident, the unit desperately wanted to get back to the prison. "The info I had was that he was MIA," Mark says. "We thought he was wounded. The old creed is that we never leave a guy behind." The Regulators wanted to find the prisoners who had killed Spann and attacked a second CIA man who was questioning the Taliban. "We begged," Mark says, "but we were told to stay away." (In the end, the Regulators wouldn't get clearance to enter Qala Jangi until the uprising was over.)

Commander Abdul Karim Fakir, who was in charge of the fortress while Dostum was in Kunduz, had worked with the Green Berets since they landed in Afghanistan. "I saw this look in Fakir's eyes," says Mark, "like, Why didn't you help?"

DOSTUM HAS NOT BEEN HOME IN FIVE YEARS to the village of Khvajeh Do Kuh. His father is old. Two weeks after Dostum descended on Balkh, things have calmed down, so the warlord climbs into the front passenger seat of a sedan, and we head across a sandstorm-blasted desert. This time there is no convoy; just a son paying his respects to his father. As we drive through a drought-ravaged wasteland, he points out battlefields and the sites of ambushes and skirmishes. Dostum tells me that he has fought on every inch of Afghan soil and can recite the names of his men who have died, describe each battle in detail, and tell you what he has learned from every encounter. He says it sadly.

A few yards before the turnoff to Khvajeh Do Kuh, he gestures to a place where 180 of his men died fighting the Taliban. All I see is brown dirt and men on donkeys leading camels along the road. Nothing of the war, death, exile, and victory that have shaped the man sitting in the front seat. There is an emotional landscape here I cannot see.

As we approach the village, the men and boys are lined up in a perfect row a hundred yards long, waiting to greet Dostum. The general gets out of the car and goes down the line, trying to embrace and talk to each person, but it is getting dark. The crowd of men follows Dostum into his father's compound.

In a tiny, sparse room are his father, Dostum's former teacher, and a village elder. The old men are frail, with deeply lined faces. The teacher giggles, his white beard shaking with joy. Dostum's father talks to his son as though he were a child, telling him that he and the teacher have been praying for his success. They reach out to shake his hand, to embrace him. The men in the room try to act formally, but as Dostum starts to leave, some begin to cry. An old man yells, "God bless you. We are alive thanks to you." As Dostum stands on the porch, looking at the place of his birth, he chokes up.

He takes me to the hilltop above the village. It's a high, lonely place. When war first came to Afghanistan, two decades ago, he built his first stronghold here to guard the village. Dostum points to the fresh dirt of new graves in the cemetery. "The men who first defended this post with me are all dead now. The new graves belong to those who were fighting terrorists." He is silhouetted against the slate-blue sky, the long tails of his silver turban whipping in the wind.

For a brief moment, the general stands triumphant, the conquering hero, the bringer of peace, the warlord who has ended war in the north—and, therefore, perhaps eliminated his own reason for being. As he leans into the Afghan wind, the light falls, and a moment in history fades.

Dostum must now change his focus from fighting to rebuilding his country. (Within a week, he will be named deputy minister of defense for the new interim government of Afghanistan.) Now, on most mornings, Dostum emerges from his house, squinting into a crowd of turbaned men waiting for an audience. They sit patiently for hours, clutching tiny pieces of paper, seeking his aid. Dostum's meetings do not end until well after midnight.

Not long before I'm to leave, Dostum asks for help with a letter of condolence to the widow of Mike Spann. The task inspires him to try to express his feelings about the past two months. He confesses that he had worried at first how the Americans would handle Afghan warfare: "It was cold; the food was bad. The bread we ate was half-mixed with dirt. I wondered if they could adapt to these circumstances. I have been to America and know the quality of life they enjoy. To my surprise, these men felt at home."

And more than that: The Afghan warlord and his tiny band of American soldiers had clearly formed a bond that only men who have been through combat can understand. "I now have a friend named Mark," Dostum says, referring to the Green Beret captain. "I feel he is my brother. He is so sincere; whenever I see him, I feel joy." He pauses for a moment, lost in reflection. "I asked for a few Americans," he says finally. "They brought with them the courage of a whole army."

Down the road at the Regulators' makeshift barracks, a call comes over the Motorola: "Pack your shit." The men quickly gather their gear, as they have so many times before. Within hours, they are gone.

MARCH 2002

II.

SEXY BEASTS

AMONG THE MAN-EATERS

By Philip Caputo

The name Tsavo means "Place of Slaughter." The lions that prowl its plains
are famous for their enormous size, the males' lack of manes, and their taste
for human flesh. The author, a Pulitzer Prize winner and ex-marine,
set out to meet these carnivores face to face.

THERE ARE FEW WORDS AS DISTURBING as "man-eater." Instantly, it dissolves hundreds of thousands of years of human progress and carries us back to our humble beginnings, when we were puny hominids, slouching across the African savanna, huddling in fireless caves, waiting for death to rush us from out of the long grass. The thought of being devoured offends our sense of human dignity, subverts our cherished belief that we are higher beings, "the paragon of animals," to borrow a line from *Hamlet*. The man-eater's actions say to us, "I don't care if you're the President of the United States, the Queen of England, the inventor of the microchip, or just an ordinary Joe or Jill; you're no paragon in *my* book, but the same as a zebra or gazelle—a source of protein. In fact, I'd rather hunt you, because you're so slow and feeble."

We didn't know if the big male lion in front of us had ever tasted human flesh. He did inhabit a region of Kenya that had given birth to the two most infamous man-eating lions in history, and that still harbors lions with a proclivity to hunt man: Only two years ago, a cattle herder had been killed and devoured by a lion not far from where this male now lay looking at us with eyes that glowed like brass in firelight. He must have gone 400 pounds, and he was ugly in the way certain prizefighters are ugly—not a photogenic, Oscar De La Hoya sort of lion, but a Jake LaMotta lion, with only a scruff of a mane, his face and hide scarred from the thorny country he lived in, or from battles with rival lions, or from the kicks of the zebra and buffalo he killed for food. He was only 25 feet away, but we were safe—provided we stayed in our Land Rover. Panting in the late afternoon heat, his gaze impassive, he rested in the shade of a tall bush beside the carcass of a young Cape buffalo killed the night before. Around him, well fed and yawning, five lionesses lazed in the short yellow grass. Two cubs licked and nibbled the buffalo's hindquarters, the ragged strips of meat in the hollowed-out cavity showing bright red under the black skin. Nothing else remained of the animal except the horned head, the front hooves, and a few scattered bones.

Photographer Rob Howard and I were taking pictures from the roof, using it to support our bulky 300-millimeter lenses. Inside, my wife, Leslie, observed through binoculars, while our guides, Iain Allan and Clive Ward, kept an eye on things.

I ran out of film and dropped through the roof hatch to fetch another roll from my camera bag. Rob stood up, trying for another angle. Immediately, the drowsy, indifferent expression went out of the male's eyes; they focused on Rob with absolute concentration. Rob's camera continued to whir and click, and I wondered if he noticed that he'd disturbed the lion. Now, with its stare still fixed on him, it grunted, first out of one side of its mouth, then the other, gathered its forepaws into itself, and raised its haunches. The long, black-tufted tail switched in the grass.

"Say, Rob, might be a good idea to sit down again," Iain advised in an undertone. "Move slowly, though."

He had barely finished this instruction when the lion made a noise like a man clearing his throat, only a good deal louder, and lunged across half the distance between us and him, swatting the air with one paw before he stopped. Rob tumbled through the roof hatch, almost landing on top of me in a clatter of camera equipment, a flailing of arms and legs.

"Jesus Christ!" he said, obviously impressed. The big male had settled down again, although his tail continued to sweep back and forth.

"The short, happy life of Rob Howard," I wisecracked. "It's embarrassing to see a man lose his nerve like that." A bit of bravado.

We were going to spend only part of this safari in a vehicle. For the rest, we would try to track and photograph lions on foot. How would my own nerve hold up then? Perhaps Rob was wondering the same thing about himself. He asked Iain if the lion could have jumped on the roof.

"Could have, but he wouldn't have," Iain replied, a smile cracking across his rough, ruddy face. "That was just a demonstration, to let you know the rules. Of course, you had no way of knowing that."

THERE WAS A LOT WE DIDN'T KNOW about these Tsavo lions—practically everything—and we had come to Kenya to begin filling in the gaps in our knowledge. After hiring Iain, whose safari company, Tropical Ice, is one of the most experienced in the country, we journeyed by Land Rover from Nairobi to the eastern section of Tsavo National Park—the largest in Kenya, with an area of 8,034 square miles (the size of Massachusetts). Here, some 200 miles southeast of Nairobi, you can get at least a taste of the wide-open wilds that Isak Dinesen described in *Out of Africa* and that aviator/adventurer Beryl Markham explored by air. It is the Africa that's all but vanished from the rest of Kenya's national parks and game reserves, which have become vast outdoor zoos, except that the animals are free while the visitors are caged in minivans.

Iain loves Tsavo—the dense palm and saltbush forests of the river valleys, the endless red and khaki plains. "Africa without any fat on it," he called it. "It's raw and primitive and it doesn't tolerate fools or forgive mistakes."

But Tsavo also has a dark history that's centuries old. Its name means "Place of Slaughter" in a local language—a reference to intertribal massacres committed by Masai warriors in the distant past. Ivory traders told spooky tales about men who vanished from their midst when their caravans stopped at the Tsavo River for water and rest. The traders blamed the mysterious disappearances on evil spirits.

The region's forbidding reputation spread worldwide in 1898, when two lions literally stopped the British Empire in its tracks by killing and eating an estimated 140 people, most of them workers building a railroad bridge over the Tsavo River, in what was then called the East Africa Protectorate. The predators' reign of terror lasted nine months, until they were hunted down and shot by the British Army engineer in charge of the project, John H. Patterson. Working as a team, the lions sneaked into the camps at night, snatched men from their tents, and consumed them. Patterson, who'd had considerable experience hunting tigers in India, devised ingenious traps and ruses to bring the animals to bay. But they outwitted him time and again, proving so crafty that the workmen—mostly contract laborers imported from India—came to believe the ancient legends about body-snatching demons, adding their own anti-imperial spin to the myth. The lions, they said, were the incarnate spirits of African chieftains angered by the building of a railroad through their ancestral lands. The workers would lie in their tents, listening to the beasts roar in the darkness. When the roars stopped, the men would call out to each other, "Beware, brothers, the devil is coming!"

In 1907, Patterson, by then a lieutenant colonel, published a book about the ordeal, *The Man-Eaters of Tsavo,* which is widely regarded as the greatest saga in the annals of big-game hunting. Still in print, it has inspired two feature films, *Bwana Devil* in 1952 and *The Ghost and the Darkness* in 1996, with Val Kilmer portraying Patterson.

While lecturing in the United States, 17 years after the book's publication, Patterson sold the lions' skins and skulls to the Field Museum of Natural History in Chicago. A taxidermist turned the hides into lifelike mounts and they were put on exhibit, where they have been ever since, a source of grim fascination to countless visitors. I saw them when I was in high school, and though I can't remember any other exhibit I looked at that day, I've never forgotten those two lions, poised on a replica of sandstone, one crouched, the other standing with right paw slightly raised, both looking intently in the same direction. They had no manes, and the absence of the adornment that gives postcard lions such a majestic appearance made them look sinister. It was as if nature had dispensed with distracting ornamentation to show the beasts in their essence—stripped-down assemblies of muscle and teeth and claws, whose sole purpose was to kill. But it was their eyes that impressed me most. They were glass facsimiles, yet they possessed a fixed, attentive, concentrated expression that must have been in the living eyes when they spotted human prey, decades before, on the plains of Africa.

Patterson's account of their raids reads like a gothic novel. Here's how he describes his discovery of the remains of his Sikh crew leader, Ungan Singh, who had been seized by one of the lions the previous night: "The ground all round was covered with blood and morsels of flesh and bones, but the head had been left intact, save for the holes made by the lion's tusks. It was the most gruesome sight I had ever seen."

Singh was one of the lions' early victims, and his ghastly death sent Patterson in avenging pursuit. He didn't know what he was in for, but he found out soon enough. The construction camps were scattered up and down the railroad right-of-way: The lions would strike at a particular camp one night and Patterson would stake it out the next, waiting with his .303 rifle—but the cats always seemed to know where he was, and would attack elsewhere.

The workmen, meanwhile, surrounded their camps with high *bomas*, or protective fences, made from thorny *Commiphora* shrubs. For a while, the attacks stopped. One night a few workers figured it was safe to sleep outside their tent but inside the boma—a bad decision. One of the lions forced its way through the fence and, ignoring the stones and firebrands that the workers threw, grabbed a man and dragged him through the thorns. It was joined by its partner, and the two savored their meal within earshot of the man's friends.

Perhaps Patterson's worst memory was of the night when he was in his boma and both lions carried their most recent kill close to him. It was too dark to aim and fire. He sat there, listening to the crunching of bones and to what he described as a contented "purring"—sounds that he could not get out of his head for days.

Patterson finally got the upper hand in December 1898. He lashed a partly eaten donkey carcass to a tree stump as bait, built a shooting platform for his protection, and waited. When the lion crept in, it ignored the bait and instead began to circle Patterson's rickety perch. Patterson blazed away into the brush; the lion's snarls grew weaker and weaker, and finally ceased. The next day, the first man-eater's body was recovered. It measured nine feet, eight inches from nose to tail tip, and was so heavy it required eight men to carry it back to camp.

To dispatch its partner, Patterson tied three live goats to a length of railroad track, then hid in a shanty nearby. The lion came just before dawn, killed one of the goats, and began to carry it away—along with the other two goats and the 250-pound rail. Patterson fired, missing the lion but killing one of the goats. The lion escaped.

The dogged Patterson stalked it for the next two weeks, and finally managed to wound it. He and his gun bearer followed the bloody spoor for a quarter mile until at last they spotted their quarry. Patterson took careful aim and fired. The lion charged. A second shot bowled it over, but it rose and charged again. Patterson fired a third time without effect. He then joined his terrified gun bearer in a nearby tree, from which he finally dropped the lion with a fourth slug. When he climbed down, he was stunned to see the lion jump up and charge him again. He pumped two more rounds into it—one in its chest, another in its head—and the huge cat went down for good. The reign of terror was over.

THROUGHOUT HISTORY, THE BEAST with a taste for human flesh has been regarded as an aberration, even as an outlaw. Patterson's book often refers to the lions in terms commonly applied to criminals or psychopaths. Even the more objective scientific literature tends to explain man-eating as the exception that proves the rule: Humans are not normally on the predator's grocery list. Lions are generally believed to turn to man-eating only when injuries or old age prevent them from pursuing their usual prey.

It's true that old, sick, or wounded lions have been responsible for most attacks on people. However, a team of researchers from Chicago's Field Museum headed by Dr. Bruce Patterson (no relation to the colonel) has come up with—well, it would be an exaggeration to say "evidence"—tantalizing *hints* that there may be some lions with a more or less genetic predisposition to prey on humans, even when strong and healthy enough to bring down a zebra or a buffalo. The explanation for this behavior would then subtly but significantly shift from the pathological to the Darwinian: Conditions in a lion's environment, as much as changes in its physiology, can drive it to hunt people—and there's nothing aberrant or "criminal" about it.

Still, such a beast poses a mystery, and the key to that mystery may be found in the lions of Tsavo, which truly are a different breed of cat from the glorious, regal lions of, say, the Serengeti. Most Tsavo males are maneless, and larger than the Serengeti male, which measures 36 inches at the shoulder and weighs between 385 and 410 pounds. Tsavo lions are up to a foot taller and can tip the scales at about 460 to 520 pounds, giving you a cat the size of a small grizzly. They are also distinguished by their behavior. On the plains, the adult male's role is to mate and protect the pride, leaving the hunting to females. In Tsavo, where scarcity of game makes prides smaller, males share in the hunting, and may even do most of it.

"There's no doubt in my mind that Tsavo lions are different," Iain told us on the drive from Nairobi. "They're total opportunists, killing machines that will attack and eat even little African hares. They're also more cunning than pride lions, often killing from ambush instead of stalk-and-spring. There's something sinister about them."

Iain is not a big-cat biologist, but 28 years of leading walking and driving safaris in Kenya and Tanzania have given him the kind of direct experience that compensates for any lack of scientific training. And he's never had an experience more direct, or more terrifying, than the one he had on a Tsavo safari last July.

It was early in the afternoon, the time when he usually checks in with his Nairobi office by satellite phone. He ambled down to the wide, sandy banks of the Galana River, where reception was better than it was in his tree-shrouded tent camp. As he chatted with his secretary, he observed a bushbuck poke its way through a saltbush thicket some distance downriver, then begin to drink. Suddenly, the animal raised its head and froze; an instant later, a lioness sprang from the saltbush still farther downriver, and the bushbuck bolted in Iain's direction, the lioness in pursuit. When she was about 50 yards from Iain, without breaking stride she veered off and headed straight for him, bursts of sand flying behind her as she ran. In a microsecond that seemed like minutes, Iain realized that he needn't worry about her teeth and claws; he was going to be killed by the impact of 300 pounds of sinew and muscle smashing into him at 25 miles an hour. When she was only 20 feet from where he stood, she veered again, kicked sand all over him, and vanished.

Iain suspects that the lioness charged him because she was confused, annoyed, or curious. "That," he said, "is the closest I've ever come to getting killed."

If he had been, he would have joined a long roster of Tsavo lion victims, the most recent being that cattle herder, taken in July 1998. Are the lions of Tsavo predisposed to prey on people? Do they represent a subspecies of lion? Why are they maneless? Why are they larger than average? Can they tell us anything new about the king of beasts? Those are the questions that prompted us to go to Tsavo.

ON OUR FIRST DAY, after settling into Iain's tent camp on the Voi (Goshi) River, we drove down a red laterite road to the Aruba Dam. There is a small lake behind the dam, where Samuel Andanje, a young researcher with the Kenya Wildlife Service, directed us to the scar-faced male and his harem of five females. They were part of a pride of 23 lions, said Andanje, who spends his nights locating the animals by their roars and his days tracking them in a Land Rover.

Shortly after the male had sent Rob tumbling back into our truck, the females, with the cubs in tow, moved off toward the lake to drink. They made a fine sight in the golden afternoon light, walking slowly through the dun-colored grass with movements that suggested water flowing. Scarface remained behind to eat his fill of the buffalo before the jackals and hyenas got to it.

As the sun lowered, we heard a series of throaty grunts from the male lion, which Clive said were a call to the females and cubs to return. Clive Ward is 56 years old, tall and spare, with the face of an ascetic and a clipped way of speaking that sometimes leaves the words trapped in his mouth. Like the 52-year-old Iain, he has guided safaris for years, and is an alpinist by avocation. He and Iain have led countless parties of trekkers up Mount Kilimanjaro and Mount Kenya, and have scaled many of the world's major peaks together. Over the years, they have developed a relationship that seems to combine war-buddy comradeship with the easy familiarity of an old married couple; they bicker now and then, and needle each other, but beneath the bickering and needling, you sense an abiding bond knit on sheer rock faces and icy crags and long, hot tramps through the African bush.

As the lions padded silently through the grass, we left—it was growing dark—and came upon a lone lioness, lying at the junction of the road and the two-track that led to camp. She didn't move as the Land Rover passed within six feet of her. She seemed to regard the intersection as hers, and, of course, it was.

The big storks roosting in the branches of trees along the Voi riverbed looked ominous in the twilight. Up ahead and across the river, waterless now in the dry season, the glow of kerosene lamps and a campfire made a more cheerful sight.

Iain believes that you don't need to practice being miserable: His safaris hark back to the stylish roughing-it of a bygone age—commodious wall tents with cots, a large, communal mess tent, outdoor showers, portable privies in canvas enclosures, laundry service, and a six-man staff to do the cooking and camp chores. On an open fire, Kahiu, the cook, whips up meals equal to anything served in Nairobi restaurants, and you wash them down with South African and Italian wines, making you feel pretty *pukka sahib*.

After dinner, we sat around the campfire on folding chairs, and once, when the wind turned, we heard lions roaring in the distance. The sound inspired Iain to offer a sequel to the tale of his encounter with the charging lioness.

"After she disappeared, I had the feeling that she'd come into camp, so I ran back and told my clients to get in their tents and zip them up, and warned the staff that a lion was in camp. Well, they looked at me as if to say that the old boy had had too much sun, and when I didn't see the lioness for a while, I figured they were right. I was about to tell my clients that they could come on out when I turned around and saw eight Africans running like hell for our pickup, with the lioness running among them—not after them, but *right in the middle of them*. The men leaped up to the truck bed in one bound. I think that old girl was very confused: She'd started off chasing a bushbuck, ended up in a camp full of people, tents, vehicles—things she'd never seen—and must have wondered, 'How did I get into this mess?' She ran out, but stopped at the edge of camp and stayed there all day. Just sat there, like the lioness we saw a little while ago."

"What good did zipping up tent flaps do?" I asked. "She could have shredded that thin canvas if she wanted to."

"Lions don't recognize a closed tent as anything; they can't be bothered," Iain explained. "Just last August, in Zimbabwe, a young Englishman, the nephew of an earl, was on a camping safari. He went into his tent and fell asleep without closing the flaps. Sometime during the night, a lioness got close to his tent. He woke up and ran out, scared as hell, right into a mob of other lions. Lions like things that run, same as any cat. When they got through with him, I don't think there was anything left."

This was not a bedtime story to tell in lion country. When Leslie and I went to our tent, we not only secured the flaps, we zipped up the covers to the mesh ventilation windows—and could barely breathe the stifling air. I wasn't encouraged by Iain's assurance that lions couldn't be bothered with tents. Hadn't the man-eaters of Tsavo barged into the tents of the construction crews? But maybe the workmen hadn't closed the flaps, I thought. My sole armament was a K-bar, the ten-inch trench knife issued to me when I was in the Marine Corps in Vietnam. It was resting in its sheath on the night table next to my cot, but it seemed to me that the best thing I could do with it in the event of a lion attack would be to fall on it and save the lion the trouble.

"JAMBO!" A STAFF MEMBER CALLED from outside our tent: hello in Swahili. "Jambo," we answered, and got dressed by lantern light. After breakfast, and with dawn erasing the last morning stars, we rolled out to the Aruba Dam to look for Scarface and his family.

They were not where we had left them. We drove along slowly, looking for pugmarks in the soft, rust-colored earth, until we heard a deep bass groan that ended in a chesty cough. It was so loud we thought the lion was only 50 yards away. We set off in the direction of the sound, bouncing over a prairie of short, dry grass tinted pale gold by the early morning sun, Clive, Rob, and I standing with our heads poking out of the roof hatches.

"Ah, there he is," said Iain, at the wheel.

"Him all right," Clive seconded.

I spend a lot of time in the woods, and am not bad at spotting game, but I had no idea what they were talking about.

"It's the ears, you look for the ears sticking above the grass when you're looking for a lion," Iain said, driving on. And then I saw them—two triangles that could have been mistaken for knots in a stump if they hadn't moved. We were 20 or 30 yards away when he stood up, with a movement fluid and unhurried, and I thought, Christ, if you were on foot, you would trip over him before you knew he was there, and that would be the last thing you would ever know in this world. Ugly-handsome Scarface went down a game trail at the leonine version of a stroll, then up over a rise and down toward a marsh, its green swath spread between the tawny ridges. We stayed with him all the way, keeping a respectful distance. He was one big boy, and if he was a man-eater, this is what he would do after he killed you: flay off your skin with his tongue, which is covered with small spines that give it the texture of coarse-grained sandpaper and are used to bring nutritious blood to the surface; next, he would bite into your abdomen or groin, open you up, and scoop out your entrails and internal organs and consume them, because they are rich in protein, your liver especially; then he would savor your meatiest parts, thighs and buttocks, followed by your arms, shoulders, and calves. The bones would be left for the hyenas, which have stronger jaws. Vultures and jackals would take care of your head and whatever scraps of flesh remained, so that, a few hours after your sudden death, it would be as though you had never existed. There is a terrible thoroughness to the mechanics of death in Africa, and we are not exempt.

Scarface led us right to his harem, and then, after posing on a knoll, he moved off into the marsh, the lionesses and cubs following soon after.

"That's that for now," said Iain. "Have to come back in the late afternoon. Let's look up Sam and try to find the rest of this pride."

Sam Andanje led us to a remote stretch of the Voi, and we followed his Land Rover through *Commiphora* scrub. I mentioned the bomas that Patterson's laborers had constructed, and how the lions had found ways through them, with the canniness of trained guerrillas infiltrating an enemy's barbed wire. Four-footed killers with above-average IQs.

"I don't doubt but that the lions had the whole thing totally wired," Iain remarked. "The difference between people and animals is that we can see the big picture, and figure out how to survive in any environment, but within their area of specialization, most animals are as smart as we are, maybe smarter." He paused, chewing over a further thought. "Take a look at this country. It's sparse and harsh—there aren't any huge herds of wildebeest, like the kind you get in the Masai Mara or the Serengeti. Tsavo lions have to take what they can get, whatever comes along. I'm convinced that they have territories they know as well as you know your backyard, with their ambush places all staked out. They're clever. They know where to be and when."

We found no lions, and by 10:30, the quest was hopeless. It was nearly 100°F, and the cats were laid up, deep within the thickets. In the late afternoon, we returned to the marsh near the Aruba Dam. There, Scarface's harem lolled with the cubs on the slope overlooking the marsh, where a solitary bull elephant grazed. Iain parked about 30 yards from the lions, and we began observing and photographing.

Later, as the sun dropped below the Taita Hills and a sundowner began to blow, the lions stirred. A small herd of Grant's gazelles daintily walked down into the marsh to graze, and the biggest lioness, the dominant female, raised her head and fastened her gaze on them.

"She's looking for a slight limp in one of the gazelles," Iain observed. "Any sign of weakness—but gazelle isn't a lion's favored prey. They're so fast, and there isn't much meat on them, so it's hardly worth the effort. Lions are lazy hunters." Gesturing to the marsh, he returned to the theme of feline intelligence. "A lot of thought went into choosing this position, above the swamp and with most of its prey upwind, so they can see or scent almost anything that comes along. It's perfect buffalo country. The sun's lowering, they're rested, and the lions will be getting hungry soon."

ON OUR FOURTH MORNING IN TSAVO, Iain's staff struck the tents, in preparation for moving to his "walking safari" campsite at a place called Durusikale, on the Galana River. If you want to experience the Africa of Isak Dinesen, then you have to do it on shank's mare.

Roused at 4:30 a.m. by another "Jambo," we breakfasted under the Southern Cross, and then drove northward, down a road paralleling a riverbed called the Hatulo Bisani, where we had seen a large herd of Cape buffalo the day before. It was Iain's theory that a lion pride might be trailing them. During the long rains of November, the Hatulo Bisani would be a torrent; now, with a mere trickle flowing between wide swaths of bright green sedge, it resembled a river of grass.

We found fresh pugmarks in the road, followed them for a while, then lost them when they angled off into the scrub. A short distance ahead, the buffalo, maybe 600 of them, grazed in the riverbed, their gray-black bodies looking like boulders.

We sat there eyeball to eyeball with one of the biggest, strongest, fiercest animals in Africa—an animal that helps to explain why Tsavo lions are so big, and why they're likely to turn man-eater. Cape buffalo are among the most numerous of Tsavo's herd animals, and lions prey on them. Lions elsewhere do so only when deprived of easier game, and even then only in large bands; no average-size lion will take down a 1,500-pound Cape buffalo alone. In other words, the lions of Tsavo are big because their favored prey is big, and because the dense, brushy country compels them to hunt in small groups. Still, no matter how hefty a lion gets, hunting buffalo is a risky business. Recently, Andanje found a lion stomped to death by a buffalo. More frequently, the cats suffer broken bones and puncture wounds; they then turn to easier prey, like livestock—and the people who tend it.

Tom Gnoske and Dr. Julian Kerbis Peterhans, members of the research team from the Field Museum, have discovered an interesting twist to such behavior: A lion that becomes a man-eater because it's injured doesn't go back to its traditional prey even after it recovers. Eating people, Gnoske says, "is an easy way to make a living."

Intriguingly, one of the Tsavo man-eaters Patterson killed had a severely broken canine tooth with an exposed root. The tooth was well worn and polished, and the entire skull had undergone "cranial remodeling" in response to the trauma, indicating that the injury was an old one. It's in the record that at least one man-eater had been prowling about Tsavo before Patterson and his bridge-building gangs arrived in March 1898. A railroad surveyor, R.O. Preston, lost several members of his crew to a man-eater near the Tsavo River early in 1897. When Preston and his men searched for remains, they found the skulls and bones of individuals who had been killed earlier still. There is no proof that an injury was the lion's "motive" for turning man-eater, but it's a plausible explanation. He might have been kicked in the jaw by a buffalo and lost a tooth; he stuck to preying on humans after the injury healed, having found out how safe and convenient it was. The arrival of the railroad workers, packed into tent camps, would have been manna from leonine heaven.

But what about his partner, who was in prime health? The Field Museum researchers speculate that an epidemic of rinderpest disease may have played a role in the lion's change of eating habits. In the early 1890s, the disease all but wiped out buffalo and domestic cattle. With its usual prey eliminated, the starving lion had to look to villages and construction camps for its meals.

Another, more disquieting, explanation lies elsewhere—with the elephants of Tsavo.

WE TURNED OFF THE Hatulo Bisani road and started down the Galana river road toward the campsite, some 25 miles downstream. Partway there, we stopped to climb one of the Sobo rocks, a series of sandstone outcrops, to scan with our binoculars for game. The Galana, fed by melting snows on Mount Kilimanjaro, showed a brassy brown as it slid slowly between galleries of saltbush and doum palm toward its distant meeting with the Indian Ocean. Beyond the river, the scorched plains rose and fell, seemingly without end. And on a far-off ridge, we saw one of Africa's primitive, elemental sights—a procession of elephants, raising dust as they migrated to the river to drink and cool themselves in the midday heat.

Forgetting our lion quest for the moment, we returned to the Land Rover and cut cross-country toward the herd, drawing close enough to count the animals—about 60 altogether, the calves trotting alongside their mothers, a huge matriarch out front, other old females guarding the flanks and rear, tusks flashing in the harsh sunlight.

Iain and Clive are elephant enthusiasts. When they saw the herd shambling toward the Galana, they drove off to a spot on the river where we had a good chance of observing the animals at close hand. We picnicked in the shade of a tamarind tree, with a broad, sandy beach in front of us. Twenty minutes later, the elephants arrived, moving within a hundred yards of where we sat. They came on down with a gliding, stiff-legged gait. The marvelous thing was how silent they were, passing through the saltbush with barely a rustle. It seemed to us that we were beholding Tsavo's wild soul made flesh.

With cat-burglar creeps, we positioned ourselves on the shore, watching and photographing for almost an hour. The animals' trunks curved into their mouths or bent back to spray their heads with water. An incredible organ, the elephant's trunk: It contains 40,000 separate muscles and tendons, and serves the elephant as a hand that feeds, a nose, a drinking straw, a built-in shower, and a weapon, all in one.

Tsavo elephants have all the reason in the world to fear and hate people. Slaughtering them for their ivory is a very old story, going back to ancient times. And the caravans that once passed through Tsavo laden with tusks may hold another explanation for the man-eating tendencies of Tsavo lions.

Dr. Chapurukha Kusimba, an anthropological archaeologist, grew up in Kenya hearing the story of the man-eaters and Patterson's epic hunt. Now an associate curator of African anthropology at the Field Museum, he began working with the Tsavo lion research team in 1994. Studying the traditional caravan routes from the interior to the coast, Kusimba learned that the caravans carried slaves as well as ivory. The Tsavo River was an important stop, where traders refreshed themselves and restocked their water supplies before moving on. However, historical texts suggest that they disposed of unnecessary cargo first: Captives too sick or weak to travel farther were abandoned there to die.

With so many corpses around, predators in the vicinity would have had an abundance of people to feed on. From there, it wouldn't have been a big step for the cats to go after living people. That may explain the myths about "evil spirits"—the men who mysteriously disappeared from the caravans' campsites had been seized not by devils but by lions. The slave and ivory caravans had passed through Tsavo for centuries—and that leads us to the truly disturbing aspect of the theory. *Panthera leo* is a social animal, capable of adopting "cultural traditions" that are passed on from generation to generation. If a lioness is hunting people, her young will grow to regard them as a normal part of their diet, and pass that knowledge on to their own young. The upshot is that Patterson's man-eaters may have done what they did not because they were handicapped by injuries, or even because their traditional prey had been wiped out, but simply because they came from a man-eating lineage so long that an appetite for human flesh was ingrained in them. Stalking and devouring the "paragon of animals" wasn't the exception, but their rule.

That's just a theory, but if you're in a tent in lion country it's the kind to make you wake up at two in the morning and hear the pad of a lion's paws in every rustle outside; to mistake your wife's breathing for a lion's; to picture him creeping up on the thin canvas that separates you from him; and to know that he isn't there out of curiosity or because he smelled the food in the cook's tent or because he winded a zebra herd beyond camp and is only passing by, but because he's scented *you* and *you* are what he's after; the kind of supposition to make you imagine the horror of what it's like to feel him bite down on your ankle or shoulder with his strong jaws and then drag you out and run off with you, wonderful, indispensable you, apple of your mother's eye, and you screaming and scratching and kicking and punching, all to no avail, until he releases his grip to free his jaws to crush your windpipe, and the last sensation you have is of his hot breath in your face.

SUCH WERE MY WAKING NIGHTMARES that night. And yet, only that afternoon, I had been as captivated by a lion as Joy Adamson had been by Elsa. We had left camp on a game drive, and rounded a bend in the road a few miles downriver, and suddenly she was there, walking purposefully ahead of us. There was nothing beautiful about her: Old scratches and cuts marred her skin like sewn rips in a threadbare sofa, and her ribs showed, though not in a way to suggest starvation so much as a spare toughness. If the sleek pride lions of the Serengeti are the haute bourgeoisie of the leonine world, Tsavo lions are the proletariat, blue-collar cats that have to work hard for a meager living. I recalled Iain's description of Tsavo as a land intolerant of fools and unforgiving of mistakes. This lioness blended right into such a landscape; she looked neither tolerant nor forgiving, but very focused. We trailed her, but she was never alarmed. Now and then, she threw a glance at us, just to check on our distance or our behavior. If we edged too close, she simply angled away, maintaining a space of perhaps 15 yards. A lady with a mission, she went on through the intermittent saltbush with the steady, unflagging pace of a veteran foot soldier.

After she covered some two miles, the lioness began to call with low grunts. We figured she was trying to locate her pride, but if they answered, we did not hear them. Another quarter of a mile, and she stopped and called more loudly—a sound that seemed to come from her belly instead of her throat, part moan, part cough. *Wa-uggh, Wa-uggh.* In a moment, two cubs bounded from a saltbush thicket a hundred yards away. They leaped on their mother, licking face and flanks, and she licked theirs.

With her cubs following, the lioness retraced her steps, and we again followed. The wary cubs often stopped to stare or hiss at us. Iain speculated that she had stashed the cubs in the saltbush to go scouting. Now she was leading the cubs back to the pride.

It would be good if she led us to the pride; our four-day foot safari was to begin the next morning, and knowing where the pride was would give us an objective. I love walking in the wild, but I love walking with a purpose even more. The lioness pressed on with her journey, and then she and the cubs pulled one of the vanishing acts that seem to be a Tsavo lion specialty. We looked for ten minutes; then, as suddenly as they'd disappeared, they reappeared, wading across the river. They stopped on a sandbar in midstream. There the cubs gamboled for a while, one mounting its forepaws on its mother's hindquarters and allowing her to pull it along as she looked for a spot to complete the crossing.

"All we need now is background music from *Born Free*," Iain remarked, but I thought of Santiago's dream in *The Old Man and the Sea*, his dream of lions on the beach.

The lioness plunged into the river and swam the channel, the cubs paddling after her. The three climbed the bank and were swallowed by the saltbush. We were sorry to see the lioness go; for all her scruffy appearance, we had grown fond of her and her self-possessed air. Still, she looked awfully lean, and I said that I would have felt better about her prospects if I had seen her and the cubs reunited with their pride.

"Don't worry about her," Iain commented. "She's in complete command of her situation."

I'm not sure how, in the span of a few hours, I went from feeling sorry for a real lion to being in abject terror of an imaginary one. At two in the morning, the rational brain doesn't function as well as it does at two in the afternoon, and you start thinking with the older brain, that cesspit of primeval dreads. Or maybe my heebie-jeebies were a reaction to another of Iain's bedtime stories, told over another of Kahiu's superb dinners: grilled eggplant, pumpkin soup, and bread pudding with hot cream.

A Texas couple and their two sons were on safari with Tropical Ice. One midnight, Iain was awakened by the parents' screams: "Iain! They're here! They're coming in!" He tumbled out of bed, unzipped his tent flap, and saw a lioness walk past him. Worse, he could hear other lions in the underbrush near camp—and the crunching of bones. Iain shouted to his clients to get on the floors of their tents and cover themselves with their mattresses. More lions appeared, playfully batting at the couple's tent, as if to tease the frightened occupants. Iain, who was trapped in his own tent, yelled to his two armed Masai guards, who had managed to sleep through the commotion. As they approached the thicket in which Iain had heard the hideous crunching noise, they were greeted by growls. The Masai did not live up to their reputation as fearless lion hunters; they fled in panic. It turned out that the lions were guarding their kill, which wasn't a person, but a warthog. Iain attempted to drive them off by clapping his hands—a sound that normally frightens lions, because no other animal makes it. It had no effect on these lions, who eventually just sauntered away.

The next day, as Iain brought the pickup around, he saw what he termed "a horrifying sight." A lioness was strolling alongside the woman's tent, which was open at one end. As calmly as he could, Iain told her to come out, but not to run, and get in the car. She had no sooner jumped in and shut the door than the lioness rounded the corner and walked into the tent. Had the woman still been inside, the lioness would have killed her. "Maybe not eaten her," Iain added, reassuringly, "but definitely killed her, because she would have tried to run."

DANGERS IMAGINED ARE ALWAYS WORSE than dangers confronted. I was in good spirits the next morning, and actually looking forward to facing a lion on foot, if for no other reason than to conquer my fear. To protect us, Iain had contracted two Kenya Wildlife Service rangers, Adan and Hassan, who were armed with semiautomatic assault rifles. Dressed in jaunty berets, camouflage uniforms, and combat boots, they looked more like commandos than park rangers. Only safaris with special permission from the park's senior warden are allowed into the vast area north of the Galana; the guards are strongly recommended.

I hoped that Adan and Hassan would not imitate the behavior of the Masai in Iain's story. If they did, we didn't have much else in the way of self-defense: my trusty K-bar; Iain's Gurkha kris, a souvenir from a trek in the

Himalaya; and Clive's Masai short sword, called a *simi*. African lore is full of stories about strong men who have killed lions with knives, but lions weren't the only dangerous game we might encounter. The saltbush forests easily conceal elephants, Cape buffalo, and the hippopotamus, which kills more people in Africa than any other mammal. Since Tropical Ice started running safaris in 1978, Iain's guards have rarely had to fire over the heads of elephants, and have never shot a lion, but they have had to kill six hippos, which are very stubborn and very aggressive.

With Hassan on point and Adan as rearguard, we waded the warm Galana to the north side, Iain instructing us to stay close together so that we would sound not like seven average-size things but like one big thing—an elephant—to deter crocodiles. We saw one of the reptiles, a nine- or ten-footer, 15 minutes after we'd forded. We continued upriver toward the Sobo rocks, and ran into a dozen hippos, entirely submerged except for the tops of their dark heads and their piggish, protruding eyes. They tolerated our photographing them for a while, but when we crept closer, one big bull lunged from the water with astonishing speed, his cavernous mouth open and threatening. A warning, which we heeded by moving on.

The morning was overcast and breezy, but by ten o'clock the air was hot and searing—reminiscent of Arizona in July. We had the whole immense wild to ourselves, because most tourists are unwilling to walk miles in triple-digit temperatures, and too timid to confront wild creatures on foot. What a difference, to observe game animals on their own terms. To photograph them, we had to read the wind as a hunter does, practicing stealth and watching for the slightest motion. We stalked up close to a band of Cape buffalo and a small elephant herd, and the experience was far more satisfying than driving up to them. Sweating, exercising caution and bush-craft, we earned the right to bag them on film.

We were on the last mile of the trek when we found pugmarks in the sand, leading straight along the shore toward a grove of doum palms some 300 yards away. They were deep and well-defined—that is, recent. Iain and I fell into a discussion as to just how recent. Clive, looking ahead with unaided eye, said they were very recent, because two lions were laid up under the palms. Clive pointed, and Iain and I raised our binoculars.

"It's a log," I said. "A big palm log."

Iain concurred.

"I am telling you, lions," Clive insisted peevishly. "Two bloody lions. One's maned, too."

Then Adan said, "Lions, 100 percent," but he spoke too loudly. The log lifted its head.

My binoculars framed an atypical Tsavo lion, a Metro-Goldwyn-Mayer emblem with a golden mane, lying in the shade with his companion and gazing straight back at us. With the palms overhead, the scene looked biblical.

The easterly wind favored us. We began a stalk, heading up over the embankment to approach the lions from above, Rob and I with our cameras ready, Adan with his rifle at low port, prepared to shoot if necessary. Hassan's was braced on his shoulder, the muzzle pointing backward at the rest of us. Iain pushed the rifle barrel aside. Hassan shifted the gun to the crook of his arm, holding it upside down as if he were cradling a baby, and sauntered along like a man strolling in Hyde Park, instead of in Tsavo with two big lions just ahead. A less than reassuring guard. I decided to grab his rifle if I had to.

We filed along a game trail between the saltbush and the riverbank, closing the distance. The idea was to capture an image of lions up close—while on foot. All right, what was the difference between a picture taken from a car and one taken on foot? I don't know, only that there seemed to be a difference. Listen to the ancient Roman Stoic Epictetus: "Reflect that the chief source of all evils to man, and of baseness and cowardice, is not death, but the fear of death." Still true, I'd say. The real point of life is to be brave; it is to master fear of death, which is the genesis of all fears. And one of the exercises by which you can steel yourself to that fear is to confront something that could break your neck with one swipe of its paw.

I don't wish to exaggerate the emotions of the moment. None of us was trembling. Instead, we were apprehensive, in the old sense of the word. We apprehended, in a state of heightened awareness—alert to every sound and movement. Coming abreast of the palm grove, Iain walked in a crouch, and we followed suit, trailing him and Hassan over the lip of the embankment to look down into the pool of shade beneath the trees. I raised my camera.

The lions were gone. They must have fled at the sound of our voices, though we never saw them move. Their tracks disappeared into the brush. It was as though they had dematerialized.

TWO HOURS INTO THE NEXT DAY'S TREK, we found evidence of an old lion kill: the skull and horns of a big Cape buffalo, resting in the grass beside a *lugga,* or dry streambed. Iain and Clive poked around, studying the area like homicide detectives.

"Probably an old bull, alone," said Iain. "The lions were down in the lugga, behind that big bush, three of them. They sprang at the buffalo from the side, just as he was about to come down the bank."

But that was all the evidence we saw of lions that morning. By eleven o'clock, with my shirt soaked through with sweat and my eyeballs feeling sunburned, we crossed back to the south side of the Galana, where we were picked up in a Land Cruiser—and were told that we need not have walked ten miles to find lions; they had found us. Soon after we left, four males had appeared on the north side of the river, almost directly across from camp. By now they had moved off.

I took a nap after lunch, took some notes, then sat shirtless and shoeless in my camp, my baked brain a perfect tabula rasa. Iain appeared, walking fast over the Bermuda grass. Gesturing, he told us in a whisper to follow him, and to be quiet. The four lions had returned.

With cameras and binoculars, we ran on tiptoe. Across the river, between 200 and 300 yards downstream, two of the four were crouched on the bank, drinking. Their hides so perfectly matched the sand and beige rock that they seemed made of the same stuff. I put the binoculars on them. They lacked manes, and I would have thought they were females, but their size suggested otherwise. Thirst slaked, one turned and padded up the bank, and it was clear that he was a male. He disappeared into a clump of doum palm; the second drank a while longer, then joined his friend. A moment later, the first lion emerged to walk slowly into the saltbush behind the palms, the other following shortly afterward, and then a third.

"See how relaxed they are?" said Iain, softly. "They're not acting as if they're aware we're here. If they are, and they're this casual about it, we may have some major problems tonight."

Just as I got out of my seat to fetch my field notes from my tent, the fourth lion showed up. He caught my movement and stopped, turning his head to face in our direction. Carefully raising my binoculars, I eased back down, and had the unsettling impression that I was staring into the lion's face, and he into mine, from a distance of, say, ten yards. Crouched low, the joints of his bent forelegs forming triangles, his shoulders a mound of muscle, sinew, and tendons, he was so still that he could have been a carving. Like the others, he had no mane.

No one knows the reason for this characteristic. It is thought by some that it evolved in Tsavo males because a mane is a liability in such thick, thornbush country. Another theory is that pride lions on the plains sport manes as symbols of power and health to attract females and warn off rival males. A mane would be useless for those purposes in Tsavo, where vision is often limited to a few yards. However, bald male lions do occur throughout sub-Saharan Africa, though they tend to be found most frequently in harsh scrub-bush habitats similar to Tsavo's. What's really intriguing is that some experts in leonine behavior believe they have identified a historical trend in man-eating, which can be traced geographically to such environments. If they are correct, it could mean that maneless lions are more likely to prey on humans.

You can ask Wayne Hosek about that. Hosek, a 56-year-old California estate planner and hunter, was born in Chicago; he had also seen the Tsavo man-eaters in his school days, and had become mesmerized by Patterson's saga. Many years later, in 1991, he was on a shooting safari near Zambia's Luangwa National Parks, a region of dense bush. People in the town of Mfuwe, near where Hosek was hunting with a professional guide and trackers, told him that they had been terrorized by a huge lion that had killed and eaten six of their neighbors. They thought it was a female, because it had no mane. Local hunters had shot six lionesses, believing each was the one responsible, but the attacks continued. The villagers pleaded with Hosek to rid them of the menace. For the next week, he and his guide virtually relived Patterson's experiences. Tracks told them that the lion wasn't just big, it was enormous. But it also was canny, outsmarting them time after time. It always seemed to know where they were and how to avoid them. As Hosek describes it, the experience ceased to be a sport and became a kind of war. Finally, concealed in a ground blind, Hosek killed the lion with one shot, from a range of 70 yards. The lion indeed was without a mane, but it was a male—and huge. Four feet at the shoulder and ten feet, six inches from its nose to the tip of its tail, it weighed 500 pounds—the biggest man-eating lion on record.

The nature of the environment, the size of the lion, the absence of a mane—Hosek's trophy fit in with the theories. I reflected on that, gazing at the big fellow across the river. He crept down to the edge of the bank, lowered his head, and drank, pausing to look at us again. He then leisurely climbed back up and lay down in the shade. If he was concerned about us, he didn't show it.

"What did you mean, if they know we're here and are casual about it that we could be in for problems tonight?" I whispered to Iain.

"They won't attack, but they could come into camp." He didn't say what led him to make such a prediction, and I didn't ask.

That night, as we sat around the campfire, the lions began to roar from across the river. It was deep and resonant, a sound like no other.

THE FINISH LINE FOR THAT DAY'S WALK was the starting point for the next. Driving there, we saw two of the lion quartet on a beach, quite a ways off, but they were soon gone. From eight in the morning till noon, we trudged ten miles to Sala Hill, which rises as a perfect pyramid out of the savanna, but we could not find the pride that the four males and the scruffy lioness belonged to.

We made a more concentrated effort the following day, beginning at the spot where we had seen the female and cubs cross the Galana. Distinct pugmarks were printed in the fine sand near a stand of doum palm. The strong sundowner winds in Tsavo scour animal tracks pretty quickly, so the prints must have been made last night or early in the morning. There were more on the sandbar, where the cubs had cavorted with their mother three days earlier, and on the opposite bank. One set of tracks led us into the saltbush, and to a lion's day bed—a patch of flattened grass and dirt—but we lost them farther on, where the earth was like pavement and covered with foot-high yellow grass.

"You can see why that movie called them ghosts," Iain said, referring to *The Ghost and the Darkness*. "They're always in ambush mode. They stay hidden, come out to hunt and kill, then hide again. They are ghosts."

His commentary was borne out a little farther upriver, when we struck the track of the two males spotted from the truck the previous day. Again we followed it; again we lost it. The lions could have been anywhere or nowhere. As Adan pushed into the saltbush, his rifle at the ready, I mentally compared Tsavo lions not to ghosts, but to the Vietcong: masters of concealment, of hit and run, showing themselves only when they chose. I was beginning to appreciate what Patterson had endured a century ago. It was an adventure for me to track these lions, but I would not have wanted to be charged with the task of finding and killing them.

We continued upriver. Then Adan found another set of prints. "These are very new," whispered Iain, pointing at one. "This is now."

A DRY WIND BLEW THROUGH the acacias, the palm fronds rattled. I flinched when a sand grouse flushed five feet away. Great predators can make their presence known, even when they aren't seen or heard. When such monarchs are near, your senses quicken, for the simple reason that your life may depend on it. I had experienced that keenness of perception several times in Alaska, coming upon grizzly tracks, and once in Arizona, crossing the fresh prints of a cougar while I was quail hunting, but I'd never experienced it as deeply as in those haunted thickets of Tsavo. There was something else as well. To walk unarmed in the lion's kingdom demands a submission not unlike the submission required of us in the presence of the divine, and it graces those who walk there with the humility that is not humiliation. I was acutely aware of being in a place where I, as a man, did not hold dominion, but had to cede dominion to a thing grander, stronger, and more adept than I.

"I believe that if one of us, right now, tried to walk back to camp alone, we wouldn't make it," Iain said. "The lions would study you, see that you're alone and defenseless, and attack." Suddenly, he stopped, wrinkled his nose, and said, "Smell that?"

I shook my head. My sense of smell was the only one that had not been heightened; I suffer from allergies and my head was stuffed. In fact, one of the things I'm allergic to is cats.

"A kill. There's something dead, rotting in there," said Iain, gesturing at a thicket.

The wind eddied a bit, and I caught it—a little like skunk, a little like week-old garbage.

Adan and Hassan pushed into the saltbush, while we who were unarmed waited in the open. When the two rangers emerged, several minutes later, they reported they had found nothing except hyena and jackal tracks, indicating that the carcass, wherever it was, had been abandoned by the lions and was now the property of scavengers.

The trek ended at the palm grove across from camp, where the four males had laired up. A lot of pugmarks, and some stains in the sand where the lions had urinated, but nothing more.

"MAKE A PERFECT MOVIE SET, wouldn't it?" Clive whispered. It was two days later, and we had just made our way through the saltbush and entered a grove of old doum palm. The trunks of the high trees were worn smooth where elephants had rubbed up against them, and the lanes between the trees were like shadowy halls, some blocked by flood-wrack from the rainy season—barricades of logs and fronds behind which a dozen lions could have lurked unseen. We expected to hear a low, menacing growl at any moment, an expectation that was not fulfilled until, making a circle, we came out of the trees and reentered the saltbush. The sound wasn't a growl, however—more of a loud grunt or bellow.

What happened next happened all at once. A cloud of dust rose from behind a thicket, Adan whipped around, leveling his rifle, and Iain said, "Get behind me!" to Leslie and me. Just as we did, certain that we were about to be charged by a lion, an elephant appeared, not 20 yards to our right. It was a young female of some two or three tons, shaking her head angrily, her ears flared. She stomped and scuffed the earth, then started toward us. Adan fired a shot over her head to scare her off. She stood her ground and let out a trumpet, her ears flaring again, dust rising from her feet, dust spewing from her hide as she tossed her great head back and forth. Iain yelled to Adan in Swahili. Adan fired again, and for an instant I thought he'd shot her—some trick of light made a puff of dust flying from her shoulder look like the impact of a bullet. In the next instant, as the female ran off, I realized that he'd put the second round over her head.

Iain lit into Adan, all in Swahili, but it was plain that the ranger was getting a royal dressing down. I couldn't understand why.

"Rangers are supposed to know that you don't have to shoot at an elephant to scare it off," Iain explained. "That female was old enough to have seen other elephants shot by poachers. You had to have been here in the eighties to appreciate it. Elephants are traumatized by the sound of gunfire. They're very intelligent animals, and it's not necessary to fire over their heads. A handclap will do it, or just shouting. What we try to do on a foot safari is to observe without disturbing the animals, and move on without them ever being aware that humans are around."

BEFORE HEADING BACK TO NAIROBI, we made a pilgrimage to the "Man-eaters' Den." After Patterson had eliminated the two "brutes," as he called the lions, work resumed on the Tsavo River bridge. While waiting for a shipment of construction materials, he took a break to explore some rocky hills near his camp and to do some recreational hunting. He was in a dry riverbed, pursuing a rhino, when he spotted something that stopped him cold.

"I saw on the other side a fearsome-looking cave which seemed to run back for a considerable distance under the rocky bank," Patterson wrote. "Round the entrance and inside the cavern I was thunderstruck to find a number of human bones with here and there a copper bangle such as the natives wear. Beyond all doubt, the man-eaters' den!"

After taking a photograph, he left his find, and from that day in early 1899 until recently, its location was lost to history. Patterson's characterization of it as a lion's den has aroused controversy and skepticism among naturalists and zoologists for a century: Lions are generally not known to be denning animals (the tale of Daniel in the lion's den notwithstanding).

In 1996, the Field Museum team endeavored to determine who or what had been the cave's true occupants. That year and the next, Kusimba, Kerbis Peterhans, Gnoske, and Andanje made extensive searches southwest of the

Tsavo River bridge—the direction Patterson said he'd followed on his excursion. Nothing was found until April 1997, when Gnoske, after rereading Patterson's descriptions and comparing them to the landscape, realized that Patterson's directions had been way off: The "rocky hills" mentioned in the book were not southwest of the bridge, but northwest.

The day after making that determination, Gnoske, Kerbis Peterhans, and Andanje found a cave in a shady riverbed only a mile from the bridge. It perfectly matched the one in Patterson's photograph. After 98 years, the man-eaters' den had been rediscovered.

But was it the man-eaters' den? The next year, the team sifted through the dirt to recover human bones and examine them for teeth marks; if there were any, the researchers could determine if they had been made by lions, hyenas, or leopards. They looked for the copper bangles Patterson had seen, as well as for human teeth to distinguish between Asians and Africans; Asian teeth would be all but incontrovertible proof that the victims had been the Indian railway workers.

The result of that work was surprising, though inconclusive. Kusimba believes that the legendary cave was never a lion's den, nor any sort of den, but in all likelihood a traditional burial cave of the ancient Taita people, who once inhabited the Tsavo region. Gnoske and Kerbis Peterhans, on the other hand, favor a theory that the bones in the cave were, in fact, the remains of lion victims, though they were probably dragged there by hyenas.

Earlier in the trip, when Rob was shooting pictures at park headquarters, Kusimba took him to the cave. Now Rob would show it to us. Iain and Clive, who had never seen the cave, were as eager for a look as Leslie and I. So, with Rob in the lead, the guides became the guided. After thrashing around for a while, we came to a ravine. Rob shouted. And there it was, with a corridor between two big boulders leading beneath an overhang and into a cavern.

"Well, I don't think it looks so fearsome," said Iain, who doesn't have a high opinion of Patterson, considering him to have been an imperial martinet, a so-so hunter, and something of a grandstander.

I agreed that the cool, shady spot was almost idyllic. Then again, we were not trying to build a bridge in the African wilderness and, at the same time, hunt down two clever cats that were using our workforce as a fast-food restaurant. To Patterson, with his memories of his workers' screams, of his crew leader's gruesome remains, of the tense, interminable nights waiting with his rifle, the cave could well have appeared "fearsome." And given the ignorance about lion behavior that prevailed in his time, it was understandable why he may have mistaken a burial cave for a man-eater's den. Imperial martinet or not, he did pretty well with what he had.

That said, I did find Patterson's characterization of his adversaries as brutes and outlaws objectionable. I recalled our second to last morning in Tsavo, as we sat in camp and watched a zebra herd warily come down to the far bank of the Galana to drink. They had been waiting on the ledge above the river for a long time, suffering from what Iain termed "the paradox of survival." The animals were parched, but feared that a lion or crocodile was waiting for them at the river's edge—lions and crocs know that zebras must drink eventually. And so the whole herd stood still, gazing at the river with what seemed to us equal measures of longing and dread, until the desperation of their thirst overcame their fear. Even so, they did not rush down with abandon, but watered in orderly stages. A dozen or so animals would drink, while the others waited their turn and the stallions stood watch. If one group got greedy and took too long, the stallions would let out a series of loud, sharp brays. It was a strange, distressful sound, falling somewhere between a whinny and a bark.

A layman should not anthropomorphize, but to me, the stallions seemed to be saying, "You've had enough, get a move on, we don't have much time." In a way, I identified with them. They were prey; and, out there, so was I. But that recognition did not offend my sense of human dignity. The offense was to my human pride. Nothing wrong with a little pride, except when it becomes excessive. If I had been in Patterson's boots, I would have pursued the lions with as much determination as he—after all, his first responsibility was to finish the bridge and protect his workers' lives—but I don't think I would have regarded the lions as savage brutes violating some law of heaven. If anything, they were only obeying the fundamental law of all creation, which is survival.

To realize that I shared something in common with the wary, anxious zebras was merely to acknowledge my true place in nature where nature is wild, the stage on which the drama of predator and prey is played out.

MAY/JUNE 2000

STOMPING GROUNDS

By Paul Kvinta

India's elephants are squeezed for living space, stressed by overdevelopment, and taking their anger out on rural villages. Only one thing prevents these pachyderms from receiving a serious dose of blowback— they also happen to be deities.

DESPITE ITS TREMENDOUS SIZE, the elephant was stealthy, and Lasman Bumiz struggled to see him. It was after sunset, and in the shadowy torchlight, the ten-foot tusker possessed the seemingly magical and decidedly unnerving ability to appear and disappear suddenly. One moment he was in front of Bumiz, the next he was behind him. Bumiz was a small man, not five feet tall, but if he didn't act soon, the elephant would materialize inside the residential compound nearby, and it would be too late. So the villager sucked up his courage and did what he'd done all week—he raised his torch high into the air, unleashed a blood-chilling shriek, and rushed the animal dead-on. Bumiz drew confidence from his friends, the men sprinting alongside him, swinging axes and machetes, banging empty cooking oil tins, whooping louder than partisan lunatics at an India-Pakistan cricket match. He knew that they were all in this together, that they somehow had to repel this superior invading force. But in a split second the tusker wheeled about and lunged at them, a terrifying feint that scattered the men like billiard balls and sent Bumiz back-pedaling into the darkness, scared and confused. What scared him the most, actually, what petrified him, was that he was confronting not a mighty animal, but something much greater. Bumiz was at war with a god.

All week the residents of Phulaguri, a rice-farming village in India's northeastern state of Assam, had debated how many elephants were laying nightly siege to their community. Some guessed more than a hundred. Others figured 60 or 70. The pandemonium each night made counting impossible. What the villagers did know was that five homes had been reduced to dusty heaps of thatch and mud and that the Assam Forest Department had failed to rescue them. It was no secret, of course, what two things the migrating elephants wanted from Phulaguri: the recently harvested rice stalks—known as "paddy"—that people stored in conical stacks in their courtyards, and the paint-peeling moonshine that some of them brewed from fermented rice. For a stiff drink, elephants would blast through walls.

Desperate for solutions, someone suggested making a *puja* to Lord Ganesha. In the crowded Hindu pantheon, Ganesha is the well-loved "remover of obstacles," and he would certainly save them. So the villagers offered up bananas, oranges, and sliced coconut, touched their foreheads to the earth, and prayed for relief from this unfathomable plague. The curious fact that Ganesha has the head of an elephant struck no one as particularly ironic. Most residents made little distinction between actual elephants and Ganesha himself.

But the puja failed to yield the desired results, and on December 28 Bumiz and his neighbors found themselves battling the tusker. At some point amid the chaos, Bumiz sprinted ahead into a bamboo patch, a flanking maneuver nobody noticed. Later, others would only shrug when speculating as to why he had chosen this ill-advised tactic. When the tusker finally turned and bolted, the group gave chase, and that's when they found Bumiz. He was pressed deep into the mud beyond the bamboo, his teeth shattered, his eyes glazed over. The elephant had stampeded right over him. Somehow, he was still alive, and he requested water. "There was no blood," says Jimmy Gothorp, the local schoolteacher. "I think his back was broken." They loaded him into a truck, where he died en route to the hospital.

Two days later, in the Bumizes' courtyard, the dead man's four-year-old son is bawling, and his pregnant wife is tugging my arm and repeating, trance-like, "What will I do now? What will I do now?" I ask some gathered neighbors why the government shouldn't simply kill Assam's wild elephants. "No, no!" the group insists. "The elephant is still God," one man says. "Even if an elephant destroys our paddy, destroys our houses, kills our people, we must respect him as a god." They believed that because God had taken Bumiz's soul directly, they didn't need to burn his body in the Hindu tradition, a process that releases the soul. Instead, they buried him. Some villagers claimed that the tusker had returned to pay respects, that they'd seen him kneeling at Bumiz's grave. Gothorp takes me to the grave and points to an indentation in the dirt. "There," he says. "They believe Ganesha knelt right there."

I ARRIVED IN ASSAM 12 DAYS EARLIER, curious about something called "human-elephant conflict," a concept that to Western ears sounds like late-night comedy material. But Christy Williams assures me it's no joke, and when we pull into a village called Da Parbatia at the start of a two-week itinerary, nobody here is laughing. On the contrary, all hell is breaking loose. "There's no organization here," grumbles Williams, pressing his way past overwrought villagers. "Someone could get killed." As director of the World Wildlife Fund's Asian Rhino and Elephant Action Strategy, Williams has witnessed elephant drives before. He has even provided fuel and firecrackers to local officials of the Assam Forest Department for this one. But what we see startles him.

Before us, a crush of seething villagers jostles at the edge of a thicket, ignoring two policemen attempting crowd control. Each time an elephant head pokes warily out of the trees, the mob surges forward, howling and cursing, banging cookware and launching firecrackers. Behind us, something resembling a block party is unfolding, with hundreds of curious onlookers from neighboring villages clogging the main road. We're standing in what was once someone's grove of banana trees, but the trees have been trampled into kindling, thanks to the unwanted visitors hiding in the thicket. Suddenly, from beyond the vegetation, explosions rip the air, and a herd of 18 elephants crashes out of the bush and rumbles across the paddy field to our right. People run screaming in every direction. On the heels of the herd are three domestic elephants ridden by several men with sticks and smoking guns. It's the Forest Department, and they chase the herd to the other side of the field, where they are met by another scrum of fist-shaking villagers. "Great," groans Williams. "They're shifting the problem from one village to the next. That makes it worse."

We elbow our way to the road for a better view. Gazing south over the open paddy fields, we watch the fleeing herd as it zigzags toward the Brahmaputra River, stopping at angry village after angry village. Williams sighs. He's a tall man, a 34-year-old Tamil from South India, eloquent and self-assured, but right now he's frustrated. "We're fighting a rear guard action," he admits, between thunderous blasts of walnut-size firecrackers. Today's conflict is merely a symptom of a greater problem, he says, one driven by habitat loss. Asian elephants are migratory animals, he explains, forest dwellers that require tremendous space. At the time of the Pharaohs, herds were found from Iraq to China, inhabiting a continuous forest belt that extended over five million square miles. Today, just 5 percent of that habitat remains. As Asia's skyrocketing human population forces herds from their last forest redoubts, the result isn't surprising—a brutal death match between man and beast. In India alone, home to three-quarters of the world's 40,000 Asian elephants, the animals have stomped or gored to death some 4,000 people in the past two decades. Meanwhile, elephant populations have mostly plummeted in the 13 countries where they reside, a result of retaliatory killings, poaching, and accidents involving railroads and highways. Laos was once called "the land of a million elephants," but now the Southeast Asian country has just 2,500. Vietnam's population has plunged to 114.

But no place has been rocked by the conflict more than India's Northeast, especially Assam, where 5,000 jumbos roam. From 1990 to 2003, the hostilities claimed 586 people and 255 elephants. If there's a ground zero for Assam's carnage, it's the district of Sonitpur, where Williams has brought me. In one week here in 1993, elephants killed more than 50 people. Then there was the three-month period in 2001, when unknown perpetrators poisoned some 30 elephants with pesticide, one of the biggest massacres of the animal in recent history.

That mass poisoning still haunts conservationists. Could it signal an attitude shift in a people who have traditionally revered elephants? Certainly, the one great force restraining this Hindu nation from exterminating its marauding herds isn't the endangered species law. It's the nearly 2,000-year-old cult of Ganesha, the elephant-headed god, along with India's rich traditions surrounding domestic elephants. "This cultural aspect has saved elephants in India," Williams says. In Sumatra, where Williams is conducting a similar campaign, "they have no elephant culture," he says. "They've brutalized their elephants." But as he and I loiter among the angry villagers outside Da Parbatia, it's clear that feelings toward elephants in Assam are at a tipping point. If villagers continue getting hammered year after year by rampaging elephants, how long before they snap?

Williams doesn't want to find out. His team has just concluded a study that identifies critical elephant migration corridors and hard-hit conflict zones in several districts north of the Brahmaputra River, including Sonitpur. In the long term, he plans to lobby government officials to protect those corridors. But over the next two weeks, he wants to drop into the maw of the conflict, to help the Forest Department's frontline troops develop village-level strategies to protect both elephants and villagers. "We can't win this in two or three years," he concedes. "But we can have an impact."

We're still watching the herd when a commotion breaks out behind us. Approaching the road is a pair of stragglers, a massive female elephant and, wobbling 30 feet behind it, a tiny calf, no bigger than an overstuffed ottoman. Williams reckons the calf is less than a month old, and as it stumbles over the paddy field's ridges, Mom drops back for some gentle coaxing.

It's a touching scene—and for reasons that may go beyond mere anthropomorphism. Elephants live about as long as humans and exhibit some of the most advanced social structures observed among mammals. Tight-knit families composed of a mother and her offspring belong to large matriarchal herds. Elephant young spend some 15 years learning their society's complex social behaviors, and individuals seem to demonstrate a sense of history, recalling important individuals and events. Relationships are fiercely loyal. Williams tells me a story about a mother and two calves that were part of his Ph.D. research in northern India. One calf found itself stuck on a railroad track, and the mother tried repeatedly to free it as a train rumbled toward them. Unable to dislodge the baby, she finally stood between her offspring and the oncoming train, trumpeting, trying to scare the train away. All three elephants were killed. "I've never heard of a mother being more protective of her young," Williams says.

As we watch the straggling mother and calf approach the road outside Da Parbatia, a weird energy courses through the crowd. Some people jeer. Others, seemingly delighted, call out *"Ganesh baba! Ganesh baba!"* Suddenly someone from the retreating mob slingshots a large firecracker that explodes in the mother's face, causing her to spin around in a panic. Amid the smoke and confusion, she locates her calf, and the shaken elephants amble off after the herd. Williams is livid. "I don't like seeing little calves tortured like that," he fumes. "The little thing must be exhausted." Then, after some thought, he adds, "What are the prospects for that calf, growing up like this?"

THE FOREST RANGERS OFFER ME betel nut, but I beg off, and they proceed to smear betel leaves with lime paste, wrap each leaf around a nut, and stuff the wads into their mouths. "The villagers were out of hand yesterday," one ranger mumbles, chewing vigorously and then arching a bright red stream of spit across the driveway of the Forest Department's Sadar Range Office. "The elephants could have hurt someone. People should stand back and let the *kunkies* through." Kunkies are domestic elephants, I learn, and the dozen men raining betel juice around me—these unshaven, middle-aged, balding foresters with baggy eyes and teeth stained red and black—are the brave-hearts I saw riding to the rescue yesterday, the Kunki Cavalry, so to speak. Admittedly, they lack a certain swashbuckling, save-the-day aura—there's not a uniform or pair of boots among them—but they do shoo away rampaging elephants, or try to, even if villagers mostly hold them in contempt. "The people do not treat us with respect," one of them complains. "They assault us because of what the elephants do to them."

Villagers aren't the only ones who disrespect the Cav.

"My men must pay for ammunition and firecrackers out of their pockets," complains Range Officer Shahdat Ali, explaining that he hasn't received funds from the state in months. "We have only one vehicle, but we need three. How can we manage?" I'm clearly looking at a shoestring operation. Exposed wires run like varicose veins across office walls that needed paint 20 years ago. There are holes in the floor and mosquitoes in the air, and using the bathroom means stepping just outside the back door.

It's December 2003, and the Cav has already conducted 96 elephant drives this year. Today the men are planning a drive aimed at the herd we saw yesterday, and they prepare as for a military campaign. Huddled beneath a naked lightbulb, the group pores over faded maps. Someone produces a couple of rusty shotguns, while someone else carefully counts out shells, handling them like priceless gems. Another guy taps and shakes several handheld radios, trying to determine which ones work. Christy Williams offers one of his jeeps, without which half the Cav would be staying home. We pile into the vehicles and speed toward the Brahmaputra River, where we'll meet the kunkies.

Assam is primarily a long, flat river valley, tucked south of the towering Himalaya and split in two by the Brahmaputra, one of the world's largest rivers. In winter, when the water is low, hundreds of low-slung, narrow islands stretch for miles in the braided waterway, divided by shallow channels. "Those fishing villages are seasonal," Williams says as we gaze from the north bank at some makeshift huts on one of the islands, where men are drying fishing nets in the afternoon sun. Each summer this dreamy scene turns into a nightmare as the monsoon-swollen river leaps its banks, obliterates thousands of huts, and kills scores of people. But it also washes millions of tons of silt down from the mountains, and this nutrient-rich soil produces the tasty, riverside grasses that have lured migrating elephants for generations.

More than half of Assam's 5,000 elephants live in the forested foothills along the state's northern border with Bhutan and the state of Arunachal Pradesh. This greenbelt, a nearly unbroken string of wildlife sanctuaries, national parks, and forest reserves, parallels the Brahmaputra for hundreds of miles. Each fall and winter, the elephants migrate south across the broad plain between the mountains and the river to graze along the Brahmaputra's banks. As agriculture spread across this plain during the 20th century, so did conflict between cultivators and migrating elephants. But full-scale war has erupted only recently, as illegal settlers have ravaged Sonitpur's northern forests, flushing herds from their last sanctuaries. These elephant armies, often a hundred strong, march across cultivated land, skirmishing with villagers and raiding the fields throughout the harvest season. For poor Assamese farmers, the loss of a harvest is devastating.

At a village near the river, we meet a man named Anwar Hussein and his nine-foot-tall *kunki*, Rajeshwari. Hussein is a *mahout*, or elephant driver, and for 3,000 rupees, or $66, a day, the Cav hires him and Rajeshwari, along with two smaller elephants and their mahouts. A dark, wiry man with a serious expression, Hussein barks a command, and Rajeshwari slowly drops to her knees, allowing a couple of the Cav to scramble aboard. The men then review their battle plan. Yesterday, they drove the 18-elephant herd away from a cluster of north-bank villages and onto a nearby river island. Today, they'll push the herd several miles westward down that same island, farther still from the villages. Meanwhile, a scouting party will locate a strategic spot along the north bank where the herd can be steered back onto the mainland. The goal, ultimately, is to prompt the elephants to migrate north across the plain and home to the hills.

Williams and I motor off with the scout team, and we soon pass a gleaming military truck with soldiers in pressed olive uniforms and snappy berets, a ubiquitous sight in Assam. The scene is a reminder of the other war here, a war the Indian government has no problems funding and one that exacerbates the elephant conflict. On a map, Assam is shaped like a scorpion, linked tenuously to the rest of the nation by a spaghetti-thin land corridor that noodles between Nepal and Bangladesh. Perpetually overlooked and underdeveloped, Assam and the six other states of the Northeast are a country apart from "mainland" India. The region is home to some 400 tribal groups—a Dr. Seussian jumble of ethnicities including the Khasis, Kukis, and Karbis; the Nagas and the Nishis; the Tiwas and the Tagins—that often explode in ethnic conflict and separatist uprisings. Several armed militias are currently fighting the Indian government, and some indigenous leaders have encouraged their tribesmen to relocate inside protected forests and parks to solidify their territorial claims. This deluge of settlers has devastated vast stretches of prime elephant habitat in northern Sonitpur.

"The best way to clear forest encroachers is to introduce a man-eating tiger," Williams muses at one point. He tends to say outlandish things, only half jokingly, whenever he judges Assam's political chaos and booming population to be harmful to elephants. "Maybe SARS isn't such a bad thing after all," he suggests at another time.

We're standing atop a bluff near the north bank of the river with some of the Cav, waiting for the kunkies to steer the herd back onto the mainland, scanning the wide floodplain with binoculars. As the sun begins to set, we're startled by explosions near the river. In the distance, against a palette of golds, reds, and blues reflecting off the glass-calm Brahmaputra, a legion of elephants storms across the plain in a furious cloud of smoke and dust, elephants of all shapes and sizes, legs churning, heads bobbing, ears flapping. They've crossed the river and are rumbling straight for us. "I count more than a hundred!" says Williams, binoculars glued to his eye sockets. Somehow, between yesterday and today, 18 elephants have morphed into 105. I look through the binoculars. Just behind the thundering herd rides Anwar Hussein and the boys of the Cav, hurling firecrackers and screaming like, well, wild Indians. "Amazing what three kunkies can do, huh?" says Williams.

By the time the herd rushes past us, it's pitch-dark. The kunkies backtrack for a straggler, but when they return, nobody's sure where the herd went. We drive north, fanning our spotlights, but after two hours of searching, the Cav remains clueless. The men scratch their heads and finally go home.

Somehow, they've lost a hundred elephants. It didn't seem possible.

I OFFER RAJESHWARI A CHUNK of dried molasses, but her daughter, Nagini, swipes the treat with her trunk, prompting Hussein to swat the teenager and triggering great laughter among the assembled children. We're in the village of Kataki Chuburi photographing the three kunkies that have toiled so diligently of late. Rajeshwari just wants breakfast. Her feet are chained to those of her offspring—Nagini and Suman—but she simply reaches out with her trunk, uproots a nearby banana tree, strips the bark, and devours the snowy white center. If the 45-year-old elephant were still wild, she'd need at least 40 square miles of forest to satisfy her colossal diet—300 to 650 pounds of vegetation daily, plus 60 gallons of water.

Hussein and two other mahouts unchain the elephants and saddle them with thick burlap pads. Then, in one graceful motion, Hussein somehow levitates onto his standing mount and positions his bare feet behind her ears. He's taking the elephants to the river for a bath this morning, and, with two dozen children in tow, the kunkies parade past the colorful adobe houses of Kataki Chuburi. Everyone nods appreciatively at Hussein and his kunki. Assamese mahouts are the Marlboro Men of India: rugged, individualistic cowboys roaming an uncertain frontier, masters of all elephant lore. They're icons of a glorious elephant culture that reaches back 5,000 years.

The earliest evidence of elephant taming appeared in the third millennium B.C., when the Harappan civilization of what is now Pakistan and northwest India produced stone engravings depicting elephants draped in cloth. Later, the Vedic texts and epic poems of early Hinduism describe kings riding fabulously ornamented elephants. More than status symbols, the animals were also the first weapons of mass destruction. The Mauryan dynasty of the fourth century B.C. employed 9,000 war elephants, the largest force ever assembled. Elephants were used to steamroll opposing infantry, although they were sometimes a terrifying source of friendly fire. When Alexander the Great attacked the forces of King Porus in present-day Pakistan in 326 B.C., Alexander's arrows so infuriated Porus's 200 elephants that they went berserk, squashing friend and foe alike.

In Assam, with its huge elephant population, knowledge about the animal was so vast that in 1734 A.D. King Siva Sinha commissioned the most comprehensive treatise on elephants ever written, the *Hastividyārnava*, "sea of elephant lore." The work is an enchanting blend of poetry, ethno-medicine, and animal husbandry. To wit:

"The elephant with a short body and tail, with a head like a broken basket, whose rutting matter smells like a mādhoi mālatī flower, should be mounted by a rider with broad chest, big ears, and with youthful vigour. In order to tame them, they should be fed with the rider's feet-dusts, mixed with smoky dusts. When they suffer from fever, three sparrows are to be placed in a cage below the elephants, and when these birds twitter, the elephants get relieved of their illness."

By the late 19th century, Assam had become the leading source of elephants for the British Empire, with as many as 4,000 wild elephants being captured each decade, most destined to labor in the timber trade.

Rajeshwari, Hussein's elephant, was captured decades ago, and has spent her life ever since in the company of tough men like Hussein, a mahout for 30 years. "When you're starting as a mahout, the elephant doesn't listen to your commands," Hussein explains. "You must work hard for 20-hour days in the forest. You must sleep under the stars. You don't know where you will end up each day." As we progress through the village, we're approached by a pious-looking woman in a pink sari holding a basket of rice. Hussein stops, and the woman reverently offers the grain to Rajeshwari, who promptly inhales it. Hussein orders his elephant to kneel, and the woman smears red dye across Rajeshwari's forehead, anointing her with the sacred mark known as a *tilak*. She then presses a five-rupee note into Hussein's hand, and we move on.

Here I am seeing the cult of Ganesha firsthand; in Rajeshwari, the woman is seeing not a mere animal, but a divinity that has been revered for 2,000 years. Images of the elephant-headed, potbellied deity are everywhere in India today—in temples and hotel lobbies, on calendars and bumper stickers. Ganesha is a rock star.

Apart from Ganesha, however, there is little left of Assam's once great elephant culture. Christy Williams and I watch one of its last remnants: Hussein bathing his kunki in the Brahmaputra. Dismounting, the mahout strips down to his *dhoti* and orders Rajeshwari into the shallow water, where he proceeds to scrub her vigorously head-to-toe with the back of a coconut shell. The long-cherished relationship here between man and elephant began deteriorating over the past century, as 95 percent of the plain between the Brahmaputra and the northern hills was cleared for agriculture, and one sprawling elephant population fragmented into many small ones, some of them barely viable. The Indian government stanched the bleeding in 1974 when it declared elephants endangered, and it later banned logging in Assam and outlawed the capturing of elephants. A government conservation program called Project Elephant has also helped. Assam's wild elephant population has stabilized at 5,000, but, ironically, the logging ban rendered most of the state's 2,500 domesticated elephants unemployed. Many are malnourished, with owners unable to afford their upkeep, and Hussein tells me he has to supplement his modest income by growing subsistence rice and vegetables. "This whole culture will probably be gone soon," sighs Williams. "Being a mahout is hardly a worthwhile profession."

WHEN WE ARRIVE WITH THE CAV at the Rupajuli Tea Estate, the sleepless laborers who live and work here turn out in droves, desperate to see results. For three days, some 81 elephants have terrorized this place, and two homes lie obliterated at the edge of a field of Guatemala grass. Later I ask one man whose home has been destroyed how the perpetrators should be handled. He chuckles uncomfortably. "The elephant is Ganesha," he says. "We don't want to hurt him." I notice that both shattered houses reek of home brew. Apparently, for the elephants involved, the past few days have amounted to one big frat party.

Rupajuli retains a distinctly colonial air, with manicured rows of dark green tea bushes and dapper whitewashed buildings. The tea pickers lead us to a swath of Guatemala grass, a rotational crop used to increase soil fertility. This patch is the size of four football fields, with a wide path running up the middle. The grass is ten feet tall and seemingly impenetrable, but the workers assure us that the elephants are lurking in there. Judging from the bread-loaf-size droppings and the cement fence posts crushed to powder, they seem to be right. Regrettably, to save $66, the Cav is kunki-less today, which means nobody is up high enough to locate the elephants. A tea picker volunteers to shimmy up a tree, and he excitedly begins blurting out herd logistics. The Cav jumps into action. First, they creep around the right side of the field, then the left, and when their quarry eludes them, they change tactics and march straight up the middle path in a brazen show of force. Several policemen accompany us today, and these guys start chucking oversize firecrackers willy-nilly into the grass, like schoolboys. It's impossible to judge our effectiveness, but when we reach the end of the field, we spy the herd huddled beneath some shade trees just outside the grass patch. From there, it should be easy to drive them away. But then, inexplicably, someone lobs an explosive at them, and all 81 elephants rush back into the grass.

"Who threw that?" demands Williams, throwing up his hands. "We had them!"

Everyone starts talking at once. Intricate plans are laid. For the next two hours, the Cav blindly chases the herd from one corner of the field to another. At one point, Williams and I take a breather, and we're gazing down the center path when an elephant head suddenly pokes out of the grass. It looks carefully both ways. Finally, the coast clear, the elephant gingerly crosses the path, as if tiptoeing. Thirty comrades follow.

It's pretty clear who's winning this engagement.

By nightfall, the Cav succeeds in moving the elephants to the exact place we originally found them, beneath the shade trees. But now it's too dark to drive them away, so we pile into the vehicles and leave. When we reach the front gate, however, we're blocked by a drunk, growling mob. "Don't get out of the vehicle," Williams tells me. One of the policemen gets nose-to-nose with the leader of the crowd, a man unfazed by the cop's rifle. He's spitting mad. "Those are your elephants!" he screams. "They don't belong to us, they belong to you! Get them out of here!" People push in menacingly, but the cop stands firm. After much snarling, the crowd reluctantly parts, and we speed away.

EVERY DAY, CRIES FOR HELP stream into the Cav office. Trampled crops, smashed homes, crushed limbs, and worse—the devastation swirls around us as the villages of Sonitpur come undone. The elephants would call, too, if they could. They're taking casualties as well.

What Christy Williams fears most is a repeat of the poisoning incident of August 2001, when dead elephants first began appearing in and around Nameri National Park in northern Sonitpur. None of the carcasses had any external injuries, although there was a particularly eerie quality about most of them—they were slightly blue. Officials suspected some sort of disease outbreak, but then tissue analyses revealed something startling—the elephants had ingested Dimecron, a powerful pesticide used on tea estates. Asked by reporters how this was possible, Apurba Chakraborty, the veterinarian who conducted the postmortems, noted the elephants' "affinity for liquor" and speculated that "they were given country-made liquor mixed with the pesticide by unscrupulous elements."

"It was targeted," Williams says, noting that all the carcasses were found in a relatively small area. "Maybe someone's family member was killed by an elephant there." The culprits, whoever they were, had chosen an especially brutal means of death. Dimecron would have ravaged an elephant's nervous system before weakening its entire body and causing unquenchable thirst. The biggest challenge for the killers was masking the pesticide's smell. "It was trial and error," explains H. P. Phukan, a divisional forest officer working in Nameri at the time. "They tried fruit, food, liquor. The villagers worked to get it right."

By November the death toll had exceeded 30, and the outcry was spreading among environmentalists and journalists around the world. Even Bollywood superstar Madhuri Dixit weighed in, urging officials to "stop this mass murder, which is shocking the world." State officials assigned a one-man commission to investigate the killings, but the Forest Department insists that uncooperative villagers undermined the effort. In the end, no arrests were made.

We hear one day that a tiny calf, not a month old, has been separated from its herd. Considering the time and place of its rescue, it's possibly the same calf we saw our first day, during the chaotic elephant drive near Da Parbatia. The vets say its chances are slim. We discuss traveling to the wildlife rehabilitation center to see the calf, but then an even more urgent call comes in from Amdenga, a village to the west.

When we arrive, the body of Birtiala Tirky is still lying on the ground in her compound, wrapped in a straw mat. The night before, a group of elephants had slipped past the men protecting the village and stormed the Tirky compound.

They were attracted to something Birtiala, 45, kept in her bedroom, a jar of rice flour for making flatbread. When an elephant crashed through the wall, Michael Tirky pulled his wife into a corner, but Birtiala panicked and ran. Two steps out of the hut, she was stomped on. The elephant then flung her limp body across a field.

Such homicidal behavior isn't unusual, Williams tells me. It stems from confusion elephants experience while raiding. They're disoriented, scared, and hungry, and thus dangerously unpredictable.

He gently asks Michael if officials have informed him of the 20,000 rupees, or $465, the government owes him for his loss. Tirky looks at him blankly. We then back off as a solemn crowd loads Birtiala's body into an oxcart. Williams whispers to me, "It's so important to give these people something immediately. There's an anger threshold. Once it gets crossed, you start getting dead elephants."

Before they wheel the cart away, Anslem Tirky, Birtiala's grown son, stands alone before his mother's body. He buries his face in his hands and weeps.

"WE HAVE AN ELEPHANTINE PROBLEM," admits Pradyut Bordoloi, Assam's dapper young forest minister, in his office in the state's capitol. Nonetheless, the minister has developed a program he believes can end human-elephant conflict in the region. First, he'll establish special elephant reserves; the government has already demarcated five of these. Admittedly, they're already seriously encroached, but Bordoloi has a plan for that, something called "joint forest management." Under this philosophy, once the encroachers are removed, villages bordering the reserves will play an active management role with the Forest Department. They'll replant deforested areas with banana trees and other elephant favorites. They'll line their paddy fields with plants elephants dislike, like mustard and chilies. New economic development programs will reduce the incentive for illegal timber cutting. Villagers will feel such ownership of the reserves, Bordoloi asserts, that they'll evict returning encroachers themselves.

How will he fund this, given that his men barely scrape by now? "There are many hurdles," Bordoloi concedes. "Unfortunately, the fiscal situation in Assam is not very good."

His plan sounds great, though I'm having trouble envisioning the Cav pulling it off. The Forest Department has tried to implement ambitious plans before and failed, most notoriously in 2001, when officers tried to erect a 50-mile-long electric "elephant fence" along the contiguous southern boundaries of three protected forests in northern Sonitpur. Elephant fencing has succeeded in other places, but only in situations with targeted goals, like protecting a specific village. Designed to deliver a 10,000-volt warning, most such fences rarely extend more than a couple of miles, and locals must participate in constant maintenance. Assam's epic barrier, in contrast, was the Berlin Wall of elephant fences, designed, apparently, to stifle what local herds naturally do—migrate south to the Brahmaputra. Worse, the fence had limited local support. "We discussed it with villagers," says R. K. Das, project overseer, "but they didn't accept it." The fence was built anyway.

The structure cost $36,000—a small fortune in Assam—and wasn't up six months before the generators and fence posts disappeared.

"We're fools," one forest officer told me. "Call us fools."

The only thing worse than the department's incompetence is its corruption. For years, officials have accepted bribes to ignore illegal logging, or have been involved in timber smuggling themselves. Bordoloi concedes he has a problem. "There are lots of allegations," he admits. "I have suspended 52 officials in the last two years. These people are being investigated."

ON A TRIP TO THE BALIPARA RESERVE FOREST, in Assam's northern greenbelt, I see what Bordoloi is up against. Not far into this 188-square-mile area, the forest abruptly disappears on both sides of the road, yielding an apocalyptic wasteland of gnarled stumps, charred earth, and pitiful lean-tos of branches and plastic. The people here belong to the Bodo tribe, which has long battled for an autonomous homeland within Assam.

Assam has a long and dubious tradition of settling people inside its "protected" forests. But the settlements exploded in the early '90s when militant Bodo leaders started recruiting people from around the region to move here illegally in order to strengthen the tribe's bid for an ethnic homeland. From 1996 to 2001, encroachers seized a chunk of forest larger than Rhode Island, and officials today estimate that Assam's northern protected lands collectively are 70 to 80 percent encroached.

There is an acrid, burning smell in the air as we approach one of the lean-tos. Two women inside cut cabbages and eye us warily, while four barefoot children watch from atop a stump that must measure five feet across. A man agrees to talk but won't give his name. "I used to cut timber," he says, "but now I grow paddy." Until recently, he says, he had a house here. But last May forest officers and police came with a team of kunkies and bulldozed everything. It was the 21st time he'd been evicted from this site. "They destroy our houses, break our pots and utensils," he says. "They damage our fields."

"The idea is to destroy their economic viability so they won't return," says Anindya Swargowari, district forest officer for western Sonitpur. But despite being backed by an order from India's Supreme Court, the eviction drives ignited a political firestorm. In April 2002, a crusading Bodo legislator and his followers torched a government antipoaching camp in Nameri National Park. Though the legislator was arrested, the incident stalled the program's momentum. Today, the evictions are sporadic, and, without resources for monitoring, officials can't prevent encroachers from returning immediately. (The whole sorry story reminds me of another one of Christy Williams's politically incorrect musings: "Democracy's OK," I heard him mutter at one point, "but a benevolent dictatorship might be better.")

I ask the Bodo man if he thinks his presence hurts the elephants.

"They are part of the forest," he states matter-of-factly, "and we live here, too." He likes Ganesha, he says, but kunkies smashed his statue of the god during the last eviction.

Basically, I'm talking to a man—follow closely now—whose elephant-headed god was destroyed by elephants attempting to reclaim the forest for elephants made homeless by the elephant-worshiping man.

There's poetic justice in there, somewhere.

MANJU BARUA IS A BEAR OF A MAN, with a bushy beard and a commanding presence, and as he pours us whiskey on the porch of his bungalow, he heaps scorn on Forest Minister Bordoloi's "joint forest management" idea. "It's the beginning of the end," he says with an incongruous grin. "When it falls apart—when the forests are gone—the government can lay half the blame on the people." Barua is one of Assam's most knowledgeable ecologists and a man who has used his advisory position on India's National Board of Wildlife to write blistering letters to Assam officials disparaging their folly. It was Barua who first told the world conservation community of the poisonings in Assam. We're at Wild Grass, the lodge he owns near Kaziranga National Park, one of the jewels of India's park system, home to endangered one-horned rhinos and hundreds of elephants, and a place guarded fiercely against poachers and encroachers by proud Forest Department personnel. It's about the only spot in Assam that draws international adventure travelers; why it can't be replicated elsewhere in the state is a tragic mystery.

This evening Barua has hired some traditional Assamese dancers to entertain his guests around a campfire. I'm not sure if it's the chanting from the performance, the shadowy light on his porch, or the whiskey, but Barua's words have an eerily prophetic quality. "What we're seeing here is the beginning of the next worldwide mass extinction," he insists. Habitat is fragmenting as fast in Assam as in any place on Earth. Crop depredation by elephants is rising. Naturally, he says, "the villager response will be to kill them." In fact, Barua reckons there's a connection between the fence fiasco and the poisonings, that encroachers north of the proposed fence feared an increase in crop depredation by trapped elephants. So they took action. "Anyone with an iota of foresight would have predicted that this fence would provoke cultivators to express their outrage in some volatile form," he says.

Barua explains that India's highly stratified society has always shunted the poor to marginal areas, to the forests and hills, forcing them to use their only available resources in an unsustainable manner. The nation's middle class condemns this behavior while demanding more wood products as they adopt consumer-driven, Western lifestyles. The Assam Forest Department can't possibly reengineer these society-wide trends, he insists, nor can nongovernmental organizations. Ultimately, solving human-elephant conflict would require all of Assam's governmental departments working to remedy several social and economic problems, including poverty and soaring birth rates. Barua chuckles at such a pipe dream and wags his finger. "The elephants will go first," he predicts. "But mark my word. People won't be far behind."

CHRISTY WILLIAMS'S VIEW couldn't be more different. "We have to fight this well into the future," he says, before leaving for Sumatra for another elephant project. He appreciates the conflict's complexities, he insists, but he also believes that NGOs like the WWF can make a difference, particularly as supporters of ragtag forest departments. "Sure, some of these guys are bad," he says of the forest service. "Some are corrupt. But at the end of the day, these are the guys who have to tackle this."

These two weeks have sparked many ideas for Williams on how to reduce pressure on villagers. Early warning systems must be established. He'll buy another vehicle for the rangers we tagged along with, and he's contemplating financing several kunki teams and basing them near heavy conflict zones across Sonitpur. There's much to do.

After Williams leaves, I visit the Center for Wildlife Rehabilitation, near Kaziranga National Park. The rescued elephant calf is here, the one we heard about earlier in the week. "I've never seen a calf so traumatized," says the vet. "Usually in two or three days they snap out of it. It's been a week. He's not settled yet." The calf was only a week old when foresters found him in a trench in a tea garden, his still-attached umbilical cord bloody and infected.

"I'd give him a fifty-fifty chance," he says.

He invites me to peer through a window into an adjacent room. Inside, there's a man standing in the center of a dimly lit eight-by-eight-foot enclosure. He's holding a baby bottle, and staggering around him is the little elephant. The tyke is three feet tall, and there's a wool blanket draped over him. His big brown eyes are glassy. He walks around and around in that tiny room, and he can't stop trembling.

AUGUST 2004

THE WHALE WARRIORS

By Peter Heller

———————

Before the world was introduced to Paul Watson and his radical brand of environmentalism through books, movies, and a television show, the author traveled with his band of eco-pirates hell-bent on saving the whales.

W HAT WOKE ME AT 3 A.M. on Christmas morning was the bow of the ship plunging off a steep wave and smashing into the trough. The hull shuddered like a living animal, and when the next roller lifted the stern, I could hear the prop pitching out of the water, beating the air with a juddering moan that shivered the ribs of the 180-foot converted North Sea trawler. We were 200 miles off the Adélie Coast, Antarctica, in a force 8 gale. The storm had been building since the previous morning. I lay in the dark and breathed. Something was different. I listened to the deep throb of the diesel engine two decks below and the turbulent sloshing against my bolted porthole, and felt a quickening in the ship.

Fifteen days before, we had left Melbourne, Australia, and headed due south on the *Farley Mowat,* the flagship of the radical environmental group the Sea Shepherd Conservation Society. The mission of her captain, Paul Watson, and his 43-member, all-volunteer crew was to hunt down and stop the Japanese whaling fleet from engaging in what they considered illegal commercial whaling. Watson had said before the trip, "We will nonviolently intervene." But judging by the preparations conducted over the past week, it seemed he was readying for a full-scale attack.

I dressed quickly, grabbed a dry suit and a life jacket, and ran up three lurching flights of narrow stairs to the bridge. Dawn. Or what passed for it in the never night of Antarctic summer. A murky gloom of wind-tortured fog mingled with blowing snow and spray. White eruptions tore off the tops of the waves and streamed their shoulders in long streaks of foam. The sea was chaos. When I had gone to sleep four hours earlier, the swells were 20 feet high and building. Now monsters over 30 feet rolled under the stern and pitched the bow wildly into a featureless sky. The timberwork of the bridge groaned and creaked. The wind battered the thick windows and ripped past the superstructure with a buffeted keening.

Watson, 55, with thick, nearly white hair and beard, wide cheekbones, and packing some extra weight underneath his exposure suit, sat in the high captain's chair, on the starboard side of the bridge, looking alternately at a radar screen over his head and at the sea. He has a gentle, watchful demeanor. Like a polar bear. Alex Cornelissen, 38, his Dutch first officer, was in the center at the helm, trying to run with the waves. Cornelissen looks too thin to go anyplace cold, and his hair is buzzed to a near stubble.

"Good timing," Cornelissen said to me with the tightening of his mouth that is his smile. "Two ships on the radar. The closest is under two miles off. If they're icebergs, they're doing six knots."

"Probably the *Nisshin Maru* and the *Esperanza*," Watson said. "They're just riding out the storm." He was talking about the 8,000-ton factory ship on which the Japanese butcher and pack the harpooned whales, and Greenpeace's flagship, which had sailed with its companion boat the *Arctic Sunrise* from Cape Town more than a month before and had been shadowing and harassing the whalers for weeks. Where the five other boats of the Japanese whaling fleet had scattered in the storm, no one could say.

I stared at the green blips on the main radar screen. Was it possible? Had Watson found, in hundreds of thousands of square miles of Southern Ocean, his prey? It seemed against all odds, even with the recon helicopter he'd picked up in Hobart, Tasmania, on his way south. Even with the Antarctic storm that was now veiling his approach from the unwary whalers. Even with the informer onboard the *Esperanza* who had secretly relayed the fleet's general position to Watson just two nights before. Because in those two days the fleet could have sailed 500 miles away. I looked at Watson in his red exposure suit and began to pull on my own. Watson turned to Cornelissen. "Wake all hands," he said.

IN 1986 THE INTERNATIONAL WHALING COMMISSION (IWC), a group of 66 nations that makes regulations and recommendations on whaling around the world, enacted a moratorium on open-sea commercial whaling in response to the fast declining numbers of the Earth's largest mammals. The Japanese, who have been aggressive whalers since the food shortages following World War II, immediately exploited a loophole that allows signatories to kill a certain number of whales annually for scientific research. In 2005, Japan, the only nation other than Norway and Iceland with an active whaling fleet, decided to double their "research" kill from the previous year and allot themselves a quota of 935 minke whales and ten endangered fin whales. In 2007 they plan to kill 50 fins and 50 endangered humpbacks. Their weapon is a relatively new and superefficient fleet comprising the 130-meter [427-foot] factory ship *Nisshin Maru,* two spotter vessels, and three fast killer, or harpoon, boats, similar in size to the *Farley Mowat.*

Lethal research, they say, is the only way to accurately measure whale population, health, and response to global warming and is essential for the sustainable management of the world's cetacean stocks. The director general of Japan's Institute of Cetacean Research (ICR), Hiroshi Hatanaka, writes, "The legal basis [for whaling] is very clear; the environmental basis is even clearer: The marine resources in the Southern Ocean must be utilized in a sustainable manner in order to protect and conserve them for future generations." Though the ICR is a registered nonprofit and claims no commercial benefit from its whaling, critics scoff, pointing out that the meat resulting from this heavily subsidized research ends up in Tokyo's famed Tsukiji Fish Market and on the tables of fancy restaurants. By some estimates, one fin whale can bring in 1.5 million dollars.

Each year the IWC's scientific committee votes on whaling proposals, and at its annual meeting last June, it narrowly passed a resolution that "strongly urged" Japanese whalers to obtain their scientific data "using nonlethal means." The whalers' response was silence, then business as usual.

While this resolution is not legally binding, much of the public was outraged that the whalers would patently disregard it. The World Wildlife Fund contended that all the research could be conducted more efficiently with new techniques that do not kill whales. New Zealand's minister of conservation, Chris Carter, among others, called the Japanese research blatant commercial whaling. Even dissenters within Japan protested: Greenpeace Japan's Mizuki Takana pointed to a 2002 report by the influential *Asahi* newspaper in which only 4 percent of the Japanese surveyed said they regularly eat whale meat; 53 percent of the population had not consumed it since childhood. "It is simply not true that whaling is important to the Japanese public," Takana said in a statement. "The whaling fleet should not leave for the Antarctic whale sanctuary."

To Watson there is no debate: The Japanese whalers are acting commercially under the auspices of "bogus research" and therefore are in violation of the 1986 moratorium. Even more contentious, the whaling occurs in the Southern Ocean Whale Sanctuary, an internationally ordained preserve that covers the waters surrounding Antarctica as far north as 40° S and protects 11 of the planet's 13 species of great whales. While research is permitted in the sanctuary, commercial whaling is explicitly forbidden. The whalers are also in clear conflict with the Convention on International Trade in Endangered Species (CITES). And though the killing area lies entirely within the Australian Antarctic Territory, the Australians, while protesting, seem to lack the political will to face down a powerful trading partner. It irks Watson that Australian frigates will eagerly pursue Patagonian toothfish poachers from South America in these same waters, but will turn a blind eye to the Japanese whalers. "It sends a message that if you're rich and powerful, you can break the law. If the Australian Navy were doing its job," he says, "we wouldn't be down here."

Watson has no such diplomatic compunctions. He says: "Our intention is to stop the criminal whaling. We are not a protest organization. We are here to enforce international conservation law. We don't wave banners. We intervene."

Whaling fleets around the world know he means business. Watson has sunk eight whaling ships. To the bottom of the sea. By 1980 he'd single-handedly shut down pirate whaling in the North Atlantic by sinking the notorious pirate whaler *Sierra* in Portugal and two of the four ships in the Spanish whaling fleet, the *Isba I* and *Isba II*. He sank two of Iceland's whalers in Reykjavík harbor and three of Norway's whaling fleet at dockside. To his critics he says: "I don't give a damn what you think. My clients are the whales and the seals. If you can find me one whale that disagrees with what we're doing, we might reconsider."

Watson's ship radiates both nobility and menace. The ship is black, stem to stern, and it flies under a Jolly Roger. The only color is a nod to public relations—the yellow letters on the side of the ship that spell SEASHEPHERD .ORG. Forward of the bridge, the *Farley* is low-slung, and the main deck holds three fast Zodiacs, or inflatable outboard motorboats, and two Jet Skis in their cradles. In the old fish hold beneath the deck, under a steel door, is a flying inflatable boat, or FIB, a kind of Zodiac with ultralight wings and a motor, which Watson hoped to use for reconnaissance. From the main deck, the bow sweeps up to a gracefully rounded bludgeon of black steel. The hull is ice reinforced, meaning strong enough to push through moderately thick ice, and ideal for ramming. Water cannons bristle off the bow and the aft helicopter deck. They are there to prevent unwanted boarding.

Four days out of Melbourne, the *Farley's* two welders got busy and began to build something that looked to me like a giant blade. It was. It was called the "can opener," and it was constructed with steel I beams and welded to the starboard bow; a seven-foot, razor-sharp cutter designed to gut the hull of an enemy ship.

I think it was then that I realized my assignment was not a game. Watson takes great pride in having never injured anyone, neither his crew members nor anyone else. The ships he has sunk have all been in port. He insists, "We are nonviolent. We disable property used in criminal activities." But his critics include prominent members of the mega-environmental organization Greenpeace, which Watson co-founded in 1972 and whose board he left five years later because, he says, "they wanted to 'bear witness' and protest. I didn't want to protest anymore. There were international laws, regulations, and treaties I wanted to enforce." Watson's dark eyes flash. "I once called them the 'Avon ladies of the environmental movement' and they never forgot it. It was a reference to their armies of door-to-door fund-raisers."

Watson didn't want to lead a large bureaucracy that spent much of its energy raising money and waving banners. He wanted to get in a ship and physically intervene. He said of the Antarctic campaign, "Greenpeace has a fast ship that could stop the whalers cold. I can't see watching whales being tortured and dying in abject agony while I 'bear witness.'"

In 1977 Watson started the Sea Shepherd Conservation Society and for the past 25 years has been running almost continuous campaigns at sea to stop illegal whaling, drift netting, long-lining, dolphin slaughters, and sealing. The Washington State–based organization spends no money on fund-raising but gets donations through media attention and word of mouth. Pierce Brosnan, Martin Sheen, and Christian Bale are generous supporters, as are John Paul DeJoria, CEO of the Paul Mitchell hair products company; Yvon Chouinard, founder of Patagonia; and Steve Wynn, Las Vegas hotel and casino operator. Watson quipped, "With James Bond, the President, and Batman on my side, how can I lose?"

WE SAILED OUT OF MELBOURNE on the morning of December 10, and it didn't take long for me to realize that the campaign was quixotic, even anachronistic. The 50-year-old *Farley* was ready for retirement and could average only a paltry ten knots. She crawled and rolled into the roaring forties. The ship's first engineer, Canadian Trevor VanDerGulik, ran a test of the water cannons and one dribbled, while the standpipe of another burst, gushing water over the bridge. I looked more closely at the crew. Three of the deckhands, Justin, Jeff, and Joel—"We're the J Crew," they'd told me—would be among the frontline soldiers in any battle. Though they were brave and dedicated animal rights activists, they'd never been to sea and were prostrate with motion sickness on the two-day run to Tasmania.

Not to say that some of the crew weren't skilled and experienced. Chris Aultman, the helicopter pilot from Orange County, California, was a tried and excellent pilot when taking off from solid ground—he'd just never flown off a moving deck. VanDerGulik, Watson's nephew, was a master ship's engineer used to supervising large dry-dock repairs with 500 mechanics under him. Marc Oosterwal, another Dutchman, was a top-notch welder. And Dave DeGraaff was a master electrician from Melbourne and a shop steward for his union, responsible for dozens of electricians. He and other workers had seen the *Farley* docked from a high-rise construction site nearby and got curious. DeGraaff took a tour of the ship and promptly signed on. Soon more construction unions in Melbourne were lining up behind Sea Shepherd, and thousands of dollars' worth of steel, welding rods, and expensive rubber for the heli-deck was showing up daily.

As for other crew members, the razor edge of their commitment scared me a little. Allison Lance Watson, the captain's wife, a lean 48-year-old blonde from Orange County who had once been married to an outlaw biker, had recently gone before a grand jury in connection with the Animal Liberation Front (ALF), a radical animal rights group that is in the sights of the FBI's domestic antiterrorism units. She refused to talk but was charged with perjury. Two years ago, she and first mate Cornelissen were arrested for leaping with knives into a frigid, net-caged bay in Taiji, Japan, where locals corral and slaughter an estimated 23,000 dolphins every year. They freed some dolphins and were promptly carted off by police. Both claim they would sacrifice their own lives for the life of a whale without hesitation. Julie Farris (whose alias, or "forest name," as she calls it, is Inde) was a 26-year-old deckhand who, in her other life, spends weeks at a time dangling 150 feet up in Douglas-fir trees as part of Earth First actions against logging. Many of the crew had been arrested while protesting in support of their beliefs. It was a committed bunch. Oh, and the food, three meals a day, was strictly vegan. No meat, no cheese, no eggs. One cold morning I loaned the gentle 22-year-old cook, Laura Dakin, a pair of shoes. A former Australian equestrian endurance rider, she had come to the Antarctic with only flip-flops, a flowing print skirt, and a lip ring. Before taking them, she asked, "Are they vegan?"

The Sea Shepherd's courage and rashness began to dawn on me. Watson was taking this rusting hulk into the most dangerous, remote seas on Earth to wage a kind of war. A place where a man overboard had minutes to live. Half of his troops had no training at all. Before leaving, his only plan for finding the Japanese whaling fleet in the vast Southern Ocean was to run helicopter reconnaissance flights and hope crews supplying the various Antarctic research stations would give him intel. Contact with Greenpeace's two pursuit ships was the best hope, but the organization responded to Watson's repeated pleas for cooperation by keeping its ships' coordinates off its Web site. Watson believed it was a deliberate attempt to foil him and his radical methods.

What Greenpeace wasn't counting on was that some of the rank and file on board their ships were also frustrated and disgusted by what they were witnessing every day. The killing of a whale by the most modern methods is cruel beyond description. An exploding harpoon, meant to kill quickly, rarely does more than rupture the whale's organs. The animal thrashes and gushes blood and begins to drown in its own hemorrhage. It is winched to the side of the harpoon ship, a probe is jabbed into it, and thousands of volts of electricity are run through the animal in an attempt to kill it faster. The whale screams and cries and thrashes. If it is a mother, its calf swims wildly beside her, doomed to its own motherless death later on. Often the electricity fails to dispatch the whale, so it takes 15 to 20 minutes of this torture before it drowns and dies. No matter what one thinks of whales' high intelligence, the advanced social structures, the obvious emotions, and the still mysterious ability to communicate over long distances, this method of slaughter would not be allowed as standard practice in any slaughterhouse in the world. This is what the Greenpeace crew had been watching day after day and were constrained from stopping. One of the crew had had enough and began to e-mail Watson with sporadic updates of the fleet's position.

This is how Watson knew, within a few thousand square miles, where the fleet might be on Christmas morning.

AT 3:50 A.M. ON SUNDAY, DECEMBER 25, 220 miles north-northeast of Antarctica's Adélie Coast, the *Farley* labored up the back of a 35-foot wave and plunged down the other side. Green water poured over the bow and flew up in a white explosion that battered the windows. We were running with the gale. It howled out of the south-southeast. The ship creaked like frozen trees in a blow.

I was wedged against a small chart table and a bulkhead on the port side of the bridge, straining to see into the fog and thinking that my family on the other side of the dateline was just now gathering for Christmas Eve lunch. In the midst of the storm's fury, an intense and eerie quiet had come over the bridge. After many months of preparation and planning, Watson was sneaking up on two vessels in a vast, empty sea in a near hurricane. The radio was silent. No one spoke. Hunter had become hunted and the bridge held the taut expectation of ambush.

Ahead I saw a dark shape in the murk. It was Greenpeace's *Esperanza,* a former Russian fire-fighting ship, moving slowly with the waves, under seven knots, riding out the storm. As we closed and passed, I could see the bright blue of her hull and her festive rainbow paint job. She looked like the *Life Aquatic* ship on steroids. We left her behind and she was swallowed in the fog.

A few minutes later we saw it. Through the mist the huge bulk of the factory ship. First just a dark shape, then the spillway ramp cut into her stern where they winched up the dead whales, the tall white superstructure of her cranes, and the words NISSHIN MARU, TOKYO. Running down the length of her hull, visible when she corkscrewed on a swell, was RESEARCH, in large block letters.

She was a sitting duck. Almost idling at 6.8 knots, riding it out. They had to have seen us moving up on the radar, but they must've figured we were the *Arctic Sunrise,* Greenpeace's other boat, a matter of no concern. Nobody had even bothered to look. I couldn't believe it. We were pulling alongside her stern.

Cornelissen, at the helm, looked level at his captain. "Do we want to ram them? Punch a few holes in their ship?"

"No, we'd sustain a lot of damage. I think the best tactic here, Alex, is the prop foulers." Watson said he didn't think the *Nisshin* could go too much faster in these seas. He wanted to cut across her bow and deploy the prop foulers— long strands of rope, steel cables, and buoys that would slip under her hull and catch and tangle her propeller.

"We could ram her up the spillway if you want. What do you say, Paul?"

"No, we're gonna do this."

He turned to VanDerGulik. "Tell them to get the prop foulers ready on the stern. Tell them to stay down, stay hidden. Don't deploy them until I blow the horn."

I looked at Watson. He seemed to be protecting his crew. No sane person wanted a collision in these seas.

Just then the whalers woke up. I can only imagine how the *Farley* must have looked materializing out of the fog and mountainous seas: an all-black ship running under a gale-stiffened Jolly Roger. It was as if the *Nisshin Maru* jumped in surprise. Someone put the hammer down and she began to pull away off our port side.

"OK," Watson said to Cornelissen. "Do it if you can. Up the spillway."

It was too late. VanDerGulik, the first engineer, had the engines tweaked, and the *Farley* was straining with all she had, 11, 11.6, 12 knots. But the *Nisshin* was too powerful. She came up to speed and began to flee at 14 knots.

And then her skipper seemed to snap. Captain D. Toyama had been whaling in the Antarctic for decades. He had been harassed for weeks by Greenpeace. Its Zodiacs swarmed his killer boats. His harpooners had shot whales right over their heads. And here, out of the fog, was a ship with a terrifying reputation. He'd had enough. A quarter mile away, I watched in amazement as the *Nisshin* turned to starboard, angled across our bow, and slowed down. Toyama seemed to be saying, "OK, you wanna mess with me? Bring it on."

Cornelissen matched the turn, about 30 degrees of it, so as not to fall behind the *Nisshin*'s stern, and set a collision course. I watched him. He was completely calm. So was Watson, who stood with a hand on the lever that controlled our speed looking relaxed. This wasn't his first rodeo. He had been shot at and depth charged by the Norwegian Navy. And he'd faced down a Soviet frigate off Siberia, refusing to halt with the Soviets just yards away and about to let loose with machine guns; the sudden, miraculous appearance of a gray whale surfacing between the two vessels defused the standoff.

Now we caught the crossing seas on our starboard side, and the *Farley* slammed over to port in a 40-degree roll that sent a videographer crashing across the bridge. The *Farley* righted and slammed to the other side. Cornelissen looked at the radar. He turned to the boatswain, Kalifi Ferretti-Gallon, a fey 22-year-old from Montreal who happened to be his girlfriend, and said, "Tell the crew, collision in two minutes."

Most of the crew was gathered in the mess in their exposure suits, aft of mid-ship, below the deck, and a long hallway away from the main hatch exit.

The *Nisshin Maru* was on our port side, and the two ships approached each other at an acute angle. In a typical collision situation, the law of the sea dictated that we had the right-of-way, as we were on her starboard. I watched with awe as the *Nisshin*'s bow, as tall as a three-story building, lunged off a 35-foot wave, airborne, and crashed down like a giant ax. The hole it tore out of the sea vaporized, the spray driven downwind. The gap closed. Three hundred yards, 200. Now we could hear the blare of the *Nisshin*'s horn through the tearing gale. Repeated blasts, short and long, enraged.

"Collision, one minute."

I remember reaching down and tugging on the waterproof zipper of my dry suit and having one very clear simple thought: You're going to be wet and cold in about 20 seconds. The hammering bow loomed, 200 feet away, aimed mid-ships, at our belly.

It was the most impressive sight I've ever seen. Cornelissen glanced at the radar, then at the juggernaut, and held his course. He was focused, intent. A deadly game of Antarctic chicken. One hundred fifty feet away. He blew the horn, which was the order to unleash the prop foulers. A squad on the stern stood, braced themselves, and whipped several hundred feet of mooring line off a big spool, enough to tangle any propeller.

And then the *Nisshin* blinked. Whoever was at their helm threw it hard to port. For an agonizing second the two ships ran parallel, and then the Japanese were pulling away, fleeing back into the fog. As they ran, Watson pulled down the mic on maritime channel 16, and barked, "*Nisshin Maru, Nisshin Maru,* this is the *Farley Mowat.* You are in violation of an international whale sanctuary. We advise you to get out. Time to go now, you murdering scumbags. Now move it! And run like the cowards you are."

I looked at my watch: 5:42 a.m.

Everybody breathed. Later I pulled Cornelissen aside.

"If we had collided," I asked, "Would we have been badly damaged?"

Cornelissen is always in motion, but when he stops, he gives you all his attention. "A ship that's ten times as heavy as your own ship," he said, "that hits you midships with its bow—it's gonna basically slice your ship in half. It will completely destroy your ship in a matter of seconds. Everybody inside would have had a very hard time getting out."

I nodded. "There was a point there where it was up to him whether we were T-boned or not."

"Yes, he definitely had that choice and he didn't take it. If he would've ended it there, that would've probably ended commercial whaling. But I still believe that not sacrificing people for that, in that way, is probably a better choice."

"But personally for you as an activist, you're willing to make that choice every day? You're willing to make that trade-off: your own life for, say, stopping whaling?"

"Absolutely. But I'm not going to engage in a suicide mission. It's gotta be a calculated risk."

I turned to the captain. He said, "We've won every game of chicken we've ever played."

Peeling off my dry suit, I let the adrenaline wash through me. I thought, Watson is the anti-Ahab. More bearish, more charming, but just as terrifying in his fearlessness and in his willingness to put everything on the line, including our lives, to save the whales.

By 6:05 a.m. the ever media-savvy Watson already had a press release posted on his Web site that began: "No whale will be killed on Christmas Day."

A certain somberness took over the ship. The storm raged. Watson showed me the weather fax. "Looks like a freight train," he chuckled. "Never really seen one like it." A line of five *l*'s for "low"—tightly packed storm systems—marched one after another west to east along the 62nd parallel. We turned south again, both to shake the storms and because Watson knew that the Japanese would eventually return to the edge of the ice cap, where the whales were most numerous. The skies lifted a little, and we sailed into a landscape that reminded me of Monument Valley, except that the flat-topped monoliths scattered across the horizon were great blue-shadowed icebergs.

That night in my bunk, I lay in the dark and thought about the exchange the Sea Shepherd Conservation Society had just invited the whalers to make: all hands lost for the end of Japanese whaling. I knew that to much of the world, Watson would be deemed insane. Maybe he was. Certainly, from the bridge of the *Nisshin Maru,* watching the much smaller ship hold its course to the brink of destruction must have sent a chill of cold horror through her officers. Honor was one thing, murder and suicide on the high seas another. But I also thought about the whales, swimming tonight in their pods through the islands of ice, families and groups of families, in numbers that for many species are just a tiny fraction of what they were just a hundred years ago. I thought about a whale Watson had tried to save from a harpoon off Siberia, that in a struggle for life had crashed down beside his Zodiac. Just before death, the animal pulled itself deliberately away so as not to crush the little boat, protecting Watson as if it understood that he was there to help. I did not think Watson was exactly insane.

Countries around the world pledged to protect the whales and codified that promise in treaties and regulations, and yet the protections were all on paper. In reality the whales of the Southern Ocean, of all the oceans, were as vulnerable as if there had been no treaties at all. The Japanese whalers allotted themselves whatever number they wished to kill, endangered and nonendangered species alike, and they came down and took them. They shot them right over Greenpeace's head. The whales could not advocate for themselves. They had no ally on the entire planet that was willing to intervene at all costs, even death, except Watson and Sea Shepherd. Human beings are willing to lay down their lives for territory, resources, national honor, religion. Why not for another species?

Whatever one said about Watson's methods, they were relatively effective. His campaigns against the English, Irish, and Scottish seal hunts in the early eighties helped shut them down for good. His battle against the Canadian seal hunt, which brought Brigitte Bardot to the ice for her famous picture, helped end the slaughter of baby harp seals in 1987. Still, Newfoundland sealers killed more than 300,000 adults last year, 98 percent of those under three months old. Watson is philosophical and dogged in his fight for threatened species. He says, "The victories are always temporary but the defeats [extinctions] are permanent."

JANUARY 2, MIDNIGHT. The constant harassment was getting to the whalers. They had been running for eight days, ever since the encounter on Christmas. The informer on the *Esperanza* said the *Nisshin Maru* was moving erratically, generally west, and that they were not whaling. There was no sign of the killer ships. He said they seemed afraid.

The black *Farley* was lumbering steadily westward along Antarctica's frozen edge in a world of fog and ice where squads of Adélie penguins swam with great speed. When the skies cleared, Chris Aultman took me on a three-hour chopper reconnaissance along the ice edge. The world below was black-and-white. Pure and lonely. That's what it is about Antarctica: You are either hot-blooded and hungry or you are a cold element. You are water or ice. There is no middle ground here, no compromise. It seemed apt. In Watson's war on the whalers, there were no conditions for truce.

A week before, Hatanaka of Japan's Institute of Cetacean Research sent an open letter to the head of Greenpeace Japan: "The Sea Shepherd boat, the *Farley Mowat,* has already foolhardily tried to approach the *Nisshin Maru* and deployed a mooring line with the intent of entwining her propeller. These are extremely dangerous actions. It is widely known that Sea Shepherd has engaged in criminal and violent activity in the past, such as setting fire to and sinking whaling vessels in Iceland and Norway and fishing vessels in Spain and other countries. Sea Shepherd is a terrorist organization. . . ." The Japanese government was rumored to be sending down a warship.

Ian Campbell, Australia's environment minister, said Watson's threats to attack the Japanese fleet reflected poorly on legitimate antiwhaling groups and "risk setting back the cause of whale conservation many years."

Greenpeace disavowed any link with Sea Shepherd. In a press release, Watson countered that "the enemy of my enemy is my ally" and that it was the whalers who were the criminals, violating, by his count, at least six international laws. Claiming authority under the UN World Charter for Nature, he ordered the whaling fleet to return to Japan. Articles by the Associated Press, and in the *Washington Post,* the *Guardian,* the *Australian,* and the *New Zealand Herald,* among others, trumpeted all sides of the developing whale war.

Watson was in his element. With every media and government attack he seemed to get friskier, firing off press releases that said, "The [Australian] government says that the Japanese do not recognize the Australian claim to the Antarctic Treaty. In 1942 they did not recognize Australia's claim to Australia." Talk about hot buttons. If he wanted to stir the pot, he was.

On the chugging *Farley,* the pace slowed. Laura Dakin, in the kitchen, cooked up vegan sausages and chocolate cake while the crew assembled in the lounge to watch *Miss Congeniality* and *Forces of Nature* in surround sound. (The ship's artist, Geert Vons, had a crush on Sandra Bullock.) The deckhands sorted smoke bombs and manufactured prop foulers. The J Crew, who, it turns out, were all semiprofessional gamblers from Syracuse, New York, played endless rounds of Texas hold 'em. We even had a haiku contest to pass the time. The winner, by Kristian Olsen, described the overloading of a Zodiac in Hobart on a run to get cases of beer: "Hobart. Beer falls in. / Splash. That's rum. Lost one boat too. / Saving whales is hard."

During these quiet moments, Watson enjoyed torturing the young officers of his watch by blaring Celtic and Canadian folk music from the bridge. He sat in his captain's chair, feet up on the sill, and read from his own writings. Raised on the rocky coast of New Brunswick, Canada, Watson is an autodidact who ran away to join a Norwegian merchant ship when he was 17. He has published five books and is in the process of writing four more. One of his works in progress is a scholarly history of the papacy, another a treatise on organized religion, called *God's Monkey House.*

On January 5, Watson got a message from his insider on the *Esperanza* placing the fleet at 63° 45′ S, 72° 20′ E, along with the simple message, "They're killing whales today."

There were several astonishing things about this news. One was that the whaling fleet was so far to the west. They had run to the very western edge of their "research area," which was at 70° E, north of Cape Darnley. Watson said, "They can't go much farther. They've run for 3,000 miles. I can only think they're running from us." The second startling inference was that the Japanese had not whaled since at least Christmas Day. For 11 days no whales had been killed. Third, they were more than 700 miles from our current position, and we were running low enough on fuel to keep VanDerGulik sounding the tanks and repeatedly calculating the distance to Cape Town—about 20 days. The safest thing would be to return immediately to Perth, about 18 days away. But Watson rarely did the safe thing. "Two and a half days and we'll get 'em," he said, then ordered Cornelissen to keep moving west.

ON JANUARY 6, the U.S. Office of Naval Intelligence detailed the *Farley Mowat*'s run-in with the *Nisshin Maru* on its piracy watch. Online I found the ONI report: There was Sea Shepherd on the Civil Maritime Analysis Department's communiqué titled "Worldwide Threat to Shipping Mariner Warning Information." At the same time, Watson's mole on the *Esperanza* reported 13 minke whales and one endangered fin whale killed that day. In New Zealand, the whaling controversy was the top story on television news, and the minister of conservation, Chris Carter, said, "the program the Japanese are undertaking in the Southern Ocean is not about science, it's about hunting and killing whales to supply meat markets." He added that New Zealand would be upping the pressure on Japan to stop whaling and that the New Zealand Air Force would be sending Orion surveillance aircraft to monitor their activities.

I went out onto the main deck to clear my head. The engine throbbed. The fog had lifted and the seas were as calm as they'd been the entire trip, a gentle roll out of the southwest. Then I saw it: a plume of mist just off the starboard bow, and another, smaller. A long, mottled lateral fin gestured out of the water, and I saw the two glossy dark backs, mother and calf, dive under the boat, the mother's articulated, graceful fluke disappearing last. Farther off starboard were three more blows, the hot mist trailing gently downwind. Behind them were more and more. Spouts of steam rising and drifting. I stared, almost stricken. All the way to the horizon, where two flat-topped icebergs marked the edge of the world, were humpback whales swimming slowly east. Pairs and small groups rolled around each other, showing fins, flukes, eyes, and then moved on. They swam past the boat on both sides. Hundreds of whales. Could they know? Could they be swimming away from their hunters to the west? They were not concerned with us at all.

JANUARY 8 WAS A GOOD DAY TO DIE. For the crew of the vegan pirate ship the *Farley Mowat*, that was the consensus. The morning brightened over a sea of silk and glass. On the port and starboard Zodiacs, the tarps were off, the prop foulers coiled and stowed; the crew had been manufacturing them night and day. The Jolly Roger was raised and flapped lazily over the bow.

At 10:15 a.m. the main radar was lit up with ships. At 10:59 the factory ship *Nisshin Maru* was visible, long and dark, lying across the mirrorlike water. It wasn't moving. The *Esperanza* was there to the south of it, hanging some distance away. We came out of the east at 9.5 knots, heading straight for the target. At 11:47, with the gap narrowed to under four miles, an irate Scandinavian-accented voice exploded onto channel 16: "You idiot! Read the rules! Read the rules! Get out of the [expletive] way!" It was the usually courteous Arne Sorensen, captain of Greenpeace's *Arctic Sunrise*. Then we saw a curious thing. From behind the huge factory ship appeared another ship, also black-hulled and just as big. It moved away to the south, to our left. Two harpoon vessels, on their way in when the *Farley* showed up, slipped out of radar range.

What we found out later was that the big freighter was the cargo ship *Oriental Bluebird*. It had been tied up to the *Nisshin,* and they were in the middle of transferring whale meat from the factory ship for transport back to Japan. Since the whalers had doubled their quota from the year before, they did not have enough room on the vast *Nisshin* to store the tons of meat they were harvesting. It was a startling illustration of the scale of the hunt.

Greenpeace was bearing witness to the transfer and protesting by maneuvering the *Arctic Sunrise* near the *Bluebird* and sending in Zodiacs to paint her side with long-handled brushes: WHALE MEAT FROM SANCTUARY, in big white letters. The Japanese ignored them and continued loading—until Sea Shepherd came into visual range. Then they panicked. They dropped the lines, and in the ensuing rush to disengage and run, they rammed Greenpeace's *Arctic Sunrise*. An e-mail from the informer on the *Esperanza* to Watson said, "Very frustrating indeed. All of this right under our noses, because they know we will not ram or endanger them. At least when you show up, they run like cowards!"

They did. They ran. From the bridge, Watson watched the *Nisshin* gather speed and charge north, the *Oriental Bluebird* fled east. From a window he yelled, "OK! Get moving!" He slowed the *Farley* long enough to lower the port and starboard Zodiacs into the sea, then throttled ahead as soon as the 18-foot rubber boats unhooked and sped away. He liked to blast Wagner's "Ride of the Valkyries" from the big outside speakers in times like these, but the gale had shorted the speakers. Two minutes later the helicopter lifted off the heli-deck, tilted hard forward and accelerated toward the fray. Up ahead we could see two orange Greenpeace Zodiacs in the water and its orange Hughes 500 chopper circling overhead. It was a melee. At 9.5 knots all the *Farley* could do now was follow and watch as the fastest Zodiac ate up the distance. The *Nisshin* was clearly expecting a fight—its water cannons were blasting steadily over the stern and sides.

"Our Zodiac is going 30 knots," Cornelissen said from the main radar screen.

The second, slower Zodiac, came behind it. We watched as the first caught up to the *Nisshin,* skirting the veil of blasting water from the cannons. The second reached the side of the ship. Its crew threw two prop foulers against the hull, and then the temperamental old outboard began to balk.

For a ship the size of the *Nisshin,* there is no way to replace a fouled prop; the parts are too massive. In the event one was disabled, the ship and her crew would have to be towed to the nearest port. The process could take weeks, and the rest of the fleet, devoid of a cargo ship, would have to return home. That was Watson's hope. Wessel-Louis Jacobsz, 24, a South African master scuba diver and captain of the first Zodiac, was going to do whatever he could to make that happen. Through binoculars I watched as he ran the Zodiac up under the bow of the ship. Even on the smooth water there was a low swell, and the outboard hit those waves and skipped airborne. The prow of the *Nisshin* towered over the little boat, pushing up a bow wave that the Zodiac rode. The whalers tried to stab the inflatable with flensing knives on long poles (for processing whale meat), but couldn't; Jacobsz and crew were under the overhang of the bow and too far away. At times the Zodiac was no more than a man's length from the *Nisshin*'s nose. J Crew Joel Capolongo, 29, and former 101st Airborne soldier Steve Sikes, 31, deployed the prop foulers. When they'd released them all, they tied a piece of scrap steel to a buoy with a long cable and threw that over as well. Then Jacobsz slid the Zodiac away in a swooping arc and circled to the stern where they picked up the buoy and sped forward to deploy it again. A false move and they'd be flattened under the *Nisshin Maru* like so much roadkill.

Two hours later, lagging farther and farther behind, Watson called the Zodiacs back to the *Farley.* None of the prop foulers had engaged. By 3:30 p.m. the *Nisshin* was 16 miles away and fleeing at 14 knots. The Japanese fleet had vanished in all directions. The sun began its slide to the horizon and reefs of clouds lowered in from the north and east. The seas doubled in height every hour.

That night, steep swells churned in from the east. Whole wheat chapatis and poker chips slid off the tables. Snow blew horizontally across the decks. Sleepers were thrown from their bunks. Watson came on watch at 8 a.m. and the *Farley* moved gingerly into a sea of scattered icebergs and fog. At 9:05 the captain was lecturing the bridge on the fall of Jerusalem during the Crusades. "The Templars and the Knights of St. John couldn't take it. The guy who finally

took Jerusalem was an excommunicant from the church . . ." When the quar-
termaster reported the new blip on the screen Watson swiveled in his chair.

"Range?"

"Sixteen miles, sir."

"Speed?"

"Ten knots."

The fog was so dense, it wasn't until we were 1.6 miles away that we could
see the black shape extending from behind the island of ice. I scanned with
binoculars and made out the white letters that I knew said WHALE MEAT FROM
SANCTUARY along the starboard side. The *Oriental Bluebird*.

They never moved. I'll never know why. Cornelissen was woken up and
took the helm. He turned to his girlfriend, the boatswain: "Tell everyone we're
gonna hit. Seven minutes." The crew was ordered to the higher decks and
armed with smoke bombs and bottles of butyric acid, which are mega stink
bombs. I thought how Sea Shepherd actions always seemed like a strange mix
of a Jack Aubrey attack and *Animal House*.

A few hundred yards from the freighter Watson took over the helm. He
aimed midships and charged full speed. We were bow to bow, starboard to starboard. Just before contact he threw the wheel over to port so the can opener—
the seven-foot steel blade on the starboard bow—raked the *Bluebird*'s side. The
Farley lurched with impact. There was an agonizing claw-scrape of steel and
then another shove as the stern swung in and hit. The can opener crumpled,
leaving a long scratch in the *Bluebird*'s thick hull like a keyed car. Watson
picked up the mic: "*Oriental Bluebird*, or should I say, the S.S. *Whale Meat*,
please remove yourself from these waters. You're in violation of international
conservation regulations. You are in a whale sanctuary, and you are assisting an
illegal activity. Remove yourself from these waters immediately."

At the same time he swung to port in a tight arc and came back across the
freighter's bow. The prop-fouling squad was ready to run out mooring line off
the stern and lay a tangler across the ship's path. By now the *Bluebird* was fleeing.
Again I watched in awe as Watson drove the *Farley* within 60 feet of its high,
hammering bow. It was like running a red light in front of a moving semi. Had
the *Bluebird* kept up her speed, she would have T-boned and sunk us. It was as
if that's what Watson was tempting her to do. But their skipper, in all prudence,
jammed his engines into reverse and groaned past our stern. The deckhands
released the fouling line, but it did not get sucked up. By the time Watson could
get around again, the *Bluebird* was running due north at 15 knots. He turned to
the officers on the bridge. "We need to come back with a faster ship," he said.

The international reaction was immediate. The Japan Whaling Association's president, Keiichi Nakajima, accused Sea Shepherd of being "circus performers" and "dangerous vegans." The *Age* newspaper out of Melbourne reported that Japan was considering scrambling police aircraft to the Antarctic to defend its whaling fleet and might ask Australia for protection. The Maritime Union of New Zealand announced that it would not service any Japanese ships having anything to do with whaling. On a live round table broadcast shown across Australia with Watson (participating via satellite phone), Australian Environment Minister Ian Campbell, and others, Watson was aggressively unrepentant.

"It is a criminal operation, it's illegal, it has no business being there," he railed. "There's no difference between them and ivory poachers or drug traffickers."

Campbell fired back that Watson was a "lunatic" and a "rogue pirate on the seas." Watson dispatched a press release that he would stop his attacks if the governments of New Zealand and Australia would initiate legal action to stop the whaling. Campbell scoffed. Watson issued a press release saying, "Let's get serious; this guy is lame."

But the truth was, Watson had no more attacks to launch. His old ship was nearly out of fuel. VanDerGulik came onto the bridge in his blue coveralls, decibel-reducing earmuffs propped on his head, and said, "We might make it to Cape Town on fumes if we don't encounter too much bad weather."

On January 10 the *Farley Mowat* turned away from the whales and limped northward into another gale. There was nothing more she could do. The Japanese could hunt again without intervention. I spent days by the stern chains watching the acrobatics of the petrels and albatross. The rougher the weather got, the more fun the birds seemed to have. I thought they were like Watson. One image from the trip kept coming back to me. It was when Chris Aultman took me up in the chopper, and we ran along the desolate false coast of the ice edge. Returning to the ship, we climbed to 4,000 feet and ran across open water into a sheen of low sun. Then I saw the ship, a jaunty, compact, black shadow on the taut blue sea that curved to the horizon. It looked so completely self-sufficient and alone.

MAY 2006

PLACES OF DARKNESS

By Kira Salak

---

*In the northeast region of war-torn Congo, volunteers have risked—and lost—
their lives for decades to save the mountain gorilla. As poaching and encroachment accelerated at an unsustainable rate, one reporter raised an uncomfortable
question: When is a primate's life worth more than a human's?*

I. Rutshuru, North Kivu Province,
Democratic Republic of the Congo (DRC)

"How are your gorillas?" Colonel Bonane asks. The brigade commandante
of the RCD (Congolese Rally for Democracy) rebel forces terrorizing eastern
Congo, he steps out of a night so complete and starless that it is as if the
darkness itself has produced him. Well over six feet tall, wearing camouflage
fatigues with a green beret folded neatly under an epaulette, he has the powerful, arresting physique of a warrior. All of us—including the park warden, a
Congolese mountain-gorilla conservationist named Vital who is acting as my
interpreter, and an RCD official assigned to monitor me—stumble out of our
plastic chairs, give deferential bows, smile lavishly and painstakingly. We need
the colonel to like us. This man can, with a word, save or destroy us.

Bonane is pleased by our display, entreats us to sit down, make ourselves comfortable. "And you," he demands in French of me. "Why are you here?" There is
instant silence around the table; his officers level sharp, steady stares at me.

Vital jumps in, explaining that I'm a journalist come to Congo, to their
war, in order to see the mountain gorillas. Or, at least, what's left of them. I
don't reveal my own, deeper interest: that I'd like to know what motivates
people, such as the late Dian Fossey, to save these animals in an area of the
world that seems hell-bent on its own destruction.

"Ah, the gorillas!" Bonane laughs. His laugh is deep, resolute, like the crack of a whip. We all come to attention at its sound, wait for whatever is expected of us. "The gorillas!" Bonane exclaims. "I love the gorillas!" He grins and sits back in his chair. His men squeal in laughter: It is a joke. All of the men with me, many of whom have devoted their lives to saving the rare gorillas and who work for the Dian Fossey Gorilla Fund Europe (DFGFE), laugh along with him. You do not want to piss off the colonel.

Overhead, a single fluorescent bulb hums and spits out light; large moths dive into it like kamikazes. The RCD soldiers eye me, their AK-47s leaning daintily against their chairs like parasols. I glare back at them, match their filmy gazes with my own. I don't know what's a more incongruous sight in this seedy outdoor restaurant in this war-exhausted town: a white journalist interested in the gorillas, or a woman. The women in these parts are noticeably absent after dark; they hide themselves to avoid being gang-raped by drunken RCD soldiers. The RCD has almost total control of this area, and I know that only the official presence of the town mayor (a high-ranking RCD crony) and the RCD government monitor keeps me in a safe, hands-off status. My two protectors are starting into yet another large bottle of Primus beer, slurring their words, sharing *mzungu* (white person) jokes with some of the soldiers nearby. I look into the darkness to the south, where the gorillas are. I wonder if they are hiding, cringing in the shadows of their jungle home. I know I would be.

It is hard to talk about the mountain gorillas and not talk about the chaos surrounding them. Perhaps more than that of any other animal on Earth, these creatures' fate is inexorably tied to war. There are only about 650 of them left. Fewer than half are in Uganda's Bwindi Impenetrable National Park bordering Congo; the others reside farther south in the Virunga Mountains, on a mere 166 square miles of protected land where Rwanda, Uganda, and the Democratic Republic of the Congo (formerly Zaire) meet. Both populations live in the heart of one of the world's most violent and unstable regions, a place rife with corruption and greed, with unchecked exploitation of natural resources and an unfathomable disregard for human life. It was in 1994 that the world got its first enduring taste of this region with the Rwandan genocide. The conflict spilled into neighboring countries as the Hutu militias, known collectively as the Interahamwe—whose war with the minority Tutsi tribe left about 800,000 dead in 100 days—fled into the jungles of eastern Congo to regroup and launch further cross-border assaults. Rwanda and Uganda sent their armies in after them in 1996, ushering in the Congolese civil war. It is a conflict that drew in the armies of Zimbabwe, Angola, Namibia, and other countries, and has created an unending nightmare for the UN. Only educated guesses about the number of dead can be made in a region that hasn't had an official census since 1984, but it is estimated that the war has claimed as many as 4.7 million people—the worst reported loss of life in an armed conflict since World War II.

And the war shows no sign of stopping. Local tribes, assorted militia groups, and clandestine army factions from neighboring countries have found the fighting lucrative beyond all expectation. In a country like Congo, where the average person can expect to earn no more than $120 a year, fortunes are made hourly by whoever controls mineral-rich areas. More profitable than gold or diamonds is the rare substance columbite-tantalite, known as coltan, an essential ingredient in microchips and cell phones. Found almost exclusively in eastern Congo, it can bring in $400 per kilo on the international market, giving rebel factions and neighboring governments a financial reason to keep the war going indefinitely. Only when the Congolese conflict caused a temporary suspension of coltan mining did the Western world feel the reverberations of a war it had all but forgotten: Sony was forced to delay the launch of its PlayStation 2.

As for the mountain gorillas, the animals have so far been blessed: The mineral hasn't yet been found in their habitat. Where it has been found— most notably in the eastern Congolese park Kahuzi-Biega—the population of eastern lowland gorillas has been decimated by as much as 90 percent and the park's jungle elephants, once numbered at 350, are down to *two*. With so much wealth being pulled out of the ground, no one, neither human nor animal, is safe. "Once the gorillas cross into unprotected [Congolese] areas, we don't know what will happen to them," says Fortunate Muyambi, field staff coordinator for the Mountain Gorilla Conservation Fund (MGCF) in Uganda. If the war goes on, he says, "there will be extinction in a very short time."

The main reason for the animals' continued survival is the tourist dollars they bring in to the area. Quite simply, they have been worth more alive than dead. In Rwanda and Uganda, prewar gorilla tourism was a significant source of revenue. Back when it was still Zaire, Congo had a thriving, lucrative tourist industry that included upscale lodges, gorilla safaris, and jungle treks. Now, with the lodges destroyed, the hiking trails frequented by the genocidal Interahamwe, and tourists banned altogether, Congo has lost all of its revenue from the gorillas—and thus the incentive to safeguard them. Though there is a national park authority, in eastern Congo it is run by RCD-appointed

bureaucrats. Vital, a straight-talking ecologist who recently won a conservation award from the BBC, explained it to me bluntly: "It's a crony government. These people don't have any interest in conservation. The first purpose
of RCD officials is achieving economic gain." The RCD does not want its
exploitation of the parks publicized or interrupted—hence the man sent to
monitor my every interview, to keep me always within his sight. I am not supposed to let my focus waver from the gorillas.

Before I came to Africa, I spoke with a representative of Doctors Without Borders who criticized the way people give more attention to the plight
of the mountain gorilla than they do to the tragedy of the human beings. It
seemed a valid and important concern. Can the gorillas' story of survival be
seen as a classic parable of hope? Of grace rising like the spring of new leaves
from a landscape devastated by war? The thought is grossly romantic, makes
me shake my head before Bonane and his men. Grace? *Here?* I know this: A
staggering 82 Congolese park rangers have been killed since the war started,
making mountain-gorilla conservation one of the most dangerous professions
on Earth. Yet the people who have devoted everything to work with these animals tell me that there is something ineffable about them. One Rwandan park
ranger, named Jean-Bosco Bizumuremyi, who endured an Interahamwe attack
to return to his gorillas—he showed me a machete scar across the top of his
head—said, "Unlike us, the gorillas do not try to kill each other."

Colonel Bonane sees me writing in my notebook, and he waves angrily at
me, issues an immediate decree. An apologetic Vital whispers in fervent English: "Stop! Don't write anymore! Close that book."

I close it.

Bonane sighs and waxes nostalgic: "Ah, the gorillas . . ."

LATER IN THE EVENING, in the dank cement cell of a room where I'm spending the night in Rutshuru, chair propped against the door, my knife out on the
table beside me and opened to the largest blade, I reread Dian Fossey's *Gorillas
in the Mist*. Fossey was the first person to launch a crusade to save the gorillas,
under the tutelage of the famous paleontologist Louis Leakey, back in 1966.
With very limited funds, she went alone into the Congolese Virungas to set
up a base camp to study what was then a dwindling population of only 240
animals. Even then, she observed that "one of the greatest drawbacks of the
Virungas is that it is shared by three countries, each of which has problems far
more urgent than the protection of wild animals." After barely a year in her
new home, she was forced to flee when war broke out. She soon returned to

the Rwandan Virungas, to set up the now world famous Karisoke Research Center. To pay for increased patrols in the Virungas, she established the Digit Fund, named after her favorite silverback, who had been killed by poachers.

I met Fossey's successor Ruth Keesling in the lobby of the posh Hotel des Milles Collines in Rwanda's capital, Kigali. Shortly after Fossey's death in 1985—two assailants, believed to be local poachers, killed Fossey with a machete blow to the head—Keesling took over the Digit Fund, changing the name to the Dian Fossey Gorilla Fund Europe. These days, she runs the Mountain Gorilla Conservation Fund. Flashing bright brown eyes and an impish grin, the 73-year-old Keesling greeted me with the unwavering energy you'd expect to find in a woman half her age. For the past 19 years, the American has made frequent pilgrimages to Rwanda and Uganda in order to meet with the leaders of both countries and negotiate on the gorillas' behalf. If in-your-face coercion was Dian Fossey's specialty, Keesling's secret weapon is congeniality. Having experienced firsthand the rare influence she had over people, I could think only this: Here is someone who can get anything she wants. Which has been good news for the gorillas. Though few outside of animal conservation know her by name, her campaign has been one of the main reasons why the gorillas have survived into the 21st century.

Most notably, she hasn't let central Africa's unrest stop her. "I don't worry about things like that," she told me over her customary pre-dinner double Chivas, waving the instability aside. She recalled arriving in Kigali the day the genocide ended and the Tutsi liberated the city from the Hutu Interahamwe— there were bodies rotting on the streets, buildings pocked with bullet holes, corpses filling the basement of her beloved Hotel des Milles Collines.

"I just didn't think a thing about it," she said of her decision to fly in under such circumstances. "We came here all the time."

Keesling explains her commitment to the gorillas by saying that she likes "solving problems," but her love for the animals is undeniably profound. She knows many of those in the Virungas by name, refers to one adored silverback, Shinda, as her "boyfriend." Her tale of how she met Fossey in 1984 is a favorite of hers, told so many times that it now has the rote ring of legend: "I met Dian at a dumpy hotel in Rwanda. She was dynamic, in control. I was so impressed by her mission. And Dian said to me, 'Ruth, there are only 248 mountain gorillas left in the world. They're all going to die, and I'm going to die with them.' " Keesling brought Karisoke its first veterinarian in 1986, and in later years raised enough funding to see poaching almost completely eradicated from much of the gorillas' habitat.

After our introduction in Kigali, Keesling and I went to visit Fossey's grave and the remnants of the original Karisoke Research Center, all located above 10,000 feet in Volcanoes National Park in the Rwandan Virungas. On the way up, we passed large tracts of farmland—all well within the official park boundaries—that had been cut from virgin rain forest. In the years after the Rwandan genocide of 1994, international pressure called for the repatriation of thousands of refugees who had fled to camps in Congo. Only when civil war erupted in Congo did many of the refugees return, some resettling on the only uninhabited land they could find: around the fringes of Volcanoes National Park. The result is the severe deforestation of the lower portions of the park's mountains.

We trudged up the muddy path, reaching moist montane forest filled with giant hagenia trees draped in a kind of Spanish moss. The 14,000-foot peaks of the volcanoes lorded over the countryside, revealing themselves through breaks in the clouds. I half expected some gorillas to come loping toward me from out of the brush. Instead, from some faraway point in the jungle, a male gorilla thumped his chest and let out a deep bass tremolo that echoed across the mountains.

The animals' extreme habitat has been their only real defense against humans. They weren't known to European explorers until 1902, when Oscar von Beringe, a German, shot two members of the first group he discovered. In the 1920s, whites decided that the rare gorillas ought to be kept alive rather than killed, and so the Belgian government, then Rwanda's colonial ruler, formed Africa's first national park, Albert National Park, in the Virungas. By not overlapping with the habitat of other large primates, the mountain gorillas have naturally quarantined themselves from such diseases as Ebola, which is currently decimating the chimpanzees of Uganda, and they have so far avoided being caught in the bush-meat trade that has ravaged the populations of the less glamorous lowland gorilla all across central Africa.

Still, their status as a highly endangered species hurts them in unexpected ways: Wealthy outsiders with their own private menageries have offered poachers upwards of $25,000 for the capture of a single baby, which can entail killing several of the adults protecting it. There were two attempts in 2002 to steal babies—one in Uganda's Bwindi Impenetrable National Park, the other in Rwanda's Volcanoes National Park—which resulted in the capture of two babies and the murder of six adults; luckily, one of the babies was recovered and successfully assimilated into another gorilla group. Yet there are concerns that the lawlessness and instability on the Congolese side of the Virungas will make it easier to steal babies from this vulnerable population. "In the spring of this year, we saw a general increase in the wildlife trade in this area from Congo," says Gil Grosvenor, a DFGF International board member and chairman of the board of the National Geographic Society, "and the [seizing of gorilla babies] suggests that there is now a focused attack on the mountain gorillas." To counter poaching, Karisoke staff and Rwandan and Congolese wildlife authorities now engage in trans-boundary patrols.

We finally reached the meadow of Karisimbi, which Fossey describes in her diary as "the most fantastically gorgeous country I never dreamed existed." It was, indeed, an enchanting place, ancient hagenia trees rising like wizened sentinels to stand vigil over the site of Fossey's life work and grave. Appropriately, she was buried alongside her gorilla cemetery, a martyr for the very animals that had consumed her life. I read the bronze plaque on the headstone—a gift that Keesling had made in Fossey's memory. Around us, workers for the Rwandan government were busy replacing Fossey's gorilla grave markers, adding fences and footpaths, and covering Fossey's grave with a neat patio of lava rock: upgrades for the tourists. Fossey and her mountain gorillas were about to go commercial; the Rwandan government had plans to charge $50 per person for permission to visit the grave.

Of Karisoke itself, little remained—just some cement foundations and rotting wooden frames. The jungle had already started to reclaim the site, beautifying its recent unsavory history with a cover of new greenery. After the Rwandan conflict erupted nearly a decade ago, the Interahamwe repeatedly pillaged Karisoke, finally using the area as a base camp for launching raids from 1997 to 1999. Miraculously, Karisoke's rangers continued to monitor the gorillas on the Rwandan side during most of the hostilities, and only three animals were killed. In Congo, however, as many as 17 were lost.

Given the continued threat of poachers and Hutu rebel encroachment, Rwanda appointed an entire army battalion to protect the animals and the tourists who visit them. I met the leader of Battalion 69, Major Kirenga, who said that the Interahamwe has not been in the park since 2001. "I don't think they will come back to this area," he said, "because when they were here in 2001, they suffered." François Bigirimana, warden of Volcanoes National Park, was less sanguine: "Now the situation is OK, but for only a short time. The Interahamwe keeps coming back."

Few in gorilla conservation can forget the widely publicized 1999 incident in Uganda's Bwindi Impenetrable National Park, home to more than 300 mountain gorillas, a spectacular area of jungle-covered peaks that the locals have long called the Place of Darkness. The name took on a more sinister meaning as the Interahamwe crossed into the region from Congo and attacked a tourist camp, murdered a warden, and led 16 foreigners on a march into the jungle. Eight were hacked to death. To the locals, numb to such atrocities, it was business as usual—but it was the first time in years that Western civilians had been direct victims of the region's horrors. The massacre took a devastating toll on Uganda's tourism industry. Today, tourism has rebounded to be the country's second largest revenue source. Bwindi now boasts a 76-person-strong ranger force with paramilitary training. Still, just a couple of miles from Bwindi's park headquarters, over some nearby hills, sits Congo.

II. Jomba, North Kivu Province, Eastern DRC

I see about renting a few RCD soldiers to "protect" me on my journey to visit the mountain gorillas. Assorted militia groups, bandits, and warlords have been staging frequent ambushes on passing cars. The latest attack on this road, I am told, was just last evening—we had been fortunate to miss our turn.

The last time Ruth Keesling visited this place, in 1998, she, her adult son, a woman from Ohio's Columbus Zoo, and a couple of local veterinary students were captured by Interahamwe child soldiers. Keesling recalled it in her typically deadpan way: "I thought, OK, we're going to get it—I might as well die with the gorillas." The soldiers held AK-47s to everyone's heads and accused Keesling's group of spying for Rwanda's Tutsi government. Everything looked hopeless, but luck intervened: They had been giving a ride to a former official of the Zairean government, who used his influence to persuade the soldiers to set the captives free. Keesling has not tried to see the Congolese mountain gorillas since.

I have no difficulty finding RCD soldiers willing to be "volunteer" protectors—all you have to do is offer them enough U.S. dollars and promises of free beer. Vital chooses three individuals who don't appear to be drunk or stoned, and our large group, including three armed Virunga National Park rangers and the three hired soldiers, presses into the ancient Toyota minibus I've rented. We head into the countryside, past overgrown fields and mud-and-wattle huts. "There are two types of ambushes here in Kivu Province," Vital tells me. "The first is the 'political ambush,' the second the 'soft hit.' " He explains that in the former, everyone in the vehicle is shot dead in order to make a statement of protest; in the latter, people are robbed or maimed but otherwise left alive. "Soft hits," Vital assures me, "are the better ones."

We pass through frequent RCD roadblocks; at each one, the park warden or government monitor leaps out of the van to shake hands and cajole the officer on duty. The notion of our going to see the gorillas always creates a profusion of laughter. I stay in the back of the van, by the window, returning the stares of children who have the stoic, circumspect countenances of adults. Only the very youngest give emphatic waves or smiles, and the soldiers mock their earnestness.

Our minivan groans and perseveres down the boulder-strewn track past villages of round thatched huts and banana trees. Women walk along the road, wearing wraps of printed cloth and carrying washtubs or cords of firewood on their heads. Their eyes settle nervously on the RCD soldiers inside, a wave of fear passing over their faces. All you can taste in this country is fear. An inescapable vortex of it. I hope these gorillas will be spectacular, more fantastic than anything I could have imagined.

We near the Virungas. I can see mountains of jungle rising from a series of deforested foothills. The land resembles a crude checkerboard: square, empty fields baking in the sun. With no buffer zone between pastureland and jungle, there is nothing to prevent further encroachment into the park from the Congolese side. Farmers and refugees have cleared the jungle toward the cloud line; the gorillas now very much inhabit the mists.

We reach the end of the road and park the van at an outpost called Jomba. Only two weeks ago, the Interahamwe came through this area, which perhaps explains why nobody is out tending the fields. To reach the Jomba park headquarters, we begin a long hike uphill through grassy, deserted fields. "In 1994," Vital says to me, "these fields were covered with jungle and giant trees." Ten years ago, Vital worked here for a large, five-star tourist lodge; it is now a pile of burned-out rubble that we pass on our way up. It is hard for me to picture this place as a stable environment, with foreign tourists resting on lawn chairs and sipping cocktails before a majestic view of the Congolese Virungas.

Jomba headquarters—a collection of a few small huts—sits on top of a lonely, tree-stripped hill at about 7,500 feet. The jungle-covered peaks of the volcanoes act as a backdrop. It is a vulnerable spot in which to live, with no immediate cover and an imposing spread of jungle nearby that might hide militiamen, snipers, ambushers.

When I reach the round cement building that acts as the base, a group of men in olive-colored uniforms comes out to greet me: the park rangers. They smile shyly; it is not often that they receive visitors, particularly foreigners. These men confirm what I already know: No one is paying them. Not the government in Kinshasa, capital of the Democratic Republic of the Congo, and certainly not the RCD. During better periods, they receive funding from

UNESCO, which allows them to feed themselves and provide for their families. But it barely suffices. It is these men who have lost 82 of their own in the past few years. I'm shown the photo of one of their most recent casualties, a man named Jean de Dieu—John of God.

While gorilla populations in Rwanda and Uganda have slowly climbed in recent years as a result of conservation efforts, most experts agree that the number of mountain gorillas in Congo has dropped significantly. They have been caught in snares, hunted with impunity by poachers, or killed in crossfire. An estimated 15 to 17 individuals have been lost since the war started. For such a fragile population totaling only about 355 in all the Virungas, a loss of 15 to 17 members is dramatic. "If you kill only 10 percent of them," says Tony Mudakikwa, senior veterinary officer for the park authority of Rwanda, "and that's only 35 individuals, I can't imagine they'd have the genetic viability to survive extinction." It is already a concern as gorillas are starting to be born with webbed fingers—a possible sign of inbreeding.

Dominique Bavukai, chief of patrols for Jomba since 2000, says that just a few months ago one of his men was kidnapped by the Interahamwe and never heard from again. A week later, the same Hutu militiamen attacked the station again. A lengthy firefight ensued, but the rangers were able to hold them off. Still, they lost another man during the battle.

"No one knows where the enemy is," Bavukai says to me, and he glances out of the hut at the surrounding countryside. His eyes look weary, resigned. "But our mission is to protect the gorillas as long as they are at risk of extinction."

"Some people in my country might wonder why you don't get a safer job," I say to the men. "Is there a reason why you've stayed?"

I am hoping for a certain kind of answer, I realize. A lofty reply about wanting to preserve the heritage of the mountain gorillas for future generations, about the inherent grace and beauty of a creature that must be saved at all costs. But Bavukai's reply is practical rather than poetic: "There are no other job opportunities out here in this war zone. It would be hard to just quit this job and find another."

OUR LONG COLUMN SNAKES its way toward the jungle and the gorillas, through barren farmland overtaken by weeds. Each soldier rests his AK-47 on a shoulder, fist around the muzzle. The higher we climb, the closer the clouds come to touching me, coating my face with mist. We finally approach a thick jungle that stretches to the very tops of the volcanoes, an unbroken spread of primeval green.

Some trackers who monitor the mountain gorillas walk over to greet us. They are stationed far from the Jomba site, on the edge of the jungle. We all head into a mass of trees and vines that requires more pushing and shoving than actual walking, the men hollowing out a path with machetes. The head tracker waves to me, and I follow him into a grassy clearing. I'm so busy looking around that I nearly walk into a giant silverback named Rugendo. He is lying on the ground, his chin resting on his hands, staring at me with liquid brown eyes. He is gigantic—his shoulder span alone is wider than two grown men's—and his enormous face studies my own with eye-blinking fascination. Two of his females, smaller and furrier, seem paralyzed with wonder as they gaze at me through the bamboo.

I kneel down and stare at them all. "Hello," I whisper, our eyes meeting.

The mountain gorillas were the first gorilla species to be habituated to a human presence. Inexplicably. It is this innate trust that fascinates me. With what other jungle animal can a person readily gain such close, intimate access? Surely this helps explain why so many tourists will fly halfway around the world for a mere hour's visit with these creatures, and why, through war and famine and unrest, so many individuals and organizations are determined to save them. But there is something beyond this: These animals, with their trusting and peaceful natures, caring family units, and unconditional acceptance of others, reveal to us humans just how far we've strayed.

The females come toward me, slowly at first and then faster as the tracker attempts to wave them off with a stick. They are determined to touch me. The tracker tries to explain their strange behavior—"They haven't seen a white person before"—but I'm not sure I believe him. Rather, they seem to want to greet me, welcome me. The females regroup for another approach, but the tracker is too fast for them. He explains that the gorillas are at risk of catching human diseases, and so only researchers, who are quarantined for two weeks upon arriving here, should interact with them.

Rugendo rolls onto his back—his enormous potbelly facing up, his legs splayed and toes wiggling—and yawns. Casually, he grabs some young bamboo and gnaws on it, glancing peacefully at me and the trackers as he chews. Humans could do anything to him right now, but he simply scratches his great belly, farts, and sighs, closing his eyes to us.

I can only wonder what will happen to him. Two weeks ago the Interahamwe crossed through this park, and they will cross through it again.

My hour is up, and the females take one more daring advance toward me before the tracker intervenes and shoos them away. Reluctantly, I follow the men out of the jungle, back into the desolate fields.

DR. THÉOGÈNE RUDASINGWA, the Rwandan President's chief of staff, sits calmly in the heavily guarded presidential compound in Kigali, fingertips touching lightly. When I ask him about his country's commitment to protecting the gorillas, he says, "Our agenda, first and foremost, is to protect the people. The protection of the mountain gorillas has been at the back of our minds. But it's in our interest—and the gorillas'—to establish more security in Congo and Uganda, as well as Rwanda."

In the name of "security," Rwandan and Ugandan troops first entered Congo (then Zaire) in 1996, igniting its bloody civil war. Rwanda pulled out its troops in 2002, but not before establishing local armies and governments—such as the RCD—to do its bidding. Uganda soon followed suit. The two countries now battle each other through proxy armies for control of Congo's lucrative natural resources.

The worst of their playing fields is in eastern Congo's Ituri Province, where Uganda and Rwanda frequently flip-flop in supporting the militias of the Lendu and Hema tribes, who busily engage in tit-for-tat massacres with each other. At least 50,000 people have died in Ituri since hostilities began there in 1999, most of them civilians; half a million others have been displaced. Various relief organizations characterize this conflict as an all-out genocide, in which rebel groups take the machete to anyone—man, woman, or child— with the wrong ethnic identification. Little wonder that the mountain gorillas are on the Rwandan government's back burner.

I decide to go to Ituri Province, the epicenter of the violence, to see how bad it is. Whatever happens there can have a domino effect on this whole region, destabilizing entire countries, killing untold numbers of people, and bringing species caught in the middle—like the mountain gorillas—to extinction.

III. Bunia, Ituri Province, Eastern DRC

"Hey, journalist! I will kill you, journalist!" The boy looks at me with blood-colored eyes—he could not be older than nine or ten—and waves the muzzle of his AK-47 in my face. He is drugged-up, gone. He wears a red T-shirt and a sardonic grin, his camouflage pants new and stiff-looking, hanging from his body like oversize pajamas. The back of the truck is full of others like him, child soldiers: a 13-year-old with a rocket launcher, a couple more teenagers with assault rifles. The driver, another kid, grinds the gears of a Toyota, trying to learn hands-on how a manual transmission works. I pause on the side of the street, intent on not showing fear. Fear is what they want, these children in control of Bunia. Show a trembling hand, throw a sidelong glance for assistance, and this weakness instantly registers in their brains. You can see the grins widen, the hands tighten around the weapons. They know they have you.

But these boys are busy with other matters. They have a truckload of looted furniture to take somewhere, and so the truck jumps into gear and roars off down the pitted street. I watch them go, still not moving. Only when they are safely out of sight do I let out my breath.

"Jesus," I whisper.

Farther up the street, a United Nations peacekeeper in a light-blue helmet and a flak jacket—a Uruguayan soldier—sits on top of an armored personnel carrier, elbow resting over the stock of his machine gun. Watching. These 700 peacekeepers, primarily Uruguayans and none battle-tested, aren't mandated to interfere militarily unless UN personnel or property are directly threatened. (Technically, they are authorized to defend civilians as well, though to do so could invite overwhelming retaliation.) They remind me of actors going through the motions of soldiery. But they are not unaware of their impotence: A number of them, obligated to simply watch the unraveling slaughter, have had nervous breakdowns and been evacuated.

Since the peacekeepers' arrival in April 2003, civilians have continued to be killed within sight of the UN's main compound; rebel soldiers have been seen adorning their weapons with the organs of their victims. Cannibalism is rife; militias go into the jungles to hunt the local Pygmy population for "bush meat." A week ago, the Rwanda-backed UPC (Union of Congolese Patriots) guerrillas, who are allied with the Hema—those who had just wrested the town of Bunia from the Uganda-backed Lendu—tossed a mutilated corpse into the UN compound to remind the peacekeepers of their uselessness. Each day, more stories of mass killings and atrocities reach the UN ears in Bunia, while hundreds of refugees pack into its makeshift camps and hospitals with their limbs cut off or their bodies shot up, telling the same gruesome stories: how family members were killed in front of them, how they were forced to eat human flesh. The UN does nothing. It will tell you that its hands are tied by its Chapter 6 mandate.

I enter one of the crude hospitals run by Doctors Without Borders. It sits on the outskirts of Bunia near the airport, adjacent to a large refugee camp full of people—mostly Hema civilians—who are lucky to have escaped their Lendu attackers alive. In two rooms, the walls are lined with foam mattresses, most of which are occupied by children and adults in bloody wrappings and casts: the victims of machete or gunshot wounds, land mines, mortar fire. The head of the DWB mission here, who for political reasons asks that his name not be used, tells me that a handful of doctors are doing 120 to 150 new consultations a day, a staggering 3,000 a month. The Doctors Without Borders physicians and staff look haggard, yet the sheer numbers of new patients keep them almost constantly on the move and force them to send even the worst casualties on their way after a few days.

I leave the hospital and start walking past Bunia's decaying buildings, riddled with bullet holes, and the emptiness of side streets that speak of something hushed and awful. It is as if death leers from every direction. It stares out at you from the faces of the refugees in the tent camps. You hear it in the voices of the child soldiers roaring by in their stolen trucks. You smell it in the cholera-infested latrines and on the disinfectant-coated floors of the makeshift hospitals. In Ituri, to the rampaging rebel soldiers, life isn't cheap; it's irrelevant. They claim a monopoly on it, decide who lives and who dies based on the lottery of their mood.

I think back to the people trying to save the mountain gorillas. How seldom I heard them mention the region's human casualties. There seemed to be a rejection of an all too common premise: that a human being's life is more valuable than any animal's. People here have explained the carnage to me as a "loss of humanity," of humans becoming "animals." I remember Rugendo, the silverback I met in the Virungas. No: We do not become animals. We become the worst that is in ourselves, what is purely, unequivocally human.

THE QUESTION OF WHO'S TO BLAME for this mess leads one down a lengthy path of culpability. The Hema and Lendu peoples lived relatively peacefully together for centuries in Ituri until the Belgians colonized Congo in 1908 and declared the Hema as racially superior, thus relegating the Lendu to a permanent lower-class status. When the country gained its independence in 1960, the favored Hema ended up in charge of Ituri's land, businesses, and government offices. Enmity grew between the Hema and the Lendu, but tensions escalated to wholesale violence after Western powers discovered that Ituri is home to some of the largest gold reserves in the world.

I meet with Col. Daniel Vollot, commander of UN forces in Ituri. He is a tall, middle-aged Frenchman with a crew cut and a wiry frame, looking in every way like the career soldier. I repeat to him one of the most blaring allegations made by Rudasingwa, the Rwandan president's chief of staff: that Interahamwe responsible for the Rwandan genocide are now "linked to Uganda" and are finding "safe haven" in Ituri. This is news to Vollot; he says he's seen no evidence of it. But when it comes to finger-pointing in this part of the world, the veracity of claims is immaterial as long as they effectively get the blood boiling. Vollot is not an optimist; he has an unmistakable look of defeat in his eyes. After he describes a UN plan to send a thousand French troops here with a beefed-up mandate that authorizes the use of force, he quickly shoots it down. "We can't solve the problem of pacifying Ituri with a thousand troops."

As we speak, I think of all the civilians being maimed and massacred across the countryside. "Doesn't it bother you," I ask Vollot, "that all of these atrocities are going on right now and you can do nothing about it?"

"Yes, it's frustrating!" he declares. "But I can't change the world. I do my best here. The press's negative comments about our mission in Congo—it's scandalous. Every day we do our best."

The UN information officer who has been monitoring our interview stands up now, trying to end it. Vollot ignores her and leans close to me: "There was an old woman, 85 years old, who was brought in with both her arms cut off. Eighty-five years old. Sometimes I want to kill. Really. Now, I'm like a beast. It's not a problem for me. I see it, I get used to it. But that's not normal behavior. Whenever I leave this country—if I leave this country—when I have a normal life, all of these things will begin again in my brain. This will be very difficult for me, I'm sure."

I ARRANGE TO GO ON THE UN's Alpha Route patrol to the north of Bunia, in the company of three military observers: an Indonesian, an Indian, and an enormous Zambian, nearly seven feet tall, who has surely missed his true calling as a linebacker. My request was reluctantly granted: UN officials told me that it would be bad press if a journalist was killed by rebels, especially after two of their own monitors had just been slaughtered in the Ituri countryside.

The observers give me a light-blue flak jacket and helmet to wear, and I get into the backseat of their Toyota 4Runner. With the Indonesian driving, we pass through the razor wire barriers protecting the UN headquarters, entering the long main drag of Bunia, with its omnipresent UPC child soldiers. Noticing that none of my companions has a weapon, I mention this to the observer from India.

"We can't use weapons unless we're defending ourselves," he explains. "It's against our mandate."

"Yes," I say. "So why don't you carry weapons to defend yourselves?"

"We do not want to be seen carrying weapons. It will give a bad impression. We want to remain neutral."

"We have this," the Zambian says, holding up a radio. "We can call in if we have trouble."

"You can call in so they know where to pick up your dead bodies," I say, half joking.

But the Indian nods. "That's right," he says. "So they can get our bodies."

We drive past the airport, leaving behind the UN's radius of protection. With no jungles around Bunia, we enter rolling green grassland, following a dirt road that curves to the north. A large contingent of Lendu fighters is supposed to be massed behind some approaching hills, regrouping in order to try to retake Bunia from the UPC-backed Hema. The Indian explains to me that his patrol has orders to conduct reconnaissance to find out more about this gathering from the locals.

We pass a man riding a bicycle, and the Indonesian stops our vehicle and flags him down. "Him," he tells us. "We will ask him." But the three men just look at one another. It turns out that none of the peacekeepers speaks French, the usual means of communication with the Congolese. I am assuming the UN commanders knew this when they sent these men out—yet here we are.

The Indian turns to me. "Do you speak French?" he asks.

"Somewhat," I say.

"Good. You can be our interpreter."

I find it unsettling that any potentially critical information for the UN must rely on my French language skills, but I give it my best shot. I ask the man if he's heard anything about the Lendu, inquiring about numbers of fighters, possible troop movements. He says that, for sure, a large number of them, perhaps as many as a thousand, are gathered behind the hills, but to his knowledge they haven't started moving forward yet.

The Indonesian stops me. He's angry. "What are you asking him?"

I tell him.

"Don't ask him that," he says.

"I thought that's what you wanted to know."

"We're only supposed to ask them 'What's the situation here?' Do not mention Lendu or troop movements."

"We want to stay neutral," the Indian explains.

When we stop another man on the road, I ask only what I'm supposed to ask: "What's the situation here?"

The Congolese man looks at me, puzzled, then gestures around him. "It's fine," he says.

I tell the Indonesian.

"Good," he says. He turns the vehicle around and we head back to town.

EACH EVENING I RUN the usual two-block gauntlet from where I'm staying—a room in the guest house of some Belgian priests—to the UN compound and then back again, passing down the pitch-black streets of Bunia, never knowing who or what waits in the shadows ahead. I'm reminded of childhood games of tag. My senses become sharp, fixed on sounds and sights. If I see UPC soldiers coming, I step behind a tree or the corner of a building and wait for them to pass. I have become a gambler, wagering my safety each night on the whims of the soldiers and their sporadic gunfire cracking across the otherwise silent town.

Tonight I have made it once again to the UN compound. If this is a game of tag, then the goal is the armored personnel carrier sitting on the lit-up corner before the rows of razor wire. By now, I recognize the Uruguayan soldier on top, and he invariably greets me with a smile and a wave from behind his .50-caliber machine gun.

"*¡Hola!*" another soldier calls out from aboard the armored personnel carrier.

"Hola," I say to them, relieved to be near them and their guns. "*¿Qué tal?*"

Whereas during the day these men stick stoically to their job, the nights are different. The darkness, its increased danger, does something to them, turns them into consummate flirts. They will ask me quick questions, delighting in my lousy Spanish, then watch me head to the gate of the UN headquarters for my meeting with the information officer, who often doesn't receive news reports until evening. When I return afterward and pause again before their APC, they greet me as usual, only this time I have lost my enthusiasm to talk with them; before me sits the long black corridor to the safety of Father Jo's place, two blocks away. Two interminable blocks of darkness.

I start walking quickly down the street. I'm hoping the Uruguayans will keep watching me, will come to my assistance if I run into trouble, but it isn't long before their white APC becomes barely discernible behind me. I hear voices. Some young UPC soldiers step out from a building, see me, rush over, and surround me. I remember the UN warnings: that the rebels want to capture or kill journalists. These men—drunk, drugged-up adolescents—ask for cigarettes or money. I glance behind me and see the Uruguayan soldier behind his machine gun, but does he see me? Do I yell out? But that would be revealing my fear to these men. I keep walking, the soldiers forming a pack around me, demanding money.

"OK," I say to them.

I pull out a wad of dirty Congolese money and shove it into their hands. An argument erupts, and I use the opportunity to shove through them, run to the priests' compound, and bang on the metal gate. A caretaker opens it. The game is over for tonight. Safety.

IF MOST OF THE PEOPLE IN ITURI HAVE "lost their humanity," it is all the more remarkable that the two Belgian priests have managed to cling so strongly to theirs. Father Joseph Deneckere—known as Father Jo—is a legend here. I do not exaggerate: He has a saintly light in his eyes. Age 58, he's lived in Ituri for going on 33 years. He and his colleague, Father Jan Mol, are two of the only foreign priests who have stayed on in Bunia through all the chaos and killing. Father Jo has been threatened numerous times, but he earned a reputation as someone to be reckoned with when some soldiers burst into his compound and trained their guns on him. They decided to play with him before they killed him, so they shot bullets around his head, made him temporarily deaf. In what Father Jo describes as a moment of heavenly intervention, he gained superhuman courage and strength, grabbed the burning-hot muzzles of their AK-47s and tossed them aside, and yelled at the soldiers like a schoolmaster chastising pupils. As he puts it, "They became afraid of me because I was not afraid." Father Jo is now known throughout the countryside as the White Father who tossed death's guns aside.

He is a large, gray-haired, bespectacled man who can be found at the end of each day holding his usual cigarette and bottle of beer. He and Father Mol maintain a guest house with impeccably clean rooms, as well as a flower and vegetable garden, and a chapel in which a black Jesus on a cross gazes down with wincing eyes. Father Jo, fluent in Swahili and Kilendu, speaks to victim and perpetrator alike with a gentle hand on their wrist. He is endlessly patient, tolerating the demands of the strung-out journalists staying at his place, shrugging it off when we noisily enter the compound after curfew, reeking of whiskey and Primus beer. And he sits for long interviews, giving the same answers again and again to the usual questions from the stream of reporters who come and go: Why such chaos in Bunia? What happened?

I am curious about other things, though. For example, how Father Jo keeps that light in his eyes, given all that he's seen. Two weeks ago, two Congolese priests in Bunia, along with 20 refuge seekers, were trapped in a building surrounded by Lendu attackers preparing to kill them. One of the priests phoned Father Mol, begging him to send UN troops to his assistance. Father Mol spent hours persuading Colonel Vollot's forces—which were occupied protecting 18,000 refugees—to intervene, stressing that the priests were only a half mile away. In the end, 22 people died, most of them killed by machete. Five hours after Father Mol's frantic appeal, Father Jo accompanied Father Mol to identify the bodies. There were men, women, and children.

"I often ask 'Where was God?' " Father Jo tells me. "I think God was not in that killing. God gave the world to mankind, and if we follow the gospel of charity and love, it must go good once more. *God is love.*"

But Father Jo admits that his faith has been tested. He tells me Thomas Lubanga, leader of the UPC rebels, once was a seminary student, had wanted to become a priest.

"How do you explain this?" I ask him.

"People here believe they will be killed, and so they do the same thing to others that they're afraid others will do to them."

Father Mol offers his own explanation, his words coming out with deliberation. I can tell he has thought about this many times. "Do we ever convert people really? The light and darkness are always present in a person, and there are moments when the bad things are reigning more strongly than the good things. These soldiers, warlords, are all victims of the political and social situation here. What is good and what is bad? I think that humiliated people will react by doing horrible things. They're asking, 'Can we be recognized as human beings?' "

THE NEXT MORNING, I hear news of a Cessna that has arrived in Bunia and is bound for Entebbe, Uganda. I have no business in Uganda, and Entebbe is a long way off, but I ask a UN official to give me a lift to the airport so I can get a seat. Anyplace in this world seems better than Bunia. While I wait for the pilot to finish up his business, I see the head of the Doctors Without Borders mission overseeing the unloading of supplies from a cargo plane. He recognizes me and comes over to say hello. I notice how old his face looks, how grave, though he's only in his 30s.

"So you're leaving," he says.

"Yeah. I'm running out of my nine lives."

He nods. "Yesterday," he says, "we had to amputate a girl's arm. We had to wait an hour with it because we weren't able to bury it. The arm was just sitting there in the bucket—we tried not to look at it." I don't know why he decided to tell me this; it is as if he were telling me about the weather. I wonder how long it will take before he allows himself to feel again.

"Is this the worst you've ever seen, here in Bunia?" I ask him.

"No. I was in Angola. Liberia. Sri Lanka."

"So do you think there'll be peace here?"

"I don't like to lie," he says. "No." The pilot is heading toward the Cessna, so I say good-bye and get in the plane. We taxi down the runway and surge into the air, but the dangers are not over yet: The pilot must gain a high altitude and avoid flying over roads or villages to protect us from any anti-aircraft fire. Gradually, Bunia and its problems shrink below us. I see that it's better to view this land from afar, muted by clouds and distance. Then I can pretend there's beauty, at least. I can forestall heartache.

BACK IN VOLCANOES NATIONAL PARK, I sit high on a slope of jungle, watching a family of mountain gorillas climb down from their trees to greet us humans. Some British tourists, perched farther below, wave their camcorders around like frenetic conductors as they try to capture their first communion with these animals. Each person has flown to Africa and spent $250 for this one-hour visit, but from the awed look on their faces they're obviously not disappointed.

I rest above them, out of the way. A gorilla baby beats his chest at us and swings from a branch. Trackers busy themselves with cutting a path higher up the slope, hoping to lead us to the silverback father. I recall a photo I saw of a gorilla touching Dian Fossey: the first known physical contact this species had ever made with a human being. Fossey's face had looked radiant, blissful. She had stepped outside of herself. You could tell from looking at that picture that she would never be the same again.

I am so busy recalling that image that I don't notice a female appearing from the brush nearby and coming directly toward me. The trackers haven't noticed her either, and they yell and rush up the slope. But it's too late. She's nearly reached me, is as large as I am, with long, wild black hair, a wide, flat nose, and those liquid brown eyes. I have never been this close to a wild animal before, and I don't know what to do. Fear rushes through my body, and I freeze, holding my breath. She ambles forward on her knuckles and stops just inches away from me, her eyes running over my face. As if from some other universe, faint and distant, I can hear the trackers scream and scold me—still, I can't move. All at once, she raises her arm and rests a black, clammy hand on my cheek.

The head tracker yells—he is a few feet away now—and the gorilla (her name, I learn, is Mbere) promptly drops her hand and retreats to the forest.

I watch her go, discovering that there are tears in my eyes. As a young baby climbs up the slope ahead of her, she stops to take an enigmatic look at me over her shoulder. If I could, if it were not already too late, I would follow her back into the state of wonder.

DECEMBER 2003/JANUARY 2004

EMPERORS AT THE END OF THE EARTH

By Peter Matthiessen

On an expedition to Antarctica's largest colony of emperor penguins, a two-time National Book Award-winning writer prowls the frozen shores of the Ross Sea and ponders one of nature's most enigmatic creatures.

AFTER SO MANY YEARS of Antarctic reading, I am eager to visit the region of James Clark Ross's epochal discoveries, including the live volcano that he named Mount Erebus and the daunting ramparts of the Great Barrier, a vast ice plateau at the south end of the Ross Sea that forbade farther navigation toward the Pole and thus became the starting point for most polar expeditions of the late 19th and early 20th centuries—the so-called heroic age of Antarctic exploration. Among Ross's finds were the first "great penguins" ever brought back from Terra Australis Incognita for the enlightenment of the Known World.

In the days before icebreaker travel, a Ross Sea journey (other than flights to McMurdo and the South Pole station) was all but impossible to arrange. But by 2001, zoologist Victor Emanuel had organized a group of birders eager to be part of an emperor penguin safari, and I signed on at once. Setting out from Tasmania aboard the *Kapitan Khlebnikov*, we would sail nearly a thousand miles to Macquarie Island, a subantarctic stronghold of marine birds and mammals, and to the Ross Sea a few days later. Ours would be the first voyage by an American bird-tour company to the remote colonies of the great emperor.

Just why I wished to make the long journey to the ice was an intricate question. "To see the emperor penguin" was not good enough. I might mutter uncomfortably that Antarctica is monumental, an astonishment. Perhaps (if pressed) I might declare that its excruciating purity and vast healing silence ring with creation, ancient and yet new and fresh beyond imagining. More than any region left on Earth, I plead, Antarctica is immaculate, a white fast-ness of pristine air and ice and virgin glacier at the farthest end of Earth, where frigid seas abound in marine creatures in a diversity still marvelously intact—all true, all true. Yet there is something else.

A LOW-PRESSURE FRONT OF HEAVY WIND and rain is forecast for the region. The ship flees before it, for the ice is still thick in those Ross Sea approaches that must be penetrated if we are to reach Terra Nova Bay and the redoubts of the emperor penguin before their colonies disperse into the ocean. Clearing Point Hurd in early afternoon, the *Kapitan Khlebnikov* moves out of Macquarie's lee into the wind, as the steep-sided rock ridge in her wake—the lonely summit of unimaginable drowned mountains—subsides gradually into the sea.

By mid-afternoon, the sinking island far astern is smothered by incom-ing mists. Leaned against the bulkhead out of the wind, I am eased into near somnolence by the ship's roll, watching the birds gather from the distances to glide across the blue churning of the wake.

In the ocean deeps beneath the hull is a dark realm of plateaus and abysses created by the rupturing of the Earth's crust. From marine charts on the bridge, I roughly estimate the time when the ship will pass over the Macquarie trench; that hour comes in mid-afternoon. The knowledge that an astonishing abyss lies three miles below is stirring. The lone sentinel island, the eastering seas, the infinite horizons all around the ocean sky: All is beautiful and wild and free—the beauty "that is inconceivable because it runs through all eternity," as one Antarctic chronicler described it.

Oddly, time draws to a stop, as in that moment at the crest of the flood, the lunar pause before the slow turn of the tide toward its ebb. Out of that suspended moment, like a held breath, rises again the question of how and why this corpus with my attached name and history came to fetch up here in just this moment of a fleeting life, on a lone vessel in the farthest reaches of the Southern Ocean, bound for an ice-locked continent a thousand miles beyond the horizon.

Some deeper quest must lie beneath this pilgrimage to behold the emperor penguin. In my case, the quest must have something to do with a lifelong need not to simplify my life—though I need that, too—but to "simplify my self." In the sea rhythm and the wind on deck, I fill my lungs with ocean emptiness and the pure wind circling the Earth; in hard weather, driven below, I kneel on the spare bunk and peer out of my window at the waves, awaiting the passage of light-boned ocean birds, astonished anew by those ancient adaptations that align them with the elements so that waves, wind, and wings all move as one. And to the degree that I am able to let go of mind and body, I soar with them.

SNOW MISTS AND DARK SHADOWS SHROUD the Transantarctic Mountains to the west. The *Kapitan Khlebnikov* is 40 miles north of the great emperor colony under Mount Melbourne, making good speed through new ice toward the year-round open water, or polynya, in Terra Nova Bay. She enters the polynya in early afternoon, under a thickening sky.

Soon the black headland of glacier-capped Cape Washington juts from the mist, and numerous snow petrels circle the ship, distressed by its intrusion. The small white birds touch lightly down and float like bits of ice on the black sea.

Groups of emperor penguins are turning up in the open water, on small floes, and finally in a long black crescent fringing the edge of the fast ice—the heavy older ice that does not drift away on tides and currents, having become fastened to the land, as in "stuck fast." Fast ice, usually in the shelter of a cliff or headland, and often miles from open water, is the habitat required by the only bird species that never sets foot on land at any point in its life cycle.

Files of birds appear on the snowy ice, coming and going from the rookeries, as an outlying colony takes shape under the headland; a mile inland, a broad area of discoloration identifies the main colony. With a flock estimated at 20,000 pairs, Cape Washington is thought to be one of the largest of the 42 emperor colonies, most of them small, scattered around the enormous circumference of Antarctica.

From the deep water off the shelf, the *K* drives herself onto the fast ice with repeated surges. As the edges shatter, her spoon bow gains the older, harder ice, until at last, on the third run, having penetrated almost her entire length, she is safely "stabled." Within minutes, she lowers her gangway to the ice, permitting passengers to disembark. A safe route over the pressure ridges and through knee-deep snow is scouted by the staff, after which the ship's company is free to make the half-mile trek out to the rookeries at any hour of the day or sunshined night.

The larger colony may extend four miles, curving gradually around the half cirque formed by the high ridge behind the cape and the Campbell Glacier, which flows down from Mount Melbourne. The near tip of the flock points at the open water; one loose gang, or crèche, of chicks, clustered for mutual warmth as well as protection against marauding skuas, is already less than a half mile from the ice edge.

Even our most seasoned birders, astounded by the riotous phenomenon on this dead snowscape, are fairly yipping with excitement. Ready at the rail in snow boots, doubtless emitting a yip or two myself, I am one of the first off the ship, and I head out to the rookery in my own custody, having learned that rare experiences in nature, while great fun to share, can be leached away by loose talk and exclamation.

Everywhere gray woolly young trail restless adults. In neckless penitential plod, eyes cast down, the chicks seem to dread some future leopard seal or orca. Some are chivied along well-worn paths leading to and from the water, while others loiter in loose crèches. All perk up at the approach of large, upright mammals in red parkas. Though visitors are instructed to keep a discreet distance, the chicks themselves transgress the rule, hurrying forward like windup toys in that stiff penguin toddle, flippers wide as if to welcome a good hug. Some come within 20 feet or so before mystification gets the better of their curiosity, at which point they inquire about our intentions in a musical three-note chirrup. In its seeming innocence and curiosity, in its childlike locomotion on the ice, the gray wool chick, black eyes bright in a snow-white face peeping out from under its black hood, has no peer that comes to mind among even the most winning of young animals.

IF 70-POUND ADULT EMPERORS, as befits their imperial eminence, are larger than mere king penguins, they are also less regally attired, showing a pale yellow-orange in those areas of head and breast where kings display a flaming orange gold. The pink feet are huge, with long, sharp claws that provide a purchase to propel them over ice; the three-toed tracks in the soft snow might be those of small Gondwanan dinosaurs in ancient muds. The flippers used so powerfully underwater serve little purpose on the ice except for balance in rough places; the stiff wing tips, touched down light as ski poles, steer the penguin as it coasts along on chest and belly, using kicks of its short, jointless legs and formidable feet, set far back on the body. An emperor I see at a distance, moving flippers like forelegs as it crosses the white plain against the mountains, looks like nothing so much as a huge antediluvian tortoise.

Ninety years ago, at the time of Apsley Cherry-Garrard's polar classic, *The Worst Journey in the World*, almost nothing was known about *Aptenodytes forsteri*, and, relative to more accessible species, not much has been learned since—or, rather, not much that is not also true of other penguins. Like all of its tribe, the emperor is hard-eyed, hard-feathered, and hard-boiled, being no less instinct-driven and pitiless than any other animal, not excluding such sentimental favorites as lovebirds, pandas, whales, ducklings, and kittens. It is only in its hardihood, its breeding cycle, and its domestic accommodations that *A. forsteri* is aberrant and extraordinary.

Each emperor is the solitary product of an extended reproductive cycle that begins in the austral autumn (March and April) rather than the spring. These penguins start congregating at the colony when all other Antarctic birds have departed, following the ice pack northward toward the open water. In mating, the huge emperors, like cranes and other noble birds, perform deep ritual greeting bows and vocalize in unison in loud trumpeting calls to strengthen the pair bond, until that dark winter day in May when the female gathers herself to lay her prodigious ivory-colored egg. Presenting it to her partner, she departs forthwith, trekking and tobogganing across the ice toward open water to forage and regain her strength, feeding at sea.

The abandoned male, which has not eaten during the two months of courtship and will fast throughout two more months of incubation, rolls the egg off the ice onto his feet, nestling it against the bare skin of the brood patch on his belly while covering any exposed shell with a special flap of feathered skin. For the next 62 to 66 days, hunched in polar dark and searing cold, he broods his egg. The emperor's plumage is inevitably denser than that of any other bird, and he conserves heat by huddling close to his brethren, forming an enigmatic mound that will not move more than a hundred yards all winter. Even while seeking the leeward side, each male finds himself spun out to windward to the very outside of the ball, all the while keeping his precious egg up off the ice.

NOT UNTIL LATE WINTER, in July, abiding by her strict internal clock, does his mate return. To reach the rookery, she may have ambled, slid, and tottered a hundred miles or more through savage darkness, miraculously arriving just in time to witness the emergence of her near-naked chick. Even so, she is more fit than the male, which has lost a good third of his body weight. Yet it is the male that offers the first food to the chick, pumping into its throat a fat-and-protein secretion saved up for the occasion in his esophagus; this "penguin milk" will last no longer than ten days. In the intensity of his paternal instinct, he may at first be too weak and addled to relinquish his chick to its mother, but shortly his mate straightens him out and sends him off to restore himself at sea.

After the male reappears, the pair takes turns feeding the chick, which will join a crèche in about six weeks. For a time, the parents will continue feeding their offspring, but in early autumn, they commence their molt, producing fresh feathers for renewed insulation against cold winter seas. As soon as the molt is completed, they will depart for good, leaving the chick peeping at the ice edge. Even now it appears that a few parents are moving their offspring closer to the water, squawking at them from behind or sliding out in front, as if to encourage the doubtful chick to follow.

SOME OF THESE FIVE-MONTH CHICKS are already frequenting ice edges, sections of which, in the next weeks, will break free as floes and carry them away on northward currents to the open sea; they remain on their floes until the gray down is replaced by the dense plumage that permits them to enter the frigid water in pursuit of fish. In the ocean, the young emperors disperse; where they go is little known. Four out of five may perish in their first year, since even those that learn to feed themselves successfully may not escape the leopard seal or orca. In four or five years, the survivors, now new adults, will return to this home rookery under Mount Melbourne. Those that form pairs will produce a single egg every second year of the long breeding cycle required for reproduction in bitter cold, fierce wind, and winter darkness.

The photographers especially are delighted by the crew's flexibility in permitting us to walk out on the ice at any hour to observe penguins, and Victor Emanuel is relieved that we are here before the great colony can disperse. In the sunny evening, I accompany him to the stranded iceberg that hides a smaller rookery under the headland. Along the snow path, we meet numbers of adult emperors. The adults have a portly walk, bowing and calling as they go; exhilarated by encounters with other emperors, they may slap flippers and bump chests like football players.

Near the moat that forms around the base of a trapped berg, three Weddell seals snooze in the snow; each opens a nostril or bland eye as we pass. Like the emperor, the big Weddell makes its home here in the fast ice. Not having to defend a horizontal territory, the bull Weddell is the same size as the females, which is also true of the other polar seals—the rare Ross seal, the leopard, and the crab-eater. Since it seldom leaves the inner ice, the adult Weddell has no natural enemies, not even the orca. These animals have seen no other men this year—we may even be their "lifer" Homo sapiens—and yet they appear indifferent to our presence, seeming quite content to doze off in our faces.

A second iceberg stranded near the ice edge ascends to a high arch capped by a snow dome of sun-filled icicles, and beyond the icicles, against a blue sky where blown snow turns to crystals, snow petrels circle. These pure white birds, as has been remarked about wild fishes, are "silent messengers of a planetary depth that makes us cry out, or go on voyages." I long to know what sense impressions pass through their white heads—none, you say? Very few, perhaps? Limited to human consciousness, unable even to interpret our disturbing intuitions, say, about the trapped intelligence in the eyes of our own dogs, how can we fathom the myriad intelligences of other beings?

To penetrate the consciousness of a wild creature would surely illuminate some vital secret of sentient existence, of pure *being*. On the other hand, why seek to know? The need for mystery, someone has said, is greater than the need for any answer. Better, perhaps, to be humbly grateful for those last hidden secrets that science has yet to poke into the open.

NOVEMBER 2003

III.

PERSONAL JOURNEYS

COMING OF AGE AT BAND-I-AMIR

By Scott Anderson

At age 14, the author set out on a yearlong road trip across Europe and Asia with his inscrutable father. Beside a remote lake in the heart of Afghanistan, he finally got the chance to prove that he wasn't just along for the ride.

W E STOOD ON THE EDGE OF THE BLUFF, my father with his morning cup of instant coffee, and watched the light creep down the cliffs on the far side of Bamian Valley. It would be some time yet before the light reached the two giant Buddhas carved into the rock wall opposite, longer still before it reached the valley floor. For now, both the statues and the mud-walled town below were obscured in the murk of dawn shadow and smoke from early hearth fires.

Every few minutes an Afghan man on foot or bicycle would appear over the lip of the bluff and pass by our campsite. They were workers at the ramshackle hotel at the far end of the escarpment, coming up from town to start their day, and even though we'd been in Bamian for less than 48 hours, my father seemed to know all of them by name.

"Hey, Amin. You're up early," he'd call out in his broad Western drawl. "Mornin', Mohammed. Damned cold last night, wasn't it?"

That none of these men spoke English, nor my father a word of Pashtu, didn't seem a problem for anyone. To his incomprehensible greetings, the men would grin and shout back something equivalently incomprehensible, to which my father, evidently working off some inscrutable set of visual cues, would either laugh or give a hearty thumbs-up signal.

"You got that right, pal!" or "You can say that again!"

During one brief lull in all the banter, my father turned back to the view, took another sip of his coffee, and his face settled into a more somber expression. "So you really got your heart set on this, don't you?"

I nodded.

"This" was Band-i-Amir, a string of five pristine lakes improbably set in the high desert some 50 miles to the west of Bamian. For reasons I couldn't fully explain, even to myself, I'd been obsessed with going to the lakes ever since we'd arrived in Afghanistan a month earlier.

My father had never been as enthusiastic about the idea and had grown markedly less so in recent days. Fifty miles may not sound like much, but this was Afghanistan, and the road to Band-i-Amir, we'd been told, was a rugged dirt-and-rock track through river gorges and over several high passes, including one of nearly 10,000 feet. In a four-wheel drive, the journey might take three hours each way, but we were traveling in a low-slung Volkswagen camper. What's more, if we did run into any trouble out there, it could be a long time before another vehicle came by. Even though it was only late October, winter was coming on fast in the Hindu Kush—the previous night, the temperature had dropped to well below zero in Bamian, freezing our water tank and making sleep nearly impossible—and everyone was starting to hunker down. During our time in Bamian, my father had acted as a one-man Band-i-Amir tourist rep, trying to entice any of the few foreigners still lingering there to accompany us to the lakes. He'd found no takers.

But to the extent that any of this presented a duel of wills, the deck was pretty heavily stacked. To one side, you had a headstrong 14-year-old boy. To the other, you had a 52-year-old man whose entire life had been given over to finding out what lay around the next bend in the road.

"Well, all right then," my father said. After one last glance over the bluff, as if making sure no one was trying to sneak past without a morning chat, he dumped the rest of his bad coffee in the dirt and started for the car. "I guess we better get going."

THE EVENTS THAT BROUGHT me to that morning in Bamian had been set in motion five months earlier, on a weekday afternoon in May 1973. Finding me lounging in our living room, my father had asked if I felt like taking a drive. We ended up in a small seaside town on the coast of Dorset, the county in southwestern England where we were then living, and he suggested a walk along the pebble beach.

A year earlier my father had abruptly quit his job with the United States government and moved the family—my mother, me, my four siblings—to Dorset with the vague notion that it would become our new home. That this scheme hadn't really taken root was apparent even to me, a particularly oblivious adolescent, and I suspected the purpose of that morning's walk on the beach was to fill me in on where we might be headed next.

Of course, the importance of this father-to-son talk didn't mean it would proceed without intermissions; from force of long habit, my father felt compelled to call out cheery, if inane greetings to everyone we passed on the beach. "Hi there, how ya doing?" "Nice day for a walk, isn't it?" or alternatively, "Kind of a lousy day for a walk, isn't it?" because engagement was his goal, not consistency.

Despite all the interruptions, what gradually emerged was that our family now stood at the cusp of something very different. Not just another move like all those that had come before; instead, a kind of scattering.

My father explained that my mother and two younger sisters would soon be leaving for Florida, where my mother had been offered a university teaching job. My eldest sister would attend college in France, while my 16-year-old brother would stay on in England by himself to finish his last year of school. As for my father, he was planning a trip—quite a big trip. Completely unbeknownst to me, he had recently put in an order for a new Volkswagen camper from the factory in Germany; once it arrived and everyone else had been packed off to their various destinations, he intended to spend the next year or so tooling through Europe and the Middle East, ultimately driving all the way to India.

On the beach, my father drew up to face me. "So your mother and I have talked it over, and we figure you're old enough now to make your own decisions. You can either go to the States with her, or you can come with me."

Weighing this choice—moving to Gainesville, Florida, versus spending a year on the road; starting my freshman year in high school versus no school at all—probably took the better part of a nanosecond. For however long it took my disbelief and glee to exhaust itself on that beach, I was probably the most excited 14-year-old kid on the planet.

Afterward, my father struggled to assume a properly paternal demeanor. "One thing that does concern me, though, is what this'll do to your education."

"What education?" I countered. "I barely go to school anyway."

I had him there. Having been bounced through five different school systems in four different countries by the eighth grade, my formal education lay in tatters, and I'd done my utmost to keep it that way; through a combination of truancy, illness—both real and feigned—and sheer recalcitrance, my absences in any given school year generally fell in the 60- to 80-day range. In fact, as I reminded my father on the Dorset beach, that very day constituted what was commonly referred to as a "school day," as had the previous two, and I'd stayed home for all of them.

"Well, OK," my father said. "Those are all good points." He fixed me with his wide grin and draped an arm around my shoulder. "Welcome aboard, pardner."

Did it occur to me that there might be something slightly odd in all this? That a set of parents would blithely scatter their teenage children across the globe, leaving one here, one there? Or for that matter, that a man married for over two decades would choose to embark on a journey where he wouldn't see his wife for a year? Nope, not at all. Not on that morning with my father on the beach or at any point in the next 12 months we spent knocking around Europe and Asia. I simply never thought about it.

That's because everyone's childhood is perfectly normal to them, and mine had been one long series of arrivings and leavings, an ever changing blur of schools and countries and friends. And in this, even my family had lent no constancy; someone was always heading off or being left behind somewhere. We led lives of permanent impermanence, and this was merely the next chapter. The big difference this time was that, of the various straws my siblings and I had drawn, I'd been the luckiest.

BAMIAN VILLAGE WAS JUST beginning to rouse, the first shepherds moving their flocks out to the surrounding fields, the land still coated in white from the thick morning frost. The men opening the *chaikhanas* along the main street stared vacantly after us as we passed. Even at that early hour, the familiar scent hung heavy on the air—a blend of charcoal smoke and dust and animal dung with something vaguely perfumed, like sandalwood—the scent of Afghanistan.

The dirt road cut west across the valley. From a distance, it appeared to have nowhere to go, that it would simply end at the base of the sheer western cliffs. But then a narrow cleft appeared in the rocks, a gorge just wide enough for a fast-flowing stream and the one-lane track.

The shadows in the canyon were far deeper than they had been in the valley—deeper, I think, than any I'd encountered before. With the cliffs towering hundreds of feet overhead and just a thin ribbon of sky visible far above, it was like a place of perpetual twilight, one that cast the rocks, the water, even our skin, in a peculiar blue-gray gloom. The higher we climbed, the narrower the gorge became, and I was struck by the irrational thought that we were no longer on a road at all but passing deeper into some ever closing cave, its walls squeezing in around us, that we might simply be swallowed up in there.

In my growing claustrophobia, I thought of telling my father that maybe we should skip it, that maybe we should go back to Bamian. Something prevented me. Part of it was pride—I'd made too big a deal out of this trip to turn back now—but I was also held by the sense that the journey was important in a way that I still could not articulate. So I said nothing and we continued on into the tightening twilight.

THE FIRST ONE WAS EVA. She was 21 and very pretty, a college friend of my eldest sister, and when Eva heard that my father and I would be stopping off briefly in Vienna during our ramble across Europe, she insisted that we stay with her. It was a welcome break from our usual car camping in the van, and each morning, I set off on my own to explore the city. I went to museums, saw the Lipizzaner stallions. I didn't much know or care what my father was doing and was quite content when our stopover, originally planned for three days, stretched to a week. My most distinct memory of Eva is from the morning we finally left Vienna. As we started away, down the quiet street of dignified Habsburgian town houses, she flung open the windows of her fourth-floor apartment and, amid great wailing and sobbing, begged my father to come back. I remember he grinned up at her, blew a kiss and then fluttered his fingers in farewell. At the end of the block, Eva's continuing cries at last growing indistinct, my father noticed my questioning stare.

"Austrians," he shrugged, "they're very emotional people."

Even with the maturity or cynicism of the intervening years, I'm not sure my father actually had an affair with Eva; if I had to put a bet down, I'd still tilt toward no. Rather, I think she was just the first person—and during that year on the road there would be many more—to fall under his peculiar spell.

He was handsome, but it was more than that. He had an open-faced friendliness, a wide grin and warm blue eyes that combined quite nicely with his large frame and his Western twang. He also had a very limited notion of personal space. When talking with someone, whether a longtime acquaintance or a complete stranger, he had a habit of standing close and constantly reaching out with his right hand as if to take hold of them by the arm or shoulder, and was only truly content when he had succeeded in doing so. It sounds kind of creepy, I realize, but I can't recall anyone ever taking offense.

I think it was because he had a genuine and uncomplicated fascination with people, a curiosity they found deeply flattering. He would pepper them with questions about their lives, where they were from, what they did, what they hoped to do next, and if this was especially pronounced around pretty women, it was, in fact, quite indiscriminate. Waitresses, soldiers, rickshaw drivers, old ladies selling vegetables, my father would schmooze anybody. He was Clintonesque before the word existed.

And, of course, it paid dividends. Ill-tempered guards at the most notorious border crossings waved him through with cheery smiles. Haughty maître d's fawned over him. He might well have been the only Westerner in history to get the better of rug merchants in Turkey, Iran, and Afghanistan, and left them happy at having been taken advantage of.

In short, his personality was perfectly suited to the unusual life he had chosen. Because at his core my father was a wanderer, and wanderers everywhere ultimately must live by their wits and their charm, by instinctively knowing how to read people.

He was born in Fresno, California, into a ranching family with deep roots in the San Joaquin Valley, and whatever it was about that environment—the pastoral setting, the comfortable ease of it all—he'd gotten the hell out the instant he had the chance. Within days of graduating from high school, he had set out across the country with a buddy in an old Model T, then spent a couple of years working construction jobs in the South Pacific. After World War II—during which he served in the Navy, naturally—he'd drifted around the West for a while, until he had the good fortune of meeting my mother, a kindred adventurous spirit, but one with a more practical side. It was she who convinced him to go to college on the GI Bill; coming out with an agronomy degree and a specialty in coffee cultivation, he was hired on by the U.S. government as an agricultural adviser and, through the 1950s, they bounced from one foreign posting to another in Central America and the Caribbean.

Before long, though, my father's innate restlessness started kicking in again, the burning itch to go somewhere completely different. By the time I, their fourth child, came along in 1959, he'd already set his sights on Asia and was busily reinventing himself as a rice expert. It worked; by my ninth birthday, we'd lived in Korea, Taiwan, and Indonesia.

But even if he was happier in Asia than he'd been in Latin America, the wanderlust still worked on my father's insides like a disease. One of the most recurrent memories of my childhood is of him sitting in his armchair in the evenings, poring over atlases the way other fathers read newspapers or books. He also had the habit of musing aloud at the dinner table about where we should maybe live next. "What would you all think about going to Jordan?" he might say. "Or how about somewhere in Africa?"

Instead, it all came to an ugly end. In 1969, after nearly two decades of adroitly jumping from one foreign assignment to the next, my father finally drew the death card: Washington, D.C. Moving from Indonesia, we settled in a northern Virginia suburb, and for the next three years he dutifully took the commuter bus to his downtown office every day, his perseverance fueled only by the hope of another foreign posting that didn't come. Viewed in this light, it was really not all that odd when my father quit the whole deal and moved us to England; the job had always been more a means to an end, what he had to do to keep himself—and by extension, us—on the road.

The difficulty, at least in my case, was that I didn't have my father's personality. The peculiarities of my childhood, of constantly moving through so many different cultures, of always being the outsider, may have made me extraordinarily self-sufficient, but it had also bred a certain detachment, a sense that the world was a place to explore rather than truly inhabit. This manifested as a kind of shyness, even timidity.

If anything, my passivity seemed to grow even more pronounced during the trip with my father. In the company of such an outsize personality, it was very easy to stay quiet, to always let him make the first overture. I was quite conscious of this and tried to counteract it, but the farther east we drove and the more alien our surroundings—Western Europe giving way to Eastern, Europe left behind for Turkey and then Iran—the more detached I became. To me, the world had always felt a bit like a collection of moving pictures passing before my eyes, some pleasant, some not—but now it had truly become that, and I was just along for the ride.

THE CEMETERY SPREAD over the entire hillside, the graves mere mounds of gathered-up stones. Wedged between these stones were poles to which flags and ribbons had been tied. These pennants were all different colors and sizes, and they beat so furiously on the windswept hill that they made a sound rather like that of water cascading onto rocks.

We had at last climbed out of the river gorge and emerged into the sunlight of the steppes, and then there had been the long, slow climb up 9,950-foot Shahidan Pass. It was while coming down off Shahidan that we had rounded a bend in the road and suddenly, implausibly, come to the cemetery. We hadn't seen a person or a car since leaving Bamian, and it was easy to imagine we were all alone out there in the sweep of hills and rock.

For some time my father and I walked among the graves. From that vantage point we could see many miles in all directions, but everywhere was the same: great expanses of rolling brown steppes, jagged snowcapped peaks beyond, but nowhere a house, a village, any sign that a person had ever come this way save for the narrow scar of the road and the graves. It was as if a city had once been here, but even its ruins had been swept away, leaving only the dead behind.

We continued on. I don't remember what we talked about, if we really talked at all or just dwelled in one of those long, comfortable silences that often held between us on the road. Whenever we came to high ground, I watched for a flash of blue in the brown distance, for some sign that we were getting close to the lakes, but I think I already knew it wouldn't happen that way, that, like the cemetery, they would simply appear as if by miracle.

EVEN AFTER ALL THESE YEARS, I still remember the first person I saw in Afghanistan.

We were very late crossing the Iranian border, dusk settling over the barren scrubland, and my father was speeding down the empty, arrow-straight highway in hopes of reaching the city of Herat before nightfall. In the far distance, I noticed a small, stationary object alongside the road, darker than the surrounding desert, the only break in color for many miles around. As we neared, I saw that it was a man standing stock-still on the edge of the blacktop. He was in his 30s or 40s with a long, black beard and a white turban, a rifle slung over his shoulder. What struck me most were his eyes. They were dark and very intense—fierce, even—and for that brief moment as we whizzed by, they locked onto mine. Friendly? No. But not really unfriendly, either. Something altogether different, a look I'd never quite seen before: challenging and guarded and opaque, all at once.

Other questions arose in my mind. What was he doing out there in the middle of nowhere? What was he watching for? And in these questions that had no answers, I had an intimation that we'd just crossed into a land utterly unlike any I had known.

We camped that night in the garden of a small hotel in Herat, and in the morning we set out to explore the city. It was an assault on the senses—dusty, smelly, shockingly poor compared to Iran—and wherever we went, packs of young boys followed us, shopkeepers watched us with the same hard stares as the man on the highway. Yet, I didn't feel intimidated, I didn't tuck in behind my father. Instead, I felt a deepening affinity, as if I'd finally come to a place that, on some subconscious level, I'd always hoped existed. Afghanistan was medieval, feral, severe. For a certain kind of 14-year-old boy, it was a dream come true.

My father's plan was for us to spend a couple of days in Herat, then overnight in the southern city of Kandahar before pushing on to Kabul; from there it was just a quick run down the Khyber Pass to Pakistan. By the end of that first day in Herat, however, I'd neatly scuttled that itinerary. While roaming through the bazaar, I'd come across a small bookstore, and there I'd found a dog-eared guidebook to Afghanistan written by someone named Nancy Hatch Dupree. By that night I'd already read most of the book and marked a dozen places where we had to go.

"Just so you know," I informed my father over dinner, "it's going to be at least a month before we get to Kabul."

What transpired over the following days was an incessant series of negotiations. My father would patiently remind me that we still had a lot of ground to cover, that whatever we missed on this pass through Afghanistan we could see during our return trip in the spring. For my part I drew on the mulishness I'd honed during my eight-year anti-school campaign to wring out every concession I could: one more day here, one more side trip there. Our stay in Herat stretched to a week, Kandahar to nearly as long, and when at last we reached Kabul, I had another whole expedition mapped out for the northern part of the country.

"First off, Nuristan," I began that haggling session, "also known as Kafiristan. Alexander the Great's men settled up there and were cut off for 2,000 years. It's still one of the most isolated places on Earth."

"That's because there's no roads up there," my father pointed out.

"Right, so we can hike in. We're looking at two, maybe three weeks."

My father shook his head. "We are not hiking into Nuristan in October. What else have you got?"

That was O.K; I'd floated Nuristan as a loss leader anyway. "The Buddhas of Bamian," I said, sliding the tattered guidebook across to him. "Dupree says they're not to be missed."

My father skimmed through the pertinent pages, arched an eyebrow in interest. "All right, we'll go to Bamian. Is that it?"

I shook my head. "Band-i-Amir. It's this wild series of lakes to the west of Bamian."

"Lakes?" My father winced. "Christ, you want to see lakes, I'll take you to Crater Lake when we're back in the States."

I shook my head again. "If we're already going to Bamian, then we've got to go to Band-i-Amir." I pointed to the guidebook. "Dupree says they're not to be missed." I had taken to citing Nancy Dupree the way some Christians quoted the Bible.

My father sighed. "All right, we'll see about the lakes. No promises. We'll have to find out about the road, but we'll see."

I think my desire to go to Band-i-Amir had less to do with actually seeing the lakes or with whatever it was I imagined I might find there, than it was a symptom of how I'd changed since reaching Afghanistan. The land had roused a fascination in me, an engagement with my surroundings. On this trip, I was no longer merely along for the ride. For the first time, I was pointing the way, leading my father.

"WELL, I'LL BE DAMNED," my father called. "Come take a look at these guys."

We had parked in a meadow just below the last lake of Band-i-Amir, and he had strolled over to the little stream nearby. I walked to his side, looked down to where he was pointing. In the pool below, perhaps three dozen extremely large fish, brown with orangish speckles, lazily circled. I asked if they were trout.

"Hell if I know," my father replied. "But they're close enough to trout for me." He turned and hurried for the camper.

An avid trout fisherman, he'd carried his fly rod all the way from England, but over the 7,000 miles we had traveled so far it had only come out twice and to disappointing effect. In Switzerland he had no sooner begun casting into a mountain stream when a farmer showed up to run him off. The one fish he'd hooked in a fast-moving river in eastern Turkey had been so large it snapped his leader. Beside this brook in Band-i-Amir, he excitedly set to work assembling his rod, debating which fly to try first.

"Those fat bastards aren't gonna know what hit 'em," he said merrily. "Gonna be like shooting sheep in a field."

We had reached Band-i-Amir by late morning. At least for me, the journey had definitely been worth it. Each of the five lakes was a distinctly different color—one turquoise, another jade, a third almost milky white—and the eeriness of their setting, simply dropped down amid the empty brown hills, was made even more unearthly by the enveloping stillness; not a bird, not a person.

I think my father, worn out from the hard drive there and no doubt already contemplating the grueling return, was considerably less impressed. For that reason I was pleased when he found the fish.

Standing over the stream, he whipped his line through the air a few times and gently set his fly down in the middle of the pool. Some of the fish lolled over to check it out, then swam slowly away.

"Maybe they don't like flies," I said.

"They love flies. They're just being cagey."

He cast a few more times. The fish seemed more disinterested with each attempt.

"You know," I said, "they're moving so slow we could probably just go down there and catch them with our bare hands."

"Shut up," my father instructed. "You're spooking them with all your dumb-ass talk."

I don't know who saw them first, but over a hillside perhaps half a mile away there suddenly appeared five horsemen galloping down in our direction. They were coming on so fast that they kicked up a great cloud of dust behind them, and there was something in their urgency—or perhaps it was that they were the first people we'd seen all day—that carried an ominous note. For a little while, probably not more than 10 or 15 seconds, we simply stood there, watching them bear down on us, and I imagine we both had the same thought: that there was no getting away before they reached us, that we could only wait and see what might happen.

"You better get in the car," my father finally muttered.

I turned, dutifully took a couple of steps, but then stopped. "No. I'll wait here."

"Get in the damned car," my father raised his voice at me for the first and only time on the trip.

"No. It won't make any difference anyway."

I think part of it was that I felt responsible. I'd brought us to Band-i-Amir, so whatever was about to happen was my doing. I suppose there was also an element of pride; I wasn't going to sit in the car like some little kid while my father dealt with the situation.

And then I did something without really thinking. As the horsemen closed in on us, I stepped away from my father and walked out toward them. I didn't go far, maybe 30 feet, and then I stopped. The horsemen drew up before me. Each had a rifle slung over his shoulder. The horses were panting and snorting, and the riders peered down at me with that same opaque, intense stare I'd seen on that first man at the border, which I'd now seen a thousand times across the breadth of Afghanistan. I tried a smile, but I could tell it was hesitant, not at all the easy welcoming grin of my father.

"Mornin'," I said, trying to put some of his Western twang into it. "How ya doing?"

It got off to a rocky start. One of the men proceeded to shout at me in whatever his native language was, punctuated with angry gestures toward my father and clicks of his tongue; the others just glared. Gradually, though, I came to understand that the stream was sacred water and that the fish in it were not to be caught—not that my father was actually doing that, but I suppose it was the principle of the thing.

"You've got to stop bothering the fish, Dad," I called to him.

Once he put away his fly rod, the mood became far more relaxed. The men dismounted their horses and gathered around to peer into our camper as if it were the most exotic thing they had ever seen. My father brought out a jar of peanut butter and crackers, made mini-sandwiches, and passed them around; the horsemen ate them out of politeness, but with expressions ranging from bewilderment to revulsion. After a few minutes and a hearty round of handshakes and backslaps all around—by now, we were all fast friends—the five men mounted up and galloped away with the same urgency as when they'd come. My father watched them recede with a weary shake of his head.

"Christ's sake, here we are in the middle of Afghanistan, and we still can't get away from the fisheries types."

The shadows were growing longer on the surrounding hills, and we packed up for the return to Bamian. As he started the car, my father reached over and patted me on the shoulder. "Nice work, pal," he said. "You handled that really well."

MY FATHER AND I WERE ON THE ROAD for eight more months. Leaving the camper in India, we flew on to Southeast Asia, went as far as Taiwan, and then turned around and started the long drive back. On the return through Afghanistan, I managed to get to a couple of the places I had lobbied for the first time, but nothing very ambitious. I think at that point even I was a bit tired, ready to get on with whatever was coming next in my life.

In hindsight that was a mistake. Shortly after we reunited with my mother and sisters in Florida in the summer of 1974, my parents divorced; my father took off by himself, and that fall I found myself starting tenth grade at Gainesville High School.

It was not an easy adjustment, and it was made more difficult by my father's periodic phone calls from the road. Each time he had a new plan, a new place he was thinking of heading, and he wanted to know if I was in. Fiji was one that lasted for a while.

"We'll get a little place on the water, buy a sailboat, sail to some of the other islands. What do you say?"

But then Fiji was replaced by Alaska—or maybe Argentina or Portugal. Each time, my hopes of escaping Gainesville were raised, and I'd come up with my own schemes of what I'd do in my new home—be a spear fisherman, a gaucho—but then it always fell through. I didn't really blame my father. I knew he was drifting and that he missed me, but after a while I told him to stop, that if he wasn't coming back to get me, he should quit talking about it. By the end of that school year I'd pretty much reconciled myself to my fate and decided that sticking it out through high school was kind of like serving out a prison sentence: not fun, certainly, but things would only get worse if I tried to go over the wall early. In all this, the trip with my father hung like a peculiar curse: the greatest experience of my life, but one that had ended and that in all likelihood would never be repeated. In my own way, I suppose I did try to replicate it. Right after graduating from high school, I took to the road myself and spent the next four years drifting around the country, taking any odd job—fruit picker in Michigan, casino worker in Reno—that would allow me to keep drifting.

In 1981 my father had a stroke that left him partially paralyzed on his left side. He had remarried and was living in Arizona at the time, and I went out there to help him with his therapy. I watched him learn to walk again, took him up to the municipal pool every day so he could swim. Whether due to the medication he was on or the damage to his brain, he was a very different man than I had known, given to crying jags and violent rages. After two months I decided my staying on wasn't doing either of us any good. On the day I was leaving, he came into my bedroom at 3 a.m. with a rifle in his hands. For a moment I thought he was planning to shoot me, but it turned out I had it backward: He wanted me to kill him.

"Because I can't live as a cripple," he said. "How can I travel if I'm a cripple?"

I took the gun from him and helped him sit on the edge of the bed. I tried to cheer him up, assured him that he was getting better, but he kept shaking his head.

"We never should have come back, you know that?" he said. "We should've just kept moving, kept moving, kept moving."

He started talking about our trip and his spirits lifted. He even chuckled at some of the things that had happened. Eventually the conversation turned to Afghanistan, to that day in Band-i-Amir.

"Remember those guys on horseback coming down off the hill?" he said, smiling now. "Damn, you were scared shitless."

"What are you talking about? I bailed you out. If it hadn't been for me, they'd have strung you up."

"Yeah, yeah," he laughed. "Punk-ass kid facing down the fish wardens; what, you want a medal?"

For a moment his face creased into that broad, happy grin I remembered so well, but then it was gone, and he slipped back into somberness. He shook his head again. "We never should've come back. That's where we screwed up. We should've just stayed out there forever."

I didn't know what to say, so I put my arm around him. I thought of telling him that, in a way, we hadn't come back, we were still out there, but I didn't say this because I wasn't sure it would be helpful.

EVENTUALLY MY FATHER MADE an almost complete recovery from his stroke and lived for another 19 years. Marrying for a third time, he moved to Maui—or more accurately, that's where he set up his base camp, for he was always in the midst of planning his next trip, poring over his atlases. These trips were no longer to places like Afghanistan, but to easier destinations: England and New Zealand.

What never changed was his habit of cornering anyone who crossed his path into conversation. Supermarket checkout girls, Maori truck drivers, honeymooners strolling the beach in Maui—no one was safe from this compulsion.

"I just like people," my father said. "And damn it, they sure as hell better like me."

In the summer of 2000, at the age of 78, he died from a brain aneurysm. He was planning a trip to Ireland at the time.

MAY 2007

PRISONER OF HILL 52

By Philip Caputo

A Vietnam vet returns to his old battlefields to make peace with the memory of the 23-year-old platoon leader he once was—and with the ghosts that haunt him still.

WE ARE IN A VILLAGE CEMETERY, among low hills west of Da Nang, but not all the dead here lie in the ground. Some wing above us, swooping and circling with distressful cries. My wife, Leslie, mistakes them for birds—they look like plovers, she says, observing their black, brown, and white markings and long slender legs. She knows a few things about avian species, and speculates aloud that these birds are making that strange cry, at once mournful and alarmed, because we're disturbing their nesting area.

"Those are the souls of the dead," Thieu says, correcting her identification. "Both Vietnamese and American, and they're crying out their sorrow to the living."

NGUYEN QUANG THIEU IS A POET, but he isn't speaking metaphorically; among the Vietnamese, the threads of the mystical are spun tightly into the weave of daily life, and the supernatural world is as real as the one they can see and smell and touch. Every other family can tell you that they have been visited by an ancestor dead for a hundred years, and the whole country, from the mist-shrouded hills near the Chinese border to the broiling marshes of the Mekong Delta, celebrates *Trung Nguyen,* Wandering Souls Day, on the 15th day of the seventh lunar month. That is when offerings of fish, meat, and fruit are laid at domestic altars and in public temples to mollify spirits made itinerant because they have been forgotten by the living.

I had an encounter with a restless Vietnamese ghost 34 years ago, in a village only a mile from where I now stand. The five of us—Leslie, Thieu, photographer Rob Howard, and Thinh, a guide from the East Asia Tourist Company in Da Nang—spent the morning in that village. It is called Hoai Nhon, and it looked much as I remembered it—a hundred-odd houses with thatch and tile roofs clustered along a dirt road, in the shadow of jungle hills that I recall by the numbers that designate their height in meters on our military maps: 327, 268, 264. At the southern edge of Hoai Nhon, shaded by old trees, is a long bungalow, made of concrete block and stucco, that serves as the village school. It served the same purpose in 1965, although there were no desks or blackboards or students in it then. Wartime. School was out indefinitely.

My thoughts travel back to a night of relentless rain and monsoon wind in mid-December, when a squad of marines from my platoon and I were inside the schoolhouse, smoking our smokes, drying off and resting up after a night patrol. The villagers had warned us to stay out of there at night. Years before, during the French-Indochina War, the local teacher had been executed by Vietminh guerrillas for his loyalty to the French colonial government, and, the villagers said, his unquiet ghost often returned in the hours of darkness. We ignored their warning, though not necessarily because we were skeptical about the ghost's existence. With such an abundance of enemies from this world—those flesh-and-blood phantoms called the Vietcong—we couldn't worry about those from the world beyond.

But around two in the morning on that December night, the schoolhouse door began to rattle and bang. At first, we thought it was the wind, but we quickly dismissed that explanation: The door was shaking as though someone were trying to force his way inside. "Who's there? Who goes there?" the squad leader, a sergeant named Pryor, called out. No response. A second later, the door shook so violently it seemed about to be ripped from its hinges. I drew my pistol, Pryor leveled his M-14 rifle, but we held our fire, because another squad was standing guard on the perimeter outside, and we were afraid of hitting one of our own men. We pulled the bar back and shouldered the door open, but saw no one. Shining flashlights on the ground, we searched amid the boot prints made by marines for the smaller prints that would have been made by a Vietcong infiltrator. There weren't any.

Next moment, three drenched marines came up to report that they had heard the sound of footsteps in the mud near their foxholes; yet no one was there. Pryor and I went back into the schoolhouse, barred the door, and waited several minutes, testing to see if the wind had been the cause after all. The door didn't budge, and as the wind groaned and the palm fronds rasped and the rain crackled against the roof, we looked at each other but did not say what we thought.

The next day, a villager told us that when he'd left his hut the previous night to relieve himself he'd seen a wraithlike form, drifting down a ravine toward the schoolhouse. Months in the bush had bred within us a certain credulity. Vietnam, we'd learned, was a land where anything could happen, where just about any story was plausible. We were convinced that we had been visited by the teacher's ghost.

Nothing since then has changed my mind, which is why I don't believe my wife and do believe Thieu: The souls of the dead, both Vietnamese and American, have taken the form of birds to cry their sorrow to the living. I don't know the names of the Vietnamese dead, but I do know the names of some American dead, 16 altogether, and the names merge in my memory into a single name, as the faces merge into one face of a young marine who will never know the indignities of old age:

FankhauserFernandezGautierGuzmanLevyLockhartManningMuirPageReasonerSimpsonSisslerSnowSullivanWarnerWest.

Their ghosts are here, along with another, and its name is Phil Caputo: the ghost of who I used to be, a 23-year-old rifle platoon leader in the Third Marine Division, a man I am sometimes proud of and sometimes ashamed of, but proud or shamed, a man I must accept as he was then, a warrior, a killer, carbine in his hand, knife and pistol hanging from his belt, his rucksack and cargo pockets filled with the implements of his lethal trade—hand grenades, smoke grenades, flares, compass, maps in acetate covers with patrol routes and checkpoints and concentrations of preplanned artillery fire marked in grease pencil.

I am here to make my peace with him, and with the biggest ghost of all, the ghost of a past that haunts me still.

I MADE MY PEACE WITH MY FORMER ENEMIES nine years ago, when I and seven other American veterans who had become novelists and poets were invited to Vietnam by the Vietnamese Writers Union to meet with Vietcong and North Vietnamese Army veterans who had become novelists and poets. "We are writers of blood and fire," said one of our hosts at the opening conference in Hanoi, sounding a note of brotherhood. "We saw war with the naked eye, but holding a pen is a thousand times more difficult than holding a rifle."

Da Nang was where the war began for me, on March 8, 1965, and I had a strange feeling of homecoming when our group of warriors-turned-writers traveled to that crowded, noisy port on the South China Sea. That evening, at a dinner hosted by the local chapter of the writers union, a poet named Ngan Vinh made a brief speech and then read one of his works, "After the Rain in the Forest." He was a striking man, tall for a Vietnamese at five feet nine, with a lean, muscular build and a shock of thick, black hair graying at the temples. During the war, Vinh had been a platoon leader like me, commanding 42 men in the first battalion, 40th brigade of the North Vietnamese Army, and his poem was about carrying a wounded comrade to safety after a battle in the monsoon in 1967. The words and imagery—the weight of the man on his shoulders, blood mixed with rain spilling into the mud of the trail—astonished me because they were so like the words and images of a poem I had written in 1966. It was called "Infantry in the Monsoon," and it was about carrying wounded comrades in the rain. I mentioned this coincidence to Vinh after the meal. He asked me to read the poem, but I didn't have it with me; nor could I remember more than a few lines, which I recited at his request. We got to talking, discovered that his battalion and mine had operated in the same valley southwest of Da Nang in early 1966, and though we determined that we had never fought each other, that was close enough. Vinh filled two glasses with vodka and said we had to drink together. We tossed our glasses back, and then Vinh embraced me and said, "You and me, Philip, we are brothers in arms," and that night, June 21, 1990, was when the Vietnam War ended for me.

There remained only one piece of unfinished business. In one of his poems, Rudyard Kipling wrote, "We've only one virginity to lose, and where we lost it there our hearts will be." I had wanted, in 1990, to return to the battlefields where I had lost that virginity, and where my friends had lost far more—their arms, their legs, their lives. I made an attempt, got as far as the village of Hoai Nhon, but no farther. An irate village chief turned me back because I did not have the proper authorization to visit the area. Also, no one had notified him that I would be coming, which insulted his dignity and violated protocol. I told him I was in Vietnam at the invitation of the writers union, and with the blessings of the government, but that cut no ice with him. There is an ancient proverb in Vietnam: "The emperor's power stops at the village gate."

For this trip, I went to some pains to obtain all the correct documents and imprimaturs, and, through the good offices of the writers union, made sure the local authorities were told about my visit. Now, wearing the same canvas-and-leather jungle boots I wore more than 30 years ago, I am going to walk down the same paddy dikes that were once exposed to snipers, down the same muddy trails once sown with mines and booby traps, then through the swales of elephant grass that sawed the skin, and on up into the mountainous jungle beneath whose soaring canopy men with rifles once waited in patient ambush. But I am not on an adventure. This is more in the nature of a pilgrimage, to make peace with myself, yes, but something more. I am thinking of a line Ophelia speaks in Act 4 of *Hamlet:* "We know what we are, but know not what we may be." In Vietnam, some cherished image we Americans had of ourselves as an essentially virtuous people came apart. My own flattering self-image was shredded here. I thought I was one thing, and discovered that I had become a person I never wanted or expected to be. I had found a darkness within myself, a kind of evil twin I hadn't realized was in me. I am here to confront him as well, that aspect of my youthful ghost that I am ashamed of.

And so I lead this rather strange patrol that consists of my wife, a photographer, a poet, and a tour guide toward Hill 22, which was a forward outpost that my company, C company, First Battalion, First Marines, had occupied between November 1965 and February 1966. If there is much that's familiar—the peasants in conical straw hats plowing with water buffalo or bowing and stooping in the rice paddies; the hamlets shaded by banana palms; and far off to the west, the brooding slopes of a cloud-capped mountain called Nui Ba Na—there is more that's unfamiliar. Flowers, for one: bougainvillea, hibiscus, and frangipani, along with scarlet and saffron blossoms I cannot name. Birds, for another; not just the birds Thieu identified as grieving souls, but green and turquoise birds, and egrets with feathers as white as angels' wings. I do not remember seeing birds and flowers during the war. Had the birds been driven out by the fighting; had the flowers died for lack of tending? Or had I simply not noticed them, my soldier's eyes blinded to beauty? Maybe so. In my Vietnam memoir, *A Rumor of War,* I had written about the peculiar vision of an infantry officer: "Landscape was no longer scenery to me, it was *terrain,* and I judged it for tactical rather than aesthetic value." But now I can look upon the Vietnamese landscape as landscape. For the first time, I see Vietnam not as a battlefield, nor as a metaphor for disaster and folly and waste of lives, but as a country.

Which is why I cannot find Hill 22. The hill in my memory, stripped of vegetation, is a brown, muddy height ringed with barbed wire and scarred with foxholes, bunkers, trenches, and mortar pits, while all the hills before my eyes are covered with trees, mostly eucalyptus planted since the war.

Then a scrawny farmer in a checkered shirt sees us looking around in confusion and asks what we are looking for. When I tell him, he says, "Oh, sure,

Hill 22. I'll take you there." My glance falls on the tattoo on his arm. It says "USA." The farmer, who gives his name as Pham Van Thang and his age as 51, tells us that he is from these parts and had served with the South Vietnamese Army and been wounded by artillery fire.

Leading us to Hill 22, Pham says that there are quite a few former Vietcong in the neighboring hamlets and that he and they get along just fine. I am not entirely convinced that he is speaking the whole truth, and I ask Thieu's opinion about Pham's veracity.

"He and the Vietcong were soldiers," says Thieu, who is short and stockily built, with a thick mustache that looks as if it's made from carbon fibers. "They talk and get along. They're not like the presidents of countries. Fuck all the presidents."

We climb a wide path through the eucalyptus, but the only thing familiar to me is the heat, and even that is not as severe as I remember it, probably because I'm not wearing a 17-pound flak jacket and carrying 40 pounds of weapons, ammo, and gear.

In a little while, something about the way the land unfolds stirs a memory, and I look off to the side of the path and see a round depression in the ground—the remnants of an old foxhole or mortar emplacement—and then a rectangular one: an old bunker. When we reach the crest of the hill, overlooking terraced rice paddies and tiered hills rising westward toward Nui Ba Na, falling southward toward the Thuy Loan river, I finally know where I am. Yet there is still a strangeness, brought on by the absence of the sounds that had become so grooved into my eardrums that I could not sleep without them for a long time after I came home from the war: the ominous rumble of distant artillery and bombing, the intermittent *tickety-tack* of automatic-weapons fire, the eerie noise, similar to an owl's hoot, made by parachute flares drifting downward in the night.

A LITTLE WAY DOWN THE SLOPE, at what's known in the soldier's trade as the "military crest," is a hole in the ground about eight feet square and six deep, half filled in with earth and partly overgrown with weeds, in which lies a rotted, stiffened, olive-drab poncho. I know—not with brain knowledge but with bone knowledge—that it's what's left of the bunker where I used to huddle with my radioman, Jones, under a roof composed of bamboo logs with three layers of sandbags on top. I climb in and, gazing through a kind of temporal telescope, see a blurred image of Jones and me, sitting with our backs to the muddy walls, listening to patrol leaders calling in situation reports in code-word jargon.

Climbing out, I observe a small, freshly painted pagoda a short distance away, and it flips another switch in my memory. I share the recollection with my wife and companions: "That was a ruin during the war, just a few jagged walls," I say. "It was a few yards outside our perimeter wire. One night, a couple of VC sneaked inside and lobbed grenades, or maybe they shot at us; I don't remember exactly. Didn't hit any of us. We dropped a 60-millimeter mortar round on them. Didn't get them either. They were already long gone. All we did was blow a few more holes in the pagoda."

My audience looks at me expectantly. They are waiting for the punch line, for some point to the story. There isn't any, or, to put it in other words, the story's pointlessness is the point. It's a quark-size microcosm of the war.

I have another memory, but it is not one I share with my wife and the others. I have shared it with the approximately two million people who have read *A Rumor of War,* but I find myself unable to utter it face-to-face to anyone. It's certainly not a story to tell your wife, lest she begin to wonder just who and what it is she married.

Pretending that I have to take a leak, I walk a few yards toward the pagoda, then stop and in fact do take a leak. I'm not sure I'm peeing on the exact spot, but I know I'm close to it: the minuscule patch of alien earth where I stood, in the early morning blackness in late January of 1966, and said "How do you do!" to my own personal Mr. Hyde, the secret sharer of my soul.

Let me establish something: I don't really want to be here. I would rather be home in Connecticut, observing the quiet glories of a New England spring, than on this heat-stricken hill on the other side of the Earth, resurrecting ugly memories better left interred. I'm sick to death of thinking about the Vietnam War, dreaming about it, and, above all, writing about it.

But here I am, so I might as well, in what I hope is a last farewell and a final repudiation, piss into Mr. Hyde's face just to let him know what I think of him. Of course, it's my own face, so really I'm letting myself know what I think of me as the stream splashes on or near the ground where I stood laughing over the corpse of a 19-year-old Vietnamese boy killed by one of my patrols. He was one of two killed that night, in a hamlet called Giao Tri, about two kilometers from Hill 22. Earlier, an informer in the village had told us that both young men were members of a Vietcong sapper team—booby-trap-and-demolitions experts—and though I had ordered the patrol to capture them if possible, kill them if necessary, in truth I hoped my marines would find a reason to kill them. I wanted them dead, and to this day I believe that the patrol knew I wanted it, because they wanted it; wanted it because 34 men from our 140-man company had been killed or wounded in the previous month, nine from our platoon, and almost all the casualties had been from mines and booby traps.

And so we laughed over the corpse with the gaping hole in the side of its head, from which blood and brains leaked out. We roared hysterically when a marine kicked it in the ribs and said, "Oh, excuse me! Hope that didn't hurt." Yeah, we'd sure paid old Charlie back. Ha-ha, ho-ho, for "Merry it was to laugh there," as the World War I poet Wilfred Owen wrote, "where death becomes absurd and life absurder. For power was on us as we slashed bones bare, not to feel sickness or remorse of murder."

And murder it was. The two Vietnamese turned out not to be Vietcong, but South Vietnamese draft dodgers seeking refuge with relatives in the village. I said earlier that I did not know the names of the Vietnamese dead whose souls had become birds to cry their sorrow. Well, I do know the names of those two: Le Dung and Le Du, and we killed them because we thought they were the enemy, when in fact the enemy was us and what we had become.

WE CALLED IT PURPLE HEART TRAIL, because so many marines had been killed and wounded on it. It wasn't a single trail, but a skein of paths and tracks that led through the jungle galleries bordering the Thuy Loan.

The next shrine on the pilgrimage is on the trail; it's the place where my platoon was ambushed on Christmas Eve, 1965. I can see it in my mind—a rice paddy with the river to its back, foothills to its front, a tree line on each of the other two sides, a dead tree standing where the rice paddy ended and the high ground began, a sagging barbed-wire fence running from the tree back toward the river. That description could fit any one of a thousand places around here, and I am once again disoriented by the changes in the landscape. Since the end of the war, the Vietnamese government has made great efforts to settle the rural areas, and what I remember as a hideous tangle of bamboo thickets interspersed with meadows of elephant grass is now under cultivation, mostly with sugarcane and tobacco. What had been a footpath is now a dirt road, big enough to handle motor vehicles, and new villages have sprung up along it. Electrical towers march across the countryside, bringing the blessings and curses of electricity to places that 30 years ago were lit only with oil lamps. Looking through one window, I see kids watching their new Sony TV.

We pass a shed (its roof supported by bamboo trunks with old GI helmet liners resting on their tops), cut across a sugarcane field, and come to the river, shallow in the dry season. The river is the only thing I recognize. I sense that everyone is wondering what we're looking for, and why, so I describe the ambush: the dead tree exploding—there was an electrically detonated mine concealed at its base—the eruption of automatic-rifle fire from the tree line, marines firing back, and the whole thing over in 15 seconds. I was knocked down by the blast, but wasn't hit, the back of my flak jacket having taken the shrapnel. Five of my men were badly wounded, one with a sucking chest wound that brought a pink froth to his mouth, another with one arm hanging by a single strand of muscle, a third's face looked as if it had been clawed by a wildcat. I describe carrying the casualties to a landing zone through the rain (this was the inspiration for my poem), calling in the medevac, the rhythmic chop of helicopter rotor blades.

As I tell this particular war story, a handful of Vietnamese gather around. This is still a remote part of the country, and foreigners are a very rare sight. One of the onlookers is a middle-aged man on crutches, wearing a gray shirt and gray trousers, the left leg of which is folded and pinned back to the stump of his thigh. He asks Thieu who we are and what we're up to. Thieu tells him I'm an American veteran, visiting the scenes of battles long ago. The man, who says that his name is Doan Thu, nods and then tells us his war story.

"In 1973, when I was 13 years old, I was bringing our cow home from the fields. The cow stepped on a land mine. The explosion killed it outright. My leg was badly mangled. I was taken to the hospital in Da Nang, where the doctors cut it off."

End of story, and I am sufficiently humbled to watch my words from now on.

A FEW KILOMETERS UPRIVER, closer to the somber loom of Nui Ba Na, lies the village of Hoi Vuc. People who have read the histories of the war are familiar with its big events, like the battles of the Ia Drang valley and Hamburger Hill, the Tet Offensive, and the fall of Saigon in 1975; but for the great majority of men who fought it, the war was mostly a matter of small unit actions in obscure places that are not in the history books and never will be. Hoi Vuc, a village of perhaps a hundred families near the fork of the Thuy Loan and one of its tributaries, was one of those places: a hard-core, nasty place where an American patrol was all but certain to get into a firefight, or run into an ambush, or trip a booby trap, or come under sniper fire. "Holy fuck! Hoi Vuc!" the marines in C company would groan whenever their mission took them within a kilometer of the village. There, early one evening in the monsoon, my own platoon had battled a platoon of main-force Vietcong, the rain-swollen

Thuy Loan preventing them from closing with us and us with them, so all we did was shoot at each other for ten minutes or so. We killed three without suffering a casualty ourselves, but we came under heavy mortar fire that night and called in artillery on the VC positions, our shells falling so close they were as much a danger to us as to the enemy, the air rent by screeches and blasts and shrapnel cracking overhead with a sound like snapping whips.

Hoi Vuc was a morass, and one day our regimental commanding officer took me aside, showed me his tactical operations map, and because I had fought in so many actions around the village, asked for my opinion of a plan he was devising to subdue the place once and for all.

"See these hills overlooking the *ville,* lieutenant?" the colonel said. "I'm thinking I'll put marines and snipers on 'em, and then I'll call a B-52 strike in on the place. Carpet bomb it, and if anybody lives through that, they'll come running out and the snipers will get them."

It was one of the moments when I did something I'm proud of. I talked the colonel out of his screwy scheme, pointing out that, one, he was unlikely to get authorization for a B-52 strike on one small village; two, even if he did, carpet bombing would slaughter innocent women, children, and old men right along with the VC; and three, the hills were so close to Hoi Vuc that the huge bombs would likely kill the marines he planned to station on them.

We have difficulty finding the village, once again because the landscape has been altered, and also because its name has been changed. Thinh, the tour-company guide, discovers that it's now called Hoa Phu. He makes a few inquiries, and then leads us to it and to the village chairman, Truong Van Cuong, a small, 46-year-old father of four who cordially invites us to dinner and to spend the night in his house. This hospitable offer is so far from the greetings I was accustomed to receiving in Hoi Vuc that I don't know how to react to it.

Although Truong is village chairman, he is obviously not getting rich off his job. His house is like the ones I recall—a palm-thatch roof, bamboo-and-rattan walls, a dirt floor trod to the hardness of concrete, a household shrine with a bowl of joss sticks and a picture of Truong's deceased mother flanked by candles in blue-and-white ceramic holders, a couple of beds with reed mats laid over wooden slats, a small, fenced courtyard where roosters nibble on corncobs. There are three items that evidence a measure of prosperity: a small TV, a radio, and an electric desk fan to combat the stifling heat.

As Truong's wife pedals off on her bicycle to the local market to buy a chicken and some vegetables, we drop our packs and sleeping bags in the courtyard and settle down to wait for the cool of evening to descend. While we wait, admiring the flowers the Truongs have planted around their fence, an emaciated, middle-aged man wearing a green army shirt approaches us, and, after learning from Thieu who we are, tells us that his house was burned down six times by U.S. troops, beginning in 1967, and that he was arrested three times, interrogated, and released.

He makes this declaration without rancor or bitterness, and then adds in the same matter-of-fact tone: "But I was never tortured. I don't blame the troops for what happened; I blame the U.S. government."

"I have to say, I'm just angry with my country," Leslie comments later. She is nearly 13 years younger than I, and remembers accompanying her mother to a candlelit antiwar vigil when she was in high school. "What were we thinking? This country was a threat? These people are lucky if they have a water buffalo!"

The questions are addressed to me, but I don't have an answer. Sometimes, events that are bewildering while we're living them acquire meaning in retrospect; but the more the Vietnam War recedes into the past, the more senseless it becomes to me, and it has never seemed so senseless as it does at this moment, as I wait to be feted by the chief of a village our colonel once wanted to annihilate with B-52s.

Evening falls, the blessed time in Vietnam, when the sun's curse is lifted. Peasants are coming in from the cane fields and rice paddies. A young man with the torso of a bantamweight prizefighter drags a heavy boat up the Thuy Loan; he will pick up a load of sugarcane and float it downriver, and tomorrow, do it all over again. The scene takes me out of the past and into the present, which is none too bright in rural Vietnam, where, despite electrification and new roads, life remains a brute, stultifying struggle to survive from harvest to harvest. The legacy of a half century of warfare is partly to blame; so are customs and attitudes hardened in the concrete of ancient traditions; and so are the repressive policies and economic mismanagement of the government, which, like that of China, is attempting to institute free-market reforms while maintaining a one-party dictatorship.

"You see Truong's floor? It's dirt," Thieu murmurs to me while Thinh and Truong's wife prepare dinner in the dark, smoky cooking shed. "Farmers and villagers [who are] like him, if they have a child in university, don't have the money to surface their floors. They don't know how to dream. They have no dreams beyond having enough clothes, enough rice to see them through to the next harvest. In many villages, the saying is, 'Pray for three bowls of rice a day and three shirts in the winter.' In my poetry, I try to show people how to dream. That should be the mission of all Vietnamese writers."

At 42, Thieu is one of Vietnam's "young writers," meaning that he was too young to have fought in the war. He's also young in the sense that he's daring enough to question the policies of the Communist Party, whose often ruthless discipline helped Vietnam win the war. When I met him nine years ago, he frequently took me aside to deliver invectives like the one I've just heard. But, I ask him, hasn't the government liberalized considerably since 1990?

It has liberalized, but not considerably, Thieu says, then adds, "There is still no real freedom of speech in Vietnam. I cry for my country in my poetry, but I have to cry quietly."

DINNER IS A FEAST OF CHICKEN, pork, rice, eggs, eggplant, cooked greens, and—this delicacy tests Leslie's and my capacities to be good guests—the chicken's claws, boiled and sticking up out of a bowl. Truong fills our glasses with a Vietnamese rice vodka that tastes vaguely of almonds, and we drink toasts. He seems reluctant to discuss his memories of the war, saying only that his mother once invited some marines into her house to eat sweet potatoes, but they declined. He and two other villagers who join us after dinner are more eager to talk about the here and now. The acronym "NGO" comes up frequently. Nongovernmental organizations are seen here as a last hope for salvation from poverty. Perhaps an NGO will fund the building of a clinic for Hoi Vuc, or a new school, the men say. There are so many kids in the village now that they have to go to class in shifts. As I listen, I think of an article I read recently in a newspaper: The latest thing in the America of the booming nineties is to own a swimming pool with stereo speakers that play underwater and that are disguised as rocks to give that natural effect. We're not just rich; we're obscenely rich.

The Truongs' generosity doesn't end with the meal. They insist that Leslie and I sleep on their beds. We protest, and not just for the form of it, but the Truongs are adamant. Honored guests, even those with sleeping bags and air mattresses, do not sleep on the ground or the floor. Before bedtime, the Truongs turn on their TV, and several villagers come over to watch a drama with them. I wish I had a cell phone so I could call a few old war buddies and tell them that I'm in Hoi Vuc, the guest of the village chief, and I am watching television with him, his wife, and his neighbors. I'm glad, when the program is over, that no one changes the channel to CNN: The culture shock would kill me.

At two in the morning, answering nature's call, I pad outside through the courtyard gate and down a pitch-black path. If ever I'm going to suffer a flash-back, it would be now, but I don't. Hearing crickets sing and frogs chirrup near the riverbank and in the paddies, I recall listening to those sounds on watch; listening for them to fall silent. When the frogs and crickets stopped, it meant that someone—or a whole battalion for all you knew—was moving around out there in the black unknown beyond your foxhole, and you waited with every sense alert, every nerve tensed for a burst of gunfire, a grenade to come arcing out of the underbrush. But now the chorus goes on without interruption, the ceaseless song of ordinary and peaceful night.

IN THE MORNING, shouldering our backpacks (I'm *backpacking in Vietnam,* for Christ's sake!), we slosh across the Thuy Loan and trek for two miles through wooded foothills, coffee and banana plantations, and isolated hamlets to the tiny village of An Loi, at the foot of Nui Ba Na.

In the past, local villagers called it Lord Mountain, for its height and the inaccessibility of its shadowed forests, spreading a canopy 200 feet above the jungle floor. Ba Na belongs to the Truong Son mountains, the rugged range that forms the spine of central Vietnam and that's known to geographers as the Annam Cordillera: a tropic wilderness that looks as you imagine the Earth looked at the dawn of time. Whenever I think of Vietnam, that mountain is the first thing I remember. Soaring almost from sea level to an altitude of 4,800 feet, with mist rising through the trees, it became the emblem of everything I found alluring, menacing, mysterious, and indomitable about Indochina. The mountain's crest, a long, serrated plateau, was the first to catch the light of sunrise; in the garish sunsets, it glowed like a volcano; at night, its massive bulk occulted the stars in the lower heavens and its blackness looked like a hole in the sky, a tunnel into the void beyond the cosmos. Tigers prowled the mountain's forests. Wild elephants had been seen there by reconnaissance patrols. Amethyst pythons thick as a man's leg coiled in the branches of the trees, and at the summit, we had heard, were the ruins of an old French resort, where colonial planters and merchants were said to have gone to escape the heat. The resort became legendary to us in 1965 and 1966, like the tale of some lost city. It was one of the riddles of Vietnam: How did the French build a vacation spa way up there? How did they get to it? There were no roads marked on our maps, only a few trails used by woodcutters and Catu tribesmen, the primitive, mysterious montagnards who hunted with crossbows.

Sometimes, looking up at it, we wanted to go to the top for the same reason the French did: According to what we'd heard, it was as cool as springtime up there, amid the mist and clouds. No chance of that. Ba Na was then deep inside "Indian country," which was what we called territory controlled by the enemy. We talked about returning to Vietnam in peacetime to climb the mountain and see if the ruins were really there or if they were merely another myth of the war.

And now, climb it is what I'll try to do, although I don't need to confirm the tales about a Lost Resort. Thinh has told us that it indeed exists. A 22-room hotel and 200 stone-and-brick villas had been built there by Vietnamese labor gangs between 1919 and 1930. Tourists were carried up a winding footpath to the peak on sedan chairs borne by four to eight coolies. Ba Na is once again a resort, Thinh informs us, operated by the Ministry of Tourism. A road has been built along the old route, and links up with a road that connects An Loi with Da Nang, some 25 kilometers away.

A van from the East Asia Tourist Company meets us at An Loi, where we are refreshing ourselves with warm Cokes at a roadside stand. When I tell Thinh that I want to walk up, he gives me the facts: The road up the mountain is 15 kilometers long (nine miles), a strenuous climb for a 57-year-old man in 90-degree heat. But I insist on going on foot, making one concession to my age by tossing my backpack into the van. Thieu, who smokes two packs a day, also gets into the vehicle, telling us that he and the driver will follow, in case we decide that riding is a better idea after all.

We set off, crossing a bridge over the Thuy Loan. We have to pay a fee at a tollgate, for Ba Na is now part of a national park (sparing it from the ruthless logging that has wreaked more devastation on Vietnam's forests since the end of the war than defoliation did during it). The road goes up in tortuous switch-backs. The slopes on both sides are extremely steep, climbing on the one side, falling on the other, the land below a quilt of greens—the dark green rows of coffee plantations, the paler green of eucalyptus and bamboo forests, the almost neon green of rice paddies—with brown rivers winding through it all and the coastal hills to the east shimmering in the heat. Rob, who is 21 years younger than I and in better shape, soon bounds ahead and disappears around a bend. Leslie, Thinh, and I trudge along, sweating in the ferocious sun, delighting in the moments when a cool breeze wafts down from higher elevations.

We stop for a break in a little thatch shelter where a man and a woman sell soft drinks, tea, and, of all things, cigarettes; then we continue on and, coming around a sharp curve, gaze southward into a long, narrow valley that was called "Happy Valley" during the war because nothing happy ever happened there. It was where, on an April morning, our company received its baptism of fire, that martial sacrament. I picture the Vietcong, firing down on us from a ridge-line, Lemmon's platoon charging them in a frontal assault, while mine and

Tester's platoon, advancing behind a mortar barrage, swept around the ridge to outflank them. Looking at the valley now, more populated and civilized than it was then, serene in the sunlight, I sense something missing: the tension between beauty and danger. Without the danger, the landscape is merely beautiful; it is scenery.

After climbing another half an hour, Thinh and I calculate that we've covered only four kilometers, less than a third of the way. We're drenched in sweat, we've been guzzling freely from water bottles. The 23-year-old rifle-platoon leader that I once was would have kept on, but not his middle-aged descendant. Soon, the van picks us up. We pass Rob, cheerfully striding along. He says he'll finish the trek on foot. Switchback after switchback, the road takes us higher, past construction and maintenance gangs.

At Vong Nguyet, an old stone-walled French hill station the Vietnamese have renovated into an inn and teahouse, it is raining lightly, and feels 20 degrees cooler than down below. We have lunch and wait for Rob, giving him a round of applause when he arrives. Leslie and I decide to walk the rest of the way with him. It's less than four kilometers. Half jokingly—which is to say, half seriously—Thinh warns us that there are still tigers on the mountain. Figuring the chances of being pounced on are pretty remote, we climb through the drizzle.

The first two kilometers are easy, but we choose to take a footpath for the last two, and it isn't easy. Still, we feel the power of the jungle as the muddy yellow path twists and ascends into the clouds. Wild orchids bloom, vines and creepers festoon the trees, and then the first ruin appears, eerie in the ribbons of vapor: a roofless villa, its stone walls crumbling and pocked with bullet and shrapnel holes—from which war, we don't know. There is another ruin farther on, and another, and the jungle is reclaiming them all; they look as if they could be a thousand years old instead of merely seventy.

A final strenuous push, and we're at the summit, where we're met by an incongruous sight: a restaurant, a terrace with little tables and plastic chairs under umbrellas advertising Tiger beer, and four buildings with steeply pitched tile roofs that are supposed to resemble montagnard longhouses but look more like Swiss chalets made of Legos. A sign says, WELCOME TO BA NA RESORT. I feel a letdown. I wasn't expecting this. I'm not sure what I was expecting—maybe some mildewed bungalow with a chugging paddle fan, the ghosts of French colonials in tropical linens, sipping drinks brought by servants in silk brocade.

We sip cold Heineken brought by the restaurant staff, eat dinner while a hard rain hammers the roof, and afterward listen to Thieu recite some of his poetry, which is very sad, and then a few lines from the 19th-century Vietnamese epic, *The Tale of Kieu*. It is also sad, a tragic love story. We ask, why is Vietnamese literature all so damned heartbreaking?

"War by war, death by death, storm by storm, this is a sad country, so its poetry must be sad," he says, chain-smoking. He pauses while a gigantic brown moth—it's as big as a bat—flits around a light. Then, looking at me, he says, "Tell me tomorrow what you dream about tonight."

At dawn, he and I stand in the incandescent light, looking eastward toward the coastal plain, then westward toward the Truong Son mountains, rising and falling toward Laos. The dense mist in the ravines and gorges looks like vaporous lakes.

"I dreamed that I was attacked by a python," I tell him. "It was coiled around me, crushing me to death, but I wrestled with it and broke its grip."

Thieu lights up and nods but says nothing.

AFTER A NIGHT IN THE OLD PORT CITY of Hoi An, we drive down a rutted dirt road, through the Vu Gia river valley, some 20 miles southwest of Da Nang. We are headed for Hill 52 and Thuong Duc, the last two way stations on the pilgrimage. Whenever I feel a tendency to romanticize the war, whenever my memories become gauzy with time and I begin to see myself as a heroic character, leading marines into battle in my early 20s, I think of those two places to correct my vision.

The Vu Gia valley was an enemy stronghold, and our battalion was the first U.S. force sent into the area, in early January of 1966, on a search-and-destroy mission. It wasn't a big battle we fought here—our 850-man battalion suffered about 10 percent casualties, and I suppose we inflicted about the same number on the Vietcong and North Vietnamese army units we engaged. But, to my mind, all the pity and madness and ugliness of war are distilled into those two or three hours. Standing atop Hill 52, pitted with the remains of foxholes and bunkers, I look out across the valley, and hear the ghosts of the war more clearly than I have so far, feel them pressing closer, see them. . . .

Helicopters swooping down into a landing zone under mortar and machine-gun fire . . . two marines somersaulted through the air by a bursting shell . . . the battalion commander, the operations and artillery officers wounded, the operations chief with both legs blown off . . . my platoon, spread out on a low ridge, firing into a tree line . . . 61-millimeter shells burst in front of us, behind us; fragments whine overhead, a swarm of lethal bees . . . I call in an air strike on the mortars . . . napalm blooms . . . a lone VC, dashing across a paddy dike to escape the flames, cut down by a Skyhawk's cannon fire . . . D company pinned down by a nest of enemy machine guns dug into concrete bunkers . . . our company sent through Ha Na village to take Hill 52 and deliver supporting fire for D company . . . maddened by the fight in the LZ, we burn and blast our way through the village until there's nothing left but ashes . . . more air strikes pound the machine-gun nest for half an hour, bombs falling so near we sometimes feel the shock wave of the blasts . . . night falls, the ashes below smolder . . . D company's wounded, somewhere off to our left flank, cry out in the darkness . . . an urgent request for morphine transmitted over the radio; D company's corpsmen have run out of it . . . dawn . . . we form up and sweep eastward along the river, passing a field burned by napalm, where a pig gnaws the charred corpse of a human being. . . .

I describe all this to Leslie, Rob, Thieu, and Thinh, and my wife's expression is more one of bafflement than horror. I might as well be telling her what life was like on some ghastly planet in another solar system. She returns to the van with Thieu and Thinh, but Rob and I stay to photograph the valley, which looks—and is—impossibly tranquil now. As we walk along, we surprise four kids who are playing on the hill. I guess they've never seen foreigners before, because three of them flee when they set eyes on our strange faces. The fourth, the smallest, looks straight at me and is literally frozen with terror. Then he screams as if he's having a nightmare. I murmur soothing words, but, inconsolable, he screams and screams.

I wonder if the boy's parents or grandparents have told him stories about the terrible men with red faces and long noses who came here with guns long before his birth; wonder if I am some sort of bogeyman come to life. I feel like running too. The memories here are too vivid.

THUONG DUC LIES A FEW MILES TO THE WEST, where the valley narrows, pinched between two high, gloomy ridges. The village nudges up against foothills on the south side of the valley, the hills climbing toward a mountainside that's almost sheer. A waterfall tumbles down it for several hundred feet, the water appearing motionless with distance, like a silvery ribbon draped over the dark jungle.

We trek up the nearest hill, where the U.S. Special Forces once had an "A" camp (later turned over to the South Vietnamese, who were overrun by Vietcong and North Vietnamese in the final offensive in 1975). At the old landing zone, a young farmer and his family have built a small thatch house and grow pineapples and bananas, which they offer to us, with typical Vietnamese hospitality. As we sit eating with the farmer and his wife, I am afflicted with a weird double vision. *We are writers of blood and fire,* said our host at the writers conference nine years ago in Hanoi. *We saw war with the naked eye. . . .* Yes, we did, and blood and fire are what I see now even as I look upon the faces of my wife and companions with the eyes in my head. Those in my mind behold, on this same hilltop, a battery of 105-millimeter howitzers shelling the ridge where the waterfall shimmers. In the distance, across the Vu Gia river, a Skyhawk painted in green-and-brown camouflage screams in, drops napalm, and climbs, doing a barrel roll; all along the valley, smoke billows from air strikes and burning villages. At the LZ, radios crackle with desperate calls for medevacs or artillery fire; earlier, one of our companies ran into a battalion of North Vietnamese regulars, and in less than 30 minutes, 108 of the company's 172 officers and men were killed or wounded. The tall, patrician-looking colonel who stands beside me gazes out over the battlefield, and remarks, "My, it certainly is a lovely valley, isn't it?"

That was in April 1966, when I was serving as an assistant regimental operations officer and our regiment was sent into Thuong Duc on a search-and-destroy mission to clear the way for the Special Forces to build their camp. I helped plan the operation, though as a junior officer I did little more than dot the *i*'s and cross the *t*'s on the operation orders. But at one point in the planning, I played a more significant role, and it's another memory that haunts me to this day. Observing that the plan called for a battalion and an artillery battery to be dropped on the north side of the Vu Gia, I suggested that another battalion should land on the south side and establish a blocking position to cut off the enemy's avenue of retreat in that direction. My suggestion was taken, but with one important difference: Instead of a battalion—four rifle companies—a single company was to be committed to the blocking position. I protested vigorously, almost to the point of insubordination, telling the operations officer that to leave one company isolated, with a wide river between them and reinforcements, would be to invite disaster. *What are you talking about, lieutenant? They're gonna have a forward air controller and forward artillery observers with them. Any trouble and they'll call the wrath of God down on Charlie. Firepower, lieutenant.*

And so the company went and that was the one that ran into the NVA battalion, which taught a lesson in firepower by opening up all at once with machine guns, mortars, recoilless rifles, and rocket-propelled grenades.

Blood and fire.

WE ARE PUT UP IN THE HEADQUARTERS of the Thuong Duc People's Committee—the town hall, a spacious, two-story villa. Taking a walk in the late afternoon, as thunder booms in the mountains westward, Leslie, Rob, and I discover that we are the main attraction in town. We can barely move, besieged by a horde of laughing, squealing schoolchildren, all practicing their two words of English: *Ha-lo, goo-bye*. They grab our hands, jump on our backs. I stop and begin to teach them how to count in English, a favor they return by teaching me to count in Vietnamese. When they hear me say, "*mot, hai, ba, bon*," their delighted cries hit a level that pierces my eardrums. They are poorly dressed, a few need baths, they have no computers or visual aids in their one-room schoolhouse, only crude desks and copy books, but they are the sweetest, most innocent and playful children you'll meet anywhere.

In the evening, we feast on rice, pork, and fish in the town hall, under a bust of Ho Chi Minh (never thought I'd do that, either), and in the morning, over breakfast tea, I have a conversation with the enemy. They are three former Vietcong: Trung Cong Phu, a 70-year-old gray-haired man with a direct gaze and the dignified bearing of an Asian venerable; Nguyen Trung Chinh, an intense, restless man who's 66 but looks 20 years younger; and Nguyen Thanh Duoc, who at 50 bears a striking resemblance to tough-guy actor Charles Bronson.

All three fought for years in and around Thuong Duc with the regional Vietcong army. Phu joined the Vietminh resistance against the French in 1946, fought them for ten years, was arrested by the Saigon regime afterward because he belonged to the Communist Party, and spent another ten years in prison. Released in 1966, he immediately joined the VC, and served as a medical corpsman with a local battalion until the war's end. Three decades of war and prison, but he feels no animosity toward Americans, only a kind of puzzlement.

"I never could understand why the U.S. was fighting in the war," he says. "I couldn't understand and asked myself, Why are these people here, killing us?"

Chinh was with the VC from 1961 to 1975, sometimes as a political officer and organizer, sometimes as a guerrilla fighter. He took part in the Tet Offensive and lost a brother in the war. To him, there is no mystery about how Asian guerrillas were able to defeat the most powerful army on Earth.

"The Americans were trained as conventional forces," he says, fidgeting with a pen. "They couldn't fight in the mountains and jungles, where we could appear and disappear. They couldn't win, because this land is our land."

Nor is there any mystery for the Bronson look-alike, Duoc. Volunteering when he was only 15, he says he was ready to "suffer bombing, disease, and hunger." Duoc fought in the battle of Thuong Duc in 1975. "There were moments of doubt that we could win, but they passed quickly. We fought the Chinese for a thousand years and won. We fought the French for a hundred years and won."

Phu nods. "The Americans were free in the sky in their helicopters, we were free in the ground in our tunnels and bunkers, and we knew the U.S. could not endure a long war. We have a tradition of long wars."

I ask each what is his most vivid memory of the war. All three ponder for a while, and Chinh is the first to offer his: "The day we liberated this area, we all cried. . . . That's my clearest memory, my tears at liberation. I cried in defeat and I cried in victory."

But these three aging fighters are impatient with talk about the past. Their attention turns to the present and its intractable problems. Thuong Duc and its two neighboring villages have a population of 36,000—8,000 of whom are school-age children, they tell me. Money is needed for a new high school, and also to repair the roads between the villages, and for medical equipment in the local clinic.

Phu takes the opportunity to give me a gentle lecture: "This area was heavily damaged in the war. You as a journalist have a responsibility to write about it and to tell the world about the support we need to rebuild and heal the wounds of war."

And I promise I will.

Finally, it is time to leave. We pause for photographs, and then I shake hands with three men I would have done my level best to kill 30 years ago, as they would have done their best to kill me.

As I walk to the van for the return trip to Hoi An, Thieu takes me aside for a moment. "I've been thinking about the dream you had on Ba Na," he says. "The python was the past. By coming here, you've broken its hold."

WINTER 1999

COLTER'S WAY

By Sebastian Junger

As American life has become less risky, has it also become less fulfilling?

Late in the summer of 1808, two fur trappers named John Colter and John Potts decided to paddle up the Missouri River, deep into Blackfeet territory, to look for beaver. Colter had been there twice before; still, they couldn't have picked a more dangerous place. The area—now known as Montana—was blank wilderness, and the Blackfeet had been implacably hostile to white men ever since their first contact with Lewis and Clark several years earlier. Colter and Potts were working for a fur trader named Manuel Lisa, who had built a fort at the confluence of the Yellowstone and Bighorn Rivers. One morning in mid-August they loaded up their canoes, shoved off into the Yellowstone, and started paddling north.

Colter was the better known of the two men. Tall, lean, and a wicked shot, he had spent more time in the wilderness than probably any white man alive—first as a hunter on the Lewis and Clark expedition, then two more years guiding and trapping along the Yellowstone. The previous winter he'd set out alone, with nothing but a rifle, a buffalo-skin blanket, and a 30-pound pack, to complete a several-month trek through what is now Montana, Idaho, and Wyoming. He saw steam geysers in an area near present-day Cody, Wyoming, that was later dubbed "Colter's Hell" by disbelievers. Within weeks of arriving back at Lisa's fort in the spring of 1808, he headed right back out again, this time up to the Three Forks area of Montana, where he'd been with Lewis and

Clark almost three years earlier. His trip was cut short when he was shot in the leg during a fight with some Blackfeet, and he returned to Lisa's fort to let the wound heal. No sooner was he better, though, than he went straight back to Three Forks, this time with John Potts. The two men quickly amassed almost a ton of pelts, but every day they spent in Blackfeet territory was pushing their luck. Finally, sometime in the fall, their luck ran out.

As they paddled the Jefferson River, 500 Blackfeet Indians suddenly swarmed toward them along the bank. Potts grabbed his rifle and killed one of them with a single shot, but he may have done that just to spare himself a slow death—the Blackfeet immediately shot him so full of arrows that "he was made a riddle of," as Colter put it. Colter surrendered and was stripped naked. One of the Blackfeet asked whether he was a good runner. Colter had the presence of mind to say no, so the Blackfeet told him he could run for his life; when they caught him, they would kill him. Naked, unarmed, and given a head start of only a couple hundred yards, Colter started to run.

He was, as it turned out, a good runner—very good. He headed for the Madison River, six miles away, and by the time he was halfway there, he'd already outdistanced every Blackfeet except one. His pursuer was carrying a spear, and Colter spun around unexpectedly, wrestled it away from him, and killed him with it. He kept running until he got to the river, dove in, and hid inside a logjam until the Blackfeet got tired of looking for him. He emerged after nightfall, swam several miles downstream, then clambered out and started walking. Lisa's fort was nearly 200 miles away. He arrived a week and a half later, his feet in shreds.

Clearly, Colter was a man who sought risk. After two brutal years with Lewis and Clark, all it took was a chance encounter with a couple of itinerant trappers for Colter to turn around and head back into Indian territory. And the following summer—after three straight years in the wild—Manuel Lisa convinced him to do the same thing. Even Colter's narrow escape didn't scare him off; soon after recovering from his ordeal, he returned to the Three Forks area to retrieve his traps—and had to flee from the Blackfeet once again. And in April 1810 he survived another Blackfeet attack on a new stockade at Three Forks, an attack that left five men dead. Finally Colter had had enough. He traveled down the Missouri and reached St. Louis by the end of May. He married a young woman and settled on a farm near Dundee, Missouri. Where the Blackfeet had failed, civilization succeeded: He died just two years later.

Given the trajectory of Colter's life, one could say that the wilderness was good for him, kept him alive. It was there that he functioned at the outer limits of his abilities—a state that humans have always thrived on. "Dangers . . . seemed to have for him a kind of fascination," another fur trapper who knew Colter said. It must have been while under the effect of that fascination that Colter felt most alive, most potent. That was why he stayed in the wilderness for six straight years; that was why he kept sneaking up to Three Forks to test his skills against the Blackfeet.

Fifty years later, whalers in New Bedford, Massachusetts, would find themselves unable to face life back home and—as miserable as they were—would sign up for another three years at sea. A hundred years after that, American soldiers at the end of their tour in Vietnam would realize they could not go back to civilian life and would volunteer for one more stint in hell.

"Their shirts and breeches of buckskin or elkskin had many patches sewed on with sinew, were worn thin between patches, were black from many campfires, and greasy from many meals," writes historian Bernard DeVoto about the early trappers. "They were threadbare and filthy, they smelled bad, and any Mandan had lighter skin. They gulped rather than ate the tripes of buffalo. They had forgotten the use of chairs. Words and phrases, mostly obscene, of Nez Perce, Clatsop, Mandan, Chinook came naturally to their tongues."

None of these men had become trappers against their will; to one degree or another, they'd all volunteered for the job. However rough it was, it must have looked better than the alternative, which was—in one form or another—an uneventful life passed in society's embrace. For people like Colter, the one thing more terrifying than having something bad happen must have been to have nothing happen at all.

Modern society, of course, has perfected the art of having nothing happen at all. There is nothing particularly wrong with this except that, for vast numbers of Americans, as life has become staggeringly easy, it has also become vaguely unfulfilling. Life in modern society is designed to eliminate as many unforeseen events as possible, and as inviting as that seems, it leaves us hopelessly underutilized. And that is where the idea of "adventure" comes in. The word comes from the Latin *adventura,* meaning "what must happen." An adventure is a situation where the outcome is not entirely within your control. It's up to fate, in other words. It should be pointed out that people whose lives are inherently dangerous, like coal miners or steelworkers, rarely seek "adventure." Like most things, danger ceases to be interesting as soon as you have no choice in the matter. For the rest of us, threats to our safety and comfort have been so completely wiped out that we have to go out of our way to create them.

About ten years ago, a young rock climber named Dan Osman started free-soloing—climbing without a safety rope—on cliffs that had stymied some of the best climbers in the country. Falling was not an option. At about the same time, though, he began falling on purpose, jumping off cliffs tethered not by a bungee cord but by regular climbing rope. He found that if he calculated the arc of his fall just right, he could jump hundreds of feet and survive. Osman's father, a policeman, told a journalist named Andrew Todhunter, "Doing the work that I do, I have faced death many, many, many times. When it's over, you celebrate the fact that you're alive, you celebrate the fact that you have a family, you celebrate the fact that you can breathe. Everything, for a few instants, seems sweeter, brighter, louder. And I think this young man has reached a point where his awareness of life and living is far beyond what I could ever achieve."

Todhunter wrote a book about Osman called *Fall of the Phantom Lord*. A few months after the book came out, Osman died on a 1,200-foot fall in Yosemite National Park. He had rigged up a rope that would allow him to jump off Leaning Tower, but after more than a dozen successful jumps by Osman and others, the rope snapped and Osman plummeted to the ground.

Colter, of course, would have thought Osman was crazy—risk your life for no good reason at all?—but he certainly would have understood the allure. Every time Colter went up to Three Forks, he was in effect free-soloing. Whether he survived or not was entirely up to him. No one was going to save him; no one was going to come to his aid. It's the oldest game in the world—and perhaps the most compelling.

The one drawback to modern adventuring, however, is that people can mistake it for something it's not. The fact that someone can free-solo a sheer rock face or balloon halfway around the world is immensely impressive but, strictly speaking, it's not necessary. And because it's not necessary, it's not heroic. Society would continue to function quite well if no one ever climbed another mountain, but it would come grinding to a halt if roughnecks stopped working on oil rigs. Oddly, though, it's the mountaineers who are heaped with glory, not the roughnecks—who have a hard time even getting a date in an oil town. A roughneck who gets crushed tripping pipe or a fireman who dies in a burning building has, in some ways, died a heroic death. But Dan Osman did not; he died because he voluntarily gambled with his life and lost. That makes him brave—unspeakably brave—but nothing more. Was his life worth the last jump? Undoubtedly not. Was his life worth living without those jumps? Apparently not. The task of every person alive is to pick a course between those two extremes.

I have only once been in a situation where everything depended on me—my own version of Colter's run. It's a ludicrous comparison except that, for the age that I was, the stakes seemed every bit as high. When I was 11, I went skiing for a week with a group of boys my age, and late one afternoon when we had nothing to do, we walked off into the pine forests around the resort. The snow was very deep, up to our waists in places, and we wallowed through slowly, taking turns breaking trail. After about half an hour, and deep into the woods now, we crested a hill and saw a small road down below us. We waited a few minutes and, sure enough, a car went by. We all threw snowballs at it. A few minutes later another car went by, and we let loose another volley.

Our snowballs weren't hitting their mark, so we worked our way down closer to the road and put together some really dense, heavy iceballs—ones that would throw like a baseball and hit just as hard. Then we waited, the woods getting darker and darker, and finally in the distance we heard the heavy whine of an 18-wheeler downshifting on a hill. A minute later it barreled around the turn and, at the last moment, we all heaved our iceballs. Five or six big white splats blossomed on the windshield. That was followed by the ghastly yelp of an air brake.

It was a dangerous thing to do, of course: The driver was taking an icy road very fast, and the explosion of snow against his windshield must have made him jump right out of his skin. We didn't think of that, though; we just watched in puzzlement as the truck bucked to a stop. And then the driver's side door flew open and a man jumped out. And everyone started to run.

I don't know why he picked me, but he did. My friends scattered into the forest, no one saying a word, and when I looked back, the man was after me. He was so angry that strange grunts were coming out of him. I had never seen an adult that enraged. I ran harder and harder but, to my amazement, he just kept coming. We were all alone in the forest now, way out of earshot of my friends; it was just a race between him and me. I knew I couldn't afford to lose it; the man was too crazy, too determined, and there was no one around to intervene. I was on my own. Adventura—what must happen will happen.

Before I knew it, the man had drawn to within a few steps of me. Neither of us said a word; we just wallowed on through the snow, each engaged in our private agonies. It was a slow-motion race with unimaginable consequences. We struggled on for what seemed like miles but in reality was probably only a few hundred yards; the deep snow made it seem farther. In the end I outlasted him. He was a strong man, but he spent his days behind the wheel of a truck—smoking, no doubt—and he was no match for a terrified kid.

With a groan of disgust he finally stopped and doubled over, swearing at me between breaths.

I kept running. I ran until his shouts had died out behind me and I couldn't stand up anymore, and then I collapsed in the snow. It was completely dark and the only sounds were the heaving of the wind through the trees and the liquid slamming of my heart. I lay there until I was calm, and then I got up and slowly made my way back to the resort. It felt like I'd been someplace very far away and had come back to a world of tremendous frivolity and innocence. It was all lit up, peals of laughter coming from the bar, adults hobbling back and forth in ski boots and brightly colored parkas. I've just come back from someplace, I thought. I've just come back from someplace these people don't even know exists.

Later, when I was older, I would know what that feeling was. It was the feeling—in its simplest form—of being alive.

Spring 1999

THE RIVER JUMPS OVER
THE MOUNTAIN

By David Quammen

———

In September 2001, the author and 15 friends set off down the Colorado River, seeking challenge, escape, and a lesson in perspective. Then the world changed. The Grand Canyon did not.

LIFE IS SHORT AND THE GRAND CANYON IS LONG, especially when you paddle your way down it in a kayak. From the put-in at Lees Ferry, not far below Glen Canyon Dam, the Colorado River winds 226 miles between walls of primordial rock to a takeout at Diamond Creek, on the Hualapai Indian Reservation, dropping through dozens of major rapids along the way. Beyond that is slightly more river, more canyon, but the urgency, the majestic ferocity, and the sense of otherworldly containment dissipate down there, as the canyon walls tilt back into rubble slopes of Sonoran Desert vegetation and the water's awesome momentum dribbles out anticlimactically into flat, inert Lake Mead. The deep magic and adamantine power that make this particular canyon grander than all others on Earth lie in those upper 226 miles. My own little kayak, of stiff yellow plastic, is nine foot two.

Simple arithmetic tells me that I'll need to travel 130,176 boat lengths from start to finish. It's a ratio conducive to humility.

On water like this, each boat length of headway involves two paddle strokes and, through the more serious rapids, maybe a quick tactical brace to prevent being flipped upside down. The lovely thing about a white-water kayak is that, far beyond any other sort of watercraft, it offers maneuverability in exchange for vulnerability, a trade-off that nicely intensifies the boater's sense of intimate interaction with a river. There are no passengers, only you the practitioner, and stability is achieved, not given. Climbing into a snugly fitted kayak, wedging your butt between the hip pads, arching your knees up into the thigh braces, is more like buckling on skis than like boarding a vessel. This is a sporting tool, not just a mode of conveyance. A white-water kayak even differs drastically from a sea kayak—roughly to the degree, say, that riding a unicycle in the circus differs from pedaling a ten-speed across Nebraska. Offering so little inherent equilibrium, so many dimensions of surprise, it's therefore the perfect boat in which to explore the chaotic border zones between equilibria and disequilibria of a personal nature—which is what, for me anyway, this trip is about. I've recently been set wobbling by the end of what I'd thought was a very good, very permanent marriage. A descent of the Grand Canyon by kayak should be more robust and less piteous, I figure, than a midlife crisis.

We launch on a Tuesday in early September, with the days growing shorter but the sun still high enough at mid-afternoon to make the deepest canyon rocks radiate, into evening, like oven-fresh bread. There are sixteen of us, seven in kayaks, the rest as oarsmen or passengers on inflatable rafts, a motley assemblage of old friends and new acquaintances all centered around the trip's organizational leaders, Cyndi and Bob Crayton of Bozeman, Montana.

Bob Crayton ran the Grand Canyon 20 years ago, as a young oil-field roughneck with a full head of hair, in a clumsy old fiberglass kayak that he paddled without undue concern about what lurked around the next bend, either on the river or in life. He was so lingeringly affected by the experience that when he met Cyndi, she took it to be something worth sharing, and after the birth of their second child, she applied for a Grand Canyon permit herself. The responsible officials at Grand Canyon National Park generally allow only eight private-party launches per week, and the waiting list is lengthy. Eleven years later, Cyndi's name has come up, and her family—including a 16-year-old son, Chase, and a 12-year-old daughter, Kinsey—forms the nucleus of our expeditionary party.

By the terms of the permit, we have 18 days to cover our 226 miles. Life is short and 18 days still shorter—even if you're living out of boats, sleeping on the ground among scorpions and rattlesnakes, defecating into metal boxes, and bathing in a cold, silty river or not at all—but for an exercise in detachment from doleful confusions and mortal regrets, which is what I want, it should be sufficient.

An hour after launching, four miles downstream, we pass under Navajo Bridge, far above, and get our last glimpse for weeks of a vehicle that travels on wheels.

THE RIVER IS SLATE GREEN AND COLD, having just emerged through dam gates from the bottom of Lake Powell. We paddle the flat-water stretches and bob through several warm-up riffles, ogling the stone, elated that we're finally under way. The current slides along at about four miles per hour, and if we rode it passively, we could make a good day's distance between late morning and mid-afternoon, with no shortage of scenic amusements. Several bends downstream, we fall silent at the sight of a few bighorn ewes grazing placidly on a sand flat along river right. They ignore us. A great blue heron roosts, with the cold dignity of a pterodactyl, on a high cliff. A belted kingfisher flies along one bank, making those trapeze-artist kingfisher swoops. Rising progressively higher, the rock layers reveal themselves as distinct strata and groups of strata by their differing colors and textures, and I've done just enough homework to try to identify them.

Let's see, from the top: That must be the Kaibab formation, then the Toroweap, then the Coconino sandstone just below. I can recite the cardinal sequence, thanks to a mnemonic offered by a scientist friend before I left my home in Montana: *Kissing Takes Concentration; However, Sex Requires More Breath and Tongue.* It codes for: Kaibab, Toroweap, Coconino, Hermit shale, Supai group, Redwall limestone, Muav limestone, Bright Angel shale, and, finally, Tapeats sandstone. After six miles, I notice what seems to be a distinct formation—crumbly, rounded off, as red as dried blood—just emerging at river level. Rick Alexander, one of my kayaking friends, with a half dozen previous Grand Canyon trips on his résumé, confirms that we're now seeing the Hermit shale. I'm mesmerized by the unfolding geologic spectacle; it's better than watching a lava lamp—but then Kayaking Takes Concentration, too, and we climb out of our boats to scout the Badger Creek Rapid.

My map booklet rates Badger's difficulty as 7 (on a scale of 10) at this water level, but it looks to be nothing more than a stairway of large, breaking waves, with a tongue of smooth, green water marking the obvious line of entry. (Converted to the more standard scale of white-water rating, Class I through Class VI, with VI being unrunnable, the major Grand Canyon rapids could all be described as "Class IV, but big.") Rick's considered wisdom, after a glance, is "Hey diddle diddle, straight down the middle." And that's where we go.

Just below Badger, Cyndi has decreed, is our camp spot for the night. Because the Park Service paperwork designates her as Trip Leader, and because she has borne so much of the organizational burden, we have all stopped calling Cyndi by her name and switched to the honorific title TL. Where are we stopping for lunch? Ask TL. Which box, on which raft, has the Pringles? Ask TL. Hey, TL, thanks for the margaritas! Rising to this burdensome challenge, Cyndi will eventually take to wearing a rhinestone tiara (belonging to Kinsey, who packed it for Mom as a surprise) on select occasions, when asserting her authority.

We haven't covered much mileage but, never mind, we've consummated our escape from the realm of the dry. That we're just eight miles from the put-in is less relevant, suddenly, than the fact that we're 218 miles from the takeout.

The moon appears late as a waning gibbous shape over the South Rim. The canyon walls occlude most of the sky, like big black shoulders, but along the linear gap between them stretches the Milky Way. So there's sky enough, stars enough, world enough and time to lull even a full, busy, vexed mind to sleep. My own mind is weary and, as I've been hoping, empty.

THE RIVER IS A PATHWAY THROUGH ROCK. The rock is a pathway through time. The span of time manifest in the exposed rock of the Grand Canyon is vast almost beyond comprehension, reflecting more than a third of the total age of our planet. The Vishnu schist, a steely gray metamorphic formation lining the innermost canyon gorge with polished cliffs that rise sheer from the water, dates back 1.7 billion years. The sedimentary layers lying above it are much younger, including that vertical stack of Paleozoic strata memorialized in my little mnemonic, all of which were laid down 570 to 250 million years ago. That point bears emphasizing: that the youngest stratum atop the Grand Canyon rim derives from the end of the Paleozoic era, more than a quarter billion years ago. The Mesozoic era, with its giant dinosaurs, scarcely exists in this petrologic record—too evanescent, too young. The Cenozoic, covering the past 65 million years, shows only as latter-day scuffs and scratches, such as the river canyon itself or the spills of extruded lava that temporarily clogged it as recently as a mere million years ago. Among the more striking facts about this geological wonder—though not the single most mystifying one, which I'll come to in its turn—is that, while the rock layers are extremely old, the canyon itself is quite recent. The river's channel (or, at least, the western half) seems to have been carved to nearly its present depth within just a few million years, and beginning only six million years ago. The river cut through like a silver knife slicing cake, though the cake itself had taken eons to assemble and bake.

My own age is 53. That's risibly old on the kayaker scale and immeasurably young on the geologic one. Time is relative, Einstein taught us, and such relativity is another factor in my secret agenda of recuperation. Hey, Dave, we've got a Grand permit, Bob Crayton told me more than a year ago; want to come? Not possible, I thought; too many deadlines, too many commitments, it takes too much time, my kayak skills are in disrepair. And then, in a moment of sublime, reckless clarity, I said: Yes! No matter how old you are, I realized, if you set yourself down within the ancientness of the Grand Canyon, your elapsed years will seem like nothing. Your life itself may seem like nothing. Your woes and your moans, your disappointments and sorrows and grievances and guilts, may therefore seem inconsiderable also. Rinse yourself in the river, measure yourself against the rock; find yourself to be a tiny, wet creature, insignificant within the larger and longer scope. That's the notion that put me on the trip roster. My shoulders are still in fairly good shape (always an issue, since dislocation is a common kayak injury) and, as far as diagnostic medicine can determine, so is my heart. I'll never know how old is too old, or not, unless I find out.

Among the seven of us paddling little boats, four are essentially professional kayakers, having grounded their lives in the sport either as instructors (Al Borrego) or as sales representatives (John Kudrna, Rob Lesser, and my geology consultant, Rick Alexander) within the white-water world. Rick, aka "Rick the Stick" for his paddling prowess, is a big, burly guy roughly the size of a doorway; John is a compact white-water athlete. Rob, with more than 30 years' paddling experience, is a legendary maker of first descents on harrowing rivers such as the Stikine, in British Columbia. In addition, there's Mark Gamba, the trip photographer, whose long legs barely fit into a kayak. Mark's role obliges him to wear a camera-encasing waterproof apparatus the size of a small television (he calls it a "surf housing") around his neck like a millstone. They're all younger and better paddlers than I—all except Rob, who is older (God bless him) and (damn him) much better. Once again, as on previous kayak trips, not all of which went off without ugly moments of drama, I find myself running in fast company.

The raft oarsmen include Brian Zimmer, a schoolteacher from Bozeman, who consents to carry our groovers (mobile toilets) and accordingly christens his 18-foot yellow boat Winnie da Pooh; Jason Dzikowski ("Diz"), a carpenter from North Carolina, whose white raft is a twin to Brian's and therefore becomes Piglet; Mike Jaenish, a criminal-defense attorney from Salt Lake City, who paddles his own raft (parakeet blue, with a banana-yellow sun canopy); and Steve Jones, a building contractor and inveterate river rat who has run the Grand 14 times. These generous raft jockeys carry the freight that allows us kayakers, as well as themselves, to camp in comfort bordering on decadence: tents, lawn chairs, tables, beer, coolers full of fresh fruit and vegetables, frozen meat, many loaves of bread, many pounds of cheese, coffee, tortillas, beer, dutch ovens, cookies, eight kinds of salsa, marshmallows, I think I've said beer, dry clothes, hiking shoes, two-burner propane stoves, a pancake griddle, a fire pan, charcoal briquettes, battery-powered lanterns, some Budweiser for when the beer is all gone, and (I swear to God) a croquet set. Steve has even thought to bring four pink plastic flamingos, with stab-in metal legs, for decorating the river frontage at each evening's camp.

Compared with an 18-foot raft, a kayak has only the most modest capacity for cargo. It can carry a few items, but they had better be small and precious. My own boat contains the following: an extra paddle, in two conjoinable pieces; air bags, to keep the boat afloat if I abandon ship and resort to swimming for my life; a pair of river sandals; a water bottle; a rescue rope coiled in a throw bag; a baseball cap; a little waterproof pouch (which rides in a handy bungee-cord shelf under the front deck, just above my knees) containing my river map, a pencil, and a Rite in the Rain notebook; and a roll-top waterproof bag, holding certain important sundries. The sundries are: my wallet, my watch, one energy bar, a container of sunscreen, and two books. The books are: *Illustrations of the Huttonian Theory of the Earth,* by a Scottish mathematician named John Playfair, and *Selected Poems,* by W. H. Auden. I've chosen these two as my intellectual and emotional sustenance for the trip. Like the energy bar, they're small packets but densely nutritious.

I'll have no time to read except during stolen moments in camp, evening and morning, so the books could just as well be in my dry bag of other stuff lashed aboard Piglet. But I prefer keeping them close to me, like survival gear.

Playfair's *Huttonian Theory* is not only a classic of science explication but also a famous act of personal loyalty. James Hutton, another Scotsman, sometimes considered the founder of modern geology, conceived a revolutionary and percipient vision of how Earth's surface has been shaped and reshaped by geological processes. But the grand opus in which Hutton presented his ideas— *Theory of the Earth, With Proofs and Illustrations*, two volumes, 1795—was so turgid, so repetitious, and so poorly received that his good friend Playfair undertook, after Hutton's death, to revivify the theory by describing it in a concise, readable form. The essence of Hutton's theory centers on three points, all of which seemed outlandishly heterodox in his time: (1) Earth's surface is constantly being eroded by water, ice, and wind, which grind old rock into sediments that are carried downstream for eventual deposition on the sea bottoms; (2) sea-bottom sediments, transmogrified slowly by pressure and heat, become stratified layers of new rock; (3) heat from below (what is its source?—that remained puzzling long after Hutton's time) also causes the slow uplift of those strata, and of the molten rock beneath them, eventually forming jagged mountains, domed plateaus, granitic knobs, great rifts and warpings, exposures and juxtapositions of variously tilted strata—all of which are subject to further erosion. In short, mountains become silt which becomes sedimentary rock which becomes mountains—a cycle that seems to go on indefinitely, showing, as Hutton put it, "no vestige of a beginning, no prospect of an end."

Hutton wasn't an impious man, but his theory provoked accusations of impiety. Among its corollaries and saucy implications were that (1) marine fossils at high elevations were not put there by Noah's flood; (2) the processes affecting topography nowadays—erosion, deposition, barely detectable uplift, and an occasional volcanic burp—are the same and the only processes that have shaped the world from its beginning; and therefore (3) planet Earth is much, much older than the figure of 6,000-some years that had been calculated by biblical literalists. "Time," Hutton wrote, "which measures every thing in our idea, and is often deficient to our schemes, is to nature endless and as nothing." Most of Hutton's prose wasn't so piquant, and his friend Playfair did a breezier job of arguing the Huttonian case. Everything that rises will be torn down, Playfair explained; everything torn down will be remade into something else, equally stony, equally grand, and rise again. My copy of Playfair's book is a facsimile of the first edition, published in 1802.

The Auden volume, by contrast, is a work of consummate 20th-century modernity. Published in 1979, it samples the best of a long, vibrant poetic lifetime. Although a few of Auden's later poems are even more opaque than an 18th-century disquisition on geology, I find deep pleasure and consolation in his grim, mordant, yet bravely humane work from the 1930s. Some of it is political, some intimately personal. Certain of these poems are written in a deceptively simple style that flows like light verse. One that I've read often, and will read again on the river, begins this way:

As I walked out one evening,
Walking down Bristol Street,
The crowds upon the pavement
Were fields of harvest wheat.

And down by the brimming river
I heard a lover sing

Under an arch of the railway:
"Love has no ending.

"I'll love you, dear, I'll love you
Till China and Africa meet
And the river jumps over the mountain
And the salmon sing in the street."

Both books fit easily into the back of my boat, their waterproof bag clipped in with a carabiner, beside the rescue rope.

FOR MOST OF ITS LENGTH IN THE CANYON—say, 90 percent of those 226 miles—the Colorado River is like a giant, sleeping snake, its latent power barely intimated by a gentle reptilian snore. The current glides slowly along, with only an occasional swell or whirlpool on an eddy line reflecting the vast, merciless energy held contained. But the river drops almost 2,000 feet between Lees Ferry and Lake Mead, and about half that total occurs in short, abrupt plunges—that is, rapids. During the next couple of days, we get our first real taste of the river's wild side.

Soap Creek Rapid is another frothy chain of waves, with no holes lurking to swallow and hold a boat, so Mark takes it as an opportunity to shoot some action close-ups. He runs Soap Creek backward, bracing himself with his paddle held in one hand, deploying his camera with the other, clicking off motor-drive shots of Rob amid the churning jiggle-jaggle of the waves. Halfway through, Mark flips upside down. I watch his boat bottom from not far away, awaiting a recovery. Underwater, he drops the protective container holding the camera and gets both hands on his paddle, then rolls briskly up, only to discover that one of his surf-housing straps has failed and the apparatus—all $3,400 of it, with a Nikon F-100 inside—seems to be gone. Bad moment, bad setback, to lose such a crucial piece of equipment so early in the trip. Then he notices the thing trailing behind him on one strap, like a drag bag of beer left in the water for chilling. He reels it in.

House Rock is more serious, a right-bending rapid in which the heavy chop pushes into a rock wall on the left, and near the bottom, a pair of tall waves guard the exit line, one of them not just breaking but recirculating as a hole. For the kayakers this doesn't present much trouble. Each of us enters on the flat green tongue, angling right, and with a few strokes amid the heavy water we're able to stay off the wall, ferry rightward, and punch through the hole along its right corner. We catch eddies at the bottom and hold position, ready if needed to help with a rescue. For the rafts, so heavily loaded, so lumbering, it's a different matter. In fact, this particular rapid proves a good reminder of a truth we already know well: Some stretches of water that are easily run by a competent kayaker can be wickedly problematic for a raft oarsman—and vice versa. In their strengths and their foibles, a big raft and a little kayak are as different as a locomotive and a horse.

Brian's locomotive runs next. With the unsavory groovers strapped firmly to its frame, with Chase Crayton and his high school buddy Cole Arpin whooping in the bow, Pooh edges away from the wall, drops straight into the hole, and goes nearly vertical, 18 feet of fat yellow sausage standing on end. Diz follows the same line in Piglet, with Kinsey Crayton and Margie Penney (a nurse from Colorado, old friend of Cyndi's) dangling forward, clutching handholds, to get thrillingly drenched in the breakers. Later, Bob will confide to me that he found himself quite flustered as he sculled in that eddy, watching his 12-year-old daughter ride through the rapid. It was a new sort of white-water excitement, jangling and unexpectedly disagreeable, for the old man. This time on the big river, he realized, he had given hostages to fortune.

And then comes Mike, his yellow canopy lowered for stormy running, a straw cowboy hat on his head. His raft being the lightest and the shortest, it's the most mobile but also the least stable, and he has no passengers to help with high-siding or bailing. He begins with an angle to the right, but then some-how his boat gets swung leftward, way leftward, and slides toward the paired waves like a van skidding on ice. When he hits the waves broadside, there's an alley-oop motion and Mike is suddenly lofted into the air—then into the water, gone. A few seconds later he bobs up beside the raft, minus his hat, and catches hold of an oar. By the time kayaks converge on him, he has already hoisted himself back in and brought the boat under control, a nice recovery by any measure.

Mike has made five earlier Grand Canyon trips. Experienced and provi-dent, he appears the next day with a different hat.

BY THE END OF THE WEEK we've followed the river downward through more than a billion years of time, descending past all nine major formations of Paleozoic sedimentary rock and into the Vishnu schist, dark and Precambrian. The cliff sides are suddenly closer, steeper, more stern and chilling, like melo-dramatic pinnacles in a woodcut by Rockwell Kent. The gunmetal-gray schist is shot through with sinuous veins of pinkish, mica-flecked intrusion known as

Zoroaster granite. In their physical presence as well as their mythic evocations, the Vishnu and the Zoroaster provide a somber, eerie sense of embrace. Rick says: "Welcome to the inner canyon gorge."

I'm still wondering how the river carved its way down here so quickly. The question is made even more baffling by the geologic conundrum I alluded to earlier, which involves a mysterious surmounting of certain obstacles. "The Colorado River has cut through several major upwarps, including the Kaibab Plateau, seemingly in defiance of the laws of gravity," according to Larry Stevens, author of the map booklet I'm using. "Controversy over how and when the Grand Canyon formed has raged for a century, but every new theory seems to be missing a critical piece of evidence." The central enigma that any theory must explain is how the early Colorado River, flowing at what seems to have been a middling elevation across an area known as the Marble Platform, managed to carve its way over— and then down into—a big, elongated dome of rock known as the Kaibab Uplift. From the surface of the Marble Platform to the crest of the Kaibab Uplift, as they stand today, there's a *rise* of several thousand feet. Did the water run uphill? Certainly not. Then how did the river get over that mountainous mound?

Nobody knows. But three different hypotheses have been offered during the past century and a half, each bidding to explain the mystery without recourse to miracles.

John Wesley Powell, after his pioneering explorations of the canyon in 1869 and 1872, guessed that the river had etched its path first, along what was a natural declivity, and that the Kaibab Uplift had risen afterward, raising the land surface against the river's flow like a loaf of bread being pushed into a band saw. Later research discredited that guess by establishing that the river channel is more recent than the vaulting.

A second hypothesis, which held sway in the 1960s, was that another river essentially backed its way through the Kaibab Uplift by what geologists call headward erosion. When a lump of rock is dislodged from the brink of, say, Niagara Falls, dropping into the gorge below, the brink itself recedes upstream by an increment equal to the size of the lost lump. That's headward erosion. The Canadian half of Niagara Falls, known as Horseshoe Falls, is eroding headward at the speedy rate of about five feet per year. Moving just a fraction that fast, the waters draining off the west side of the Kaibab area might have eaten backward through the uplift in not many millions of years, uniting with and capturing the upper Colorado.

A third hypothesis, articulated by a geologist named Ivo Lucchitta, suggests that the lower half of the Grand Canyon might well have been cut by headward erosion within only the past few million years, but that the upper half is much older. That upper half must have been carved (or at least begun) during a time when the Marble Platform itself was overlaid with thick layers of Mesozoic rock, from which the river could find a downhill angle across the Kaibab Uplift. The upper layers of rock were later stripped away, by some form of surface erosion, leaving the Marble Platform overshadowed by the Kaibab Uplift. But the uplift by then had a canyon sawn through it. In this view, the river jumped over the mountain by way of a ramp, but the ramp has since disappeared.

Other ideas are still being offered, and the mystery remains.

ON THE AFTERNOON OF DAY EIGHT we beach our boats at Phantom Ranch, one of very few sites within the canyon that connect by steep foot trails with the outside world. The little compound at Phantom includes a campground for hikers from the rims, a set of rest rooms, a corral of horses, and a small store. It's the only place where river travelers can buy a glass of cold lemonade, reexperience a flush toilet, and use a pay telephone. The date happens to be September 11, 2001. Mike makes the first call, to his wife, and returns with the day's scarcely believable news.

After a few more calls to loved ones on the outside, we drink our lemonades in somber silence and then return to the riverbank. We compare what we've heard and pool what we think we know: the World Trade Center leveled, the Pentagon hit, another plane downed near Pittsburgh (or was it Camp David?), perhaps two more hijacked airliners still unaccounted for, and 30,000 to 50,000 people dead in Manhattan, which is being evacuated. The country is shut down, the military is on highest alert, and George Bush is aboard *Air Force One,* somewhere, headed for Nebraska. Nebraska, I say, that means the underground nuclear command center, at Cheyenne Mountain. Cheyenne Mountain is in Colorado, says Margie, who comes from Boulder. You're right, I say, wait, no, Nebraska is the headquarters of the Strategic Air Command. What's going on? we all wonder. I've spoken only with my frail, cheerful, octogenarian parents in Minneapolis, mostly to confirm that they're all right. They are—distraught at the news, like everyone, but not personally assailed by terrorists. You won't see anything in the sky, says my mother, the planes are all grounded.

We climb into our boats. The rafts pull out, surrendering swoonlike to the current, heading downstream for another ten days in the canyon under conditions of near total isolation. The other kayakers peel away, too, and I find myself alone on the beach. I hesitate. Is there any conceivable reason, I consider, why I should abort this journey and walk out of here? Is there anything useful I can do? Is there anywhere else, right now, I should be? Anywhere else I want to be?

No. I signed on to this trip because I craved an exercise in detachment—from my own life as it has unfolded in recent years, and from the world. So here we are, I think, with an exercise in detachment far more dolorous than I'd foreseen. My sympathies to you, dead and grieving people; good luck, America. I paddle into the heavy current and let it swing me downstream.

WE HAVE RAPIDS TO RUN: Horn Creek, Crystal, Bedrock, Upset, and other frivolous challenges to mortality. On the water, we think about the water. In camp, especially when the darkening sky fills with stars and remains peculiarly empty of airplanes, it's different. We think about New York and beyond. We ponder the fact that we're missing a slice of American history, never to be regained, synthesized, or duplicated. We relish unabashedly the simple joys of being together in this marvelous, wild, ancient place.

Me, I'm glad also for the company of Auden. That evening, I reread his "September 1, 1939." With clever hopes expiring at the end of "a low dishonest decade," says the poet,

> Waves of anger and fear
> Circulate over the bright
> And darkened lands of the earth,
> Obsessing our private lives;
> The unmentionable odour of death
> Offends the September night.

It was written, of course, to mark the day Hitler invaded Poland. But the poem is wise beyond old news.

> I and the public know
> What all schoolchildren learn,
> Those to whom evil is done
> Do evil in return.

WE'VE CAMPED JUST ABOVE a formidable rapid called Hermit, rated 8. All night, in wakeful moments, we hear its roar. We're now on the threshold of the canyon's more serious water—beginning with Hermit, then Crystal, then a string of other rapids, culminating next week in Lava Falls. At dawn on the morning after our stop at Phantom Ranch, the sky is red. I think: Sailors, take warning.

Crystal proves just difficult enough to be interesting, with a huge crashing hole at the bottom center and several offset holes farther up. Al and I choose a left line, catching an eddy halfway down along that wall, from which we watch the others run right. We peel, cross between holes, and follow. Within the next few miles, we ride the big waves of Tuna Creek, Sapphire, and Serpentine, which deliver us into camp that afternoon on a surge of white-water euphoria, overshadowed by our concern about events beyond the canyon rim.

SEVERAL DAYS LATER, we stop to hike up a side canyon called Matkatamiba, a tranquil afternoon's interlude for stretching our legs and gawking at a different sort of scenery. Digressing to explore such byways—with their slots, waterfalls, secret chambers, and polished walls—is an important part of the Grand Canyon experience, a felicity that complements the big-river rush. We've already probed a nice selection: Shinumo Wash, Nautiloid Canyon, Elves Chasm, and a dramatic waterspout called Thunder River, blasting out of its hole in a great cliff. Matkatamiba Canyon is more graceful than any of them.

We catch a blind eddy at Matkatamiba's mouth, leave the boats, and ascend between walls of smoothly curvaceous blue-green limestone, our feet sloshing in clear, warmish water. In some spots the channel, buffed smooth, is only as wide as one human foot. We wade, clamber, and walk several hundred yards before the little canyon bends sharply and, there at its crook, opens out into a natural rotunda. Walls of red rock, hundreds of feet high and undercut with galleries, rise above; the little creek tumbles along its delicate path, across a floor that resembles artfully terraced slate; California redbuds and catclaw acacias, elegantly gnarled like bonsai, stand in patches of rocky soil; and across one spring-moistened slope drapes a profusion of wild grapevines, grasses, and maidenhair ferns, offering a textural counterpoint—cool and green—to all the warm, dry stone. At the center of this extraordinary space is an island of large boulders, like a dais. The whole layout seems to have been designed, perhaps by a subtle Japanese architect, for human ceremony.

Someone says, This would be a great place to hear a concert. Someone else says, This would be a great place to get married. Alluding to a pair of our other kayaking chums, back in Montana, Rick says: "Ron and Carla did get married here."

Married here? It strikes me as an innocent, weird thought from a race of beings to which I don't presently belong. I keep my mouth shut, remembering a December day 18 years ago, when I myself and a wonderful, serious, joyous woman got married in a beautiful place—on the side of Kitt Peak, in southern Arizona, with a view of Baboquivari, sacred mountain of the Papago. Ultimately it didn't help.

AT THE BOTTOM OF UPSET RAPID, stretching wide across the main flow, is a menacing hole. At the top, just beyond the tongue, is a seemingly innocuous diagonal wave, curling off the left wall. The tongue itself isn't glassy and green, not today. Distant rainstorms somewhere upstream have brought a deluge of mocha silt, and the whole river has done a chameleon shift from olive to sullen brown. Even the whitecaps are no longer white. They look like fresh adobe.

After we've scouted the rapid and picked routes for avoiding the hole, Mike takes a leftish line of entry and then, to his shock and ours, finds his raft lifted sideways by the upper wave, which tips him, flips him, as smoothly as a single-blade plow turning dirt. He and Margie, his passenger today, tumble through the air in what seems like choreographed, Hollywood-stunt slow motion. Then they endure the full rapid, dunked through the hole and swept along, trying to catch breaths and get hold of the overturned boat. By the time we reach them, they're in calmer water but still fighting current and cold. Margie, swimming and gasping, grabs hold of my stern handle for a tow to the bank and then, as she climbs out into a jumble of boulders, nearly steps on a rattlesnake, which she hears rattling but can barely see, since her contacts have been splashed awry. I return to help Rick and John, who are bulldozing the raft toward shore with their kayaks. We get it secured and then, with ten pairs of arms lifting and pushing, flipped back upright. The only loss is a lawn chair that wasn't strapped down. Frustrated, embarrassed, Mike says, "I'm gonna take up bowling when I get back to Salt Lake."

The upset at Upset feels like a foreboding prelude. That night over dinner our talk turns with titillating grimness to Lava Falls, which we'll face tomorrow. Bob recalls it vividly from 20 years ago. Steve mentions that the right-side line is difficult at low water, and low water is what we'll have. The right side, Rick says, is always a gnarly run. Mike says, My boat needs more ballast; I'll fill the empty carboys with river water. None of the rest of us has ever seen this storied drop. It's a sinister place, with all that lava rock, says Rick. You can talk about running Lava this way or that, Steve adds, but you don't really know what you're going to do until you get there.

Bedding down on the warm sand, I embrace a few resolute thoughts. No point wasting time or energy worrying about things in advance—especially not a mere rapid on a lovely river. If I happen to drown in Lava, which is highly unlikely but possible, it's not important. If I embarrass myself, floundering, swimming for dear life and being rescued, that's even less important. If I manage to slide through with aplomb, less important still. What's important is not to have done Lava Falls but to do it. What matters is to enter the rapid and live its 10 or 20 seconds of magisterial chaos as acutely as possible.

I'm just not sensitive enough, I suppose, to be an angst-ridden person. I sleep soundly, and dream of pretty women and skiing.

WE HEAR IT BEFORE WE SEE IT. Then there's a horizon line, like beveled marble, where the whole river drops away invisibly. Just upstream of the suck, we pull ashore to scout.

A high cliff of coal-dark basalt looms on the right, a cutaway section of what once was an igneous dam, showing fudgy swirls, puckers, and long rows of columnar basaltic crystals like grinning teeth. We climb. From above on a rocky trail—just the sort of perspective that always makes rapids look deceptively small—Lava looks big. It's not so much a waterfall—despite the name—as a raging cascade. Impassable rocks on the left, a hole on the right, several curling waves, another hole, hectic zones of disorderly froth, a big sloping rock at bottom right against which a person would not want to be pinned, and just beside that, another roiling hole, in front of which is a high, tumbling wave. "Busy" is the white-water term. The right line does look uninviting. The left line doesn't exit. There's no sneak route. But there is an imaginable path, from upper right to lower left, nudging past the curlers, crossing a hurricane's eye of relatively calm water, ferrying wide of the lower hole, that each of us commits to mind like a mantra. Then it's back to the boats.

Rick disappears over the horizon line. Bob follows. John signals me from shore: Okay, DQ, your turn. I can see almost nothing as I paddle down the approach tongue. My brain is vacant of any thought more profoundly speculative than: Well, here I go. As the first waves hit, I hit back, with an aggressive right brace that seems to have been a bit too aggressive, because I find myself in mid-rapid with my head underwater on the right. Not wanting to drop entirely upside down (and set up to roll, which would take time), I hold that position for a second or three, hoping that a random upswell might lift me; then, either with such a lift or without it (who knows, who remembers?), I manage to wiggle upright off my very deep brace, finding balance, finding air. I take a few strokes, gather a little momentum, in time to punch my head sideways through the lower wave and miss the hole. As easy as that, I'm in an eddy below, my body aflush with a wave of elated relief.

We wait vigilantly, Rick and Bob and I, bobbing like flotsam in the left lower eddy, for the others. As Mike's blue raft slides neatly between the lower hole and the sloped rock, he pumps his fist with the joy of redemption. Diz, forced to run last so that Mark can shoot him in action from Piglet's own bow, finds a nifty line, bringing all our remaining Pringles through safely.

Rob comments later that I had "an exciting run," which is polite but not complimentary, and that he captured it all on video. Cyndi herself will find irony in the fact that "the most conservative boater had the most exciting run," with which I can't argue. I'm content to know that, perhaps for the first time ever, W. H. Auden (or, at least, one of his books) has taken a kayak ride through Lava Falls.

ON THE LAST EVENING, our 17th on the river, we celebrate with rum punch and begin regretting that the trip has passed so quickly, like a blink. We're in no great hurry to rejoin the world, however the world may now be. We've had almost no news, but within the past few days we've noticed planes reappearing in the sky, evidently on a route between Phoenix and Los Angeles. We can scarcely imagine, or care, what the men and women who sit behind television anchor desks have been saying. Our detachment from the events and aftermath of September 11 has been decreed by circumstance and enforced by isolation; bizarre, cold, not without deep sympathy, and salubrious. The loudest noise down here is the roar of water. Ravens, not newsmen, hover nearby like undertakers. The strata of rock and the silt in the river serve as reminders, thanks to James Hutton, that everything built will be ground down, and that all grinding provides new material for building. At least some of us feel that, with enough food, enough river, we could continue indefinitely this mode of travel and life amid this amiable company. But there isn't enough. Size is relative, like time, and in some ways the Grand Canyon is too small. The journey through it is nearly over, already.

As for my personal supplies: I've finished Playfair's *Huttonian Theory*, but there's still plenty of unread Auden, partly because I've been revisiting favorites. I've joined him repeatedly, for instance, on that evening walk down Bristol Street, past the railway arch, from beneath which comes the voice, claiming:

"I'll love you, dear, I'll love you
Till China and Africa meet
And the river jumps over the mountain

And the salmon sing in the street."

After listening through further such promises of eternal devotion, the eavesdropping poet detects a counterpoint:

But all the clocks in the city
Began to whirr and chime:
"O let not Time deceive you,
You cannot conquer Time.

"In the burrows of the Nightmare
Where Justice naked is,
Time watches from the shadow
And coughs when you would kiss."

My hands ache in the night, pleasantly, from 17 days of hard use. My shoulders are no worse than when I started. My body has found the river regimen agreeable, and my brain has been drawn outside itself. I feel rinsed, peaceful, and whole. I know the end of the poem almost by heart:

It was late, late in the evening,
The lovers they were gone;
The clocks had ceased their chiming
And the deep river ran on.

Next day, our last, we cover six miles of flat water. From the takeout beach at Diamond Creek, as we load our boats into a truck, I can hear the gentle growl of another rapid, just below, waiting to be run.

JANUARY/ FEBRUARY 2002

HELL AND BACK

By Kira Salak

---

*For centuries, Amazonian shamans have used ayahuasca as a window into
the troubled soul. When the author, dogged by depression and other spiritual
demons, participates in the ancient ceremony, she enters worlds more
terrifying—and enlightening—than she ever imagined.*

I WILL NEVER FORGET what it was like.

The overwhelming misery. The certainty of never-ending suffering. No
one to help you, no way to escape. Everywhere I looked: darkness so thick that
the idea of light seemed inconceivable.

Suddenly, I swirled down a tunnel of fire, wailing figures calling out to
me in agony, begging me to save them. Others tried to terrorize me. "You will
never leave here," they said. "Never. Never."

I found myself laughing at them. "I'm not scared of you," I said.

But the darkness became even thicker; the emotional charge of suffering
nearly unbearable. I felt as if I would burst from heartbreak—everywhere, I
felt the agony of humankind, its tragedies, its hatreds, its sorrows.

I reached the bottom of the tunnel and saw three thrones in a black chamber. Three shadowy figures sat in the chairs; in the middle was what I took to
be the devil himself.

"The darkness will never end," he said. "It will never end. You can never
escape this place."

"I can," I replied. All at once, I willed myself to rise. I sailed up through
the tunnel of fire, higher and higher until I broke through to a white light.
All darkness immediately vanished. My body felt light, at peace. I floated
among a beautiful spread of colors and patterns. Slowly my ayahuasca vision

faded. I returned to my body, to where I lay in the hut, insects calling from the jungle.

"Welcome back," the shaman said.

The next morning, I discovered the impossible: The severe depression that had ruled my life since childhood had miraculously vanished.

GIANT BLUE BUTTERFLIES flutter clumsily past our canoe. Parrots flee higher into treetops. The deeper we go into the Amazon jungle, the more I realize I can't turn back. It has been a year since my last visit, and I'm here again in Peru traveling down the Río Aucayacu for more shamanistic healing. The truth is, I'm petrified to do it a second time around. But with shamanism—and with the drinking of ayahuasca in particular—I've learned that, for me, the worse the experience, the better the payoff. There is only one requirement for this work: You must be brave. You'll be learning how to save yourself.

The jungle camp where our shamanistic treatment will take place is some 200 miles from the nearest town, Iquitos, deep in the Peruvian Amazon. Beside me are the other four members of my tour. There is Winston, the biggest person I've ever met. Nearly seven feet tall, surely over 400 pounds, he has a powerful body that could easily rip someone apart. I expect him to be a bodyguard or a bouncer; turns out he's a security guard. But there is something else about him. Something less tangible. It seems to rest in the black circles beneath his eyes, the face that never smiles, the glances that immediately dismiss all they survey. Winston does not seem like a happy man.

Then the others: Lisa, who has a master's degree from Stanford and is now pursuing her doctorate in political theory at Duke University; Christy, who just quit her job counseling at-risk teens to travel around South America; and Katherine, Christy's British friend. By all appearances, our group seems to be composed of ordinary citizens. No New Age energy healers. No pan flute makers. No hippies or Rastafarians or nouveau Druids. Christy betrays only a passing interest in becoming a yoga instructor.

And then there is me, who a year ago came to Peru on a lark to take the "sacred spirit medicine," ayahuasca, and get worked over by shamans. Little suspecting that I'd emerge from it feeling as if a waterlogged wool coat had been removed from my shoulders—literally feeling the burden of depression lifted—and thinking that there must be something to this crazy shamanism after all.

And so I am back again.

I've told no one this time—especially not my family. I grew up among fundamentalist atheists who taught me that we're all alone in the universe, the fleeting dramas of our lives culminating in a final, ignoble end: death. Nothing beyond that. It was not a prescription for happiness, yet, for the first couple decades of my life, I became prideful and arrogant about my atheism, believing that I was one of the rare few who had the courage to face life without the "crutches" of religion or, worse, such outrageous notions as shamanism. But for all of my overweening rationality, my world remained a dark, forbidding place beyond my control. And my mortality gaped at me mercilessly.

Lisa shakes me from my reveries, asking why I've come back to take another tour with the shamans.

"I've got some more work to do," I say. Hers is a complicated question to answer. And especially personal. Lord knows I didn't have to come back. I could have been content with the results of my last visit: no more morbid desires to die. Waking up one morning in a hut in the sultry jungles of Peru, desiring only to live.

Still, even after those victories I knew there were some stubborn enemies hiding out in my psyche: Fear and Shame. They were taking potshots at my newfound joy, ambushing my successes. How do you describe what it's like to want love from another but to be terrified of it at the same time? To want good things to happen to you, while some disjointed part of you believes that you don't deserve them? To look in a mirror and see only imperfections? This was the meat and potatoes of my several years of therapy. Expensive therapy. Who did what—when—why. The constant excavations of memory. The sleuthwork. Patching together theory after theory. Rational-emotive behavioral therapy. Gestalt therapy. Humanistic therapy. Biofeedback. Positive affirmations. I am a beautiful person. I deserve the best in life.

Then, there's the impatience. Thirty-three years old already, for chrissakes. And in all that time, after all that therapy, only one thing worked on my depression—an ayahuasca "cleansing" with Amazonian shamans.

OUR CANOE DOCKS ON THE BANKS of the Río Aucayacu near a large hut surrounded by jungle: the healing center. We unload our bags and supplies and a local man leads us to our respective bungalows. I share mine with Lisa. Our accommodations are without frills: a mosquito net covering a mattress on the floor, a sink, a toilet. Basic meals. Kerosene lamps. We can either bathe in the river or use a communal shower. It is a kind of asceticism, a shedding of life's little sophistications in preparation for the hard work ahead. Where we're going, all worldly goods are worthless. Where we're going, the only way out is through fear.

The head shaman for our group is Hamilton Souther, an American and the man behind the company that runs these journeys, Blue Morpho. He is 27, blond-haired, blue-eyed, exceptionally good-looking. But talk to him for even a minute, and his striking appearance quickly fades before his most obvious quality: his unconditional acceptance of everyone. You cannot make him angry. You cannot seduce him. You cannot offend him (though it is extremely tempting to try). He is like a mirror, always reflecting back your own ego, showing you your attachments, your fixations, your fears. If you end up liking him, that's great, but if you don't, it's unimportant.

How Hamilton, a young California gringo, ended up in the middle of the Peruvian jungle as a shamanic healer is a story that stretches credulity. When he was "younger" (which is to say, a young adult), he explains, he led a very troubled life. Controlled by anger, he found the world to be a depressing, hopeless place in which he was just another inmate doing time. Then on the darkest night of his life, when he was filled with spiritual despair, he says he called to God and begged him—if he did really exist—to show himself. Hamilton claims he then heard voices and saw spirits. He thought he'd gone insane. So did his psychologist. But then a trusted acquaintance suggested that he wasn't crazy at all; he'd merely opened channels to other dimensions.

One of the many spirit voices advised him to go to South America to apprentice under a shaman. He took this advice, made his way to Peru, and found two master shamans to teach him everything they knew. One of them, Don Julio Gerena Pinedo, is with us now. He is 87, has been leading ayahuasca ceremonies for over 50 years, and is widely regarded as one of the most powerful healers in the Amazon. He sits hunched over in a chair in the main hut, holding a large cigar, or *mapacho,* made from jungle-grown tobacco that is used, he says, to purify his body from negative energy. Hamilton and his three gringo shaman apprentices affectionately call Don Julio "Yoda."

On the way here, Hamilton stopped our canoe periodically to hike into the jungle to collect the fixings for our ayahuasca brew. "Ayahuasca," a Quechua word meaning "vine of the soul," is shorthand for a concoction of Amazonian plants that shamans have boiled down for centuries to use for healing purposes. Though some call the mixture a drug, indigenous peoples regard such a description as derogatory. To them it is a medicine that has been used by the tribes of the Amazon Basin for hundreds, perhaps thousands, of years, demanding respect and right intention. The main chemical in the brew, dimethyltryptamine (DMT), accounts for ayahuasca's illegality in the United States; DMT, though chemically distant from LSD, has hallucinogenic properties. But it is ayahuasca's many plant ingredients cooperating ingeniously to allow DMT to circulate freely in the body that produce the unique ayahuasca experience.

To prepare the brew, apprentices spend years under the tutelage of an elder shaman getting to know the different plant ingredients, passing weeks or months at a time learning their individual healing properties and governing spirits. These beings, they claim, teach them *icaros,* or spirit songs, which, when sung or whistled, call forth the plants' unique assistance during ceremonies. The training isn't easy; those like Hamilton who earn the title of "master shaman"—highly respected members of Amazonian communities—receive patients from far and wide. Based on the individual needs of their patients, shamans must know which plants are required for a ceremony (there are two primary ingredients, but any of an estimated 100 species have been used in ayahuasca brews), how much of them to harvest, and how to prepare them for ingestion. The plants' spirits are then said to work together to produce the most successful possible healing for each person, regardless of what ails them.

The taking of ayahuasca has been associated with a long list of documented cures: the disappearance of everything from metastasized colorectal cancer to cocaine addiction, even after just a ceremony or two. It's thought to be non-addictive and safe to ingest. Yet Western scientists have all but ignored it for decades, reluctant to risk their careers by researching a substance containing the outlawed DMT. Only in the past decade, and then only by a handful of researchers, has ayahuasca begun to be studied.

At the vanguard of this research is Charles Grob, M.D., a professor of psychiatry and pediatrics at UCLA's School of Medicine. In 1993 Dr. Grob launched the Hoasca Project, the first in-depth study of the physical and psychological effects of ayahuasca on humans. His team went to Brazil, where the plant mixture can be taken legally, to study members of a native church, the União do Vegetal (UDV), who use ayahuasca as a sacrament, and compared them to a control group that had never ingested the substance. The studies found that all the ayahuasca-using UDV members had experienced remission without recurrence of their addictions, depression, or anxiety disorders. In addition, blood samples revealed a startling discovery: Ayahuasca seems to give users a greater sensitivity to serotonin—one of the mood-regulating chemicals produced by the body—by increasing the number of serotonin receptors on nerve cells.

Unlike most common antidepressants, which Grob says can create such high levels of serotonin that cells may actually compensate by losing many of their serotonin receptors, the Hoasca Project showed that ayahuasca strongly enhances the body's ability to absorb the serotonin that's naturally there. "Ayahuasca is perhaps a far more sophisticated and effective way to treat depression than SSRIs [antidepressant drugs]," Grob concludes, adding that the use of SSRIs is "a rather crude way" of doing it. And ayahuasca, he insists, has great potential as a long-term solution.

While it's tantalizing to wonder whether such positive physiological changes took place in me when I was last in Peru, I'm also intrigued by the visions I had, which seemed to have an equally powerful role in alleviating my depression: It was as if I'd been shown my own self-imposed hells and taught how to free myself from them. What was really going on?

According to Grob, ayahuasca provokes a profound state of altered consciousness that can lead to temporary "ego disintegration," as he calls it, allowing people to move beyond their defense mechanisms into the depths of their unconscious minds—a unique opportunity, he says, that cannot be duplicated by any nondrug therapy methods.

"You come back with images, messages, even communications," he explains. "You're learning about yourself, reconceptualizing prior experiences. Having had a profound psycho-spiritual epiphany, you're not the same person you were before." But the curious should take heed: The unconscious mind holds many things you don't want to look at. All those self-destructive beliefs, suppressed traumatic events, denied emotions. Little wonder that an ayahuasca vision can reveal itself as a kind of hell in which a person is forced—literally—to face his or her demons. "Ayahuasca is not for everyone," Grob warns. "It's probably not for most people in our world today. You have to be willing to have a very powerful, long, internal experience, which can get very scary. You have to be willing to withstand that."

IT'S 9 P.M.—TIME FOR THE FIRST CEREMONY. We all meet in the main hut. Outside, night has taken over the jungle, which resounds with piercing insect calls. We will have five such ceremonies before going back to civilization. Each takes place at 9 p.m. We've fasted since lunch. One of the apprentices spreads out foam mattresses in a circle for us to lie on. Hamilton and Don Julio sit in front of us, in chairs, lighting their mapachos, with their apprentices seated on either side. Hamilton asks Lisa, the would-be Duke political theorist, to sit next to Winston, but she immediately protests.

"I don't want to sit next to any aggressive male energy," she says. "Can I change places?"

Winston glances at her forlornly. Lisa is probably the most physically attractive of the women on our tour—thin, dainty, with delicate porcelain-doll features. Winston rolls his eyes as Lisa moves away from him, and Hamilton puts me next to him instead.

Before we start, Hamilton takes out a liter of the ayahuasca he'd prepared during the day. This he hands to Don Julio, who blesses it with his mapacho, blowing tobacco smoke inside the bottle and over his body. He clears his throat several times, sounding like a horse whinnying, and hands the bottle to Hamilton to do the same. Hamilton pays homage to the ayahuasca spirits, speaking to them in Spanish and entreating them to help us.

Everyone receives a plastic basin—known ominously as a "vomit bucket"—and a roll of toilet paper for wiping our mouths after puking; this can be expected during most ceremonies, unless, as the shamans say, people are used to suppressing their feelings. Many mistakenly think that holding back emotions is a sign of strength and control; actually, Hamilton says, it's the opposite. Avoidance, a refusal to face painful feelings, is a weakness; unless this suppression stops, a person will never be healed of physical and psychological issues.

Perhaps the worst thing about taking ayahuasca is the taste. It is a thick brown sludge, gritty and triggering an immediate gag reflex. The closest taste comparison I can make is Baileys Irish Cream mixed with prune juice. The shamans say that the spirits tell them how much each of us needs to drink. The more healing a person needs, the more they get. I must need a lot of healing, then, as nearly a full cup is passed to me, versus the baby helpings poured for Lisa and Christy. The good news, I tell myself, is that no one to my knowledge has ever died from ayahuasca.

I drink it as if I were a contestant on *Fear Factor,* in two big, quick gulps. When everyone in our circle has drunk, including Hamilton, the kerosene lamp is put out and darkness fills the hut. Hamilton and Don Julio start shaking their *chakapas,* or leaf rattles, and singing their spirit songs. Nothing happens for about 20 minutes. I close my eyes and wait. Soon I start to see a pale green glow; colorful, primordial forms, resembling amoebas or bacteria, float by. Alarmed, I open my eyes. And this is uncanny: I can see the rafters of the hut, the thatch roof, the glow of the stars outside the screened windows—but the same amoeba-like things are passing over that view, as if superimposed.

"You're seeing with your third eye," one of the apprentices explains. Also known in Eastern spiritual traditions as the sixth chakra, the third eye supposedly allows for connection with other dimensions. And what if I am actually seeing two worlds at once? It seems too incredible, and I close my eyes to limit the confusion. Fantastical scenes glide by, composed of ever-shifting geometric forms and textures. Colors seem to be the nature of these views; a dazzling and dizzying display of every conceivable hue blending and parting in kaleido-scopic brilliance. But then the colors vanish all at once as if a curtain has been pulled down. Blackness. Everywhere.

Dark creatures sail by. Tangles of long, hissing serpents. Dragons spitting fire. Screaming humanlike forms. For a bunch of hallucinations, they seem terrifyingly real. An average ayahuasca ceremony lasts about four to five hours. But in ayahuasca space—where time, linear thought, and the rules of three-dimensional reality no longer apply—four to five hours of sheer darkness and terror can feel like a lifetime. My heartbeat soars; it's hard to breathe. But I have done this before. I remind myself that what I'm experiencing now is my fear taking symbolic form through the ayahuasca. Fear that I have lived with my entire life and that needs to be released.

Hamilton explains it this way: Everyone has an energetic body run by an inextinguishable life force. In Eastern traditions, this force, known as chi or prana, is manipulated through such things as acupuncture or yoga to run smoothly and prevent the buildup of the negative energies that cause bodily disease, mental illness, and even death. To Amazonian shamans, however, these negative energies are actual spirit entities that attach themselves to the body and cause mischief. In everyone, Hamilton asserts, there is a loving "higher self," but whenever unpleasant thoughts enter a person's mind—anger, fear, sorrow—it's because a dark spirit is hooked to the body and is temporarily commandeering the person's mind. In some cases, he adds, particularly evil spirits from the lowest hell of the "astral realms" take over a person perma-nently—known as full-blown demonic possession—creating a psychopathic mind that seeks only to harm others.

I work on controlling my breathing. But such thick darkness. Clouds of bats and demonlike faces. Black lightning. Black walls materializing before me no matter which way I turn. Closer and closer, the darkness surrounding me, trapping me. I can barely breathe.

"Hamilton!" I belt out. "Help me!"

"On my way, Kira," he says calmly. "Hang in there. Don't give in to the fear."

That's the trick: Don't give in to it. But it's much easier said than done. I must tell it that I'm stronger. I must tell it that it has no effect upon me. But it does. I'm terrified. The darkness presses against me; it wants to annihilate me.

Hamilton is standing over me now, rattling his chakapa, singing his spirit songs. Inexplicably, as he does this, the darkness backs off. But more of it comes in a seemingly endless stream. I see dark, raging faces. My body begins to contort; it feels as if little balls are ripping through my flesh, bursting from my skin. The pain is excruciating. I writhe on the mattress, screaming. Hamilton calls over one of his helpers—a local woman named Rosa—with directions to hold me down.

"Tell the spirits to leave you with ease," Hamilton says to me.

"They won't!" I yell out. And now they appear to be escaping en masse from my throat. I hear myself making otherworldly squealing and hissing sounds. Such high-pitched screeches that surely no human could ever make. All the while there is me, like a kind of witness, watching and listening in horror, feeling utterly helpless to stop it. I've read nothing about this sort of experience happening when taking ayahuasca. And now I see an image of a mountain in Libya, a supposedly haunted mountain that I climbed a year and a half ago, despite strong warnings from locals. A voice tells me that whatever is now leaving my body attached itself to me in that place.

Haunted mountains. Demonic hitchhikers. Who would believe this? Yet on and on it goes. The screaming, the wailing. My body shakes wildly; I see a great serpent emerging from my body, with designs on Hamilton. He shakes his chakapa at it, singing loudly, and after what seems like an infinite battle of wills, the creature leaves me. I grab the vomit bucket and puke for several minutes. Though my stomach has been empty for over eight hours, a flood of solid particles comes out of me.

The visions fade. My body stops shaking. Hamilton takes his seat again and Rosa releases her grip on me. I examine the vomit bucket with a flashlight: Black specks the size of dimes litter orange-colored foam. The shamans believe that what we vomit out during a ceremony is the physical manifestation of dark energy and toxins being purged from the body. The more that comes out, the better.

"Good work, Kira," Hamilton says to me from across the room.

My entire body hurts. My head throbs. I can hear the others in the room, whispering to each other. I had barely been conscious of their experiences, they had seemed so quiet by comparison.

"Is Kira OK?" Christy asks Hamilton.

"She just had a little exorcism," Hamilton explains with relish. "She's fine."

"Bloody hell; was that what it was?" says Katherine.

"She just picked up some travelers," Hamilton says. "We had to get rid of them."

"Bloody hell!" Katherine says again. "Is this what you'd consider a normal ceremony, Hamilton?"

"About one out of a hundred ceremonies is as intense as this one. We kicked some real demon butt tonight."

The apprentices agree that they've never experienced anything as intense as tonight's ceremony. I hope it's not true, though. It's hardly a distinction worth celebrating.

"Once you get the upper hand over demons energetically," Hamilton says to me, "they leave you without any trouble. That'll come. One thing at a time."

THERE IS PROBABLY NO HANGOVER that comes anywhere close to the hangover from an exorcism. It's the next morning and I can barely walk—not that I really want to. I have zero energy. My voice is almost gone, and I must communicate in a hoarse whisper if I communicate at all. This has proven not to be an issue as the others on the tour are so freaked out by what happened last night that they can barely mumble an obligatory "good morning" to me. Lisa has now made it clear that she doesn't want to sit next to Winston or me. I give her a wide berth as I take my seat at the breakfast table. I've never felt so vulnerable before complete strangers, and I feel embarrassed and dejected by their stares. I want to tell them that what happened last night was completely out of my control. That, somehow, it wasn't me.

But how to explain it when I don't quite understand it myself? All I can say for sure is that Hamilton's role as shaman was critical in helping me. He says he drinks the brew along with us, his "clients," so he and his army of spirit helpers can defeat our most formidable demons and guide us out of our darkness.

Shamans will tell you that during an ayahuasca cleansing they're not working with the contents of a person's hallucination but are actually visiting that person in whatever plane of reality his or her spirit happens to be. We are not, they insist, confined to the reality of our five senses, but can transcend it and enter a multidimensional universe. Their perspective is not unlike that presented by quantum theorists, such as David Bohm, who describe a holographic universe with coexisting realms of reality. To Amazonian shamans, there are an infinite number of such realms, each as distinct from one another as London or Paris, each inhabited by beings with certain appearances, abilities, and customs. To become a master shaman, they contend, one must learn to negotiate these worlds, to enlist the assistance of their various denizens, to become comfortable working in places of light and darkness. For, they will tell you, there is no doubt that there is a heaven and hell—many levels and manifestations of each, in fact—which are as real as Tokyo or Palm Beach. Yes, one finds angels and demons in such places. Hollywood got that part right.

But to the mind trained in the West, such notions of spirit travel and multidimensional reality are a long stretch for the imagination. "I do not believe that there are beings and creatures just like us who reside elsewhere in other realms," wrote Benny Shanon, Ph.D., a psychology professor at Hebrew University in Jerusalem. He drank ayahuasca in more than 130 ceremonies, studying his and others' vision experiences and producing one of the most extensive books on the subject to date, *The Antipodes of the Mind*, in which he concludes that the visions are simply hallucinations of the highest order: "Under [ayahuasca's] intoxication, people's imagination and creative powers are greatly enhanced. Thus, their minds are prone to create the fantastic images they see with the brew." In Shanon's view, as well as in those of other Western scientists, DMT-created visions are simply extraordinary reflections of the contents of the unconscious mind. Grob, the UCLA psychiatrist and ayahuasca researcher, agrees with this in part, though he adds: "Sometimes the visions are uncanny and don't seem to reflect personal experience. . . . People consistently have very profound spiritual experiences with this compound."

And this notion of a spiritual experience marks the very juncture where Western science and analytic thought depart on the subject of ayahuasca and where indigenous culture and mysticism come in. Most ayahuasca researchers agree that, curiously, the compound appears to affect people on three different levels—the physical, psychological, and spiritual—complicating efforts to definitively catalog its effects, let alone explain specific therapeutic benefits. Says Ralph Metzner, psychologist, ayahuasca researcher, and editor of the book *Sacred Vine of Spirits*, "[Healing with ayahuasca] presumes a completely different understanding of illness and medicine than what we are accustomed to in the West. But even from the point of view of Western medicine and psychotherapy it is clear that remarkable physical healings and resolutions of psychological difficulties can occur with this medicine."

WE TAKE A BREAK FOR A DAY TO recuperate. By the time the next ceremony comes along, I am enthusiastic and ready to go. We all take our seats in the main hut, Lisa sitting farthest from me. With resignation, I notice that I've been doled out a huge dose of ayahuasca, again. We all drink. Soon, the telltale green hue covers everything, and the visions begin. Dark visions. The bats, the snakes, the demon figures. Still, my body does not quake in pain and horror as before. I have learned how fear works: It only affects me, terrorizes me, if I believe the thoughts it puts in my head.

All negative thoughts, shamans believe, are dark spirits speaking to us, trying to scare us into reacting; the spirits then feed on our reactivity, growing stronger and more formidable until they finally rule over us. This is how, Hamilton suggests, addictions and psychological disorders develop in people.

"Everyone hears the voices of spirits," he tells me. "They've just convinced themselves that they are hearing their own thoughts." We must, he maintains, practice choosing which thoughts we pay attention to.

Now I'm traveling to a realm where I meet my various incarnations from past lives. We are connected to a large wheel; whenever fear energy leaves the top of my head in puffs of dark smoke, it leaves their heads at the same time. Our lives, it seems, are interconnected and dependent. Outside of linear time, all our lifetimes, all our many incarnations, occur simultaneously. "Past life" is really a misnomer; "other life" seems a more accurate way of describing it.

With some of the individuals, I can guess their historical period from their clothing. With others, I can't place them at all. There is a balding, overweight, monk-looking guy. The big muscular warrior with the pointed helmet (who, he says, gives me my present interest in the martial arts). The black woman who is a slave in North Carolina. Interestingly, there are only about 15 or so individuals; a spirit tells me that many people average less than 30 total Earth incarnations and that their souls commonly skip centuries, reincarnating only in spirit realms.

And what of the two women who aren't wearing historically identifiable clothing? "We are your future incarnations," one of them explains, lovingly.

AFTER THREE CEREMONIES I still feel that I have something big to purge. There is something stubborn in me, refusing to be released. I walk through the jungle and wade into a narrow river, dunking myself in the water. Schools of piranha-size fish, *mojaritas,* nip harmlessly at my skin, unnerving me. Earlier today I was still scared to look at myself in the mirror, still scared of the self-judgment, the all-too-familiar shame.

I report to the hut for the next ceremony. The others sit or lie in hammocks, waiting silently, fretfully. Their experiences, while nowhere near as intense as mine, have been bad enough in their view. Winston has found the darkness during his visions tedious and unrelenting. Christy actually found herself crying during the last ceremony, which is something she says she doesn't do. Lisa has found her ceremony experiences "too dark" for her tastes and blames me for creating this.

"It's her own fear she's scared of," Hamilton told me earlier. "It has nothing to do with you."

We begin the ceremony, drink the ayahuasca. I'm hoping to find myself in some heavenly realms this time, but again, as usual, the darkness. With disappointment, I find myself entering a familiar tunnel of fire, heading down to one of the hell realms. I don't know where I'm going, or why, when I suddenly glimpse the bottom of the tunnel and leap back in shock: *Me*, I'm there, but as a little girl. She's huddled, captive, in a ball of fire before the three thrones of the devil and his sidekicks. As soon as I reach her, she begins wailing, "Don't leave me! Don't leave me!" It's heartbreaking to her.

I think this must be a part of me that I lost. Long ago. The shamans believe that whenever a traumatic event happens to us, we lose part of our spirit, that it flees the body to survive the experience. And that unless a person undergoes a shamanistic "soul retrieval," these parts will be forever lost. Each one, they say, contains an element of who they truly are; people may lose their sense of humor, their trust of others, their innocence. According to psychotherapist and shamanic healer Sandra Ingerman, author of *Soul Retrieval,* such problems as addictions, personality disorders, and memory blackouts are all warning signs that a person may have lost key portions of themselves.

"No one will help me!" the little girl wails in my vision. And now she is me—I am wailing. Crying like I have never cried before. I know it as an expression of primordial terror from a time when, as a small child, I felt abandoned, set helpless before the universe. I have never felt such profound fear. How did this happen to me? the adult me wonders with fury. And why?

"The darkness was so heavy during your childhood," a spirit voice says to me, "that your soul splintered beneath the weight."

I have an awareness of having lost so much of myself. Who will I be when all the parts come home? I feel a hand on my back: Hamilton's. "I'm here to help you," he says. Suddenly, the flames trapping the little girl disappear. Everything is covered in a freezing white frost. I shiver from the intense cold.

"Julio and I have frozen the devil," Hamilton declares. "You can pull the little girl out now."

So that's why everything got so cold, I think. But wait a minute—what are Hamilton and Don Julio doing in my vision? How can Hamilton see what I'm seeing?

"Pull her out," Hamilton says to me.

I reach down and take the girl's hand. When she feels my touch, she stops crying, and I pull her up, out of the tunnel of fire. The darkness departs. We reach realms of bright white light—the first such places my visions have allowed. The heavenly realms.

"Your little girl has to enter your body," Hamilton says. "Call to her."

I do. I see her split into several little girls, each looking like me at a different age. One at a time, they appear to enter me, my body jolting backwards for each "soul part," as Hamilton calls them, that was retrieved.

As soon as they're done, I see a vision of them. Dazed by the brilliant light of their new world, the girls walk through green grass, under pure white clouds. Scores of butterflies land on them, smothering them. It is an unbelievably perfect place in which there is a sense that nothing could ever hurt me.

ONLY ONE CEREMONY LEFT and I haven't yet experienced God. The shamans say they see him all the time; Hamilton suggests I visit him. Strange: Though I can't say conclusively whether he exists, I'm angry with him. If God is out there, I have a few bones to pick with him.

The ceremony begins with the usual tedious blackness. I keep sending it away, but it reappears in its myriad forms: bats, demons, dragons.

"God!" I yell out in my vision. "Where are you?"

But only darkness. The seemingly endless darkness. I'm getting more and more aggravated. Why do religious people always say that God is there for you when you need him? Well, he's nowhere. Just serpents and those little demon guys.

All of a sudden, I realize that my fears about his not existing, about my not being able to find him, may be thoughts created by dark spirits. I release those fears and immediately I rise higher, into white realms. Through a hazy gray cloud, I can see a vision of a white-bearded man—God? Appearing like a giant Santa Claus. And while I'm sure the way he looks is a stereotyped invention of my mind, a kind of visual distillation of something wholly beyond conception, it's bizarre to be talking to him about my problems.

"Why did you hate me so much?" I demand.

"I never hated you," he says. "You hated yourself. I have always loved you as my own child. Know that suffering is the greatest teacher on Earth. It leads us out of our belief in separation."

I don't know what he means by "separation."

Darkness falls. I can't see God in my vision anymore. A scathing pain rises in my chest—the most excruciating pain I've ever felt. I squeak out a cry to Hamilton and he comes over, singing spirit songs. Legions of demons sail out of my body. I'm helpless before them; they contort me.

I'm made to see that what is being purged now is a deeply rooted belief that I don't deserve to be alive, that no one can love me and I will always need to justify my existence. Slowly I gain the upper hand over the darkness and order it to leave my body. I feel a pressure in my chest that could break all my ribs. I grab my bucket, vomit out what appears to be a stream of fire. Hamilton kneels down and blows tobacco smoke onto the top of my head. I cough violently and watch as demons burst out of me, roaring, only to disintegrate in white light.

And before me this enormous image of God. He takes me in his arms and coddles me like a child. I know, unequivocally, that I am loved and have always been loved. That I matter and have always mattered. That I'm safe and, no matter what happens, will always be safe. I will never allow myself to become separated from him again.

As the visions fade and the ceremony closes, I find myself back in the dark hut. But in my mind's eye I'm still sitting in God's enormous lap. Don Julio nods and silently smokes his mapacho. The others whisper about their experiences. Winston still didn't find a way out of his darkness and will extend his time in Peru to do more ceremonies. Katherine sighs luxuriously: She's been bathing in the heavenly astral realms, having broken through her own issues. Lisa's darkness hasn't let up and it's still my fault; she, too, will be staying in Peru for more shamanistic work.

Me, I'm ready to go home. I sit up with difficulty, as if waking from decades of sleep. It would be easier for me to call it all a dream, a grand hallucination. Then I could have my old world back, in which I thought I knew what was real and unreal, true and untrue. Now the problem is, I don't know anything.

It takes almost all the energy I have left, but I feel around for my flashlight and shine it into my vomit bucket. *No.* I lean down closer. Steady the beam of light. I catch my breath as I examine the object: A small black snake seems to have materialized from my body.

MARCH 2006

STORMING THE ISLANDS OF FIRE AND ICE

By Jon Bowermaster

Four friends, two kayaks, 21 days on some of the world's wildest seas.
The destination: the Aleutians' remote, mysterious birthplace of the winds.

DAY 1: June 14, North Cove, Kagamil Island

The 38-foot *Miss Pepper's,* out of Dutch Harbor, Alaska, shimmies violently as it plows through 12-foot seas. Peering out darkened windows, all I can see are black, ominous waves meeting black, ominous skies. Our 22-foot-long fiberglass kayaks bang atop the boat's wheelhouse; 12 hours of nonstop Bering Sea rocking and rolling threaten to set them free. The mood in the cabin is edged with foreboding as we make our way at full throttle across dangerous Samalga Pass, which separates Umnak Island from our destination, the poetically named Islands of Four Mountains.

Suddenly, an 18-foot metal skiff appears out of the black, piloted by Scott Kerr. A native New Yorker long married to a local Aleut woman, he lives on Umnak in the village of Nikolski (pop. 35), the only settlement for more than a hundred miles. Since none of us (including the captain of *Miss Pepper's,* Don Graves) has ever been to this part of the ocean, and Kerr has, we've arranged for him to guide us the last few hours through the fog and heavy seas. In exchange, we've brought him $88 worth of groceries, including a couple bags of Purina Dog Chow and a few tins of Red Man.

Kerr and his friend Rex, who looks barely awake, tie off their skiff and board *Miss Pepper's.* They smell of wood smoke and tobacco; long knives and heavy flashlights hang from their rope belts. Neither man appears happy to see us. "What are your intentions?" Kerr keeps asking as we study maps of the area where three teammates and I plan to spend the next month. We are about 800 miles southwest of Anchorage, a third of the way down the Aleutians. Kerr can't understand why anyone would want to go to this remote part of the archipelago, especially on a night like this.

Our intentions are straightforward: We're out here to test our sea-kayaking skills in some of the world's stormiest waters and to climb the volcanic peaks of the Islands of Four Mountains. The group was named by early Russian mariners who, as they sailed toward the Alaska mainland, could see to the north the snowcapped cones of Herbert and Carlisle Islands, and the twin summits of Chuginadak—thus, the Islands of Four Mountains. (The other two members of the group, Kagamil and Uliaga, which are also crowned with volcanoes, were hidden from the sailors' view.) We heard about this tiny, treeless archipelago from veteran expeditionary kayaker and author Derek Hutchinson (*The Complete Book of Sea Kayaking* and *Guide to Expedition Kayaking*), who paddled out of Dutch Harbor on Unalaska Island in the early 1970s and glimpsed the peaks of Chuginadak and Carlisle through binoculars. About a year ago a friend told me that Hutchinson regarded the Islands of Four Mountains as the most spectacular place he'd never been but had always wanted to visit. We took the most compelling destination on his wish list and ran with it.

Our journey has brought us to one of the loneliest and least known spots on Earth, a place where the Pacific Ocean and the Bering Sea meet at what the Aleuts call "the birthplace of the winds." The weather and tides will dictate our itinerary, but we'll attempt to visit each island in the group. Two big kayaks will carry the four of us and everything we need for five weeks: food, fuel, paddling and climbing gear, emergency and first-aid kits, and a small mountain of camera equipment. We can't risk caching food or gear in case one of those notorious Aleutian storms comes out of nowhere, cutting us off from our supplies for a week or more.

Success is far from assured in a region where it's common for gales to exceed a hundred miles an hour. Strong currents, ten-foot standing tidal rips, and constant winds churn the channels that separate the five islands. It's possible we've come more than 4,000 miles only to be forced into our tents by heavy storms, unable to paddle even one mile. According to the 1964 edition of the navigational guide *The Coast Pilot,* "No other area in the world is recognized as having worse weather in general than that which the Aleutian Islands experience."

I explain our motives and our goals to Scott, Rex, and Captain Graves. Scott just shakes his head. "You're gonna have your hands full."

He's probably right. Unfortunately, we don't really know what we're getting into. For eight months prior to our trip, I sought information from the usual sources. Alaskans, mostly. Men and women who study the people, weather, and history of this wild region. Boat captains, bush pilots, volcanologists, anthropologists, geologists. What I learned was . . . well . . . not much. When I contacted the resident expert on the Aleutians at the Alaskan Volcano Observatory in Anchorage, he said, "Call me when you get back, because you'll definitely know more about those islands than we do."

The last people to live here were the Aleuts some 200 years ago. To contemporary members of the tribe, the islands are an enigma, a sacred place where ancestors buried their mummified dead in caves. Today, hardly anyone visits the area in any craft, let alone kayaks.

One man I tried to track down for months, Bob Adams, finally met me at the dock in Dutch Harbor minutes before our departure. Eight years ago Adams motored to the Islands of Four Mountains to pick up an archaeological team. "It's a very mysterious, magical place," he told me, "more spiritual than anywhere else in the Aleutian chain."

At 6 a.m., off Kagamil, the motor slows as Captain Graves studies his depth gauge. "I can't get any closer," he says. "I'm dropping anchor."

Off-loading is as difficult as the run out from Dutch Harbor. Barely awake ourselves, a tad green from the rough ride, our team—Barry Tessman, Sean Farrell, Scott McGuire, and I—throw our food and gear into Kerr's boat for the ride to shore, then unlash our kayaks. Within minutes, things fall apart: The overloaded skiff nearly swamps in the surf pounding the sand beach at North Cove. One of the kayak's hatch covers has come untied during the night, and it blows into the 38-degree ocean. Sean dives in fully clothed to save it, but it sinks out of sight.

Two and a half hours later, *Miss Pepper's,* trailing the banged-up metal skiff, finally motors away into the fog.

DAY 2: June 15, North Cove, Kagamil Island

In the morning I measure the temperature of the ocean; it's between 35 and 38°F. The air temperature is in the low 40s, with windchill in the mid-20s. Not exactly swimming weather. In theory our boats, which weigh between 700 and 800 pounds when loaded, could be rolled back up if we overturned. But the reality is that if the kayaks are dumped, we'll probably end up swimming. If that happens, we'll have less than five minutes to get back in the boats before hypothermia begins to slow our hearts. It's said that the fittest Aleuts could survive 45 minutes in these waters; I give us 15 at most.

But we've got a strong team: Barry, 39, makes his living as a photographer, but in past lives he's been a raft, ski, and kayak guide. Scott, 26, tall and rangy, is an ambitious, experienced sea kayaker. Both are like human motors in the back of the boats. Sean, 31, a lawyer with the biggest firm in Orange County, California, has circumnavigated the Atlantic using only a sextant; his navigational skills with maps, compass, and GPS are crucial on this trip since we hope to do most of our paddling in foggy—and therefore less windy—conditions.

Our first test is today: a 2.5-mile crossing to tiny Uliaga for a daylong exploration of the island's 2,915-foot volcano. As we push off the beach, I'm nervous. Within minutes, Kagamil is swallowed by fog behind us; Uliaga remains invisible somewhere ahead. In rhythm, we cut through the pea soup, the current crossing our bow at a fast five to seven knots. We skirt whitecaps that mark a long line of tidal rips, where rushing water passes over shallows and creates powerful standing waves like rapids on a river. Flocks of puffins and murres fly hauntingly out of the fog. After a 30-minute sprint, the greening meadows of Uliaga emerge from the mists. My arms are exhausted. This is not Baja, a place for leisurely paddling. "Paddle for your life," is our motto.

Changing out of dry suits, we climb a steep, grassy cliff up to a meadow just beginning to bloom with buttercups, marigolds, and the bright purple flowers of Nootka lupines. When the skies clear, we are rewarded with a magnificent view back at Kagamil's dormant volcano. As we hike past patches of snow to high meadow lakes, we look southwest to see the faint outline of the 5,283-foot volcano on Carlisle and glimpses of Chuginadak's two big volcanoes, wreathed in fog and clouds. Bald eagles soar overhead. About 500 feet below the summit, we decide to head down; we need to get back in time to catch a slack tide for the return trip to Kagamil.

Back on the water at 7 p.m., we avoid the big whitecaps of a tidal rip near the shore, then plow through four-foot swells that completely submerge our 22-foot boat. "Now you see 'em, now you don't," Scott yells as we watch the other kayak disappear into deep troughs of coal black sea.

A dramatic surf landing caps our return as six-foot waves propel the boats onto shore. With relief we pull the kayaks up onto the inky sand beach. The first two crossings are behind us.

DAY 6: June 19, Eagle Camp, Kagamil

Storms pinned us in our tents for two days at North Cove, but yesterday we finally made it to the south end of Kagamil. Under sunny blue skies, we lolled on the rocks in T-shirts, unloaded the boats, and dried our gear. Today finds us 2,500 feet up the side of Kagamil's volcano—430 feet below the summit—being buffeted by 40-mile-an-hour gusts. Brown fog and noxious smells pouring from dozens of sulfur vents make the mountainside seem infernal, otherworldly.

A softball-size chunk of rock whistles by, missing Barry's head by a few feet. The scree here is loose and the falling rocks treacherous; pushing for the summit, we decide, is out of the question. As we descend below the clouds, the level, green coastline comes into view. As always, we're on the lookout for signs of the Aleuts who lived on these islands as far back as 9,000 years ago. This verdant shore looks like a promising place to search.

"How about those flats over there," says Barry as we crest a small ridge. "It's perfect for an Aleut subdivision—out of the wind."

The Aleutians were once the homeland of 15,000 to 25,000 Unangan people. They lived in coastal villages on virtually every island in the chain, and survived on marine mammals, fish, bird eggs, and plants. When Russian fur traders arrived in the mid-1700s, they renamed the Unangans the Aleuts, and nearly wiped them out with disease, violence, and slavery. By the early 1800s, fewer than one thousand Aleuts remained. Today, the native population numbers about 2,300, but only a handful of the nearly 200 islands in the archipelago are inhabited.

On our way back to camp we hike to the southeast corner of the island, which Scott Kerr told us was the site of an ancient Aleut settlement known as "the village where it is always warm." Sulfuric vents have cooked the ground here red and raw. In many places we think we can make out traces of centuries-old *barabaras,* the partially underground communal sod houses of the Aleuts. Thick, tablet-like rocks that jut out of the tundra may have once served as cairns for native seafarers.

Starting in the mid-1800s, Russian explorers reported finding Aleutian mummies—some of them hundreds of years old—in caves on several islands in the chain. The largest concentration was on the south coast of Kagamil, where as many as 50 mummies were discovered in a single cave. According to Corey Ford's *Where the Sea Breaks Its Back,* "The bodies were carefully eviscerated, stuffed with wild rye (*elymus*), and placed in a sitting position, the knees drawn up under the chin, the arms folded, the head bent forward in an attitude of brooding contemplation. The natural heat of the volcano dried and preserved the mummies: landslides and geologic disturbances sealed the entrances to the caves and locked away their secrets forever."

How was it possible that such an elaborate death ritual, practiced most notably in ancient Egypt and Peru, but in few other places, came to play such an important role in the culture of a tiny island in the middle of the Aleutians? The discovery of the remarkable Kagamil mummies and speculation over their significance still fuel scholarly debates. Some archaeologists think that the practice of mummification spread east from Egypt, and was introduced to the Aleutians by Asians migrating to the New World via the island chain. Another school of thought holds that the practice arose locally. After a century of study, no one really knows where the inspiration or expertise for Aleut mummification came from. The unanswered questions only serve to heighten the mystery of the Islands of Four Mountains.

DAY 8: June 21, Eagle Camp, Kagamil

The fog is so thick this morning we can't see the cove we know is a hundred feet beneath our cliff-top camp. It's below freezing. And on this day—the longest of the year—we'll tackle what we expect will be one of the most difficult parts of our trip: a six-mile paddle south across Kagamil Pass to Chuginadak Island.

We push off at noon just as high tide is peaking, and paddle into four-foot swells that crash over the starboard as Scott struggles to keep the boat on course. About one hundred feet ahead, Barry and Sean zigzag, trying to hold their compass bearing against wind, waves, and current.

Every time we venture onto the sea I think of what it must have been like for the Aleuts, who refined an extremely sophisticated vessel they called the *ikyak* for pursuing seals, sea lions, walrus, and whales on the open sea—perhaps the most demanding form of hunting ever practiced. The boat cover was made from sea lion skins pulled over a frame of whalebones lashed together with baleen fibers. Polished ivory or small bones were strategically inserted into the framework as joints so that every part of the ikyak was in motion as it moved across the sea. The Aleuts carved double-bladed paddles (similar in shape to the ones we're using), and wore sealskin shirts that fitted over the cockpit to keep out water (exactly like the neoprene-and-Kevlar garments we wear). The best kayakers could sustain about ten miles an hour on the open ocean in boats 15 to 30 feet long. Hunters usually went out with a partner, so that if one boat flipped, the capsized kayaker could be pulled to shore by his friend. If caught in open sea by foul weather, several hunters would lash their boats together to ride out the storm.

The Aleuts' relationship with their boats was intense. In this polygamous society, the morning after a man slept with a woman, he was obliged to lavish extra attention on his kayak. This sometimes took the form of an elaborate session of rubbing the vessel before going out to sea. If the owner did not make these signs of affection, it was believed, the kayak would become jealous, and break or capsize.

We sprint for an hour, but it looks as though we may not reach Chuginadak for another hour. My arms are tired; my feet, numb. Two orange-hooded paddlers bob in and out of troughs just ahead of us.

"How's the weather?" I shout to Barry as we pull alongside for a mid-pass conference.

"Dangerous," is his response.

DAY 9: June 22, Skiff Cove, Chuginadak

After our tiring paddle from Kagamil, we take a day off to explore our new island. At 8:16 p.m., for the first time on our trip, the wind dies.

Completely.

Just like that, out come the gnats and up comes the rank smell of sea kelp at low tide. We hear the screaming gulls and squawking murres and the wash of sea on rocks. We leave our tents, which have stopped flapping; we no longer need to shout to be heard. As the temperature climbs to 52°F, hats come off and jackets are unzipped.

It lasts an hour, and it feels all wrong. The Aleutians without wind are not the Aleutians anymore.

DAY 10: June 23, Skiff Cove, Chuginadak

The storm begins at three in the morning, with a ferocity far beyond what we've seen so far. Rains dump and 35-mile-an-hour gusts of wind pound the tent walls like a heavyweight's fist. Emerging mid-morning requires full rain gear. The cove in front of us is blue-gray with whitecaps. Beyond, in the pass, monstrous waves are whipped up by a wind hard from the east. All the beautiful waterfalls surrounding our camp are blown horizontal, or even forced back up over the cliffs.

Late in the afternoon, Sean—restless, curious—bangs on our nylon walls. Suffering from tent fever, he has taken a big hike despite the wet and cold. "Hey guys," he shouts. "I found a downed plane!"

Putting on four layers, including Gore-Tex pants, jackets, and mittens, we pile out of the tents to follow him up the treeless hills and over stony ridges and fast-running streams. "At first I thought it was a beached whale," he says as we hike into 45-mile-an-hour winds, which nearly blow us over backward. The temperature is 8°F.

As we reach the top of a hill, we peer through the swirling mists at what looks like a gleaming silver cigar lying on the tundra. When we get closer we see that it is, indeed, a plane—upside down, two-passenger cockpit smashed into the spongy moss, a single landing wheel spinning in the wind. The crash threw the propeller and one wing to the side. A metal catch-hook juts from the underside of the fuselage: This plane came off a ship. Unexploded ordnance lies half-buried in the grass. A metal ID plate riveted to the underbelly tells us that the plane was last serviced in September 1943 on Kodiak Island, about 800 miles northeast. There are no signs of human remains.

The plane is a relic of a little known event in World War II—the Japanese invasion of the Aleutians. When Japan was ready to attack Midway Island, 2,400 miles southwest, it started the battle by bombing Dutch Harbor on June 3, 1942, in an attempt to lure the U.S. Pacific Fleet north. When the Midway offensive failed, 2,600 Japanese troops landed on Attu Island at the western end of the Aleutians and another 5,000 occupied nearby Kiska to prevent the chain from being used as an Allied invasion route to Japan. In May 1943 some 16,000 Americans fought for three weeks to liberate Attu, sustaining more than 3,800 casualties, including 549 soldiers killed. (A third of the casualties were from hypothermia and frostbite, not enemy bullets.) In August an American invasion force of battleships, cruisers, destroyers, minesweepers, transports, and 34,000 troops descended on Kiska, only to find that the garrison had been abandoned a few weeks earlier.

DAY 15: June 28, Carlisle Island

The alarm goes off at 6:15 a.m., and we all quietly pray for it to rain just a little harder—then we could justify staying in our tents instead of going down to the sea. It's going to be a 30-degree day.

The temperature is 34°F as we load the boats. The drizzle is nearly snow. Dressed in Polartec 200 one-piece fleece suits, Gore-Tex dry suits, Gore-Tex Skanoraks, three layers of fleece-and-neoprene socks and booties, fleece-lined skullcaps and pogies, we push off from the beach one minute before ten o'clock.

From our boats we scout a couple of rocky beaches on Chuginadak where we can retreat if the current proves too strong. It's time to make a decision. "What do you think?" I shout to Barry. He shrugs. "Let's go!" Still riding the outgoing tide, we set off west into a channel that sounds and moves like a roaring river. Despite the waves swamping fore and aft, it's apparent halfway across the channel that we'll make it to Herbert. Still, it isn't until we hit the kelp line, which means we are out of the big currents and wind, that I'm able to breathe a sigh of relief. Herbert is our fifth of five islands. Though our expedition is only a qualified success—we still have to get back to Chuginadak for our rendezvous with *Miss Pepper's*—we have achieved one thing we set out to do: put our feet on each of the islands.

As we pull the boats onto yet another rocky beach, Barry tells me the sizable concern he had mid-crossing. "The current slingshotted us across the channel through the tidal rips," he says. "We were nearly out of control. If we hadn't made that eddy at the corner of Chuginadak, then where would we have ended up? That was definitely our sketchiest crossing."

DAY 16: June 29, Herbert Island

Rain continues throughout the day, stopping just before midnight, when skies clear and a haunting light emerges from behind the scudding clouds. It is the first night of a full moon.

We gather outside our tents. Mount Cleveland peers over our left shoulder, Herbert's distinctive blown-in-half volcano rises straight above us. As we watch from our high-meadow camp, the clouds part, exposing the moon in its perfect roundness. It lasts long past midnight, a perfect gift from the Aleutians for my 45th birthday.

DAY 18: July 1, Herbert Island

Despite the wind and rain and roar of the sea this morning, we barely think twice about whether to go. Maybe we've grown a little overconfident. This is exactly the kind of day where plenty could go wrong.

As soon as we break from the lee of our campsite cove, the winds and current begin hammering us. "Mach I," Scott shouts behind me. We are heading four miles northeast straight across to Chuginadak, and by mid-pass we know we've bitten off a big day. I get out the wind meter, which registers gusts of 20 miles an hour. With windchill, the temperature is 26°F. Peeking over my shoulder, I keep looking for Barry and Sean's orange Skanoraks; if I can see them, it means their boat is still upright.

As we pull within 1.5 miles of Mount Cleveland on Chuginadak, a fierce wind racing down the volcano's slopes crosshatches the sea. We're being swamped from the south; the boat pitchpoles into three- and four-foot waves. Even so, we have to pick up the pace as we paddle into the wind.

We finally round the northwest corner of Chuginadak and reach the relatively sheltered north shore; the winds drop and the waves subside. We are still nine miles west of Applegate Cove, but the sun comes out, exposing the island's big twin volcanoes under blue skies. Our seventh and final crossing is completed; it feels good to be coasting down the final stretch.

Ha!

Just as we clear the rocky pinnacle bracketing the west end of Applegate's black-sand beach, a riotous 30-mile-an-hour wind smacks us starboard. The near-gale literally roars from the Pacific through a slot carved between Chuginadak's volcanoes by centuries of conditions like this. Whitecaps erupt around us. When I pick my paddle out of the water, the wind almost rips it from my hands. Forward progress is nearly impossible. Each time the bow digs into a wave at an angle, I get a face full of cold water; every time I lift my right paddle out of the water, the wind carries its load directly into Scott's face.

Shouting at the top of my lungs, I suggest that we take refuge in the nearby kelp pads, the way seals do during storms, and wait for the wind to subside. Scott shouts back, "No way. It could get worse before it gets better and then we'd be stuck here for the night. Let's keep paddling." Barry and Sean are a mile out to sea, trying to avoid the ferocious wind. "I don't like what they're doing," Scott shouts. "If they get blown out, they'll be in the middle of the pass within minutes. We want to stay close to shore in case it really goes off."

We've already paddled a hard ten miles, and heading into the winds makes these last miles even tougher. There are times when I think we'll be blown back to shore, or worse, out to sea. When we reach the heart of the slot, the wind grows even stronger. We can see the canyon. It's black, filled with fog and cloud, like some kind of sub-Arctic hell.

DAY 21: July 4, Applegate Cove, Chuginadak Island

The temperature is 26°F at seven o'clock this morning as we start to climb 5,675-foot Mount Cleveland. In a direct line it's a ten-mile hike each way, straight up. Sean estimates the round-trip at 12 to 15 hours. One of 41 active volcanoes in the Aleutian arc, Cleveland has erupted more than a dozen times since 1893. The last one was on May 25, 1994, when the volcano sent a plume of ash six miles into the sky. The only known death by volcano in the Aleutians occurred on this mountain in 1944, when a two-day eruption triggered a mud slide that killed an American soldier who was part of a small Army Air Force reconnaissance team stationed on the island.

For the past three days Herbert has been buried in fog and rain; if we hadn't left when we did, we'd still be stuck there. And on the day that we chose to climb the islands' tallest peak—why not make the ascent on the Fourth of July?—the weather couldn't be better. If there is some kind of Aleutian god, today he or she is smiling down on us. We hope our luck holds until July 7—the day we've arranged for our pickup at Applegate Cove.

Two thousand feet up, we stop to put on crampons and harnesses. To the north, Uliaga and Kagamil are perfectly exposed. We see distinctly our routes between the islands, even the coves where we camped and the nasty tidal rips we skirted. It's a steep climb across soft, deep snow. We stick to the widest, snowiest shaft, traversing the mountain north to south and back again, slowly gaining altitude. A slip would mean a fast glissade until sharp, black lava rock at the bottom ripped us to pieces.

As we ascend, the wind picks up, ricocheting dry snow off our hoods. We stop to hack a ledge into the snow with boots and axes, then pull on snow pants and another layer of fleece. The view out over the Bering Sea remains magnificent, blue and clear. Forty-mile-an-hour gusts blast our precarious shelf, and within seconds we are enveloped in a snow hurricane that buries axes, crampon bags, photo gear, and bags of nuts. As quickly as the wind arrives, it subsides.

The next thousand feet are far steeper. We can't make out the peak above us but, finally, at 5,100 feet we reach a north-facing corner and there is Carlisle Island, rising out of the sea like an upside-down ice cream cone, surrounded by a skirt of green meadows. Barry and I sneak out to the edge for a clear view from west to east.

"It's unbelievable," I say with a sweep of my hands. "From here it all seems so . . . peaceful."

The next traverse takes us past a small, smoking crater just off-peak, then leads to a jumble of jagged lava rock that fringes the mountain. We remove our crampons, the summit only 50 feet above us.

Scaling those final feet is the hardest work of the day, requiring us to crawl on our hands and knees over scree in winds so violent that it's difficult to stand. I dig out my wind meter and brace myself: 51 miles an hour, windchill 2°F. Dropping to our knees, we peer over the edge of the caldera. In the heart of the volcano, an oblong hole, bubbling and yellow, is surrounded by vents leaking poisonous smoke.

We shout congratulations and trade positions so that we can see all of the views. Since it's the Fourth of July, I make a toast with a thermos cup of Gatorade to a single sentiment that helped propel us to the Bering Sea, across the channels, up this mountain, and to whatever place comes next. "To independence!" I say.

WINTER 1999

THE MOONBOW CHRONICLES

By Tim Cahill

Even after 130 years of Winnebagos and walkabouts, Yellowstone still has tales to tell . . . and mouths start foaming when 240 "newly discovered" waterfalls suddenly appear in America's outdoor wonderland.

I WAS SITTING IN WHAT AMOUNTED TO a wilderness hot tub under a 150-foot-high waterfall near the southwest corner of Yellowstone Park. It was late at night, and the moon was just about to clear the canyon. Its light would illuminate the falls, especially in that place where water exploded off the rocks below in an ephemeral mist that drifted on the evening breeze. I believed that there would be a certain very specific bending of light: a silver luminescence trembling in the vapor; the experience of a lifetime. Or the phenomenon might be entirely mythical, an incandescence out of the imagination, a goblin of the light, something all shivery to contemplate in theory but a complete no-show in the reality department.

There are a lot of strange and wondrous things happening in the largely unknown backcountry of Yellowstone. The park is big, bigger, in fact, than some states: about two and a quarter million acres, with 94 trailheads and at least a thousand miles of trail, as well as great expanses of land that aren't served by any trails at all. A man might spend a lifetime walking the backcountry and never know it all. This means there is always something to discover, and I was coming to the end of a summer of doing just that. Over the previous three months, I had trudged several hundred miles through the hidden country, propelled, in part, by a book I didn't much like.

In *The Guide to Yellowstone Waterfalls and Their Discovery*, by Paul Rubinstein, Lee Whittlesey, and Mike Stevens, published in 2000, the authors report that they "discovered" 240 unknown, unmapped, or unphotographed water-falls. No kidding? In this day and age, new discoveries! Well, not precisely. A foreword, by Dr. Judith Meyer, a geography professor at Southwest Missouri State University, puts the matter in perspective: "The title of 'discoverer' is not necessarily bestowed on someone who sees something for the first time. A discoverer discloses information to others," in the manner, for instance, that Christopher Columbus discovered America.

This is not an evil, or even a fraudulent, book. The authors may have truly found some unseen water. Maybe. But they themselves acknowledge that a few "privileged" individuals "did see some" of the waterfalls before they did. "Most of them failed, however, to write reports . . . or photograph them, or even map them" and therefore "missed their chance at credit for their discoveries."

Some of those privileged individuals, it must be said, missed their chance in the name of what I can describe only as the preservation of wonder. Certain rangers, guides, and knowledgeable hikers find the concept of credit for dis-covery disagreeable. The authors themselves note that "some wilderness advo-cates hate the idea of official names in wilderness areas and love the idea of large spaces on the maps where there are no names."

AND THAT WAS THE GIST of the argument swirling about the book on the fringes of Yellowstone Park, where I live. It was a low-level dispute: No one doubted the authors' honesty or good intentions, only the wisdom of their catalog approach to wilderness. Others, generally outside the area, just read the headlines. Friends and colleagues called from New York, curious about the 240 new waterfalls.

Which, the authors said, was part of the plan. "We hope the revelation of these beautiful natural features will spur city dwellers, who need these places for mental health and restoration more than anyone else"—nutcases!—"to use every wherewithal to protect them—by voting for environmental candidates rather than the developers, by yelling loudly whenever there are threats to these places. . . ." And so on, in admirable openhanded altruism.

It occurred to me that if these three guys could spend seven summers searching for waterfalls on behalf of the sanity of city dwellers everywhere, the least I could do for the pitiable urbanites was to spend a single summer selflessly hiking the backcountry with my friends. I'd let the water fall where it may, and later we could all go out and yell at some developers together.

Hiking Yellowstone, out of sight of any road, seems to be on everyone's unfulfilled wish list. It is often said that 99 percent of the visitors to Yellowstone never see the backcountry. Out of curiosity, I checked this out and found that the statistic is somewhat understated. In 2001, according to Yellowstone Visitors Services, the park had 2,758,526 recreational visitors, of which 19,239 applied for backcountry camping permits. That means—rounding the numbers off a bit—that, in 2001 anyway, 99.3 percent of park visitors didn't overnight in the backcountry.

I am, myself, an example. I have lived just 60 miles north of the park for 25 years and can count my overnight backcountry trips on the fingers of one hand, a shameful statistic in itself. Just another reason to get out on the trail.

As it happens, my neighbor, photographer Tom Murphy, has been a guide in Yellowstone for the past 17 years and knows it as well as anyone of my acquaintance. Together we planned three forays into the park. All of our destinations involved several days' worth of walking, an activity that both Tom and I knew buys solitude in Yellowstone.

Our first trip started at the Pacific Creek trailhead, just outside Grand Teton National Park. It led generally northeast up over the mountains of the Bridger-Teton National Forest, then into Yellowstone Park, where we passed by the Thorofare Patrol Cabin, 32 miles from the nearest road, the most remote occupied dwelling in the contiguous United States. The second trip took us to the Goblin Labyrinths, and the last was a visit to the River of Reliable Rainbows.

Chapter One: Land of the Ghost Trees

And so, on that first trip in late July, five of us found ourselves walking north toward the top of the world, the Continental Divide, at a place called Two Ocean Pass, just outside the southeast corner of the park. The divide itself runs through a marshy bog about three miles long. Pacific Creek flows out of the bog south and west. At the north end of the bog, the watercourse flowing north and east is called Atlantic Creek. As the names suggest, these two streams, separated by only three miles, empty into entirely disparate oceans.

"So," Tom explained to me, "a fish could conceivably swim up Pacific Creek, muddle through the bog, and end up swimming down Atlantic Creek." That's why Tom wanted to walk 32 miles, enduring 3,000 feet or more of elevation change, carrying his 90-pound backpack full mostly of camera gear. He wanted to see a place where a fish could swim across the Continental Divide. Tom, I should explain, grew up on a cattle ranch in South Dakota, 60 miles from the nearest town, and is prone to become excited about concepts like fish swimming over the Rocky Mountains.

We slogged northeast along the Pacific Creek Trail for several days but eventually stumbled into the bog at the top of the world. The map said we were 8,200 feet above sea level.

The bog was about half a mile across. Willows were thick but seldom more than waist high. Where the ground rose slightly, there were profusions of purple monkshood, a flower that looks pretty much like its name. Underfoot, slow-running copper-colored water made countless narrow furrows in the marshy ground, and these small streams—some of them no more than a foot wide—ran in long, roundabout, curving courses or in shorter, dithering meanders. Tom and I, along with another friend, Dr. David Long, a biochemist turned fine printmaker, postholed through the mud out into the marsh, looking for the exact place where black-spotted west-slope trout might slip over the divide and into the waters of the Atlantic.

Presently, Tom found a tiny ridgeline, about two or three feet higher than the surrounding land, and he stood there, in an area of rusty burned grasses about the size of a football field. Water to the west seemed to flow west; eastern waters east. We stood for a strangely triumphant moment on the exact instant of the Continental Divide and discussed transcontinental trout.

The narrow streams were a labyrinthine tangle—many of them hidden under willows—and none of us could say that there wasn't a connection somewhere. On the other hand, in June, during the season of snowmelt, the bog was probably more like a lake, and that, we decided sagely, is how and when fish swim over the Rocky Mountains.

Later in the day, we pushed off north and east, walking beside the outflow from the bog. Atlantic Creek dropped down through forests of burned trees, great limbless lodgepole pines, whole forests of standing dead, all of the trees weathered a ghostly silver-white. Sometimes the trail took us through meadows alive with every manner of wildflower—sego lilies, for instance, which look a bit like white tulips with round red spots on the inner petals. Eileen Ralicke, Dave's wife, who is a nurse practitioner, declared the sego lily "the most beautiful thing I've ever seen." Kara Krietlow, an emergency room nurse—Tom and Dave and I weren't taking any chances with our health, you see—agreed.

The land had risen from the west slope in a series of stair-step meadows, and now it was floating down to the north and east in meadows several miles wide where flowers grew in patchwork brilliance. This route, beyond Two Ocean Pass, is a corridor through the mountains so agreeable to travel that old-time trappers—the Jim Bridgers and Osborne Russells—called it the Thorofare.

WE CAMPED UNDER THE MOUNTAIN called Hawks Rest, just outside the border of the park. I went off by myself, bathed in the Yellowstone River, then took a shortcut back to camp, which was a mistake, because the ground was the consistency of Jell-O, and it swallowed my legs to mid-calf. I was sweating profusely and pretty much entirely filthy when I got back to camp, which required a second trip, this one on a trail, back to the river for another bath.

So I was amazed early the next morning when I saw a huge bull moose trotting on his big pie-plate hooves through the same marsh that had eaten me alive the day before. Low clouds scattered the newly risen sun in slanting pillars, an effect that is locally called God light. The moose, a deep auburn color in the God light, moved effortlessly through the mud and the flowers, great muscles rolling in his immense shoulders. Beauty finds you where it will, and I was, at the time, squatting in the bushes performing my morning necessity.

We passed Hawks Rest, crossed the Yellowstone River on a wooden bridge, walked past Bridger Lake, and entered the park where a sign had fallen from a single ghost tree standing sentinel at the trail. From here it was a two-mile walk to the Thorofare Patrol Cabin, which meant we were halfway done with the trip. It seemed ironic that it had been necessary (and, I suppose, polite) to contact the Park Service, an agency of the United States government, to secure permission to speak with the person living in the most remote cabin in the contiguous United States. A sign on the door said, "The ranger on duty has departed." So much for calling ahead.

No matter. We moved on around the three-lobed mountain called the Trident and found our assigned campsites—yes, you have to make backcountry campsite reservations—in a thick forest of unburned lodgepole pine and Douglas fir. The lodgepole gave way to a vast expanse of meadow, and that is where we set up our tents: on the very edge of the Thorofare, the Mother of all Meadows. I could see for 20 miles in one direction, at a guess, and 15 in another. A fierce wind arose, and the grasses and the sedges and the forbs and the flowers danced a brief mad fandango; then all at once everything went calm, and dusk settled over the land. The moon rose, Mars scowled down, the Milky Way spread across the known universe, and everywhere, in any direction I looked, there was not a single light.

I was still thinking about the privilege of solitude the next morning. In six days, we'd seen two hikers and two horsepacking parties, all back in the Bridger-Teton. Nobody in the Thorofare.

Suddenly, a sound like gunfire echoed off the walls of the mountains on either side of the rocky corridor that enfolded the meadow. It was a bright, windy day, and we'd been hearing these thunderclaps reverberating all about us every few hours. Tom said they were ghost trees falling in the distance, and indeed, this time we could see it. Across a narrow part of the meadow, in a fringing ghost forest on the flank of the mountain opposite, a huge lodgepole had toppled, caught on a neighboring tree for a moment, then fallen to the earth with a series of tremendous crashing echoes.

The ghost forests date mostly from the fires of 1988. New timber is growing in the midst of the ghost forests, living lodgepoles now eight and ten feet high and growing at the rate of about ten inches a year. Soon, as the older trees crash about them, the new growth will accelerate, each tree growing straight and fast, racing the others to the sun. In ten more years, the forest will be 16 to 18 feet high, and a hundred years from now the trees will be full grown, and there will be another fire. People are more than willing to argue this point—fire should be stopped, or it shouldn't be stopped, or it ought to be purposely set—but this is my reading of the history and natural history of the land: I believe we are privileged to see the forest regenerate itself in our lifetimes. We're at that point in the cycle: about a dozen years into a turnaround of a century or more.

We camped under Colter Peak and high-stepped across the marshy meadow of the Thorofare to the Yellowstone River. There was evidence on the muddy banks that this immense meadow was a Thorofare for life in general, with no particular nod to the human variety. All the tracks were fresh, but one tended to notice the grizzly first. His front foot was 12 inches across, by actual measurement. Nearby, there was a cylinder of scat with a little bit of hair in it. The wolf tracks leading away were bigger than those of a coyote that seemed to have come by later. A raven had strutted about the bank, and the beaver's track was plain enough as well: an endearing, pigeon-toed gait, with the flat rake of the tail dragging behind

THE NEXT MORNING, we woke to the deep, aching, eerie howling of wolves in the near distance. It is a sound that sends a shimmer of gooseflesh down the arms and up the back.

Tom had a special mission that day. He was going to take us to a waterfall he'd found a while ago: one that wasn't in the *Waterfalls* book. The authors of that controversial work wrote, "We would be fools to believe we have found every waterfall in Yellowstone." Once again, they were right, and we had proof of that only 10 or 12 miles out of our way. Tom, who is one of those people who would rather not clutter up wilderness maps with a lot of names, said, "You can't give the location."

"What about all the people who live in the city and have mental problems," I argued. "Giving the location and naming the falls might help them."

But he didn't care about city dwellers' sanity, not even a little bit.

It was, let us say, a goodly walk, and it took us up on top of a low plateau, where the fires of 1988 had been particularly fierce and the ghost forest stretched on forever, on all sides. A brutal wind shrieked through the bones of the forest, and we could hear the trees creaking, creaking, creaking with their craving to finally and irrevocably fall.

And, coming through the forest, moving toward us along the trail, was a man on horseback who turned out to be backcountry ranger Bob Jackson. He had a bunch of work to do and not much time to chat. He lived in the Thorofare cabin, he said, from June 1 to the end of October and had since 1978. Used to be he caught a lot of poachers coming into the park during hunting season, looking for prize animals: elk and bighorn sheep mostly. There is less poaching going on today, but there are still bad guys out there. Bob's seen their tracks, and he plans to get them. "You know," he said, "almost every poacher, when I finally caught him, he cried." Bob Jackson liked that: catching crybaby poachers.

He asked us where we were going, and Tom described the waterfall. "One of the prettiest ones in the park," Bob said.

"You mean," I asked, "you know about this waterfall? Why don't you name it and take credit for its discovery?" Bob Jackson looked at me in the manner I imagine he looks at poachers. I didn't immediately burst into tears—though, on sober reflection, I believe that would have been the proper response. "It was a joke, Bob," I wanted to call after him as he rode off through the ghost forest.

Hours later, we reached the shores of Yellowstone Lake, which stretched out blue-gray as far as the eye could see, 14 miles wide, 20 miles long, with 110 miles of shoreline. So I can say that the unnamed waterfall was only about half a mile from the lake. That doesn't narrow it down too much.

Tom found it one day when he was "dinking around," looking for a spring, actually, because Tom will fill his canteen from a spring in preference to pumping and purifying water. He'd seen a lush hillside covered over in cow parsnip and mossy rock—good signs of water—and about 150 feet above, there was water gushing out of the side of the hill. It fell 18 to 20 feet and then cascaded down some rocks for another 35 to 40 feet. I thought it was all the more appealing because it was a waterfall that started as a spring. We filled our canteens, drank greedily, and then sat suffering ice cream headaches for ten minutes or so.

And now, since we'd gone 12 miles out of our way and were moving at something less than three miles an hour, we were going to be late getting into camp. It is not usually a good idea to walk at night in the park. It's not even a good idea to walk at twilight, because, as Tom explained, bears are crepuscular, which means that they tend to feed in the half-light of dawn and dusk. I was thinking about that as we crossed a creek, and there, on the trail, was the track of a large grizzly. It was new: I could see the ridges like fingerprints on the pads of its toes. "About two minutes ahead of us," Tom said.

"You think so?"

"Look." There, beside the track, were several drops of water in the dusty soil, and they were moving forward, along with the tracks, so that it looked as if someone had been walking along carrying a wet rug, except that this was a grizzly track, and the wet rug had been a wet bear skin attached to the grizzly. We'd just crossed a creek, and so had the bear. The water drops were drying up even as I looked at them. The griz was about two minutes ahead of us.

And then the sun set, and we were walking in the dark, with headlamps, along the north side of the Southeast Arm of Yellowstone Lake, until we found our reserved campsite at about 11:30 at night. The sky was perfectly clear, the moon almost full, and waves lapped gently on the beach, so that, visually anyway, it felt as if there ought to be a palm tree silhouetted against the sky. But on this last day of July, the temperature stood somewhere to the south of 20 degrees. It was damn cold.

I left that morning, as planned. Tom stayed for another week.

Chapter Two: The Hard-Rock Circus

Three weeks later, Tom and I took our second trip into the backcountry. There were just the two of us making our way through the sagebrush-littered flats of the Lamar Valley, at the northeast end of the park, moving due south, toward Hoodoo Basin, an area that P. W. Norris, the second superintendent of the park, called the Goblin Labyrinths.

Tom and I were taking big loops around bison weighing in the neighborhood of one ton. "Two days after you left the lake, I saw something that I thought only existed in folklore," he told me. "An evening rainsquall passed across the lake, and the last of the rain hung in the air. There was a light then, and I turned to see the full moon, which was just rising, on the horizon. When I turned back and looked into what was left of the rain, I thought I could see a faint, silvery sort of line, and then it grew bigger and bent around until I was looking at a kind of rainbow in negative. A moonbow."

"Any colors?" I asked, envious.

"It was all bluish white."

I'd missed the vaporous display by 48 hours. Experience of a lifetime going on up at Yellowstone Lake, and I was down in town having a drink at The Owl.

As if to put a certain emphasis on my regret, it began to rain intermittently. Tom, as it turned out, doesn't carry rain gear. If he has to, he says, he walks wet. If it's a cold rain, he walks fast. "But . . . ," I stammered, "you're a guide. You work search-and-rescue."

"I'm not saying it's right," Tom said. "When you grow up on a cattle ranch in South Dakota, you just don't have a lot of experience with rain." He thought a bit. "Rain was good."

TWO DAYS AND 20 MILES IN, we arrived at the Upper Miller Creek Patrol Station and ran into ranger Mike Ross. He is tall and blond and handsome and is one of the few men I've ever met who didn't look like a complete dork in a ranger uniform.

Mike was one of the Park Service personnel who didn't agree with the concept of the *Waterfalls* book. "I grew up in the park," he said. "I know it pretty well, and those guys did some real exploration. But I had problems with the naming. I wrote Lee Whittlesey an e-mail and told him that the thrill he got naming and locating these falls was one he stole from every subsequent visitor." We stayed the night near the cabin and chatted with Mike until long after dark. "I don't get a lot of company here," he said. "And the people I do see usually turn back at this point."

"Why?" I asked. The Hoodoo Basin, with its weird formations, was just over the hill, about eight miles away and 2,500 feet above.

"Well, sometimes they've overestimated what they can do," Mike said. "And then it's a long, boring walk. I mean, there aren't a lot of sweeping views, and it's mostly burned. And finally, they don't want to make the 2,500-foot climb." He pointed to the forested wall behind the cabin. "We call that Parachute Hill," Mike said.

"How many people actually get to the Hoodoo Basin?" I asked.

Mike pulled out some kind of PalmPilot, scratched on it with a stylus, and said: "I downloaded this at the backcountry office a few days ago. So, as of August 26, there were three permits for the year. You guys are one of them. I doubt if 25 sets of eyes see the hoodoos in any given year."

Parachute Hill was a bastard, there's no doubt about it, a cruel set of switchbacks that took two long hours of trudging. We topped out on a grassy hillside of long, sloping meadows that gave way to cool, unburned forest at 9,500 feet. All about, lying on the ground near the trail, were obsidian chips: arrowheads and spear points and scrapers. These were tools chipped out of rock with rock by men who had found a pleasant and militarily advantageous place to work.

Tom and I walked up to the summit of Parker Peak, 10,203 feet in elevation, according to the map, and I could see the high peaks that fringed the park, which is actually the caldera of an immense and ancient volcano that last erupted 600,000 years ago. Most of the highest peaks in the Yellowstone area stand at the edge of the park, on what would have been the rim of all that molten fury.

Tom strolled down a short ridge running south off the summit. Where it dead-ended in cliffs, someone had built a small enclosure by setting rocks on edge and fitting them together with other, smaller rocks wedged into the interstices. The whole affair was about nine by six feet, an oval enclosure protected from the wind and overlooking the Lamar River to the southwest and the Beartooth Plateau to the northeast. It was a place where men came to discover what was sacred. A vision-quest site, and not on any map I know of.

WE CAME DOWN PARKER PEAK and made for the Hoodoo Basin. Superintendent Norris, in his 1880 report, noted that some prospectors working the head of the Upper Lamar River in 1870 had stumbled on "a region of countless remnants of erosion, so wild, weird and spectral that they named it the 'Hoodoo' or 'Goblin Land.' "

The trail led to a basin under the rounded, grassy summit of Hoodoo Peak. It appeared that 500 feet of vertical slope had eroded away from the mountain, leaving a haphazard labyrinth of oddly shaped reddish gray columns. There was one pillar, a hundred feet high, upon which a large rock was balanced precariously. It looked like nothing so much as a small car resting on its front bumper with its back wheels in the air. This formation was very much like one Norris sketched in the 1880 report. Could that top rock have held its position for more than 120 years? It occurred to me that I had arrived at an unfamiliar intersection between geology and acrobatics.

I moved below the permanently precarious hard-rock circus and walked around a high, flat blade of standing stone. It was growing late, and the sky above was still blue, but in the basin, where we were, shadows fell all about. I looked up at the flat rock rising 60 or 70 feet above me, and it resolved itself into a face, with a central protrusion of nose and a large pyramidal hat above, of the sort that might be worn by shamans or priests of some alien religion.

But what made me stumble, startled in the silence, was the perfectly animate pair of eyes staring down at me. They were a cool, luminescent, living blue. I believe I may have said something clever, like "Whoa," as I wheeled backward, then stood still, pinned motionless under the intense blue gaze of the rock. I lived through five very odd seconds until the eyes resolved themselves into two round holes in the flattish rock: Now I was looking directly into the blue of the western sky.

Tom and I spent two days in the Goblin Labyrinths. The nights were deliciously creepy. The moon, half full behind us, illuminated the various figures in a pale light broken by irregular shadows. The stars, cold and bright, glittered through holes in the rock. They wheeled overhead as we sat for hours watching the shadows shift so that the rock figures assumed alternate shapes: a horse's head, a fierce crouching lion, a failed saguaro cactus, a sorcerer's apprentice.

The next day, we climbed Hoodoo Peak, which, at 10,563 feet, is a thousand feet and an hour's climb above the basin. There were more goblins set higher on the mountain, and they were not as eroded as the ones in the basin, so that from a distance they looked rather like the heads on Easter Island, only bunched closely together, as if conspiring in the wind. There were some fanciful columns and balancing acts. I rather liked the one that looked like a pig on a stilt.

Still, it was the basin that drew me back at dusk the next night. I went around the front side of the flat rock and stood in its shadow in order to stare it directly in the eyes. And the damn thing winked at me. "Whoa," I said.

"What," Tom asked.

"The rock is winking at me."

I climbed up on a scree slope to get a better view. Aha! Some small bird, probably an owl, was moving in and out of one of the eyes, perching there for some moments as it scanned the ground for rodents. The owl blocked the sky and caused the rock face to wink.

When I dragged Tom to that vantage point to explain myself, the owl, of course, was gone.

Chapter Three: River of Reliable Rainbows

At the very southwest corner of the park is an area called the Bechler, named for the region's main river course. If the Bechler ever ran a personal ad seeking companionship, it would be a pretty sappy one: "If you like hot tubs and rainbows and waterfalls, you'll like me. I'm the Bechler."

On this third trip, the party consisted of Tom, Dave, me, our medical crew from the first trip—Eileen and Kara—as well as Elizabeth Schultz, a friend and local interior decorator who was in charge of camp decor. We drove to Ashton, Idaho, then down the gravel road that leads to the Bechler's entrance. "We're doing this," I reminded everyone, "in the name of city dwellers' sanity." Just in case anyone thought we were only having fun.

And maybe it wouldn't be all that enjoyable. We were certainly pushing the weather. It was late September, and though it can snow on you any month of the year in Yellowstone, September and October are famous for days of mild summer temperatures followed by heavy, wet snows accumulating sometimes several feet in a matter of 24 hours. Roads are often closed in late August due to heavy snowfall. And in 2001, it snowed pretty hard in June.

"It won't snow on us," I told my hiking companions, "because I lead a good and virtuous life."

"We're dead," Dave said.

The trail was essentially flat and took us through the autumnal grasses of the immense Bechler Meadows. It was the season of rut for the elk, and we could hear various males bugling in the distance. This is a high-pitched noise, almost like the shriek air makes escaping from a balloon when the opening is stretched flat. It moderates down in tone to a kind of pained whine, as if the animal is saying, "Mate with me, mate with me, all of you, mate with me."

Elk were mating now, the males were fighting, and they had to chase the females, which depleted the fat that animals of both sexes had accumulated over the summer and thereby diminished their chances of surviving the winter. "It would be better for the elk," Dave said as we prepared dinner, "if the females just gave it up."

All three women stared at him. A silence ensued. Dave said, "Or I could be wrong."

Coyotes yipped and howled, harmonizing with the elk, and their vocalizations sounded nothing at all like the deep, eerie sounds made by wolves. In the morning, the grasses were frosted over, glittering in the sun, and we could see the snow-covered ridge of the Tetons in the southern distance. A bull moose was trotting along on the side of the meadow, near a fringe of trees. Moving out ahead, a female was running rapidly away, and not about to just give it up at all. The male animal was making a series of revolting sounds: It started with a kind of *eh-eh-eh*, followed by a tormented swallowing, and then a repulsive noise that sounded like someone seriously vomiting. ("Mate with me! Oh, God, I'm sick. Mate with me!")

The weather held—it's my good and virtuous life—and it was actually hot at noon. We moved up Bechler Canyon, which is famous for its waterfalls. The topography is this: Centrally located in the Bechler region is the Pitchstone Plateau, which is nearly 9,000 feet high. It drops off to the southwest, and water flows down a rocky slope that terminates in a number of sheer cliffs. This is Cascade Corner. The waterfalls of Cascade Corner pitch into the Bechler Meadows or the Falls River Basin.

Ouzel Falls is north of the main trail, dropping off a rock ridge at the entrance to the Bechler Canyon. From our first vantage point, there was no sense of water moving. The falls looked like a distant mirror glittering in the sun. There seemed to be no trail to the falls—none we could find—and we bushwhacked over animal trails and down timber, then moved up a deeply wooded canyon and stood at the foot of the falls, which drops 230 feet and is one of Yellowstone's tallest. It was now three in the afternoon, and the sun had cleared the trees on both sides of the narrow canyon. Rainbows danced in the spray.

Eileen scrambled up some talus to shower in the shifting shards of color. To see a rainbow, you need a light source behind you and water vapor floating on air in front. I moved this way and that, in order to position the sun and spray to enhance the colors hanging and shifting at the base of the falls. The map suggested that a great many of the falls in and around the Bechler region face generally south, which meant the sun would shine directly on them at least part of the day. And that meant that every day in which there was sun, there'd be a rainbow or two as well. You could count on them: I thought of the Bechler as the River of Reliable Rainbows.

Over the next several days, we moved up the Bechler and courageously endured the sight of many waterfalls generating many rainbows. Colonnade Falls, for instance, just off the trail, is a two-step affair, with a 35-foot plunge above, a pool, and a 67-foot drop below. The lower falls is enfolded in a curving basalt wall. The gray rock had formed itself into consecutive columns in the Doric tradition. It has a certain wild nobility, Yellowstone's own Parthenon, with falls and a fountain.

SOME HOURS LATER, THE CANYON WIDENED, and the trail moved through a meadow where vaguely oval hot pools 10 and 20 and 30 feet across steamed in the sun. In some of the pools, there were bits and shards of what appeared to be rusted sheet metal, as if someone had driven a Model T into the water 80 years ago. In fact, the shards were living colonies of microbes.

"If you cut into them," said Dave, the biochemist, "you see that the top layer uses the longest visible light, the second layer uses less long light, and so on, until all the light is used." I stared at the cooperative colony, and it still looked like chunks of old cars to me.

We branched off the main trail and followed the Ferris Fork of the Bechler. This little-used path drops down into another narrow meadow where there are a number of hot springs and pools. Steam rose off the boiling pools in strange, curvilinear patterns. There was a spectacular terrace of precipitated material on the opposite bank of the river. Hot water from the pool above ran down the bank of the terrace, which was striated in several colors: wet brown and garish pumpkin and overachieving moss, all interspersed with running channels of steaming water and lined in creamy beige. Just at river level, the green rock formed a pool perhaps ten feet in diameter, and its surface was the color of cream.

We followed the Ferris Fork up the drainage that led to the Pitchstone Plateau. There were five waterfalls in the space of a couple hours' walk. The top falls was unnamed—another one not in the *Waterfalls* book—but the bottom four were all on the map: Wahhi, Sluiceway, Gwinna, and Tendoy. They were all shadowed in foliage and faced vaguely north, so they were not good rainbow falls.

We came back down to the meadow near the steaming terrace and sat in the river, just where one of the bigger hot streams poured into the cold water of the Ferris Fork. It is illegal—not to say suicidal—to bathe in any of the thermal features of the park. But when these features empty into a river, at what is called a hot pot, swimming and soaking are perfectly acceptable. So we were soaking off our long walk, talking about our favorite waterfalls, and discussing rainbows when it occurred to us that the moon was full. There wasn't a hint of foul weather. And if you had a clear sky and a waterfall facing in just the right direction . . .

OVER THE COURSE OF A COUPLE OF DAYS, we hiked back down the canyon to the Boundary Creek Trail and followed it to Dunanda Falls, which is only about eight miles from the entrance to the park. Dunanda is a 150-foot-high plunge facing generally south, so that, in the afternoons, reliable rainbows dance over the rocks at its base. It is the archetype of all western waterfalls. Water rolls over the lip at the top and catches in a series of notched pools just below, and these pools empty intermittently. Eileen, always one to test the shower, said that it felt like a pulsing showerhead, except that the pulse alternated between a gentle spray and a ten-gallon bucketload.

It was necessary to walk three miles back toward the ranger station and our assigned campsite. We planned to set up our tents, eat, hang our food, and walk back to the falls in the dark, using headlamps. We could be there by 10 or 11. At that time, the full moon would clear the east ridge of the downriver canyon and would be shining directly on the falls.

This evening stroll involved five stream crossings, and took us a lot longer than we'd anticipated. Still, we beat the moon to the falls.

Most of us took up residence in one or the other of the hot pots. Presently, the moon, like a floodlight, rose over the canyon rim. The falling water took on a silver tinge, and the rock wall, which had looked gold under the sun, was now a slick black, so the contrast of water and rock was incomparably stark. The pools below the lip of the falls were glowing, as from within, with a pale blue light. And then it started at the base of the falls: just a diagonal line in the spray.

"It's going to happen," I told Kara, who was sitting beside me in one of the hot pots.

Where falling water hit the rock at the base of the falls and exploded upward in vapor, the light was very bright. It concentrated itself in a shining ball. The diagonal line was above, and it slowly began to bend until, in the fullness of time (ten minutes, maybe), it formed a perfectly symmetrical bow, shining silver-blue under the moon.

Kara said she could see colors in the moonbow, and when I looked very hard, I thought I could make out a faint line of reddish orange above and some deep violet at the bottom. Both colors were very pale. In any case, it was exhilarating, the experience of a lifetime: an entirely perfect moonbow, silver and iridescent, all shining and spectral there at the base of Dunanda Falls. The hot pot itself was a luxury, and I considered myself a pretty swell fellow, doing all this for the sanity of city dwellers, who need such things more than anyone else. I even thought of naming the moonbow. Cahill's Luminescence. Something like that. Otherwise, someone else might take credit for it.

May 2002

IV.

THE OUTER LIMITS

THE VANISHING BREED

By Gretel Ehrlich

---

*In a forgotten corner of Russia, a little-known group of reindeer herders still lives
by patterns older than recorded history, shifting nomadically with the seasons.
But how long can it last?*

G ORDON WAKES ME. I had fallen asleep, even as we bumped over frozen
tundra on sleds. How many hours had passed? We'd been traveling for
days—by train from Moscow, helicopter from Arkhangel'sk, and now snowmobile from the village of Nizhnyaya Pesha in northwestern Russia. "I think
we're here," Gordon says. Dogs bark and come running. Ahead I see three large
tepees with smoke curling from their topmost holes, four harnessed reindeer,
and a group of men looking up to see who we are. One of them, a man wearing
dark glasses and a reindeer-skin tunic, hands me a piece of hard candy by way
of greeting. His wide leather belt is decorated with bear teeth and bone cutouts
of spruce trees. A scabbard hangs from two gold chains and swings with the
weight of the knife sheathed inside. "We are Komi people," he says. He is Vasily, the leader, and he seems not to notice my confusion.

We had come to this part of Russia—somewhere between the Kanin Peninsula and the Yamal Peninsula—to join the Nenets, one of Russia's indigenous groups. They are an Asiatic people and tend to have almond eyes and
black hair, far different from the Komi before us. These people are fair-haired
with blue eyes and look like Russians. No one on our team had ever heard
of them.

Vasily asks who we are. I say we are one Russian, one Alaskan Iñupiaq, and
two white Americans, and that we've come to learn about the people of the

reindeer. "In our long memory, we have never had foreign visitors," he tells us shyly. "But you are welcome to travel with us if it pleases you."

Somewhere nearby, the Komi's 2,500 reindeer are being readied to move. Camp is packed up in front of us. "We will be traveling tonight and every few days for the next weeks," Vasily says. "We are making our way to the place where the females will begin calving."

There's quiet excitement among our team of four: photographer Gordon Wiltsie, filmmaker Andrew Okpeaha MacLean, translator and naturalist Andrei Volkov, and I. To have come upon people still living according to the old ways, traveling in every season in nomadic family groups, wearing skins, and driving reindeer sleds across the tundra is completely unexpected. Unlike many indigenous families that were collectivized and segregated into "reindeer brigades" during the Soviet period, these particular Komi were forgotten. "We are people who move," they say with easy smiles. We decide immediately to join them.

Only 12 hours earlier we began this wintry day south of the Barents Sea in the ecotone between taiga and tundra. Our cavernous helicopter had lost one of its ceiling panels. Electrical wires hung down almost touching our heads. We sat on hard benches for hours. There were no seat belts, no bathroom. One man—not of our team—with a vodka hangover vomited quietly into a bag.

Green to the south, white to the north, islands of spruce trees floated in close-cropped tundra; frozen bogs and waterways separated humps of moss and lichen and spread laterally as if to the ends of the Earth. Below us a filthy river bent back on itself, almost in half, like a mind that had been lost. To the west were the Solovetskiye Islands and the infamous prison camp upon which Solzhenitsyn's book *The Gulag Archipelago* had been based, and a few miles south was the labor camp where the poet Joseph Brodsky had been detained. Now, among reindeer sleds piled high with the Komi's belongings, the darkness of those Soviet days seems long gone. We are welcome here.

ANDREI UNFOLDS HIS SATELLITE MAP on top of a sled as the men gather around to show him where we are. A finger points: 50 miles southwest of Nizhnyaya Pesha, and across the Snopa River. Tomorrow, they tell us, we will travel north again.

The women of the camp drift over to our group. They are old, in their 70s, but vigorous; all adult Komi reindeer herders drive their own sleds. They tell us that they are four families: "Just old women and our sons—and one daughter," they say, laughing. "With a few married in, and two young helpers." They have no permanent residence, and most have no memory of ever having had one. They travel year-round with their herd. The route, comprising four pastures, goes from taiga to wet tundra, where north-flowing rivers and streams bleed into the Barents Sea.

Their possessions are packed on 84 sleds. Moving with the seasons and the weather, they live in large skin *chums* (pronounced "chooms"). They don't ride their reindeer as the Sakha people to the east do, but harness them to hand-carved wooden sleds. "We can't remember a time when we didn't live this way," Vasily says, and invites us into his chum for tea.

We duck through the canvas flap. Inside, Maria, Vasily's mother, is feeding the woodstove with split birch logs. She scoops snow into a pot to melt for tea. Another pot burbles with chunks of reindeer. Our welcome is not just tea and cookies but also stew with potatoes or pasta, wild berries, and bread.

We sit on skins laid over spruce boughs at a low table. Maria pushes plates of food toward us. "You've come a long way out of the sky—you must be hungry," she says.

The chum is spacious, 25 feet in diameter. Instead of the sacred pole used by the Nenets on the Yamal Peninsula, the practical Komi set their sheet metal woodstove in the center of the chum with a stovepipe thrust up through the open hole. Maria and Vasily, her youngest son at 45, sleep on one side; Piotr, the oldest son—he's 52—sleeps alone on the other.

Through the one window, snow-encrusted spruces sway and dogs are curled up on the seats of the sleds. It's early April and still wintry, with three feet of hard snow on the ground. At 25 miles above the Arctic Circle, it's unusual to see trees. At the same latitude in Greenland or Arctic Canada there would be none, but this corner of northwestern Russia is warmed slightly by the Gulf Stream.

For Komi nomads, each year is one of frequent movement and harsh temperatures—30-below in winter, 90-above in summer with ferocious bugs. They have reindeer to eat, and reindeer from which to make clothes and shelters, with usually enough animals to sell so they can buy what they need from nearby villages. Winter is spent in the taiga's mixed forests of birch and spruce; spring and fall are on the open tundra near the Barents coast. In the summer they move up to a low mountain that is mosquito free.

The men pore over our maps, speaking of features as most would a good friend. What I see is thousands of square miles of uninhabited land. "Who owns all this?" I ask. "I guess Putin does," Piotr, the leader's older brother, says, laughing. He's tall, gaunt, and voluble. "Yes, it must be his. There are Nenets to the east near Indiga, and Nenets to the west on the Kanin Peninsula, but here, no one but us and we are not many. You see, we have no wives, no children, and the old ones are dying out—our fathers are already gone." He pauses, looks around, then smiles: "In summer the main population is mosquitoes."

By the time we finish our tea and reindeer, it is twilight. Piotr lights the kerosene lamp hanging from his wooden carving of a man's face. "Why aren't any of you married?" I ask. Vasily and Piotr shake their heads: "No women want to live this way, out on the tundra with the *oleni* [reindeer] anymore," they say. There will be no new generation to carry on this group's reindeer-herding tradition.

MORNING. BANDS OF PALE LIGHT slide down the peeled spruce poles. There are reindeer under me, reindeer around me. I sleep soundly. Someone gets up and starts the fire. The stove wood crackles. Water boils. I sit up. Maria smiles: "Good morning," she says in Komi. She is fixing the usual breakfast of stewed berries, boiled reindeer meat, and bread.

It's moving day. Outside, thick fog rolls in. Rime ice hangs in trees, on sleds, and laces the net fence—a portable corral into which the reindeer will be herded. Piotr is splitting wood. He looks toward the horizon, a gray blank: His fellow Komi, he says, "are hunting for the reindeer. They're out there some-where. But it's hard to find them in this weather."

We pack our things. Then the "village"—the three chums—is dismantled. Stick by stick, the hole to the sky is gone, the center stovepipe laid on the ground. The three spruce boughs at the entrance are stacked on top of a loaded sled. Both men and women unwind the canvas and skin coverings and pull them from the poles. Skin by skin, animal by animal—it takes 25 reindeer skins to cover one chum.

TODAY I HAVE MADE TWO NEW FRIENDS: Katya, and a dog, Moo Moo. Katya is 38. Her mother, also named Maria, is 72. They live in the middle and largest of the three chums. While her mother makes tea, Katya explains that in their one chum, two separate families have lived for over 80 years in a space divided by only the *pach*—the woodstove in the center.

"At one time there were 20 of us living in this chum—and 16 of them were children," Katya says. Currently she and her two brothers live with their mother on the left side of the chum; five men live on the other side.

"What happens if someone doesn't get along?" I ask. She looks at me quiz-zically. "That never happens. If there's a problem, we talk it out among our-selves. If that doesn't work, we send them to a village for a short time."

Katya folds clothes and patiently helps her mother pack the kitchen: Porcelain cups go into a padded wooden box with a lid, plus the plates, spoons, forks. The belongings are loaded on a sled, then the walls of the chum come down and we stand exposed to the snowy world. The spruce poles are dragged away, the kitchen table is gone, and the ashes from the woodstove are dumped.

Somewhere out on the tundra are the two herds: the gelded reindeer used for pulling sleds, and the big herd of 2,500, which includes the breeding males and the females about to begin calving.

Reindeer hunting and husbandry has always been the traditional way of life for indigenous people of Arctic Russia, since tundra can support no other crop or animal. Biologists have put Russia's domesticated reindeer population at 1.2 million. It is estimated that there are between one and 1.5 million wild reindeer in the northern tundra regions of the country. At night these animals often come and steal tamed ones away.

Tundra, which comes from the Finnish *tunturi*, meaning "completely treeless heights," has peaty gley soil carrying continuous mats of mosses with patches of lichen, dwarf willows, sedges, berries, and Arctic flowers like saxifrage and dryas. But it is the lichens that nourish and sustain reindeer throughout the winter with their abundant "lichen starch," amino acids, and vitamins.

In turn, these tundra-adapted animals, both wild and tame, sustain the lives of many of Russia's northern peoples, from the Sami in the far northwest to the Chukchi in northeastern Siberia.

THE FOG THAT CAME IN EARLIER has dropped to the ground, and it is almost impossible to see. Someone hears reindeer coming and yells, "Oleni!" The women, standing by their sleds, hurriedly pull on their *malitsas*, or skin dresses, and stuff the footbeds of their leggings with dried grass for insulation. They grab long prodding poles and rush to the corral. With their sewn-in hoods tightly framing their faces and fur mittens on their hands, they look like monastics from a bygone era.

The wait is long. The reindeer were near, but now they are gone. The women lean on their poles. The fog is a cold room that holds them now that the chums have been taken down. Hours go by. No one seems concerned that we will be making a late start. A fire is built and a pot of tea is placed over the open flame. A few chunks of reindeer meat are threaded on a stick, roasted, and passed around. The men joke about not having wives. "If we put TVs in the chums, then we could get women to live with us," forgetting that they have no electricity.

Shy Vasily, the leader, speaks up: "I will bring in a television next time we are near a village." Everyone laughs except Katya. She lives half the year in a town south of here and has seen the devastation caused by capitalism without a true democracy and by epidemic alcoholism. "We live better here than in the village," she says. "It has always been that way and will always be." When one of the men from her chum suggests building a casino in Nizhnyaya Pesha, Katya turns to him angrily: "If you play in the casino, I will kick you out of the chum."

AFTERNOON. REINDEER SWARM OVER THE HILL. In the cold their panting breath spills out in plumes. The herder glides through the middle of the reindeer on his sled as if he were floating. Flanked on both sides, the animals flood into the corral with one of the dogs barking at their heels.

The roiling mass of animals pushes at the fence and the women lean in, holding the top edge of the net high. Antlers clack, brown noses stick up out of the scrum. One huge male rises from the crowd, pawing at the animal in front of him, and kicks Katya in the face. Tears come but she waves me away, indicating that she's alright.

Antlered heads rise and fall. Strips of velvet hang from broken tines. In the chaos of the corral, several animals drop antlers to the ground. The rime ice on the net jangles.

The men take turns going into the corral. They know each animal, which ones worked last and need a rest, which ones are fresh, which ones are young and need to be harnessed to an experienced animal. Soft ropes fly: A reindeer is caught and struggles backward. Another one is caught, and another, until half a dozen reindeer are tethered together and pulled from the moving mass.

Harnessing is slow, but no one ever looks hurried. Every member of the group drives a sled and pulls a caravan of packed sleds behind them. Each driver requires at least 15 reindeer: three or four to pull the first sled, then two more between each of the six or seven freight sleds.

It's late afternoon by the time we take off, but because it's April and we are above the Arctic Circle, there will be light well into the night. Katya and I share the front seat of her sled, really only big enough for one person, but we squeeze on. Her reindeer run at first and we bounce hard, then they slow to a trot. The dogs are tied to the sides of the sleds and run along happily. Puppies get to ride.

Katya's mother starts off in the lead, followed by Vasily's mother, Maria. They are strong drivers, and the sleds glide easily on the ice-covered ponds and over the purple and rust-colored hummocks. There's a forest of snow-flocked spruces on our right, but we're still out in the open. One meadow gives way to another. The going is slow. We seem to be in another century: traveling in a wintry shroud, clothed in hides and fur, the clacking of reindeer feet setting the rhythm.

A RIVER AHEAD. Fyodor, the youngest of the group and of Nenets descent, glides up beside us, jumps off, cocks his fur hat to one side, and helps the others lift each of the sleds down an embankment. Down they go, fishtailing across the frozen river, then bump up the other side, three men pushing from behind.

Traveling again, thick trees yield to a huge meadow. We make camp at the far end. The reindeer are turned loose. It's 10 p.m. by the time the first chum goes up, the two central poles forming an A, and the other poles carefully balanced against them.

Four wooden planks—a portable floor—are put down on either side of the woodstove, and cut spruce boughs are laid around the perimeter and covered with reindeer skins. Fires are started in the sheet metal stoves, even before the hide and canvas coverings are tied on, so that later the stoves will be hot enough to heat tea water and cook the evening meal.

For the time being, the camp is a hive of activity: Logs from the forest are ferried in on reindeer sleds and firewood is cut. At our chum, Maria bosses the men as they push the reindeer-skin coverings to the top of the chum with long poles. "Not too high, down on that side . . . no . . . no, okay that's right, higher, it's going to be bad weather tonight. . . ," she yells, and her sons do her bidding. The piece of canvas that has a glass window sewn in is carefully placed at the back to let light in on the low table where they eat. The kitchen is set up: tablecloth, dishes, silverware, tea, cookies, and candies. The movable world of these Komi people is set in place again.

Afterward the men rest on the huge pile of firewood they've just cut. "Two years ago in December and January, in just this place, three wolves came into the herd and ate some of our reindeer," Vasily tells me. "There was very little snow, so the wolves could get away from us. But when they came back, the snow was deeper and we were able to shoot them. We don't eat the meat, but we use the skins."

That same year a bear attacked three harnessed reindeer near their chum. "We were inside eating when the dogs began barking," they tell me. By the time they ran outside to kill the bear, the reindeer were already dead. The bear stayed around camp all night and found their cache of meat. "He ate that too. He ate everything."

They look at the woods nearby. "Maybe we will have a bear come into camp tonight," they say, smiling. "They are smarter than we are, so watch out!"

NIGHT. NO WOLVES, NO BEARS, only Arctic sun touching down on reindeer hides. Snow falls. Maria ties a red wool scarf over her head, shuffles out away from the camp activity, scoops clean snow into three buckets, and hauls them into the chum to melt for tea. The dogs are fed and curl up under the sleds for shelter.

I follow Vasily and Piotr through the flap of the chum. It's warm inside. Vasily looks boyish, with brown bangs and big soft eyes. He tells how, when he was forced by the Soviet government to go to boarding school, he hid when the helicopter came for him. "We were on the tundra, but there were some trees nearby," he says. "I ran into the forest and dug a cave in the snow. The pilots found me and dragged me away."

The children spoke only Komi when they arrived at school. It took an extra year of classes just to learn Russian. They tell me they couldn't digest the food. "Especially porridge," Vasily says. "Before then, we had only eaten reindeer meat, fish, and berries."

As he talks, Maria makes his bed with loving care. She piles up skins, positions a large pillow against the chum wall, and lays out his sheepskin bag at a right angle to her bed so that his head is almost in her lap. At 45, he's still sleeping with his mother.

Piotr, the restless one of the two brothers, fends for himself. His bed is spartan, and he thrives on listening to the radio news from Moscow. "Do you know Tina Turner? Will you vote for Hillary Clinton?" he asks. A few years earlier he left the tundra for a job in the city of Arkhangel'sk. He didn't like city life, so he came home. "They didn't pay me enough, and I had no free time. I hated it. Not enough money to rent an apartment or have a girlfriend; no time to do carvings."

As he talks, he fiddles with his cheap short-wave radio: It issues only static. For a moment news about Chechnya comes on, then the voices fade. In frustration, he shoves the radio under a jacket by the side of his bed and pulls a single reindeer skin over himself without removing his clothes or boots. "I've always slept with my boots on," he tells me. "It's from living outside with the reindeer all my life," he says. "I'd prefer to sleep outdoors all the time."

Several miles away, Katya's two brothers are camped out with the main herd of reindeer. Despite the snow, they have no tent. From the age of 12 all Komi herders spend certain nights out on the open ground, regardless of the weather. Staying in the chum, they tell me, "would make us lazy and sleepy, and then the wolves and bears would come and eat the calves." They are on guard duty for a week, and after they come in, two other men from the camp will take over.

Soon it will be Vasily's turn to live out on the range with the expectant reindeer, but for now he's dreamy-eyed and quiet. He sits back against the tepee poles with his sleeping mother's head against his thigh. She's already snoring. He speaks slowly, with the quiet reserve of a much older man: "We like it here, living in a chum, because these poles we have carved from the forest, and these walls we have sewn together from our reindeer. That is the meaning of home."

A HARD CRUST HAS FORMED ON THE SNOW during the night, and in the morning I ski alone through the open meadow and up the Snopa River with no idea of where it might lead. Northwestern Russia was thought of as an untamed frontier. But it was neither empty nor uninhabited. In fact, the whole apron of tundra between northwestern Russia and the Pacific Ocean was as rich and diverse in culture as it was in natural resources. First contact with the indigenous peoples between the Dvina River and the Ural Mountains occurred as early as the tenth century, when fur-mongers made their way north. By the 11th century, the colonial subjugation of the Komi was well under way, and by the late 1300s, their ceremonial life had been devastated by Christian proselytizers. In 1456 a treaty "gave" these northern lands to the Muscovites under Ivan III, and by 1620, the conquest of western Siberia, all the way east to the Yenisey River, was complete.

It's hard to be in this country without thinking of subsequent terrors: the forced labor system that began in 1918 and continued through 1956; Stalin's Great Purge of 1937, during which 30 million people were imprisoned and ten million died; the collectivization of nomadic people under Communism. But when I ask my Komi friends if they were harmed during these years, they say no. "They forgot about us. We weren't collectivized like the Nenets were," Vasily says. "They left our families alone."

Alone but hardly untouched. In those times the Barents and Kara Seas became dumping grounds: At least 7,000 tons of radioactive waste and 18 nuclear reactors were sunk into the depths, giving off cesium-137, cobalt-60, strontium, and iodine worth some one million curies. One curie is enough to kill a human. The Arctic island of Novaya Zemlya just north of here was also befouled by nuclear testing. Prevailing winds blew radioactivity all the way across the Siberian tundra, only to be sucked up by lichens, which acquire their nutrients from air, not earth. These, in turn, are eaten by reindeer, and the reindeer are consumed by those who live in the path of the wind.

I ski and ski, then turn back toward camp. Under my feet the land is changing. Between the Barents Sea and the Pacific Ocean the permafrost has been melting. One of the biggest causes of exponential jumps in global warming could come from methane, which is 20 times stronger in its greenhouse effect than carbon dioxide.

Warming Arctic soils are outgassing upwards of 15 million tons of methane a year. A German climatologist, John Schellnhuber, told me, "If the big methane reservoirs get activated, then they could contribute as much to global warming as the burning of all fossil fuels on Earth." But will the reindeer mind if the tundra no longer freezes?

RAIN IN THE NIGHT. The Komi word for rain is *zer*. In the morning the white world of flocked spruce trees around us vanishes. I wash my face using water from a small iron pot hung by a chain. Camp is disassembled and the sleds are repacked. We are traveling again—one in a series of moves that will take us to spring camp, where the women of these four families will stay until June while the men tend the calving reindeer.

To live nomadically in the Russian north doesn't mean one is homeless, but quite the opposite. Home is wider than four walls; home is the wall and roof and floor of each season: white, green, and brown. It is taiga and tundra, mountain and river, lichen, moss, and berry, reindeer, river, and bog.

We travel in fog. With little visibility, the caravans become separated. We see the tail end of the last sled vanish. Snow blows onto the tracks. For a moment we're lost, and Andrei, our translator, takes a compass reading just in case we get left behind. We set off again, hoping we'll come across sled tracks.

Flat land, flat all the way to the cod-rich, polluted Barents Sea. We pass the tilted dunes of tundra. Tiny yellow berries and small orange flowers are starting to show. Another bend and another, and we see the other sleds. In half an hour we're at camp.

Already the first chum is going up. Even this close to the Arctic Ocean there are trees in view. Sun shines through the fog, but the wind is frigid. "Maybe the wind has come to take the fog away," Maria says.

We're camped near a forest island called Kol'-Ostrov, and I dream that the trees exhale gyrfalcons, brown bears, and swans. Andrei and I ski to it—he, on wide Komi skis, pushing along with a pole. We look for bear tracks, wolf tracks, but see none. Up high there are falcon nests, but they are still empty. We cross a melting cranberry bog, our skis dropping through one layer of ice and water to a second, firmer ice floor.

In the distance, lake ice booms. A swan flies into the Kol'-Ostrov. "The earth is waking up. You can hear it," Andrei says with a smile. Another small lake appears on the horizon, which the Komi call Happiness. They say that when the geese arrive, the reindeer will start calving.

Evening. Blue sky and flat tundra. Fires in every stove. Reindeer grazing in the distance. Moo Moo and another dog sit together on the seat of a sled and howl as if to say: Finally, it is spring.

SHE SWEEPS THE FLOOR OF THE CHUM with three raven wings. Earlier I had asked Katya if the feathers were a sacred amulet. She laughed at the suggestion. "No, they're just for cleaning." She's a wide-eyed beauty, vigorous, affectionate, and innocent. Outside on the tundra, in her hooded malitsa, she's a medieval nun, but in the chum, wearing black tights and a turtleneck, she's modern, efficient, quick-witted.

She lives nomadically half the year to help her aging mother and her two brothers. The rest of the time she lives in a small town. In June her older sister comes to camp and takes over. "Every year I say, 'This will be the last year,' but then I come back. They say about people like me that I have 'tundra fever.' Well, maybe I do. I love it here too much to stop coming," she says.

We re-dig the trenches that we made the day before to keep meltwater from seeping onto the floor of the chum, and lay firewood in front of the stove. Her face alternately registers excitement, sadness, and calm. "I feel very good now, inside of myself," she says. "I had bad experiences with men and also with racism, because I am not Russian. When I went to college, people made fun of me because I was Komi. And the men, well, there was always too much vodka. Now I am a woman not looking for a man, a woman who lives in two worlds. This is best for me. Yes, maybe this is the only way."

LATE AT NIGHT VASILY RETURNS from a nearby village slightly drunk. As if ashamed of him, his mother lowers a cotton curtain over their two beds. In the dark, Piotr lies on top of reindeer skins, smoking. He says that the Nenets around Indiga no longer live as families on the tundra. The men take turns going out for a month at a time, and the women live in town. They are having problems keeping their language alive among the young. "They have given up living all the time with their reindeer. We Komi are still *vödzyny*—nomads. I'm proud that I speak Komi. I prefer this way of living—always moving with the animals and our families. I lived in town once and worked. I know what town is. Living with the oleni, making everything we need, and requiring very little else—that means we are free."

He stubs out his cigarette. The night's darkness breaks into something darker. Fresh air swoops down through the smoke hole. Piotr blows out the kerosene lamp and crosses back to his thin bed. "If I had a million dollars, I wouldn't buy a house, or a car, or get a wife. I'd travel," he says. When I ask where, he says, "To the places in the world where there are reindeer—Sápmi, Mongolia, Chukotka." In other words, he would never venture far from home.

"GOOD MORNING. GET UP QUICKLY. Good weather!" Maria shouts. It's Wednesday, our last day of living at spring camp with the women. Today we will go with the men to the main herd of reindeer, who will soon begin calving. Only one man will stay behind with the five women. The puppies are playing, the men are harnessing reindeer, and the women are busy packing the men's rucksacks with extra clothes and food—fresh-baked rolls, cloudberry jam, butter, and tea. Then it's time to leave.

Andrei is calling to me to get on the sled. In the confusion I search for Katya. She has put on her malitsa for a photograph. After, we stand face to face holding each other and say almost simultaneously, though in different languages, "I will never forget you."

Andrei and I climb onto a sled driven by Red Beard, a grumpy man who handles his animals crudely. As soon as we're seated, the reindeer lurch ahead. A piece of wood supporting the runner breaks. I yell at Red Beard. He doesn't seem to care. Andrei shrugs. The sled holds.

When I turn and wave goodbye to the women, I realize that Piotr is staying behind. He'd wrapped a carving that I'd admired and put it on the sled. How could I have known it was a farewell present? I yell, "Piotr! *Spasibo!*" but he has already turned away and is cutting wood.

The route is not smooth. We tip and tilt over hummocks, crash down onto ice, slide, fishtail, slam down, dip and drop into meltwater pools, then haul up onto humps of lichen and moss, and jolt down again into water.

"How do you like 'tundra-thumping?'" Andrew, the filmmaker, asks as his sled bumps by. Being from Barrow, Alaska, he's used to traveling across this kind of open country. I raise a thumb. "Bitchin'," I say. He smiles, but when the young reindeer hitched to his sled take off in the wrong direction, veering so fast he becomes airborne, his smile disappears.

A white-tailed eagle flies up, but still we see no geese. When I ask if the reindeer have begun calving yet, Red Beard shakes his head. We follow the river south where we are going to have to make a dangerous crossing and stop on a bank above the river. I'm nervous about water and had even called my husband on the sat phone the night before. Now I see it's worse than I imagined. I step to the edge: The current is fast, the water is deep, with huge shards of broken ice crashing into each other and stacking up on shore.

I ask the men how we will cross with our animals and heavily laden sleds. They laugh nervously. "We put pieces of wood and logs under the sled runners so they float like small rafts. The reindeer swim and help pull the sleds across. But you have to be careful because the water comes pretty high."

When I ask if there will be problems, they say, "Sometimes a sled runner gets caught under a piece of ice or the harness gets snagged, and then there's trouble."

"And then?" I ask. They shrug. "Do you swim?" I ask.

"*Niet!*" they answer, laughing.

ANDREW CHANGES PLACES WITH ANDREI to ride with me. He wants to film whatever it is that is coming next—floating, swimming, drowning. We follow the river farther south, then, inexplicably, turn north onto the rough tundra again. Another sled comes next to ours: "The reindeer have already crossed. They're on this side now," Nikolai, the other driver, says. Relieved that we don't have to make the dangerous ford, we keep bumping north.

We detour into melting bogs and cross a small lake where the top layer of ice is covered with standing water. Candle ice pings and the sled runners clatter. Sun sparkle blinds me, and for a moment I can't remember where I am. A hard jolt brings me back: We are traveling downstream to find the reindeer. A second hard jolt dumps us upside down into pond water.

I call out for Andrew. His face is under water, but he's holding the camera straight up in the air. Red Beard hasn't noticed that he's lost his passengers. We run after him. Finally he stops and we get back on, dripping. There are snow clouds in the air. In polite Russian, Andrew asks Red Beard if he could slow down a bit. Red Beard growls: "You can hike if you don't like it."

Soon we're gliding up onto a good-size island amid melting ponds, and then we see: The reindeer are there—2,500 animals swarming the hillocks and swimming the narrow channels. Something black moves between an animal's legs. It's a newborn reindeer, tiny and wobbling. The mother is lying down in the midst of the moving herd, and the calf is trying to suckle. Reindeer are running past. Finally the mother gets up, lets the calf suck, then joins the others with the calf running alongside.

One of the herders has gone ahead; we hear only his high-pitched, haunting, two-note call. He's trying to get the reindeer to cross a narrow bridge, but the animals shift nervously in a wide circle. An hour goes by, and another. It begins to rain. Three geese fly up.

Finally the animals funnel over the bridge. On the other side is a surprising view: not tundra, but a narrow strip of arable land—a hay meadow beside the raging river.

We camp at the edge of its three Monet-like stacks. There's a tiny hut with a long table inside, but no stove. We pitch two tents—that's all we have. Now, at day's end, and with us wet to the bone, rain turns to snow.

The men make a big fire, whittle the ends of a forked stick, and roast reindeer en brochette. We cram into the shed, drink shots of vodka, eat berries and meat. There are ten of us, and even without a stove, the body heat keeps us warm.

"The reindeer want to go north. They'd be at the Barents Sea in a few days if we let them go," Vasily says. "But we want them to stay here until all the calves are born. This is a good place for them."

During the night snow pushes at the tent. In the morning the sky is slate over white-topped haystacks. We drink pond water tea. It is brackish, sieved through furled lichens. Breakfast is reindeer soup. The bones are fed to the dogs. Red Beard's gruffness softens as he begins to sing. I don't know why, but I ask him if he's ever been in love. He responds quietly: "Yes. I once had a wife. I have a son. They've never been here to see me," and begins singing again.

WIND IN THE SPRUCES. Swans circling. Ptarmigan squabbling in the brush. Of all the Komi men, Artur, the youngest, is the most responsible. When he goes out to check the reindeer, I ski up and down the snow road in search of bear tracks, wolf tracks, or incoming swans. "You have to stay here for a whole year before you know how we live and who we are," Artur says, passing me in his reindeer sled. I concur.

In the morning we pack. Fyodor is missing—supposedly he's been drinking in the nearby village of Snopa—so we're asked to help bring in the reindeer. The sky is clearing, but it is cold. Spring has come earlier this year, the men say, but they are happy that the cold will keep the mosquitoes down.

The reindeer are harnessed, and the men take our gear to a field on the edge of Snopa. By mid-afternoon the helicopter still has not come. We visit the sauna and the schoolhouse, where a portrait of Pushkin on the wall has replaced the one of Lenin. There's a bakery, a dairy, and small gardens between the Tolstoyan wooden houses and barns, with loose horses running across the fields bucking and pawing. An idyllic scene, except that many of the men in town are drunk.

Nikolai sees Fyodor, bleary-eyed with vodka, running between two barns but can't catch him. He's in trouble. It was an embarrassment for the herders to need our help with the reindeer. Later they shun him when he appears and tell him to come back when he is sober.

We look skyward for the helicopter. Nothing. Artur gives me a gift of a reindeer's headstall made of bone. "Everything we make is done with a knife and an ax." Bone. Wood. Skin.

"Soon we will be away from this village, and there won't be anyone getting drunk," Artur says as we walk to the edge of the river. "I'm sorry you had to see us this way. I wish you could stay. Yes, a whole year would do it. Then you would know us, and after, you could go your way."

AN ENORMOUS HELICOPTER LANDS in the bare field like a beast out of a nightmare. The herders hand up our skis and duffels. The machine lifts and shudders. Tears come. I will not be here again. Cloud shadows sprout and die. I turn my head to look: It is endless, this mosaic of rotting ice and gray-green lichen and moss. As we gain altitude I'm instantly lost. There is no village, no chum, no reindeer. The body of the tundra is bigger than all that; it hides human and animal occupation. All I see are islands and hummocks trapped in meltwater moats and a whole frozen world going soft in faint light. I strain to hear the lichens' symbiotic song and dance. Instead, cranberry bogs may cough up methane, and by the end of summer it could boil up in a million pond-pots. We hover and slide over a world of leaking vessels—as if the earth were bleeding to death.

Trees, when they appear, stain the snow with shadows that are blue; geese drop down onto water that looks like sky. Lake ice is gouged by the tracks of a passing bear. Collars of ice fold back from ponds. A tree goes down: I see it falling. Beyond, five swans land. A bend in the river dangles like a loose knee.

We land at Oma, then Mezen', then at a nameless village. As we pass again into the world of trees, I look back at the vast expanse from which we have come and see that, once this generation of Komi is gone, there will be only the wiggle-worm puzzle of melting tundra—ultimately, a whole land drowned.

MARCH 2008

THE LURE OF IMPOSSIBLE PLACES

By Tim Cahill

The world may be shrinking, but it still holds a lot of wild, extreme, incredible
terrain—and a few hopelessly impractical people who love it.

A N ARCHAEOLOGIST FRIEND OF MINE was railing against the media a
few years ago. He had been showing a reporter-photographer team one
of his digs in the mountains near my Montana home. It is a painstaking process, this business of excavating a site in which there is evidence of 9,000 years
of continuous human habitation. "Is this the oldest site in all the Americas?"
the reporter asked.

Well, no, it wasn't. It wasn't even the oldest first-Americans site within a
hundred miles.

"Well, are these the only artifacts of this type ever found?" the reporter
wanted to know. No, they were pretty typical of the period, actually. The
reporter seemed progressively more disappointed and less inclined to ask questions. The photographer packed her cameras away, and the two journalists
took their leave very soon thereafter.

"Fled like rats," I suggested.

"Like rats," my friend agreed. "And they weren't the first." We thought about
this for a moment, the archaeologist and I. "What I want to know," my friend
asked, "is why it always has to be the 'oldest' or the 'biggest' or the 'only'."

"Gee, I dunno," I said. But I did; really, I knew. We journalists think
"ultimates" make better stories. We believe people are more apt to read an
article titled "World's Oldest Human Habitation Reveals Evidence of Unique

Weapons Technology" rather than one headlined "Typical Stone Tools Found at Pretty Old Site."

I've tried, over the ensuing years, to wean myself off the journalistic search for nothing less than the unmatched or the incomparable. For example, I've spent a lot of time walking the area near that pretty old site where the typical stone tools were found. I thought for a time that I had conquered the urge to deal with the ultimate. But then it occurred to me that this was, in fact, the oldest site I could see from my front door, the oldest site on the mountain overlooking my town, and the oldest site that I personally knew a great deal about. It is my personal ultimate first-Americans site.

I have come to understand that there is something about the site that thrills me in a sense that is far more profound than any mere intellectual interest. That, I think, is the nature of the ultimate.

When the first people settled the mountain looming over my home almost ten centuries ago, it must have looked much as it does today. The last ice had retreated a few thousand years earlier, and the men and women who took up residence were matchless hunters and gatherers. Indeed, every single one of us is alive today because hundreds of generations of our ancestors were expert hunters and gatherers. I believe these talents and urges exist deep within us all, whether we call the manifestations "shoe shopping" or "making a killing in the market." So, as I walk that land, in the footsteps of the old ones, my thoughts tend to ricochet off reason and zing around somewhere near the outskirts of wisdom.

Is this thought unformed? Of course it is. But I think we are getting close to the reason humans seek out the ultimate, which is something I still do in my capacity as a journalist. On Lantau Island, just off China, at the Po Lin Monastery, there is an immense statue of the Buddha. When I was there, not long ago, I asked if it was the biggest Buddha on Earth. No, it was the "largest outdoor Buddha." I wrote that down. Actually, I was told, it was the "largest outdoor bronze Buddha." That was one too many qualifiers. I began wondering if there were bigger indoor Buddhas, as well as bigger outdoor Buddhas made of something other than bronze, and perhaps bigger inflatable floating Buddhas or even huge shipshape Buddhas. In any case, I wrote the words "pretty big Buddha" in my notebook and fled like a rat.

Another time, through no great effort on my part, I found myself standing on the sea ice at the exact point of the geographic North Pole. It was about 25 degrees Fahrenheit—not particularly cold, in other words—the sky was overcast, spitting snow, and one could see for, oh, a hundred yards in any direction.

That direction was south. Here I was, on this ultimate spot, slowly turning through 360 degrees, thinking, It's all south. Somehow, this perception did not fill me with thoughts of an exalted nature. Everyone's ultimate is different. Some places will speak to you. Others may not.

I had come to the Pole on a Russian icebreaker, and there was some swimming to be done in the black seawater under the broken ice. Water can get only so cold, so my brief swim at the North Pole was an ultimate of another sort. Perhaps I cogitated deeply on the subject. I don't recall. There were Russians and a great deal of vodka involved.

In my life, I have actually sought out ultimates of a negative sort. Not long ago, I purposely visited the most densely populated place on Earth, the Mong Kok district of Kowloon, just off Hong Kong. There are said to be 165,000 persons per square kilometer in Mong Kok, and, indeed, there was a lot of unintentional jostling and bumping of shoulders involved in simply walking down the street. But why did I go there? Anyone who knows me knows that I actively hate crowds: crowded parties, crowded restaurants, crowded streets. Give me any damn crowd at all. I curse it. I spit in its multifaceted face. *Ptew, ptew, ptew.*

Why did I go to the most crowded place on Earth? I don't know. I really don't. But if someone told you that you could have a glimpse of hell, just a glimpse, and then walk away, would you do it? Mong Kok is my idea of the final nightmare.

So, the 9,000-year-old first-Americans site is, in my mind, the way the world begins. The jostling, gasping crush of humanity swirling down the behavioral sink in Mong Kok is the way it ends.

What I mean to say here is that the ultimate holds an interest entirely untrammeled by logic or sanity. Once, a couple of decades ago, the photographer Michael "Nick" Nichols and I crossed Death Valley at its deepest point, 282 feet below sea level. This is, of course, the lowest spot in America. We then walked overland and mostly off-trail to the summit of Mount Whitney, which, at 14,494 feet, is the highest spot in the contiguous U.S. I am often asked why we did this. My standard answer is: "The reasons have never been satisfactorily explained."

I knew that the highest and lowest places in the lower 48 were separated by a mere hundred miles or so. Why not walk it? As I pointed out to my partner, the distinguished and ineffably boyish Nick Nichols, "Nothing could possibly go wrong."

"Don't say that," he said. Nick is very superstitious about things like hubris and poor planning. But, really, we had this deal knocked. Cross Death Valley, in the middle of the summer, mid-July to be exact, and you get . . . uh, well, the possibility of death. But, really, aside from that, what could go wrong?

Well, first off, the lowest place in the United States is surrounded by very high places—Telescope Peak, for instance, is over 11,000 feet—and water wants to collect in the basin of the valley. Constant winds evaporate the water—you hardly sweat in 110-degree heat—and the relentless sun bakes the land. So it's a dry walk across all that trackless sand and baked mud, right? Like hell it is.

The valley is trying terribly hard to be a lake, but the sun and evaporative wind won't let it, so the lake water hides, like a kid reading under the covers with a flashlight. As you get out toward the center and the bottom of the valley, the baked mud under your boots gets thinner—it is only a wafer crust of minerals and salts eroded from the mountains above. Walking on this stuff is like walking on crusty snow: Each step would seem to hold, then the bottom would give way and we'd plunge knee-deep into the hot mineral soup just below the lowest place in America. Then it was difficult to get the foot out of the hole with the boot on it. And so much pressure now had to be exerted by the leading foot that there was no hope of skating over the top. No, we were post-holing through this enchantment, and each step put us knee-deep into the muck. Or deeper. Often we sank up to our thighs. The shattered mineral plates on the valley floor cut up our pants and shins and then rubbed salt into our wounds.

We weren't entirely dim-witted and kept a full ten paces between us, switching the lead as often as I could convince Nick that it was his turn. We were both familiar with Daniel Cronkhite's book *Death Valley's Victims*. Cronkhite writes that there are rumors of places in the valley where men and whole wagon teams have been swallowed up without a trace. I know of no record of this actually happening. It is the folk wisdom. People have certainly disappeared in the valley and never been seen again. One description that haunts me to this day is from a traveler who claims to have found a dead man's face staring up out of the mud: "He was a Swede with yellow hair, and he stared at the sun. He sank standing up."

So Nick and I were following in each other's footsteps, and if one of us went down, it was up to the other to crawl out on the thin crust and pull him out of there. We had a thin-ice type of rescue in mind, here in a temperature near a hundred degrees at the bottom of America.

It was at this point that Nick declared that he had dropped some camera ditty or another. Anyway, it was something he needed, one of his lights. We were walking at night—about three in the morning, actually—and none of

Nick's pictures were going to turn out without the proper lights. He needed to go back and find the damn thing.

That would be easy enough. He'd just step back through our postholes until he spotted the gadget. "You don't have to come," Nick informed me.

"Right," I said. Moron.

So off Nick went, in the direction of the road we'd left quite some time ago. For a long while I could hear the *crack-splush* of his steps. Then all was quiet but for the wind. Nick was so far away, I lost sight of his headlamp in the darkness. Then, if I listened very intently, I could hear the mineral soup gurgling into our postholes. It seemed unwise to take another step in a place where a man or wagon could be swallowed up whole. I'd wait to walk. With Nick around I'd at least have a chance. So I stood still, but I could feel myself almost imperceptibly sinking into the hell soup at the bottom of America.

I am standing here at the lowest point, I thought. Everyplace was up. Somehow this had more emotional resonance than the thought that everyplace was south. The words "nadir" and "lowdown" and "depressed" and "abyss" all occurred to me, and I thought of the yellow-haired Swede who'd died standing up, staring at the sun, and I felt myself trembling on the periphery of profound thoughts.

I think that is the nature of Ultimate Places. They exist entirely on their own, not for you, or in spite of you, or because of you. They are what they are, and if you hang around them long enough, you, too, may be tempted to commit philosophy.

OCTOBER 2003

OUT OF THIN AIR

By David Roberts

After 75 years, Everest finally gave up its most closely held secret. Or did it?

A S HE SHUFFLED ALONG THE SHALE LEDGE, peering intently at his surroundings, Jake Norton heard the two-way radio inside his down suit crackle to life. "Last time I went bouldering in my hobnails," came the muffled voice, "I fell off."

Of this message, Norton caught only the word "hobnails." Immediately, he ripped the radio out of his cocoon of down and nylon, pushed the button, and spoke: "What was that, Conrad?

"Come on down." The voice was clearer now. "Let's get together for Snickers and tea."

Norton gazed across the mountain face. Fifty yards below him, some distance to the west, his friend was waving his ski pole. Norton's blood sang as he started to climb across the dangerous slabs toward Conrad Anker. Three other colleagues, scattered about the sterile mountain slope, remained oblivious. This time Anker injected some urgency into his radio message: "I'm calling a mandatory group meeting right now!"

When Norton reached his teammate, he found Anker sitting on his pack, staring at the ground in front of him. It was about noon on May 1, 1999. Norton and Anker were just below 27,000 feet on the North Face of Mount Everest. Before them sprawled a dead man, lying facedown uphill, hands raised above his shoulders, fingers frozen into the scree as if in his last moment he had been clawing at the earth for purchase. Tatters of old clothing covered his neck and lower arms, but his back and much of his shoulders were laid bare. His torso gleamed an eerie alabaster. Astonishingly, the winds that had torn loose seven layers of wool, cotton, and silk had left the man's skin intact. The body was so perfectly mummified that Anker and Norton could see the well-defined swell of powerful muscles, could even see the blue discoloration of bruises.

Later Anker remembered his thoughts at the moment of discovery: *This is what we came here to do, he mused. This is who we're looking for. This is Sandy Irvine.*

NEARLY 75 YEARS EARLIER, on the morning of June 8, 1924, George Leigh Mallory and Andrew "Sandy" Irvine set out from Camp VI, at 26,700 feet on the Northeast Ridge of Everest. Theirs would be the last possible attempt on the world's highest mountain during this, the third expedition ever to plumb its intricate defenses. The monsoon would arrive any day, enfolding the Himalaya in a four-month miasma of heavy snow.

Yet as the pair closed their canvas tent and headed along the ridge, they were filled with a keen optimism. Only four days earlier, their teammate E. F. "Teddy" Norton had reached 28,126 feet—the highest anyone had ever climbed—before turning back a mere thousand feet below the summit. Norton had made his gutsy push without the aid of bottled oxygen. Mallory and Irvine were breathing gas; though Mallory had initially been a skeptic about its efficacy, on the 1922 expedition he had learned firsthand that climbers aided by oxygen high on Everest could easily double the climbing speed of those without.

Mallory, who was ten days short of his 38th birthday, was the climbing leader on this effort. He was the only man who had taken part in all three Everest expeditions. Everest had become an obsession for him, as for no one else: If there were any way of reaching the summit that day, he would find it.

Irvine, at 22, was a remarkably inexperienced mountaineer, with only an exploratory junket to Spitsbergen under his belt. But on Everest he had proved to be tougher than several of his more seasoned comrades, an uncomplaining worker, and a delightful companion. He was also something of a mechanical genius, who had taken apart the oxygen apparatus in the field and rebuilt it in a lighter and more efficient form.

Among the rest of the team that day, only Noel Odell, climbing solo up to Camp VI in support of the summit duo, was high on the mountain. At 12:50 in the afternoon he mounted a small crag at around 26,000 feet just as the clouds abruptly cleared. Squinting upward, he was treated to a brief vision that has become, in its tantalizing poignance, perhaps the most legendary sighting in exploration history. As Odell later wrote:

"I saw the whole summit ridge and final peak of Everest unveiled. I noticed far away on a snow slope leading up to what seemed to me to be the last step but one from the base of the final pyramid, a tiny object moving and approaching the rock step. A second object followed, and then climbed to the top of the step . . . I could see that they were moving expeditiously as if endeavouring to make up for lost time."

Then Mallory and Irvine vanished into history.

As CONRAD ANKER AND JAKE NORTON studied the mummified body lying among the rocks, their three teammates made their way one by one to the site. The going was treacherous; a slip here could mean a fatal fall of 7,000 feet to the upper Rongbuk Glacier. As each searcher arrived, the gestalt of the details—the ragged edges of the torn-away clothing, the fingers planted in the scree, a thin white rope tangled about the torso, terminating in a frayed loose end—struck home. Below the base of the back, the right buttock had been eaten away by goraks—the prehistoric-looking ravens that haunt the upper reaches of the Himalaya. The birds had used this orifice to ravage the man's internal organs. The left foot was bare, the lower leg folded atop its companion, as if to shelter it from further harm—for the right leg, hobnailed boot intact, lay hideously bent, both tibia and fibula plainly broken.

"I was pretty blown away," recalled Tap Richards. "It was obviously a body, but it looked like a marble statue."

For half an hour, a sense of taboo hung over the stark tableau. At first, the five men could not bring themselves to touch the body. Instead they took photographs and pointed out nuances that might bear on how the man had met his end. Jake Norton sat down with a flat stone in his lap and began to carve a memorial to Sandy Irvine.

"It didn't hit me on a personal level until we started working on him," said Dave Hahn. "Then he became a real man."

With great care, the men used their axes to chip away at the ice that froze the victim to the slope. As they got closer to the body, they switched to pocketknives, carving with an archaeological delicacy. While Hahn and Andy Politz shot video footage, Richards and Norton bore the brunt of the excavation, as they cut away beneath the corpse in hopes of finding what might lie in his pockets. Then Norton came across a name tag on the collar of one of the man's garments. It read "G. Mallory."

"That's weird," said Norton to his teammates. "Why would Irvine be wearing Mallory's shirt?"

NOEL ODELL'S GLIMPSE FROM HIS PERCH at 26,000 feet was the last anyone ever saw of the two doomed climbers, and for 75 years climbers and scholars have wrangled over just what his sighting signified. The ultimate question remained unanswered: Could Mallory and Irvine have reached the summit of Everest, 29 years before Edmund Hillary and Tenzing Norgay made the official first ascent?

During those 75 years, only two further pieces of hard information cast any light on the mystery of Mallory and Irvine's fate, but each was as tantalizing as Odell's fugitive apparition. In 1933, on the first expedition to Everest after Mallory's, Percy Wyn Harris found an ice ax lying on a rock slab, 200 yards short of what had come to be called the First Step—thus considerably below where the pair had been at the time of Odell's sighting. Plainly the ax belonged to either Mallory or Irvine, but as a piece of evidence it was maddeningly ambiguous. Had one of the climbers dropped it during the ascent? Or had it been deliberately laid aside as unnecessary on the mostly rocky terrain that stretched above? Or, more ominously, did it mark the site of a fatal accident on the descent, as one man dropped the ax to make a futile effort to belay his falling partner?

From 1938, the year of the last British pre-war expedition, to 1960, when the Chinese claimed to make the first ascent of Everest from the north, no sanctioned Western expeditions visited the Tibetan side of the mountain. It was not until 1979 that the Chinese first granted permission to foreigners to approach the mountain through its "province" of Tibet. That year, the second tantalizing clue to Mallory and Irvine's demise came to light.

The climbing leader of the Sino-Japanese expedition, Ryoten Hasegawa, had a provocative conversation with one of its Chinese members, Wang Hongbao. Wang told the Japanese man that four years earlier, during the second Chinese attempt of Everest, he had gone out for a short walk from Camp VI, at about 27,000 feet. Within 20 minutes of leaving his tent, he had come across the body of a fallen climber. It was, he insisted, "an old English dead." The man's clothes had turned to dust and blown away in the winds of the decades. He was lying on his side, and one of his cheeks had been pecked away by goraks.

Between Hasegawa's Japanese and Wang's Chinese, the conversation took place in a linguistic muddle. Hasegawa wondered whether the dead man could have been a Russian from a long-rumored secret 1952 attempt, on which six climbers were supposed to have died; but Wang vigorously demurred, repeating "English! English!"

Hasegawa realized that the body might well have been that of Mallory or Irvine. But before he could question Wang further, the Chinese climber died in an avalanche—just a day after sharing his startling confidence.

During the last two decades, scores of expeditions have attacked Everest from the north. All of them have watched keenly for any further sign of the lost climbers, to no avail. An American mountaineer-historian, Tom Holzel, became obsessed with the puzzle, and after extensive research, narrowed down the search area to a large quadrangle on the North Face, below the ridge route Mallory and Irvine had traveled. In 1986, Holzel helped organize an expedition—the first of its kind—to search systematically for the vanished pair. The team included such first-rate climbers as David Breashears, Sue Giller, and Dave Cheesmond, but terrible weather thwarted their efforts to go higher than 25,500 feet—more than a thousand feet below Holzel's search zone. (In retrospect, it would become clear that a search in the autumn season, such as the 1986 team conducted, was doomed to fail because of the vast quantities of snow the summer-long monsoon inevitably dumps.)

Before the expedition, Holzel had synthesized all his research into a house-of-cards hypothesis that he laid out in the concluding chapter of *First on Everest: The Mystery of Mallory & Irvine* (which he coauthored with Audrey Salkeld). According to Holzel, Mallory and Irvine faced the realization that they would run out of bottled oxygen well below the summit. Mallory was, in Holzel's view, de facto the stronger climber, with Irvine perhaps daunted by a challenge well beyond any he had previously faced. In any event, Irvine gave his remaining gas to his partner, then descended as Mallory headed solo for the summit.

Carried away by his own theorizing, Holzel wrote as if recording solid history, not educated guess: "Splitting up at 1 p.m., Mallory quickly raced up the final pyramid of Everest's summit. Irvine returned past the First Step and started his descending traverse of the North Face slabs. . . . Perhaps after numerous small slips, each caught in time, Irvine lost control as both his feet shot out from under him. Turning to catch himself with his ice ax, it wrenched out of his exhausted grip. He tumbled a thousand feet to the snow terrace below."

Holzel was further convinced that Mallory reached the summit only to die of hypothermia in the bivouac he could not have avoided, or in a fall, perhaps all the way to the Rongbuk Glacier.

In the years after 1986, most informed observers doubted Holzel's asser-
tion that Mallory had made the summit. But the notion of the two climbers
splitting up, with Irvine dropping his ax and slipping to his death on the
North Face, came to be a kind of received wisdom. Thus the body that Wang
Hongbao had found near Camp VI had to be Irvine's. It was for this reason
that all five searchers last May, as they stared at the "marble statue" lying frozen
facedown in the scree, were certain they were looking at Sandy Irvine.

ONLY ONE OF TWO THINGS could settle for good the question of whether
Mallory or Irvine reached the summit in 1924. The first is that some relic—a
piece of gear, a keepsake, or a note unmistakably belonging to one of the
men—might be found on or near the top. But the hundreds of successful
summitters over the past 46 years have never found anything of that kind.
(Looking for traces of predecessors in 1953, Hillary peered down the North
Ridge and declared it unclimbable.)

The other possibility touches on the kind of wild surmise normally found
only in the pages of Conan Doyle. We know that Mallory carried a Kodak Vest
Pocket camera. If the camera could be found, and the film, deep-frozen since
1924, could be developed, a photo clearly taken from the summit—an image
of such peaks as Ama Dablam or Nuptse, for instance, invisible from anywhere
on Everest's North Face—would clinch the case. (In 1897, a three-man Swed-
ish expedition led by Salomon Andrée, attempting to balloon to the North
Pole, vanished in the Arctic. Thirty-three years later, the men's bodies were
found on remote White Island. Their pictures, perfectly preserved, delivered a
vivid testament to the trio's last days and to the mishaps that doomed them.)

During the past few years, a young German grad student in geology has
taken up the quest where Tom Holzel left off. Jochen Hemmleb, 28, is a
climber of modest abilities, but a researcher whose obsession with detail puts
even Holzel's in the shade. From a single, mediocre photo published in a book
celebrating the 1975 Chinese expedition, Hemmleb figured out that Camp VI
that year had been pitched in an entirely different place from nearly all other
expeditions' Camps VI. Studying background details, Hemmleb thought he
could extrapolate the location of the fugitive camp. A search, then, for the
body Wang Hongbao had found ought to focus on all terrain within a plausible 20-minute stroll of that camp.

A friend of Hemmleb's got in touch with Mount Rainier guide Eric Simonson, who had climbed Everest from the north in 1991. Galvanized by the
German's research, Simonson put together a climbing team and a network of

sponsors. Most of his teammates were fellow Rainier guides, but at the last moment, he snagged a genuine star—36-year-old Conrad Anker, one of the strongest and most ambitious climbers in the world. The BBC and *NOVA* agreed to coproduce a film about the expedition, and the Seattle-based Web site MountainZone.com signed on to cover the team via daily Internet dispatches.

Most observers viewed the expedition as something of a boondoggle—one more gimmick, like campaigns to raise money for medical research or to clean up other expeditions' trash, to finance an expensive outing on the world's highest mountain. Even if Simonson and Hemmleb's motives were sincere, after all the expeditions that had crisscrossed the northern slopes of Everest over the years, the chances of finding something new from the 1924 expedition seemed infinitesimal.

Even Anker had, in the middle of a 1997 cutting-edge jaunt among unclimbed towers in Antarctica, vocally derided the Everest circuses of recent years. Then, last March, on the eve of his departure for Nepal, one of Anker's friends invited him to dinner.

"What are you up to, Conrad?" the friend asked over coffee.

"I'm off for Tibet. A little high-altitude trekking."

"Kailas?" the friend asked, naming the holy mountain, object of Buddhist and Hindu pilgrimages.

"No, a little higher," said Anker sheepishly. "I'm going to Everest."

WITH THE SOLE EXCEPTION OF AMELIA EARHART IN 1937, the vanishing of no explorer in the 20th century has generated anything like the romantic speculation surrounding George Leigh Mallory's. At the core of the puzzle is not simply the mystery of what went wrong to cause the deaths of Mallory and Irvine. It is all too easy, even in the 1990s, to fall off the north side of Everest or to freeze to death high on its ledges. The paramount issue, the conundrum that every subsequent Everest climber and armchair expert has struggled to solve, is whether the two could have reached the summit. Depending on where exactly the pair was when Odell saw them at 12:50 on June 8 (and the man himself vacillated in his testimony over the decades), Mallory and Irvine might have been as close as 500 feet below the top. And at the moment, they were "moving expeditiously" upward.

No 8,000-meter peak in the world would be climbed for another 26 years, until the French ascent of Annapurna in 1950, despite a dozen bold attacks on K2, Kangchenjunga, Nanga Parbat, and Everest in the 1930s, by teams loaded with top-notch American, English, and German mountaineers. If Mallory and

Irvine summitted in 1924, their deed stands a fair claim to be regarded as the greatest climbing feat in history.

Beyond all this, Mallory himself was one of the most talented, charismatic, and at the same time enigmatic figures ever to cross the stage of mountain conquest. Born in Cheshire, England, in 1886, a parson's son, he attended Winchester school, then went up to Magdalene College, Cambridge. As a child, his sister recalled, "He climbed everything that it was at all possible to climb"—trees, walls, and buildings. He excelled in football (i.e., soccer) and gymnastics, and "did not like to lose." But it was not until the age of 18, during the summer before his last year at Winchester, that Mallory first did any real mountaineering, when a tutor, R. L. G. Irving, took him and another student to the Alps. The climbs Irving dragged his novices up were surprisingly ambitious, and during those arduous outings on Monte Rosa and Mont Blanc, Mallory discovered the passion that would center his life.

From his first years onward, two characteristics emerged that would ultimately bear on his fate on Mount Everest. Mallory had a kind of addiction to risk that skeptical observers considered simple recklessness. His sister remembered him telling her that in theory a boy ought to be able to lie on the railroad tracks and escape unharmed as a train ran over him. Some years later, after Mallory led a very experienced Austrian mountaineer up a difficult route in Wales, the visitor marveled at Mallory's "mastery of the hardest pitches," but inveighed, "That young man will not be alive for long."

The other characteristic was a chronic absentmindedness. There is a famous route on Lliwedd, the great peak in Wales, on which legend has it Mallory made the first ascent, solo at dusk, to recover a pipe he had left on a high ledge that he had reached earlier in the day by a more conventional but less direct itinerary. Even in 1922, on Everest, the expedition leader, Charles Bruce, described Mallory as "a great dear but forgets his boots on all occasions." On top of his absentmindedness, Mallory had a mechanical ineptitude so extreme he had trouble making his camp stove work.

Mallory was also possessed of extraordinary good looks. The photos capture his handsomeness, but no photo could convey the charm and magnetism that made both men and women fall in love with him, often at first sight.

Through fellow Cambridge students James Strachey and Geoffrey Keynes, Mallory drifted within the orbit of Bloomsbury. On first beholding this "Greek god," the more unabashed flouters of convention within that circle could hardly contain their rapture. Wrote Lytton Strachey to Clive and Vanessa Bell, after his first meeting with Mallory: "*Mon dieu!*—George Mallory!—When that's been written, what more need be said? My hand trembles, my heart palpitates, my whole being swoons at the words—oh heavens! heavens! . . . [H]e's six foot high, with the body of an athlete by Praxiteles, and a face—oh incredible—the mystery of Botticelli, the refinement and delicacy of a Chinese print, the youth and piquancy of an unimaginable English boy."

Once Mallory had reached his prime, his climbing technique seems to have been as *foudroyant* as his beauty, for colleague after colleague marveled at it. His close friend Cottie Sanders, better known by her novelist nom de plume Ann Bridge, remembered: "He was never a showy climber; he did not go in for the minute precisions of style at all. On the contrary, he seemed to move on rocks with a sort of large, casual ease that was very deceptive when one came to try and follow him. When he was confronted with a pitch which taxed his powers, he would fling himself at it with a sort of angry energy, appearing to worry it as a terrier worries a rat, till he had mastered it." Fear, Sanders said, was "something he had no experience of whatever."

Geoffrey Winthrop Young, the finest British climber of the generation before Mallory's, who would become the true mentor of his life, wrote, "He swung up rock with a long thigh, a lifted knee, and a ripple of irresistible movement." Robert Graves was taken climbing by Mallory as a schoolboy, long before he became a great poet, novelist, and scholar. *In Good-bye to All That,* Graves recalled that his tutor "used to go drunk with excitement at the end of his climbs."

After Cambridge, Mallory hoped to become a writer, and managed to publish a critical work called *Boswell the Biographer.* In his articles for the climbing journals, he went far beyond the dry recitations of passes gained and ridges traversed that were the norm of the day, striving for a lyrical flight to match the exaltation he felt in the mountains. Mallory's most famous written passage comes from such an account, of a difficult route on Mont Blanc, published in 1918 in the *Alpine Journal:* "Have we vanquished an enemy? None but ourselves. Have we gained success? That word means nothing here."

There is perhaps a rueful irony in the fact that the single phrase for which Mallory will forever be remembered was a spontaneous retort, in the midst of a tiring American lecture tour, to a journalist who asked him why he wanted to climb Everest. "Because it is there," snapped Mallory, passing on to posterity an apothegm as pithy as any Confucian riddle. Some of Mallory's closest friends insisted that the response was meant as an off-putting non sequitur, from a man weary in his bones of being asked the same unanswerable question mountaineers have always been scolded with.

Meanwhile, to eke out a living, Mallory took a teaching job at a boarding school called Charterhouse. He poured himself into the job, and students such as Robert Graves remained indebted to him for the rest of their lives. But Mallory was too disorganized to be a really effective teacher, too creative to be happy in his drudgerous and sedentary post.

Mallory served on the French front during World War I, where he suffered his share of close calls—a whizzing bullet that passed between him and a nearby soldier, two friends blown apart by a shell as they followed a few paces behind him.

The year before he left for the front, on a 1914 jaunt to Venice, Mallory fell in love with Ruth Turner. She was beautiful—"Botticellian" was his own word for her. They were married only four months after meeting, just as Mallory turned 28. He at once taught his bride to climb, hauling her along on far from trivial routes in Wales. By 1920, the couple had two daughters and a son. After a decade of marriage, their passion for each other seemed utterly undimmed, as their letters, collected in the archives of Magdalene College, testify.

If it weren't for Everest, Mallory might have settled down to a life of schoolteaching, dabbling as a writer, and climbing summers in the Alps. As early as 1919, however, rumors of a British reconnaissance of the approaches to the world's highest mountain were floating about. No Westerner had stood within 40 miles of its flanks. For a man of Mallory's restless spirit, this siren call could not go unheeded.

THE 1921 RECONNAISSANCE, pursued through the summer and into the autumn season, was in many respects a colossal mess. The party's talents were wildly uneven, with several over-the-hill, out-of-shape walruses in leadership positions. One of them died of dysentery long before the team had even sighted the mountain. George Bernard Shaw later memorably characterized a group portrait of the team as looking like a picnic in Connemara surprised by a snowstorm.

The personnel were further split by sharp jealousies and antipathies. Yet despite lugging such psychological balls and chains toward the mountain, the team unerringly discovered the route to the North Col, which would be the key to all attempts on Everest for the next 29 years. Mallory's own spirits swung wildly between joy and despair. Sometimes the expedition was "a thrilling business"; at other times, "a fraud." "[O]ur present job is to rub our noses against the impossible," he wrote despondently from the mountain. The man's mechanical ineptitude also took its toll, as he wasted weeks of photographic effort by having inserted the plates in the camera incorrectly. Yet the team reached the creditable altitude of 23,000 feet, and when they were forced to turn around, Mallory was the last to give up.

The next spring, a much stronger party attacked the mountain. Once more, its members were divided by tensions and disagreements, most rancorously in the debate over bottled oxygen. Mallory disdained "gas" as both unsporting and useless, and he could barely stand to don the claustrophobic face mask it required. But the other strongest climber, George Finch, proved the efficacy of oxygen, reaching, with Geoffrey Bruce, a height of about 26,500 feet, the highest men had ever climbed on Earth.

On this expedition, Mallory performed an act of great pluck and heroism when he stopped the potentially fatal fall of three teammates with a brilliant ice ax belay. Yet he would return from the mountain weighed down with guilt and opprobrium. Insisting on one last, late attempt on June 3, Mallory led a large party toward the North Col. Four days later, an avalanche engulfed the team, knocking nine climbers over a 50-foot ice cliff. Seven Sherpa and Bhotia porters, but no sahibs, were killed.

The blame for the accident was loaded onto Mallory's shoulders, not only for pushing the late attempt, but because he had approached the North Col in dubious snow conditions. Mallory did nothing to shirk his responsibility, writing Geoffrey Winthrop Young, "And I'm to blame. . . . Do you know that sickening feeling that one can't go back and have it undone?"

In 1924, Mallory hesitated to join the expedition. He was 37 years old, with children eight, seven, and three years old who, thanks to the war and Everest, had seen their father less than half the days they had been alive. According to friends, he had gloomy premonitions about a third attempt. "This is going to be more like war than mountaineering," he told Geoffrey Keynes. "I don't expect to come back."

Yet in the end, he could not resist the pull of the mountain that had come to be identified, in the public mind, with Mallory and Mallory alone. And by the time the team was reaching Base Camp, he was blithely confident of success. "I can't see myself coming down defeated," he wrote Ruth; and to veteran mountaineer Tom Longstaff, "We are going to sail to the top this time and God with us—or stamp to the top with our teeth in the wind."

From the start, however, everything seemed to go wrong. The leader, Charles Bruce, fell ill with malaria and had to give up the expedition. The weather was terrible, turning back efforts to establish even the lower camps. During one snafu, four porters were stranded in a storm above all the Englishmen, and only a truly gutsy rescue by Mallory, Norton, and Howard Somervell saved their lives. After that, 40 of the 55 porters were too frightened to be of any use on the mountain, and most of the Western climbers were ill with diarrhea or hacking coughs.

By May 31, no one had gotten higher than the North Col. In his despair, Mallory wrote Ruth, "It is 50 to 1 against us, but we'll have a whack yet and do ourselves proud."

Then the mountain laid a last spell of grace on the beleaguered team. The weather turned fine, and the monsoon held off. Mallory's plan was to use the best remaining porters to establish Camps V and VI. Then, from the higher camp, Norton and Somervell would set off on an oxygenless attempt, to be followed by Mallory and Irvine breathing gas.

On June 4, Somervell reached his limit around 28,000 feet, while Norton soloed on, traversing right into the Great Couloir and establishing a new altitude record. On the descent, Somervell nearly choked to death on an obstruction lodged in his throat, before coughing up the entire lining of his larynx.

On June 8, Mallory and Irvine made their attempt. Even here, Mallory's absentmindedness took its toll, as he forgot his compass and flashlight; the day before, he had accidentally knocked the cook stove into the void. At 12:50, Odell caught his glimpse of the pair, high on the North Ridge, before clouds swallowed the upper mountain. Late in the afternoon, he climbed above Camp VI, whistling and yodeling in hopes of getting an answer from the descending duo, before (as Mallory had ordered) climbing all the way down to Camp IV. Two days later, by now remarkably acclimatized, Odell made it back up to Camp VI. When he found the tent exactly as he had left it, he knew the worst. He laid two sleeping bags in the snow in a figure "T"—the signal to the watchers below that all hope was lost.

According to biographer David Robertson, "Ruth [Mallory] received the news in Cambridge from a representative of the press. She went out for a long walk with old friends." A month later, still beside herself with grief, she wrote to Geoffrey Winthrop Young, "Oh Geoffrey, if only it hadn't happened! It so easily might not have."

At 83, Clare Millikan, Mallory's oldest child, remembers precisely how she learned of her father's death when she was eight. "It was getting-up time," she says. "Mother took us into her bedroom. We all lay in bed together, with her arms around us. Then she told us. There was nothing confusing about it. He wasn't 'missing'—he was quite definitely dead. He wasn't coming back."

FROM THE OUTSET, the 1999 expedition was blessed with one stroke of extraordinary luck. The previous winter had seen less snowfall than any year in recent memory. When Simonson, who had been on six previous Everest expeditions, arrived at Base Camp, he was shocked and delighted to see how bare the mountain was.

The team also benefited from a long spell of good weather, allowing them to get high enough by the end of April to launch the search. On May 1, the five strongest climbers—Dave Hahn, Tap Richards, Jake Norton, Andy Politz, and Conrad Anker—left Camp V at dawn and climbed toward the zone Hemmleb had designated for the search. The area was, Simonson estimated, about as large as 12 football fields; it would be difficult for five men to canvass it thoroughly in the five hours they could afford before descending. At 27,000 feet, they fanned out in various directions. Meanwhile, at Base Camp, Hemmleb watched their every move through the eyepiece of a 200-power telescope, feeding them advice over the two-way radio.

Almost at once, Norton found an oxygen bottle. He radioed a description of it to Hemmleb, who verified that the design matched that of the 1975 Chinese expedition's equipment. Thus the climbers knew they were indeed in the vicinity of the Chinese Camp VI.

Anker found himself lower and farther west than his teammates. "I wanted to look into the Great Couloir," he recalls, "and check out the route Reinhold Messner climbed when he soloed the mountain in 1980." About an hour into his foray, Anker came across the body of a modern climber, a Petzl ascender still attached to his harness. Then, after another 15 minutes, a second body, dressed in a faded blue down suit. Both bodies lay grotesquely sprawled, limbs akimbo, torn by the violence of long falls. (The team would later estimate that some 17 dead bodies lie between 27,000 feet and the summit on this side of Everest.)

"I knew I was in a natural catchment basin," says Anker. "I could see how the natural forces of the mountain had moved the bodies. I was fresh—I hadn't overanalyzed, projecting preconceived 'facts' onto reality."

At Base Camp, Hemmleb wondered why Anker had strayed so far west, beyond the limits of his search zone. Sometime after 11 a.m., Andy Politz called Anker on his radio. "Conrad," he said, "what are you doing way out there? We need to be more systematic."

"I started to traverse back toward the other guys," Anker remembers. "I was walking the lower edge of the catchment basin. I sat down, took my crampons off, drank some water, took a cough drop. Then, as I hiked up a small dihedral, I looked over and saw some blue and yellow fabric flapping in the wind—probably the remains of an old tent. I scanned to the right. Then I caught a glimpse of white—porcelain white, not the white of snow, not the white of quartz rock. I walked over and sat down next to him. I didn't touch him. Everything seemed to be in slow motion. I thought, *This is what we came to do*. But it didn't really sink in yet."

Anker pulled out his radio and improvised his cryptic message: "Last time I went bouldering in my hobnails, I fell off." Because everyone on the mountain could listen in on the team's radio calls, the members had agreed on a code, for fear some other expedition might scoop the team by sending out to the world the astounding news of just this sort of find. "Boulder" was the code word for a body (Anker threw in the hobnails as a sly allusion to the footgear of the 1920s); "gorak" would be the code word for the camera.

Anker's stunned teammates arrived one by one, murmuring, "Good job, Conrad!" and "Wow, this is amazing!" Then, after their respectful pause, they set out to excavate the corpse. Having freed up parts of the garments on which the body lay, they started going through the pockets. They found a smashed altimeter, a pair of tiny scissors, a tin of beef lozenges, a tube of zinc oxide, a box of phosphorus-rich matches. Then Richards came across another name tag, on a seam of the man's shirt. It read "G. LEIGH. MA." The clincher came when Norton found a batch of letters neatly wrapped in a handkerchief. When Norton unfolded it, he held in his hand an envelope addressed to "George Leigh Mallory Esq., c/o British Trade Agent, Yalung Tibet." It was not Sandy Irvine the men had found. It was George Mallory.

Even as they unearthed what the team would soon call the "artifacts," they discussed their significance. A pair of goggles, bent but not smashed, found in Mallory's pocket suggested to Andy Politz that the fatal fall had occurred at dusk or later—for on Teddy Norton's attempt four days before Mallory's, he had removed his goggles during the day, only to incur a painful and disabling case of snow blindness.

Most eloquent was the rope, a three-strand braided cotton cord about three-eighths of an inch in diameter. The knot with which Mallory had tied in was frozen around his waist. The rest of the rope, though tangled about the body, stretched only some ten feet to where it had clearly broken. Thus Holzel's cherished hypothesis was out the window. Mallory and Irvine had been roped together when the fatal fall occurred, though it remained to be seen whether the two men had fallen together, only to have the rope sever over a sharp edge, or if Irvine had made a desperate belay over a projecting rock, which had cut the rope as the impact of Mallory's fall came upon it.

To their great disappointment, the searchers found no camera. And as they carefully handled the letters (one each from Mallory's brother and sister, a third from a yet undetermined woman) and a few penciled notes to and from Mallory dealing with logistical details, they failed to discover any annotation bearing upon the question of whether the two men had reached the summit.

It was dawning on the searchers, also, that the body that Wang Hongbao had found in 1975 was in all probability not this one. Linguistic confusion or no, the description seemed entirely different from the scene that now lay before them: a dead man lying on his side, not facedown; a cheek pecked away by goraks, not the right buttock. It seemed likely that Wang had found Irvine, not Mallory.

Too soon, the five men realized they must end their work and head back to Camp V. The last act of salvage they performed was to cut a small piece of tissue from Mallory's body, to serve as a DNA sample. Then, to honor the great mountaineer, and to hide the site from the inevitable high-altitude curiosity seekers who might look for it once the electrifying news was out, they resolved to bury him. Loose stones were hard to find, but the men formed a bucket brigade, passing chunks of shale and gradually interring Mallory in a makeshift grave. One of the men read a prayer of committal that the Bishop of Bristol had given the expedition to use in just such an eventuality. Andy Politz loaded the artifacts as carefully as he could in his pack. Then the five men started down the tricky slabs.

"Our emotions only really came out once we were back at Camp V," recalled Dave Hahn. "That's when what we found really began to sink in. It was . . . what? Satisfaction and amazement."

ON THE MOUNTAIN, THE CLIMBING TEAM had carried out their work in a spirit of collaborative harmony. But as the coded news of their find made its way to Base Camp, and then, decoded, to the world, controversy began to erupt. Latent tensions among the three media outlets covering the expedition—MountainZone.com, *NOVA,* and the BBC—escalated nastily, now that so much was at stake. Liesl Clark, a producer for *NOVA,* had been posting dispatches on the PBS Internet site. These were far more lucid and informative than the MountainZone.com postings, which consisted largely of impromptu radio reports from often exhausted team members.

Now *NOVA* scooped MountainZone.com in getting the news of some sort of discovery out to the world, infuriating Simonson, who thought Clark should have confined her dispatches to "educational" topics, not news. From the blow-up emerged an agreement that *NOVA* would give MountainZone .com a 24-hour lead on all reportage.

Meanwhile, to handle the frenzy for photos emanating from the offices of newspapers and magazines, the team turned over many of its best pictures to Gamma Liaison. In a bidding war for a single exclusive photo of Mallory in situ, *Newsweek* topped its American rivals with an offer that was reported to be $40,000 (several sources say the bid was closer to $15,000).

Particularly in England and its former colonies, where the bidding winners were tabloids, the expedition's decision to sell Mallory pictures unleashed a deluge of disapproval. "I'm absolutely appalled by this. Words can't express how disgusted I am," Sir Chris Bonington, who had led the landmark 1975 ascent of Everest's southwest face, told the *London Observer*. "These people don't deserve to be called climbers." Sir Edmund Hillary was of like mind, deploring the notion that "the expedition members should flog off the photograph of this heroic figure." (After the media storm broke, the team announced that all photo monies would be donated to Himalayan charities.)

Mallory's grandson, George Mallory II, who had climbed Everest by the North Ridge in 1995, weighed in: "Frankly, it makes me bloody angry. . . . It's like digging for diamonds, without having to do any of the digging."

Meanwhile knotty legal tangles hung over the artifacts and the letters, which team members eventually carried back to the States in Ziploc bags with silica gel inserted to keep them dry. To whom did the stuff ultimately belong? Was it a case of finders keepers; were the team members, in Anker's pithy phrase, "the Mel Fishers of high-altitude climbing"? Or did Mallory's estate have a prior claim? As for the letters and notes and the right to publish their contents, which copyright laws applied? The Chinese regulations of today, or Britain's in 1924?

With accusations flying right and left, with book deals in the works and Hollywood producers expressing interest, with the climbers themselves scrambling to put the best spin on their deeds and intentions, one thing was clear: This was a story that would not go away.

AT CAMP V ON MAY 1, 1999, the men who had found Mallory's body stayed up late discussing the implications of their discovery. Clearly the expedition's next priority was to search for the body of Irvine and the camera. The broken rope tied to Mallory might well mean that Irvine lay nearby.

The next day, however, it started snowing. By the time the storm had passed, several inches of new snow blanketed the North Face. "If we'd been a day later," said Dave Hahn, "we'd have never found Mallory."

The team still had as long as a month before the monsoon would arrive. Worn out by the excitement and toil of their discovery, the quintet descended to regroup with their teammates.

It would be 15 days before the team got a second chance to search. In the interim, a Ukrainian expedition got into serious trouble on the North Ridge, and the Americans went to their aid. Even so, one Ukrainian died and another suffered horrible frostbite.

Finally, on May 16, Andy Politz and Thom Pollard resumed the search, this time armed with a metal detector. There was still so much new snow on the North Face, however, that the pair decided not to look for Irvine, but to return to Mallory to make sure they hadn't overlooked anything. Pollard, hired by *NOVA* to shoot video, had set out with his teammates on May 1, but turned back when he started to have trouble with his oxygen. Thus he depended on Politz to relocate Mallory in his makeshift grave of piled stones.

This was easier said than done. "Andy just kept walking and walking, not saying anything," Pollard recalled. "After a while I said to myself, 'I know he's lost.' Finally Andy said, 'I can't find him.' 'You've gotta be shittin' me,' I said."

The pair swept back and forth across the ledges where Politz thought the grave must be; with the new snow, everything looked different. Finally, after about an hour of wandering, their labor was rewarded.

At the scene, Pollard was struck dumb. "It evoked something deeply spiritual," he recalls. "I kept thinking, *This is one of the greatest figures in the history of mountaineering*. I got down on my knees and asked for guidance. I prayed, in essence, for guidance not to desecrate the site."

Working silently, the two men unpiled the stones that covered the body. With the metal detector, Politz found an artifact the first team had missed: a wristwatch in Mallory's pants pocket. The glass was gone from its face, and the minute and second hands were broken off, but the hour hand pointed to between one and two, a little closer to two. (The hand was subsequently broken off as the watch was transported to Base Camp.) Was this clue an indication that the accident had occurred around 1:40? If so, was it 1:40 p.m., less than an hour after Odell's sighting, or 1:40 a.m., in the middle of a desperate descent in the night without a flashlight? Or had the watch ceased working before the accident, and Mallory had thrust it into his pocket?

Politz pulled off a section of the rope to carry down, and removed the hobnailed boot from Mallory's broken right leg.

Meanwhile Pollard decided he wanted to look at Mallory's face, which was still frozen into the scree. Cutting away the recalcitrant ice and dirt as carefully as he could ("It was like digging into your driveway"), at last he cleared the ice enough so that, lying on the ground, he could look George Mallory in the face.

"The face was in perfect condition," says Pollard. "It was ever so slightly distorted—pancaked, in effect—by the years of bearing the weight of snow. His eyes were closed. I could still see whiskers on his chin."

As he made his furtive investigation, Pollard found the wound that may have caused Mallory's death. "Over his left eye, there was a hole. There was dried blood, and two pieces of skull sticking out. It was as though someone had taken a ball-peen hammer and smashed in his forehead."

Finally the two men reburied the body under the stones; spoke, as their predecessors had, the Anglican prayer of committal; and started to head down. By the time they neared camp, they were descending the fixed ropes in the dark.

NOEL ODELL BELIEVED THAT MALLORY HAD CLIMBED EVEREST. So did Charles Bruce and Tom Longstaff and Geoffrey Winthrop Young. Wrote the latter, "After nearly 20 years' knowledge of Mallory as a mountaineer, I can say . . . that difficult as it would have been for any mountaineer to turn back with the only difficulty past—to Mallory it would have been an impossibility."

These men, of course, were swayed by their friendship with Mallory and admiration of his drive. The members of the 1933 expedition—perhaps for the opposite reason, for they had not ventured to Tibet to make the *second* ascent of Everest—were convinced to a man that Mallory and Irvine had not reached the top.

Over the years, despite Tom Holzel's airy theorizing, most experts doubted whether the two men could have pushed all the way to the summit in 1924. The members of the 1999 expedition were themselves skeptical when they arrived at Base Camp. But finding Mallory had a galvanic effect upon their judgment. Jochen Hemmleb now says, "I give them a 60-40 or a 50-50 chance they made the summit." Jake Norton goes even further: "Seeing George Mallory changed my mind. He was awe-inspiring in death. Maybe it's idealism on my part, maybe I just want to believe, but I'd say the odds are 75-25 he made the summit."

Once the second search had been completed, the expedition had a final goal—to reach the top themselves. All the climbers who were fit enough to go high had, in varying degrees, been bitten by summit fever. Eric Simonson, who had summitted in 1991, would have liked to be in the vanguard, but as the team leader, his intention all along had been to direct the expedition from Advance Base Camp—a task his teammates all agreed he performed in masterly fashion.

Andy Politz was willing to forgo the push because he had climbed Everest in 1991; Thom Pollard, because he felt it was his job to document the discovery. Among the other four—Dave Hahn, Tap Richards, Jake Norton, and Conrad Anker—only Hahn had previously climbed Everest, in 1994. On May 17, the day after Politz and Pollard conducted the second search, these four headed up the North Ridge, bent on pushing to the top.

But Conrad Anker had a further agenda, one that could cast an entirely new light on whether Mallory and Irvine had ascended Everest. He wanted to free-climb the Second Step.

Teddy Norton had reached a height calculated as 28,126 feet by traversing west across the upper North Face and entering the Great Couloir. In 1933, Frank Smythe exactly matched that high point, which stood, in the absence of any sure knowledge of Mallory and Irvine's achievement, as the world altitude record until 1952, when the Swiss Raymond Lambert and the Sherpa Tenzing Norgay turned back on the South Col route only 800 feet below the summit.

The Great Couloir would prove a feasible route up the north side of Everest, as Reinhold Messner demonstrated in making his astounding oxygenless solo ascent in 1980. But we can be quite certain this was not the route followed by Mallory and Irvine, because Odell saw them high on the skyline of the North Ridge.

The Second Step is a 90-foot-high, nearly vertical cliff that interrupts the North Ridge at 28,230 feet. Unless Mallory and Irvine tackled it, the first men to grapple with this formidable obstacle were the Chinese team in 1960. By their own account, which appeared in a propaganda organ called *China Reconstructs,* an initial pair of would-be summitters flailed away at the Step for a long afternoon and into the night, climbing all but the last stretch of wall, before enduring a grim bivouac in a crevice. Three weeks later, another group came to grips with the Step. According to the account, one man made four all-out attempts to surmount the final ten feet of wall, falling off exhausted each time. Finally another climber, Chu Yin-hua, took off his gloves and boots, used a shoulder stand, and had a go at the cliff barefoot. Topping the cliff after a three-hour struggle, Chu brought his comrades up on a tight rope. Three of them continued to the summit, arriving well after dark. For his heroic effort, Chu later lost his toes and parts of his fingers to frostbite.

And even at that, it's debatable whether that effort was truly successful. The account of this climb in *China Reconstructs* sounds more like a homiletic Maoist tract than a journal article. As editor H. Adams Carter dryly commented in the *American Alpine Journal* in 1961, after offering a précis of the Chinese climb, "The details are such that mountaineers in nearly all parts of the climbing world have received the news with considerable skepticism."

The next alleged ascent of the North Ridge, also by the Chinese, came in 1975, during the expedition on which Wang Hongbao found his "old English dead." Cognizant of the difficulty of the Second Step, the team hauled a ladder up to the crux and tied it to pitons pounded in place. All subsequent ascents of the North Ridge have used the ladder or the myriad fixed ropes now in place on the Step.

Mallory and Irvine, of course, had had no ladder. If Anker could free-climb the Second Step and ascertain its difficulty, that knowledge would aid immensely in judging whether Mallory could have pulled off the same feat.

Starting at 2:30 a.m. on May 17, sucking bottled oxygen, the four men headed up the North Face to the Northeast Ridge. In ankle-deep snow, Anker broke trail all the way, putting in new fixed ropes on some of the tricky sections. A lenticular cloud cap shrouded the summit, though there was virtually no wind.

Tap Richards and Jake Norton, both 25, were fit, well acclimatized, and good technical climbers. But that day they were not as mentally strong as Anker, who was 36, or Hahn, 37. Just below the Second Step, the younger pair conferred. "We were moving slow," said Richards later. "Things just didn't feel right. We'd seen what happened to the Ukrainians. There was a bit of a feeling that death was breathing in our faces."

"We decided to turn around," added Norton. "It was the hardest decision I've ever made in the mountains. I was in tears."

Before descending, the pair sat on a ledge to watch Anker tackle the Second Step. Dave Hahn belayed at the foot of the vertical cliff. To attack the wall, Anker took off his oxygen apparatus—not so much out of purism as because the gear was a hindrance on hard rock.

In his usual low-key fashion, Anker describes the climb. "The first part's a chimney. Then there's a snow cone. Then the crux—about 25 feet of vertical rock. There was an off-width crack" (so-called by climbers because it's a fissure of particularly awkward width, too large for hand-jamming, too small to chimney). "I got in one cam for protection. But I had to step on the ladder—the foothold I needed was underneath it, between the rungs. I just took one step on the ladder. Then a mantle problem, and I was up." At the time, Anker cautiously rated the climb as 5.8 in difficulty—as hard as or harder than anything that had been done in Wales by 1924. But on returning to the States and comparing the pitch to routes he led at Indian Creek in Utah, he revised the grade of the Second Step to a solid 5.10.

Tap Richards, who watched the ascent, marveled, "Conrad made it look easy, but he's so good. He just blew right up it."

Attaching his ascenders to the fixed rope, Dave Hahn climbed the ladder. "It took me as long to second as it had Conrad to lead," says Hahn, "and I wasn't even trying to free it."

At this point, Richards and Norton headed down. Below the First Step, near where Percy Wyn Harris had found the ice ax in 1933, they came across an old oxygen bottle, lying near a boulder on a ledge where climbers might well be tempted to take a rest break. Eric Simonson had actually noticed the bottle in 1991; later he would say he felt like "kicking himself" for not carrying it down then. Hemmleb later verified that the bottle was unmistakably from the 1924 expedition. It was an important find, for it further verified the altitude that we can be sure Mallory and Irvine reached as at least 28,000 feet.

Anker and Hahn pushed upward. Once more, Anker broke trail every step of the way, through snow now sometimes thigh-deep. Hahn describes that last ascent. "By the Third Step, it had started snowing hard. It was scary and difficult. You knew that if the snow sloughed 20 feet, you'd slough the rest of the 9,000 down to the glacier. And there was a cornice edge. We both knew guys who had walked right off cornices and died. Conrad just pushed up the summit snowfield. He's ten times stronger than I am. He's much more bold. We have it worked out—between the two of us, he's the leader.

"There was a tricky traverse across part of the North Face. He got 45 minutes ahead of me there. It was a lousy time to be split up, but he waited for me on the summit ridge. That was good of him.

"We summitted at 2:50. We spent five minutes there. It wasn't a pleasant summit—it was a business summit. There was nothing to look at—clouds all around us. We shook hands. We knew where we were.

"I had a lot of concern about getting down. I'm a careful climber. There's no way I could have kept up with Conrad. He could have flown down that terrain. But he waited for me again, to make sure I got across the tricky traverse OK.

"It got dark just below the First Step. We pushed on by headlamp. We radioed ahead, and Jake and Tap came up to greet us with oxygen and hot water for tea."

Hahn and Anker collapsed into Camp VI at 9:15 p.m. "In the tent," says Hahn, "I sat up rubbing my head. I said to Conrad, 'Thanks for working so hard for me.' He was flat on his back, in his sleeping bag. He said, 'I like it when I'm this tired. It's nice to just pass out when you hit camp.'"

FINDING MALLORY'S BODY, of course, does not solve the crucial mystery of whether he reached the summit. But there may be further information to be wrung from the artifacts, which the team has submitted to forensic experts. Ultimately, those humble but eloquent objects—the monogrammed handkerchief, the goggles, the length of cotton rope, the watch, the oxygen bottle—will, if the team has any say about it, find their way to a museum.

Somewhere on Everest still lie Sandy Irvine and the Kodak Vest Pocket camera. Already Eric Simonson is planning an expedition for sometime in the next two years to continue the search. Most of the climbers from last spring, as well as Jochen Hemmleb, hope to be along; but not Conrad Anker. "I'm an alpinist, not a guide," he says. "I'm more interested in doing hard climbs in unexplored ranges."

Unlike his more credulous teammates, Anker concludes that there is only a very small chance that Mallory and Irvine made the summit. The difficulty of the Second Step is the clincher, since a careful examination of the terrain convinced Anker that on the Ridge, there is no reasonable alternative to the line up which the Chinese bolted their ladder. On the descent, Anker and Hahn rappelled a fixed line over the Second Step. No trace from 1924 of any anchor or rope above the Second Step has ever been found. Mallory and Irvine would have had to down-climb it—a far more difficult proposition than ascending it.

Even so, Anker will not rule out the possibility that unusual climate conditions in 1924 could have deposited a snow cone covering the Second Step. "We need to study the 1924 photos really carefully," he says. "If there was a snow ramp covering the cliff, they could have walked right up it."

Another curious detail gives the skeptics pause. Why would Mallory have carried letters from his brother and sister, but none from his beloved wife, Ruth? Clare Millikan remembers being told at age eight that her father was carrying a photo of Ruth, which he intended to leave on the summit. Can the absence of a photo or letter on Mallory's body tell us anything about how high he climbed on June 8, 1924?

On May 17, as Anker and Hahn, near exhaustion, climbed down into the night across the downward-tilting slabs of the North Face, the image of Mallory attempting the same descent, in hobnailed boots, with no flashlight to guide his way, was constantly before their eyes. Having twice reached the summit by the North Ridge, Hahn, like Anker, doubts that Mallory could have made it. "Going up the ladder over the Second Step," he says, "I looked closely at the route. I kept saying, 'Yeah, this part is doable; so is this part.'

All the parts were doable, but to put them together is too much. Conrad and I climb for a living. We left at 2:30 a.m., and we didn't get back to camp till 9:15 p.m. We knew right where to go. Mallory and Irvine didn't know where to go—they would have had to find the key over and over again.

"And yet, when I stood there looking at Mallory's body, my emotions took over. It all became personal. You just had to root for the man."

There is no denying that George Leigh Mallory was a genius of ascent, and that Everest brought out the finest in him. The men who knew him best kept coming back to that talismanic fact. For Geoffrey Winthrop Young, grieving the loss of his friend and protégé, the summit must have been reached, in the final analysis, simply "because Mallory was Mallory." And a quarter-century after his disappearance, Young remembered a blithe route the pair had climbed in Wales: "The laughing hours chased each other unnoticed. . . . On a day like this, and in movement, Mallory was wholly in harmony within himself, and with the world, and nothing could give him pause."

FALL 1999

THIRTEEN WAYS OF
LOOKING AT A VOID

By Michael Finkel

The Sahara's Ténéré is a chunk of the planet gone dead: 154,000 square miles of nothing—except faith, war, salt, beer, speed . . . and an urgent sense of what it is to be alive.

"HELL," SAYS MOUSAKA. He raises a forefinger and circles it in the air, to indicate that he is referring to the whole of the void. I am sitting on Mousaka's lap. Mousaka is sitting on Osiman's lap. Osiman is sitting on someone else's lap. And so on—everyone sitting on another's lap. We are on a truck, crossing the void. The truck looks like a dump truck, though it doesn't dump. It is 20 feet long and 6 feet wide, diesel powered, painted white. One hundred and ninety passengers are aboard, tossed atop one another like a pile of laundry. People are on the roof of the cab, and straddling the rail of the bed, and pressed into the bed itself. There is no room for carry-on bags; water jugs and other belongings must be tied to the truck's rail and hung over the sides. Fistfights have broken out over half an inch of contested space. Beyond the truck, the void encompasses 154,440 square miles, at last count, and is virtually uninhabited.

Like many of the people on board, Mousaka makes his living by harvesting crops—oranges or potatoes or dates. His facial scars, patterned like whiskers, indicate that he is a member of the Hausa culture, from southern Niger. Mousaka has two wives and four children and no way to provide for them, except to get on a truck. Also on the truck are Tuareg and Songhai and Zerma and Fulani and Kanuri and Wodaabe. Everyone is headed to Libya, where the drought that has gripped much of North Africa has been less severe and there are still crops to pick. Libya has become the new promised land. Mousaka plans to stay through the harvest season, January to July, and then return to his family. To get to Libya from the south, though, one must first cross the void.

The void is the giant sand sea at the center of the Sahara. It covers half of Niger and some of Algeria and a little of Libya and a corner of Chad. On maps of the Sahara, it is labeled, in large, spaced letters, "Ténéré"—a term taken from the Tuareg language that means "nothing" or "emptiness" or "void." The Ténéré is Earth at its least hospitable, a chunk of the planet gone dead. Even the word itself, "Ténéré," looks vaguely ominous, barbed as it is with accents. In the heart of the void there is not a scrap of shade nor a bead of water nor a blade of grass. Most parts, even bacteria can't survive.

The void is freezing by night and scorching by day and wind-scoured always. Its center is as flat and featureless as the head of a drum. There is not so much as a large rock. Mousaka has been crossing the void for four days; he has at least a week to go. Except for prayer breaks, the truck does not stop. Since entering the void, Mousaka has hardly slept, or eaten, or drunk. He has no shoes, no sunglasses, no blanket. His ears are plugged with sand. His clothing is tattered. His feet are swollen. This morning, I asked him what comes to mind when he thinks about the void. For two weeks now, as I've been crossing the Sahara myself, using all manner of transportation, I have asked this question to almost every person I've met. When the truck rides over a bump and everybody is jounced, elbows colliding with sternums, heads hammering heads, Mousaka leans forward and tells me his answer again. "The desert is disgusting," he says, in French. "The desert is hell." Then he spits over the side of the truck, and spits again, trying to rid himself of the sand that has collected in his mouth.

"FAITH," SAYS MONIQUE. "The Ténéré gives me faith." Monique has been crossing and recrossing the void for four weeks. We've met at the small market in the Algerian town of Djanet, at the northern hem of the Ténéré. Monique is here with her travel partners, resupplying. She's Swiss, though she's lived in the United States for a good part of her life. Her group is traversing the void in a convoy of Pinzgauers—six-wheel-drive, moon-rover-looking vehicles, made in Austria, that are apparently undaunted by even the softest of sands.

Monique is in her early 70s. A few years ago, not long after her husband passed away, she fulfilled a lifelong fantasy and visited the Sahara. The desert changed her. She witnessed sunrises that turned the sand the color of lipstick. She saw starfish-shaped dunes, miles across, whose curving forms left her breathless with wonder. She heard the fizzy hum known as the singing of the sands. She reveled in the silence and the openness. She slept outside. She let the wind braid her hair and the sand sit under her fingernails and the sun bake her skin. She shared meals with desert nomads. She learned that not every place on Earth is crowded and greed-filled and tamed. She stayed three months. Now she's back for another extended visit.

Her story is not unusual. Tourism in the Ténéré is suddenly popular. Outfitters in Paris and London and Geneva and Berlin are chartering flights to the edge of the void and then arranging for vehicles that will take you to the middle. Look at the map, the brochures say: You're going to the heart of the Sahara, to the famous Ténéré. Doesn't the word itself, exotic with accents, roll off the tongue like a tiny poem?

Many of the tourists are on spiritual quests. They live hectic lives, and they want a nice dose of nothing—and there is nothing more nothing than the void. The void is so blank that a point-and-shoot camera will often refuse to work, the auto-focus finding nothing to focus on. This is good. By offering nothing, I've been told, the void tacitly accepts everything. Whatever you want to find seems to be there. Not long after I met Monique, I spoke with another American. Her name is Beth. She had been in the Ténéré for two and a half weeks, and she told me that the point of her trip was to feel the wind in her face. After a fortnight of wind, Beth came to a profound decision. She said she now realized what her life was missing. She said that the moment she returned home she was quitting her Internet job and opening up her own business. She said she was going to bake apple pies.

"MONEY," SAYS AHMED. "Money, money, money, money, money." Ahmed has no money. But he does have a plan. His plan is to meet every plane that lands in his hometown of Agadez, in central Niger, one of the hubs of Ténéré tourism. During the cooler months, and when the runway is not too potholed, a flight arrives in Agadez as often as once a week. When my plane landed, from Paris, Ahmed was there. The flight was packed with French vacationers, but all of them had planned their trips with European full-service agencies. No one needed to hire a freelance guide. This is why Ahmed is stuck talking with me.

Ahmed speaks French and English and German and Arabic and Hausa and Toubou, as well as his mother tongue, the Tuareg language called Tamashek. He's 27 years old. He has typical Tuareg hair, jet black and wild with curls, and a habit of glancing every so often at his wrist, like a busy executive, which is a tic he must have picked up from tourists, for Ahmed does not own a watch, and, he tells me, he never has. He says he's learned all these languages because he doesn't want to get on a truck to Libya. He tells me he can help tourists rent quality Land Cruisers, and he can cook for them—his specialty is tagela, a bread that is baked in the sand—and he can guide them across the void without a worry of getting lost. Tourism, he says, is the only way to make money in the void.

Inside his shirt pocket, Ahmed keeps a brochure that was once attached to a bottle of shampoo. The brochure features photos of very pretty models, white women with perfect hair and polished teeth, and Ahmed has opened and closed the brochure so many times that it is as brittle and wrinkled as an old dollar bill. "When I have money," he says, "I will have women like this."

"But," I point out, "the plane landed, and you didn't get a client."

"Maybe next week," he says.

"So how will you make money this week?"

"I just told you all about me," he says. "Doesn't that deserve a tip?"

"SALT," SAYS CHOUKOU. He tips his chin to the south, toward a place called Bilma, in eastern Niger, where he's going to gather salt. Choukou is on his camel. He's sitting cross-legged, his head wrapped loosely in a long white cloth, his body shrouded in a billowy tan robe, and there is an air about him of exquisite levity—a mood he always seems to project when he is atop his camel. Often, he breaks into song, a warbling chant in the Toubou tongue, a language whose syllables are as rounded as river stones. I am riding another of his camels, a blue-eyed female that emits the sort of noises that make me think of calling a plumber. A half dozen other camels are following us, riderless. We are crossing the void.

Choukou is a Toubou, a member of one of the last seminomadic peoples to live along the edges of the void. At its periphery, the void is not particularly voidlike; it's surrounded on three sides by craggy mountains—the Massif de l'Aïr, the Ahaggar, the Plateau du Djado, the Tibesti—and, to the south, the Lake Chad Basin. Choukou can ride his camel sitting frontward or backward or sidesaddle or standing, and he can command his camel, never raising his voice above a whisper, to squat down or rise up or spin in circles. His knife is strapped high on his right arm; his goatskin, filled with water, is hooked to his saddle; a few dried dates are in the breast pocket of his robe, along with a pouch of tobacco and some scraps of rolling paper. He is sitting on his blanket. This is all he has with him. It has been said that a Toubou can live for three days on a single date: the first day on its skin, the second on its fruit, the third on its pit. My guess is that this is truer than you might imagine. In two days of difficult travel with Choukou, I saw him eat one meal.

If you ask Choukou how old he is, he'll say he doesn't know. He's willing to guess (20, he supposes), but he can't say for sure. It doesn't matter. His sense of time is not divided into years or seasons or months. It's divided into directions. Either he is headed to Bilma, to gather salt, or he is headed away from Bilma, to sell his salt. It has been this way for the Toubou for 2,000 years. No one has yet discovered a more economical method of transporting salt across the void—engines and sand are an unhappy mix—and so camels are still in use. Camels can survive two weeks between water stops and then, in a single prolonged drink, can down 25 gallons of water, none of which happens to be stored in the hump. When Choukou arrives at the salt mines of Bilma, he will load each of his camels with six 50-pound pillars of salt, then join with other Toubou to form a caravan—a hundred or more camels striding single file across the sands—and set out for Agadez. In the best of conditions, the trek can take nearly a month.

Choukou occasionally encounters tourists, and he sometimes sees the overloaded trucks, but he is only mildly curious. He does not have to seek solace from a hectic life. He has no need to pick crops in Libya. He travels with the minimum he requires to survive, and he knows that if even one well along the route has suddenly run dry—it happens—then he will probably die. He knows that there are bandits in the void and sandstorms in the void. He is not married. A good wife, he tells me, costs five camels, and he can't yet afford one. If he makes it to Agadez, he will sell his salt and then immediately start back to Bilma. He navigates by the dunes and the colors of the soil and the direction of the wind. He can study a set of camel tracks and determine which breed of camel left them, and therefore the tribe to which they belong, and how many days old the tracks are, and how heavy a load the camels are carrying, and how many animals are in the caravan. He was born in the void, and he has never left the void. This is perhaps why he looks at me oddly when I ask him what comes to mind when he contemplates his homeland. I ask him the question, and his face becomes passive. He mentions salt, but then he is quiet for a few seconds. "I really don't think about the void," he says.

"CAMERAS," SAYS MUSTAFA. "Also videos and watches and Walkmans and jewelry and GPS units." Mustafa has an M16 rifle slung over his shoulder. He is trying to sell me the items he has taken from other tourists. I am at a police checkpoint in the tiny outpost of Chirfa, along the northeastern border of the void. I've hired a desert taxi—a daredevil driver and a beater Land Cruiser—to take me to Algeria. Now we've been stopped.

Mustafa is fat. He is fat, and he is wearing a police uniform. This is a bad combination. In the void, only the wealthy are fat. Police in Niger do not make enough money to become wealthy; a fat police officer is therefore a corrupt police officer. And a corrupt officer inevitably means trouble. When I refuse to even look at his wares, Mustafa becomes angry. He asks to see my travel documents. The void is a fascinating place—there exist, at once, both no rules and strict rules. To cross the void legally, you are supposed to carry very specific travel documents, and I actually have them. But the documents are open to interpretation. You must, for example, list your exact route of travel. It is difficult to do this when you are crossing an expanse of sand that has no real roads. So of course Mustafa finds a mistake.

"It is easy to correct," he says. "You just have to return to Agadez." Agadez is a four-day drive in the opposite direction. "Or I can correct it here," he adds. "Just give me your GPS unit." He does not even bother to pretend that it isn't a bribe. Mustafa is the leader of this outpost, the dictator of a thousand square miles of desert. There is no one to appeal to.

"I don't have a GPS unit," I say.

"Then your watch."

"No," I say.

"A payment will do."

"No," I say.

"Fine," he says. Then he says nothing. He folds his arms and rests them on the shelf formed by his belly. He stands there for a long time. The driver turns off the car. We wait. Mustafa has all day, all week, all month, all year. He has no schedule. He has no meetings. If we try to drive away, he will shoot us. It is a losing battle.

I hand him a sheaf of Central African francs, and we continue on.

"BEER," SAYS GRACE. "BEER AND WOMEN." Grace is maybe 35 years old and wears a dress brilliant with yellow sunflowers. She has a theory: Crossing the void, she insists, seeing all that nothing, she posits, produces within a man a certain kind of emptiness. It is her divine duty, she's decided, to fill that emptiness. And so Grace has opened a bar in Dirkou. A bar and brothel.

Dirkou is an unusual town. It's in Niger, at the northeastern rim of the Ténéré, built in what is known as a wadi—an ancient riverbed, now dry, but where water exists not too far below the surface, reachable by digging wells. The underground water allows date palms to grow in Dirkou. Whether you are traveling by truck, camel, or 4x4, it is nearly impossible to cross the void without stopping in Dirkou for fuel or provisions or water or emptiness-filling.

Apparently, it is popular to inform newcomers to Dirkou that they are now as close as they can get to the end of the Earth. My first hour in town, I was told this five or six times; it must be a sort of civic slogan. This proves only that a visit to the end of the Earth should not be on one's to-do list. Dirkou is possibly the most unredeeming place I have ever visited, Los Angeles included. The town is essentially one large bus station, except that it lacks electricity, plumbing, television, newspapers, and telephones. Locals say that it has not rained here in more than two years. The streets are heavy with beggars and con artists and thieves and migrants and drifters and soldiers and prostitutes. Almost everyone is male, except the prostitutes. The place is literally a dump: When you want to throw something away, you just toss it in the street.

Grace's emptiness theory has a certain truth. I arrived in Dirkou after riding on the Libya-bound truck for three days. Of the 190 passengers, 186 were male. Those with a bit of money went straight to Grace's bar. The bar was like every structure in Dirkou: mud walls, palm-frond roof, sand floors. I sat at a scrap-wood table, on a milk-crate chair. A battery-powered radio emitted 90 percent static and 10 percent Arabic music from a station in Chad. I drank a Niger beer, which had been stored in the shade and was, by Saharan standards, cold. I drank two more.

My emptiness, it seems, was not as profound as those of my truck mates. In the Ténéré, there exists the odd but pervasive belief that alcohol hydrates you—and not only hydrates you but hydrates you more efficiently than water. Some people on the truck did not drink at all the last day of the trip, for they knew Grace's bar was approaching. Many of these same men were soon passed out in the back of the bar. There is also the belief that a man cannot catch AIDS from a prostitute so long as she is less than 18 years old.

One other item that Dirkou lacks is bathrooms. After eating a bit of camel sausage and drinking my fourth beer, I ask Grace where the bathroom is. She tells me it is in the street. I explain, delicately, that I'm hoping to produce a different sort of waste. She says it doesn't matter, the bathroom is in the street. I walk out of the bar, seeking a private spot, and in the process I witness three men doing what I am planning to do. This explains much about the unfortunate odor that permeates Dirkou.

"SPIRITS," SAYS WORDIGOU. He is sitting on a blanket and holding his supper bowl, which at one time was a sardine tin. His face is illuminated by a kerosene lamp. Wordigou has joined us for dinner, some rice and a bit of mutton. He is a cousin of Choukou's, the young salt trader who told me that he does not think about the void. Choukou allowed me to join his camel trek for two days, and now, in the middle of our journey, we have stopped for the evening at a Toubou encampment. Wordigou lives in the camp, which consists of a handful of dome-shaped grass huts, two dozen camels, an extended family of Toubou, and a herd of goats. In the hut I've been lent for the night, a cassette tape is displayed on the wall as a sort of curious knickknack. Certainly there is no tape player in the camp. Here, the chief form of entertainment is the same as it is almost everywhere in the void—talking. Wordigou, who guesses that he is a little less than 30 years old, leads the mealtime discussion. He is a sharp and insightful conversationalist. The topic is religion. The Toubou are nominally Muslim, but most, including Wordigou, have combined Islam with traditional animist beliefs.

"The desert," says Wordigou, "is filled with spirits. I talk with them all the time. They tell me things. They tell me news. Some spirits you see, and some you don't see, and some are nice, and some are not nice, and some pretend to be nice but really aren't. I ask the nice ones to send me strong camels. And also to lead me to hidden treasures."

Wordigou catches my eye, and he knows immediately that I do not share his beliefs. Still, he is magnanimous. "Even if you do not see my spirits," he says, "you must see someone's. Everyone does. How else could Christianity and Judaism and Islam all have begun in the very same desert?"

"WORK," SAYS BILIT. "It ties me to the desert." Bilit is the driver of the overloaded truck that is headed to Libya. He has stopped his vehicle, climbed out of the front seat, and genuflected in the direction of Mecca. Sand is stuck to his forehead. The passengers who've gotten off are piling aboard. Only their turbans can be seen through the swirling sand. Everyone wears a turban in the void—it protects against sun and wind and provides the wearer with a degree of anonymity, which can be valuable if one is attempting a dubiously legal maneuver, like sneaking into Libya. Turbans are about the only splashes of color in the desert. They come in a handful of bold, basic hues, like gum balls. Bilit's is green. I ask him how far we have to go.

"Two days," says Bilit. "*Inshallah,*" he adds—God willing. He says it again: "Inshallah." This is, by far, the void's most utilized expression, the oral equivalent of punctuation. God willing. It emphasizes the daunting fact that, no matter the degree of one's preparation, traveling the void always involves relinquishing control. Bilit has driven this route—Agadez to Dirkou, 400 miles of void—for eight years. When conditions allow, he drives 20 to 22 hours a day. Where the sand is firm, Bilit can drive as fast as 15 miles an hour. Where it is soft, the passengers have to get out and push. Everywhere, the engine sounds as though it is continually trying to clear its throat.

His route is one of the busiest in the Ténéré—sometimes he sees three or even four other vehicles a day. This means that Bilit doesn't need to rely on compass bearings or star readings to determine if he is headed in the correct direction. There are actually other tire tracks in the sand to follow. Not all tracks, however, are reliable. A "road" in the Ténéré can be 20 miles wide, with tracks braiding about one another where the drivers detoured around signs of softness, seeking firmer sand. Inexperienced drivers have followed braided tracks and ended up confounding themselves. In a place with a blank horizon, it is impossible to tell if you're headed in a gradual arc or going straight. Drivers have followed bad braids until they've run out of gas.

Worse is when there are no tracks at all. This happens after every major sandstorm, when the swirling sands return the void to blankness, shaken clean like an Etch A Sketch. A sandstorm occurs, on average, about once a week. During a storm, Bilit stops the truck. Sometimes he'll be stopped for two days. Sometimes three. The passengers, of course, must suffer through it; they are too crowded to move. The trucks are so crowded because the more people aboard, the more money the truck's owner makes. The void is a place where crude economics rule. Comfort is rarely a consideration.

One time, Bilit did not stop in a sandstorm. He got lost. Getting lost in the void is a frightening situation. Even with a compass and the stars, you can easily be off by half a degree and bypass an entire town. Bilit managed to find his way. But recently, on the same route, a truck was severely lost. There are few rescue services in the Ténéré, and by the time an army vehicle located the truck, only eight people were alive. Thirty-six corpses were discovered, all victims of dehydration. The rest of the passengers—six at least, and possibly many more—were likely buried beneath the sands and have never been found.

"WAR," SAYS TOMBU. Where I see dunes, Tombu sees bunkers. Tombu is a soldier, a former leader of the Tuareg during the armed rebellion that erupted in Niger in 1990. Warring is in his blood. For more than 3,000 years, until the French overran North Africa in the late 1800s, the Tuareg were known as the bandits of the Ténéré, robbing camel caravans as they headed across the void.

The fighting that began in 1990, however, was over civil rights. Many Tuareg felt like second-class citizens in Niger—it was the majority Hausa and other ethnic groups, they claimed, who were given all the good jobs, the government positions, the college scholarships. And so these Tuareg decided to try to gain autonomy over their homeland, which is essentially the whole of the Ténéré. They were fighting for an Independent Republic of the Void. Hundreds of people were killed before a compromise was reached in 1995: The Tuareg would be treated with greater respect, and in return they would agree to drop their fight for independence. Though isolated skirmishes continued until 1998, the void is quiet, at least for now. This is a main reason why there has been a sudden upswing in tourism.

Tombu is no longer a fighter; he now drives a desert taxi, though he drives like a soldier, which is to say as recklessly as possible. I have hired him to take me north, through the center of the void, into Algeria—a four-day drive. We were together when the police officer forced me to pay him a bribe. During rest stops, Tombu draws diagrams in the sand, showing me how he attacked a post high in the Massif de l'Aïr and how he ambushed a convoy of jeeps in the open void. "But now there is peace," he says. He looks disappointed. I ask him if anything has changed for the Tuareg.

"No," he says. "Except that we have given up our guns." He looks even more disappointed. "But," he adds, visibly brightening, "it will be very easy to get them back."

"Speed," says Joel. He has just pulled his motorbike up to the place I've rented in Dirkou, a furnitureless, sand-floored room for a dollar a night. Joel is in the desert for one primary reason: to go fast. He is here for two months, from Israel, to ride his motorbike, a red-and-white Yamaha, and the void is his playground. Speed and the void have a storied relationship; each winter for 13 years, the famous Paris-to-Dakar rally cut through the Ténéré—a few hundred foreigners in roadsters and pickup trucks and motorbikes tearing hell-bent across the sand. The race was rerouted in 1997, but its wrecks are still on display, each one visible from miles away, the vehicles' paint scoured by the wind-blown sand and the steel baked to a smooth chocolate brown.

Joel reveres the Paris-to-Dakar. He talks about sand the way skiers talk about snow—in a language unintelligible to outsiders. Sand, it turns out, is not merely sand. There are chotts and regs and oueds and ergs and barchans and feche-feche and gassis and bull dust. The sand around Dirkou, Joel tells me, is just about perfect. "Would you like to borrow my bike?" he asks.

I would. I snap on his helmet and straddle the seat and set out across the sand. The world before me is an absolute plane, nothing at all, and I throttle the bike and soon I'm in fifth and the engine is screaming and sand is tornadoing about. I know, on some level, that I'm going fast and that it's dangerous, but the feeling is absent of fear. The dimensions are so skewed it's more like skydiving—I've committed myself, and now I'm hurtling through space, and there is nothing that can hurt me. It's euphoric, a pure sense of motion and G-force and lawlessness, and I want more, of course, so I pull on the throttle and the world is a blur and the horizon is empty, and it is here, it is right now, that I suddenly realize what I need to do. And I do it. I shut my eyes. I pinch them shut, and the bike bullets on, and I override my panic because I know that there's nothing to hit, not a thing in my way, and soon, with my eyes closed, I find that my head has gone silent and I have discovered a crystalline form of freedom.

"DEATH," SAYS KEVIN. "I think about dying." Kevin is not alone. Everyone who crosses the void, whether tourist or Toubou or truck passenger, is witness to the Ténéré's ruthlessness. There are the bones, for example—so many bones that a good way to navigate the void is to follow the skeletons, which are scattered beside every main route like cairns on a hiking trail. They're mostly goat bones. Goats are common freight in the Ténéré, and there are always a couple of animals that do not survive the crossing. Dead goats are tossed off the trucks. In the center of the void, the carcasses become sun-dried and leathery, like mummies. At the edges of the void, where jackals roam, the bones are picked clean and sun-bleached white as alabaster. Some of the skeletons are of camels; a couple are human. People die every year in the Ténéré, but few travelers have experienced such deaths as directly as Kevin.

Kevin is also on the Libya-bound truck, crossing with the crop pickers, though he is different from most other passengers. He has no interest in picking crops. He wants to play soccer. He's a midfielder, seeking a spot with a professional team in either Libya or Tunisia. Kevin was born in South Africa, under apartheid, then later fled to Senegal, where he lived in a refugee camp. His voice is warm and calm, and his eyes, peering through a pair of metal-framed glasses, register the sort of deep-seated thoughtfulness one might look for in a physician or religious leader. Whenever a fight breaks out on the truck, he assumes the role of mediator, gently persuading both parties to compromise on the level of uncomfortableness. He tells me that he would like to study philosophy and that he has been inspired by the writings of Thomas Jefferson. He says that his favorite musician is Phil Collins. "When I listen to his music," he says, "it makes me cry." I tell him, deadpan, that it makes me cry, too. This is Kevin's second attempt at reaching the soccer fields across the sands. The first trip, a year previous, ended in disaster.

He was riding with his friend Silman in a dilapidated Land Cruiser in the northern part of the void. Both of them dreamed of playing soccer. There were six other passengers in the car and a driver, and for safety they were following another Land Cruiser, creating a shortcut across the Ténéré. The car Kevin and Silman were in broke down. There was no room in the second Land Cruiser, so only the driver of the first car squeezed in. He told his passengers to wait. He said he'd go to the nearest town, a day's drive away, and then return with another car.

After three days, there was still no sign of the driver. Water was running low. It was the middle of summer. Temperatures in the void often reach 115 degrees Fahrenheit and have gone as high as 130 degrees. The sky turns white with heat; the sand shimmers and appears molten. Kevin and Silman decided they would rather walk than wait. The other six passengers decided to remain with the broken vehicle. Kevin and Silman set out across the desert, following the tracks of the second Land Cruiser. Merely sitting in the shade in the Sahara, a person can produce two gallons of sweat per day. Walking, Kevin and Silman probably produced twice that amount. They carried what water they had, but there was no way they could replace a quarter of the loss.

Humans are adaptable creatures, but finely calibrated. Even a gallon loss—about 5 percent of one's body fluid—results in dizziness and headache and circulatory problems. Saliva glands dry up. Speech is garbled. Kevin and Silman reached this state in less than a day. At a two-gallon deficit, walking is nearly impossible. The tongue swells, vision and hearing are diminished, and one's urine is the color of dark rust. It is difficult to form cogent thoughts. Recovery is not possible without medical assistance. People who approach this state often take desperate measures. Urine is the first thing to be drunk. Kevin and Silman did this. "You would've done it, too," Kevin tells me. People who have waited by stranded cars have drunk gasoline and radiator fluid and battery acid. There have been instances in which people dying of thirst have killed others and drunk their blood.

Kevin and Silman managed to walk for three days. Then Silman collapsed. Kevin pushed on alone, crawling at times. The next day, the driver returned. He came upon Kevin, who at this point was scarcely conscious. The driver had no explanation for his weeklong delay. He gave Kevin water, and they rushed to find Silman. It was too late. Silman was dead. They returned to the broken Land Cruiser. Nobody was there. Evidently, the other passengers had also tried to walk. Their footprints had been covered by blowing sand. After hours of searching, there was no trace of anyone else. Kevin was the only survivor.

"HISTORY," SAYS HAMOUD. Hamoud is an old man—though "old" is a relative term in Niger, where the life expectancy is 41. I have hired a desert taxi to take me to a place called Djado, in eastern Niger, where Hamoud works as a guide. Djado is, by far, the nicest city I have seen in the Ténéré. It is built on a small hill beside an oasis thick with date palms and looks a bit like a wattle-and-daub version of Mont-Saint-Michel. The homes, unlike any others I've seen in the void, are multistoried, spacious, and cool. Thought has been given to the architecture; walls are elliptical, and turrets have been built to provide views of the surrounding desert. There is not a scrap of garbage.

One problem: Nobody lives in Djado. The city is several thousand years old and has been abandoned for more than two centuries. At one time, there may have been a half million people living along Djado's oasis. Now it is part of a national reserve and off-limits to development. A handful of families are clustered in mud shanties a couple of miles away, hoping to earn a few dollars from the trickle of tourists.

Nobody knows exactly why Djado was deserted; the final blows were most likely a malaria epidemic and the changing patterns of trade routes. But Hamoud suggests that the city's decline was initiated by a dramatic shift in the climate. Ten thousand years ago, the Sahara was green. Giraffes and elephants and hippos roamed the land. Crocodiles lived in the rivers. On cliffs not far from Djado, ancient paintings depict an elaborate society of cattle herders and fishermen and bow hunters. Around 4000 B.C., the weather began to change. The game animals left. The rivers dried. One of the last completed cliff paintings is of a cow that appears to be weeping, perhaps symbolic of the prevailing mood. When Djado was at its prime, its oasis may have covered dozens of square miles. Now there is little more than a stagnant pond. Hamoud says that he found walking through Djado to be "mesmerizing" and "thrilling" and "magnificent" and "beautiful." I do not tell him this, but my overwhelming feeling is of sadness. In the void, it seems clear, people's lives were better a millennium ago than they are today.

"DESTINY," SAYS AKLY. He shrugs his shoulders in a way designed to imply that he could care less, but his words have already belied his gesture. Akly does care, but he is powerless to do anything—and maybe this, in truth, is what his shrug is attempting to express. Akly is a Tuareg, a native of Agadez who was educated in Paris. He has returned to Niger, with his French wife, to run a small guest house. Agadez is a poor city in a poor nation beset by a brutal desert. It is not a place to foster optimism.

Akly is worried about the Sahara. He is concerned about its expansion. Most scientific evidence appears to show that the Sahara is on the march. In three decades, the desert has advanced more than 60 miles to the south, devouring grasslands and crops, drying up wells, creating refugees. The Sahara is expanding north, too, piling up at the foothills of the Atlas Mountains, as if preparing to ambush the Mediterranean.

Desertification is a force as powerful as plate tectonics. If the Sahara wants to grow, it will grow. Akly says he has witnessed, just in his lifetime, profound changes. He believes that the desert's growth is due both to the Sahara's own forces and to human influences. "We cut down all the trees," he says, "and put a hole in the ozone. The Earth is warming. There are too many people. But what can we do? Everyone needs to eat, everyone wants a family." He shrugs again, that same shrug.

"It has gotten harder and harder to live here," he says. "I am glad that you are here to see how hard it is. I hope you can get accustomed to it."

I shake my head no and point to the sweat beading my face, and to the heat rash that has pimpled my neck, and to the blotches of sunburn that have left dead skin flaking off my nose and cheeks and arms.

"I think you'd better get used to it," Akly says. "I think everyone should get used to it. Because one day, maybe not that far away, all of the deserts are going to grow. They are going to grow like the Sahara is growing. And then everyone is going to live in the void."

September/October 2001

BEING THE BOATMAN

By Charles Graeber

It was an ad hoc journey of enlightenment: sail, row, and drag a skiff 160 miles up India's holiest river, the Ganges. The locals said such a trip would be impossible, or very simple; safe, or quite dangerous. In the end it was awe-inspiring and incomprehensible—just as Lord Shiva himself would have wanted.

MODERN TRAVEL CAN BE DISORIENTING. Strapped between tray tables in a 747, the body moves easily, zipping world to world at the speed of sound. But your soul, your sense of where you are—that travels more slowly, arriving days or even weeks later, like misrouted luggage. The result is a feeling familiar to habitual travelers: not quite here, not quite home.

So here's where I find myself when my soul finally catches up to my body: I am sunburned and barefoot and trudging along an Indian riverbank of mud and sand and human remains. This shoreline is at once sewer, sink, and cemetery for the surrounding villagers, and my tired legs are caked to the thigh in indeterminate river yuck. I hike up my loincloth and pull, staggering with the weight. The bamboo yoke across my chest is connected to 50 feet of nylon cord, which in turn is connected to the wooden skiff that has been my kitchen, bed, and conveyance for the past four days. These days have seemed to last forever.

The beach stretches to the horizon, and it is my task to walk it. Sometimes the towline snags on a water buffalo. Sometimes I sink to my thighs in mud. And sometimes the distance yields a dot, which in time becomes a man soaping himself in the current. As I approach, he freezes—toothbrush stick in mouth, suds in hair—and stares in raw amazement. His eyes do the talking: Who are you? And what in the world are you doing here? These are good questions, but I don't have the language to explain. Instead, I smile, wish him good day, and continue. The full answer, like lost luggage or a steamer-class soul, is coming to me slowly. When you're a boatman on the River Ganges, there is plenty of time to consider everything.

IT STARTED SIX YEARS AGO, on my first trip to India. The plan was for two months of solo adventure—but I was rarely solo. There were thousands of us, all there to do our India thing, and all, it seemed, carrying the same guidebooks. We were at the Monkey Temple and the Taj Mahal, lounging on the right beaches in Goa and trekking with the recommended outfitters in Manali. I thought I'd lost them in Kashmir—the civil war and all—but then, in my final week, there we all were again in Varanasi, tanned and dusty in our loose cotton clothes, and packed like penguins along the world's most holy natural feature, the Ganges.

On the map, India is shaped something like a heart, and veined diagonally across its middle is one of the most fascinating thin blue lines in the world. From its icy origin in a Himalayan glacier to its delta in the Bay of Bengal, the Ganges is the spiritual lifeblood of India, a river of heaven with 108 names.

To the devout, it is Himacalendra-tanaya—Daughter of the Lord of the Himalayas. It is Dear to Siva, and Liberator of the 60,000 Sons of Sagara. It is Melodious. It is Ocean-Flowing, and Lucky. It is White, and Happy, and Colorless. It Carries Away Fear, Brings Happiness, Destroys Illusion. And always it is Ramya—it is Beautiful. For a Hindu, it is at once a physical and a metaphysical destination. To die on its banks brings release from the tiresome chain of death and rebirth; to bathe in its waters is to be touched by God.

But I was a foreigner and a tourist, crouching in a little wooden skiff for my half-hour glimpse of pilgrims and funerals while my boatman worked the oars with hands as tough as talons. Like his father and all his fathers before him, this man knew the river, not as a must-see in a tourist guidebook but as a flowing, living product of time, like music. While I snapped photos of the sunset, the boatman scanned the roiling current with eyes wizened by lifetimes of river sun. *This* was the way to see India. Forget sightseeing; next time I wanted to be the boatman.

I had half a decade to plan my route. As glimpsed during my first trip, the natural starting point for a river journey seemed to be Varanasi, the holy city of Siva, multihanded god of destruction and regeneration. Varanasi was famous for its champion boatmen. It would be the perfect port in which to secure a vessel and a crew. For a destination, I chose the city of Allahabad, a seemingly doable 160 miles upriver.

According to my guidebook, Allahabad is famous for two things: its 419-year-old red-stone fort and the Sangam, where the Ganges is spiritually supercharged by its confluence with the Yamuna and the mythical Saraswati, River of Enlightenment. This three-in-one combination has the power to cleanse the soul and open the eyes, and true believers travel thousands of miles for a dip. If it was good enough for millions of Hindus, it was certainly good enough for me.

As far as I could tell, my quest had only three potentially fatal flaws. First, my intended journey was upriver, against the current. This one didn't bother me much—if the trip was possible, such a challenge might even add to the be-the-boatman experience.

Second was that ongoing conflict up in Kashmir. While tensions between India and Pakistan hadn't yet flared to the nuclear saber-rattling levels of this past summer, any armed confrontation that involves two nuclear powers demands that attention be paid. In this case, though, the disputed territory is in the northernmost reaches of the country—if India is a heart, this is the aorta—and it's some 800 miles from Varanasi. I decided the situation was well within my range of risk tolerance.

The final problem was harder to rationalize: None of my previous domestic camping or canoe trips even came close to the notion of taking on an Indian river of life with 108 names and a fecal coliform count that is 61,000 times higher, at Varanasi, than what the World Health Organization considers safe for drinking. Put simply, the journey just wasn't on my experiential map—and it wasn't in any of the guidebooks, either. There was, it seemed, only one path to being the boatman. You had to go, then be.

TWENTY-FOUR HOURS AFTER LEAVING NEW YORK, I was standing in Mughal Sarai station on a platform thick with shouting taxi wallahs. I chose a sleepy Sikh in an electric-blue turban, who swerved his Ambassador cab around the milling rickshaws and cows. The morning air already carried the bouquet of incense, diesel exhaust, and human business. Twenty minutes later, we crossed the pontoon bridge over the Ganges and entered Varanasi.

The streets were a maze of markets, temples, and banging funeral parades, all crowded against the ramparts overlooking the gray expanse of the river. As viewed from these 40-foot walls, the riverbank seemed to bustle like a well-stirred ant colony. I steadied myself with a cup of *chai,* then started down the narrow stone stairs toward the water.

I passed the pyres on the Burning Ghat, and the barbers with straight razors shaving the bereaved over black haystacks of hair. I edged through the crowds thronging the Goddess of Smallpox, through the begging lepers, and through the laundry men beating rags on rocks with karate-type cries. Farther on were the holy men, some twisting their penises with sticks like model airplane propellers, others covered with cow-dung ash and meditating near smoldering tree stumps. First days in India: Without a decompression period, it all can be a bit much. I double-knotted the lid of my brain box, screwed my sunglasses to my face, and continued: I was looking for a boat.

Theoretically, I didn't have to look far. As any guidebook will tell you, Varanasi is full of skiffs and boatmen who row pilgrims and tourists alike across the broad river. But these passengers are daytrippers; I was looking for a voyage. I spoke to everyone. Boatmen, scam artists, holy men, guest-house operators, hash dealers, waiters, astrologers, and vendors of ladies' silk pants. The interviews filled the better part of the day. Afterward, I sipped a sunset chai on my guest-house balcony and asked myself, What had I learned?

According to my sources, my upriver journey was impossible, very simple, would take two days, two weeks, a month. It was safe and dangerous. It was unnecessary, stupid, an enlightened spiritual quest commissioned by Lord Siva himself. After a full day of questions, only one thing was certain: Varanasi has as many answers as it does boatmen, but there is only one Baba Maghi.

That night I strolled the moonlit ghats to where a small boat nosed the riverbank. Inside the greasy tarp, a guttering lamp flickered on the shapes of perhaps a dozen men, all facing what looked like a healthy corpse: a broken back, a gray mop over a wrinkled skull, earlobes heavy with loops of gold. At a reputed 104 years old, Baba Maghi is the father of the Varanasi boatmen.

We sat in silence as Baba sucked hungrily from a clay chillum. Smoke poured from his nostrils, filling the boat with a hashish fog, while the men performed *puja* and chanted. My eyes were now used to the light, and I could see another man, a Hindu priest with bulging eyes and a ferocious grin that fully employed both sets of teeth. Baba turned to the priest and croaked something I didn't understand.

"Baba say Allahabad will be taking you nine days," the priest whispered. "Nine days upriver and hard working. For the boat and three of the best boatmen, Baba is telling you 12,000 rupees."

I reacted to the number—about $250—like I'd swallowed a bug. My quest was possible; it was even being handled seriously. That was good. But now I had to get practical. With no real information, I bluffed.

"Ten thousand rupees," I said firmly. "For a boat, water, and only two boatmen. One, two, and . . ." I pounded my chest and offered my uncalloused hands, a horse at auction: "three." The boat exploded in laughter, rolling eyeballs, and teeth. Baba laughed, too, shaking like a Muppet until he coughed up something solid.

"Oh, it is not possible," said the priest. He cocked his head. "Upriver, very hard work."

Baba croaked another phlegmy syllable. The priest brightened. "And now Baba say three boatmen—and 13,000 rupees."

This was bad. Somehow we were bargaining up, not down, with Baba pushing like a cardsharp jacking the pot. I waggled my head, futilely trying to appear relaxed and local. How to counter? Should I scramble back to Baba's first offer or hang tough?

"Baba has an old brain," the priest explained. He leaned toward me. "It's the way he is thinking."

This was Baba's trump: the crazy-old-man card. If I was going to bargain, I needed to start playing the old man's game.

"Yes?" said the priest. His smile was hypnotic. He was enjoying this.

I touched his shoulder. "Please tell Baba that I have a young brain," I said. "And young pockets."

The priest translated rapidly, apparently thrilled with the sport. Laughter, deep and good-natured, bubbled up from the darkness.

"And in this young brain there is hope," I continued. "And in these young pockets"—I shook my pants—"there are 11,000 rupees."

The priest's grin went megawatt. By now Baba himself was bobbing up and down uncontrollably. He laughed and cried and then hacked with a sound like snapping open a paper grocery sack. The priest dipped a cup into the river, and Baba took a long, slurping drink of that good Ganges water. Then he slumped and breathed like a giant lizard.

"Ha," Baba croaked finally. "*Thik hai.*" All right.

"You will have a very good journey," added the priest.

I hoped so. At this point, I had a boat and a crew of three—and no idea what to expect.

SIX DAYS LATER, I AM—WELL, WHERE AM I? I don't quite know. I am maybe 85 miles upriver from Varanasi, moving slowly, very slowly, toward the horizon along the east bank of an ancient, living river. We've been rowing, poling, and pulling our open boat steadily against the current, starting each day in the bruised light of dawn, ending bunked under the moon on the wood deck. Sometimes we pull to the banks to buy a fish or touch the local shrines and take tea with the elder of a small mud village. At the larger towns, we prowl like sailors on shore leave, bartering for chickens and powdered milk before slipping back and rowing away. But mostly we are between places, in the blank space on the map.

This morning we started on a flat bank perfect for towing, so once again I'm walking with the bamboo yoke, straining against the floated weight like a barge-pulling mule. Behind me, our boat bobs like a kite at the far end of a string. The skiff is perhaps 20 feet long, six feet in the beam, and draws less than a foot of water. It's tapered fore and aft, like a lifeboat, with a rectangular stowage where Ramesh, the youngest of the boatmen, is now mincing garlic and chilies for lunch. Cantilevered on his haunches, the tiny cook could fit inside a bowling ball bag. Up front, perched on the bow, is Uncle, as sinewy and silent as Death. Far back, on the raised stern, sits Captain, the most petite of the boatmen, pushing the tiller and calling encouragement.

"Thik hai!" he yells. "*Chalo!*" Meaning: Go.

I go. After days of towing, rowing, and pushing, I have developed the pace and mind-set of a long-distance runner. India unfolds, one foot at a time.

These banks stretch on either side in an alluvial plain perhaps a mile across and end in a green berm topped in places with a spreading tree or a small white temple. The oxbows are flat and hot and littered with things abandoned by the current—flowers and altars and a Noah's ark of skeletons. I step over the delicately bleached birds, the gnarled masses of spines and skulls and whole-horse assemblages, laid out where they fell. Occasionally there are human bodies, flotsam from burials upstream, which the monsoon tides have arranged into shipwreck poses. A week ago, this was my own personal Valley of Death. Now, none of this concerns me. My job is to keep the line tight, to keep the boat moving. So I pull.

The beach extends to the horizon. I walk it. It's followed by another beach, followed by another. Over the days and miles, a thought occurs to me: I am dead, and this is purgatory. This trip might last forever; this beach will never end. There's something about walking a bone-strewn strand, barefoot and silent and bearing a bamboo pole, that makes you think like this. Maybe it's the vastness of the horizon, the simplicity of the work. Maybe it's sunstroke. I'm trying to decide whether a beautiful purgatory would be a bad thing, whether maybe I should get a hat, when I hear Captain.

"*Bas! Bas!*"

Before I can stop, the towline goes as tight as a piano wire, snapping me to the ground.

From my new horizontal vantage I see that the river ahead has been partially closed off by a series of *bandals*—an ancient jetty system of bamboo and tarp that creates a deep, swift channel on one side and a silted backwater on the other. We've hit a submerged sandbar in the backwater, and for perhaps the 50th time, we're stuck fast. I reel in the line and wade back to the boat.

We pole backward from the bow, pinwheeling in the current, only to ground ourselves again. The bandals are funneling water hard, forcing us back and sideways. Without a motor, we can't handle the left channel, and the silted section is simply not navigable. We'll need to push through the middle.

Ramesh, Uncle, and I jump into the swift water to lighten the boat. We plant our feet in the river bottom and push from the gunwales, plowing a trench through the sand. Captain grunts over his tiller pole, pushing and shouting directions until, finally, we hit our depth and the boat bobs like a cork. We're clear. We give our ride one final push and hop back on.

It's time for the oars. Each is a long pole of bamboo fastened to a crate board with a metal pin and held to the gunwales with a wetted loop of worn twine. Ramesh starts first, his left hand on the oar butt, his right hand over the left, his feet braced in a groove in the deck. He pulls, making a slow circle, finding his zone, and I lock into his pace, pushing when he pushes, pulling when he pulls, mast to chest and back. At each stroke, the oars knock and groan in their saddles. We work slowly up the river, one hour, then another, hypnotized by the metronome, like two halves of a clean-valved machine.

AT MIDDAY WE PULL TO THE SIDE FOR LUNCH. The current is clear and strong here, cutting the banks cleanly. River dolphins breach and blow through the roiling stream, and the boatmen wash. Captain oils and reparts his hair in a cracked hand mirror, and I soap my trousers in a biscuit tin before hanging them in the raw noon sun. It has been a long morning. My lower back is trashed, and my hands are pillowed with blisters, three at the pads and a quarter-size bubble on each palm. Ramesh grins proudly.

"Thik hai," he says. This is my flesh report card, and the crew nod their approval. Ramesh mothers my damaged mitts with mustard oil before searing them over a kerosene flame. Apparently the oil will fill my blisters, forming a durable callous glove. In the meantime, they hurt more than ever.

I spend the afternoon tracing the shore with the tiller while Uncle pulls us along a flat green bank. It's a perfect, clear day. To my left, a kingfisher explodes from the heart of the river, while a white crane herds sardines in the shallows. They pulse from the water in waves. We pass thin, naked boys cartwheeling off an obliging water buffalo, cliffs peppered with swallow holes, packs of wild dogs gnawing something dead and orange. On the left bank, a group of villagers stand circled around a burning pyre. At its center is a cloth-covered body, dancing with flame.

"Old man die, family very happy," Captain says. He nods toward the bank, not looking away from his spot on the river. "Drink, dance, very happy, very nice." He thinks for a moment, shaking his head. "Fifteen year die—ten, fifteen, twenty year die—no happy. Old man die, new life."

An hour later we approach a circle of women in bright-yellow saris. They want to string a garland of marigolds across the river. How far did we think that was? How long should their string be? There are no certain answers here. We guess and continue. The river changes, becomes fast, then slow; wide, then narrow. It has never been just one thing.

Sometime in the late afternoon we stop and tie to a pontoon bridge at a village on the outskirts of Bhadohi. Suddenly, Captain has an agenda. He changes from his work *lungi* into his pants and flip-flops and motions for me to follow him onto the bank. Above the berm is a narrow dirt road flanked by lopsided mud houses, a few skinny cows, and a small group of men with bed head and hanging shirtsleeves. Captain knows this track. He cuts a sharp right at the crossroads until he reaches an enormous tree at the village's edge. Behind the tree is another mud house; this one has a door of unusually heavy wood and a single window with bars like an old-time bank.

Captain looks at me, winks, then thrusts a hundred-rupee note roughly through the bars. He steps back, cocky and slicking his hair. The village men stand apart, staring like simpletons. Arriving in his own vessel with his foreign crew, clean white shirt, and neatly parted coif, Captain is the Man.

In the darkness behind the window, I can see a shape, a bearded man rising from a stool. With equal roughness, this man snatches the money from the counter and holds it to the window, checking the watermark. A few seconds later, miniature IV bags start shooting out the barred window, smacking the dust with a hollow *plump*. I bend down and pick up one of these miracles. It's squishy and sized like a juice box, but behind the Sanskrit and seals I spy a familiar brown liquid. This, I realize, is Indian government whiskey.

When we return to the boat, a small crowd has gathered. They're hoping for a show, and Captain doesn't disappoint. He lines up metal cups on the deck, rips a bag with his teeth, and pours out shots. We pull them back hard and finish with a manly "Ahhh!" Captain shoots me another wink, takes the tiller, and we push off, laying into the oars with new strength.

By sunset we are utterly exhausted and tie under the stone ramparts of an ancient fort. There is no light here, only the moon and the pinpricks of familiar constellations at unfamiliar angles. The world is blue, silhouetted with black hills and trees, and the river whispers against our wooden hull, the same secrets told for centuries told again tonight. We sip our whiskey and huddle close on the wood floor for warmth, serenaded by frogs and the hiss of the kerosene cooker. And for the first time since I stepped on board, I realize that this trip, like all trips, will one day end.

Captain guesses that we are close, only miles away, and clinks his metal cup against mine to toast our hard work. "Cheese," he says. I smile and drink. We pass the night like this, laughing and elbowing one another under the high moon like happy crews the world over. Although I can't say exactly where I am, there is nowhere on Earth I'd rather be.

ON THE EIGHTH MORNING, we row away from the rising sun on a river of molten metal. The current is fierce, and hunks of raw earth splash into the stream, but we feel strong and strain happily at the oars. By now my blisters have hardened into honest yellow calluses, and Ramesh and I goad each other on with chants and grunts. The boat surges through the current like a water bug.

"Thik hai!" yells the captain. "Thik hai!" Even Uncle breaks a broad grin. It is not yet seven o'clock.

Slowly, very slowly, morning becomes day, and the banks of the river become a town, then a city, then Allahabad. The Ganges, the Yamuna, the mythical Saraswati: The three holy rivers form a trident. At the trinity point is the Sangam, where the water's heart boils. River of Heaven, Purifier of Souls, Opener of Eyes; I jump from the boat with the pilgrims, dunking again and again in the cool water beneath the ramparts of the red-stone fort.

According to my guidebook, this imposing post was built in 1583 by the Mughal Emperor Akbar, and you can apparently reach it from Varanasi in a few hours by train or bus, even less time by taxi. To this serviceable list I would like to add one small footnote.

This historic fort is far more beautiful, more satisfying, when approached after eight days spent traveling upriver on an open wooden boat, and is best seen in the company of the three champion Varanasi boatmen with whom you have shared a floor, ten words of Hindi, five packets of government whiskey—and no map.

SEPTEMBER 2002

THE LAST CAIRN

By Chip Brown

Johnny Waterman was the mad genius of Alaskan mountaineering, an untamed eccentric who pulled off one of climbing's most audacious feats—a five-month solo ascent of Mount Hunter. Then he vanished into the northern wilderness.

YOUNG MEN GO INTO THE MOUNTAINS all the time to discover themselves and to propitiate the ghosts of their fathers, but it's the rare father who goes into the mountains to join the ghost of his son. Guy Waterman died three years ago on a winter evening on a mountain ridge in New Hampshire. He was 67 years old, a climber, a homesteader, an author widely known in New England outdoors circles. He was also the father of three sons, and he believed in the peculiarly American myth that says there is something between fathers and sons that can be understood only in the context of wilderness. Before he sat down in the snow and froze to death on a February night, he wrote some notes to friends, hoping to explain his decision to take his own life. One was to an old pal named Brad Snyder, who knew of the special kinship Guy felt with his middle son, John Mallon Waterman.

In December 1968, when Johnny was 16, Guy had set out with his son on a grand winter circuit in the White Mountains of New Hampshire. They planned to follow the string of boarded-up Appalachian Mountain Club huts along the entire length of the Presidential Range and then to traverse the ranges west—something no one had ever done in winter. They wore snowshoes and carried 80-pound packs. The temperature when they started was 12 below zero. They soon ran into a storm, and on top of Mount Jefferson got lost in an icy cloud. Guy wrote about how they survived the bitter whiteout: "To guard against losing their way—which could have been disastrous—the son would go out from the last identified cairn as far as he could and still see it. Then the father would go out from there as far as he could without losing sight of the son, and stand there waiting for some brief lapse in the wind to try to squint forward into the fury of the storm in a forlorn effort to find another cairn."

To keep their tent from exploding in the wind, they had to stay awake most of that night holding the aluminum poles. Their clothes got soaked; their down sleeping bags had no loft. They beat a dire retreat and hiked into a town, where they found a Laundromat and dried their gear. Then—the index of their zeal—they started back in, walking up the Mount Washington Auto Road. They got to 5,500 feet when another storm hit. The temperature dropped to 26 below zero. The winds were shrieking at a hundred miles an hour.

Father and son spent four days holed up in one of the metal bivouac sheds that once provided emergency shelter for road crews: 6 ½-Mile Box it was called. To fetch water, one of them had to get completely dressed—boots, crampons, over-mitts, parka, face mask—go out into the storm, chop at an icy snow crest with an ax, hope the gales blew some of the chips into a stuff sack, then dive back inside the shed and melt the collection of ice chips. They played poker for lunch snacks with a handmade deck of cards. To his chagrin, Guy discovered that Dostoyevsky's *Notes From Underground* was no help in passing the time, whereas Johnny's trashy detective novels were riveting.

How long those hours were! And, in retrospect, how short.

Six months after the winter outing in the White Mountains, Guy let Snyder take Johnny to Alaska on a climbing expedition to Mount McKinley. The teenager became the third youngest person to stand on the highest point in North America. The ascent was the first of Johnny's many formidable achievements in Alaska and a moment of crowning pride for his father. Then, in 1978, Johnny produced his masterpiece—a 145-day solo expedition on 14,573-foot Mount Hunter, the third highest peak in the Alaska Range. Of that feat, American climber Jeff Lowe once wrote, "There is nothing else in the history of mountaineering with which to compare it." Three years later, Johnny vanished while soloing on McKinley. The grief that seized Guy never really let him go. Saying good-bye to his old friend Snyder, Waterman wrote:

"Sorry to be leaving like this, but I've tried to explain my thinking about old age prospects and other shortcomings, for me, of this life. . . . It isn't a question of going or staying—just when and how to go. Above tree line in the wind seems appropriate—I'll be joining Johnny, to whom I was always closer akin than anyone realized."

Here was the saddest sort of faith—faith not that a father and son would be reunited in the next world, but that they would always be paired in this one by the likeness of their deaths.

Johnny Waterman's reputation as the "crazy genius" of Alaska mountaineering was secured long before he disappeared on McKinley. Yet what people saw as madness in Johnny was often just Guy's intensity turned inside out or carried to extremes. Johnny had his father's passion for music, for example, but not his talent. Guy, who was gifted enough to play professional jazz piano as a teenager in Washington, D.C., was always shy about performing. Johnny, with marginal gifts, would take to the stage of a bar to honk Christmas carols on the clarinet, undaunted by booing patrons or the bartender's plugging in the jukebox. Guy's signature tam o' shanter—the very symbol of his discreet showmanship— became in Johnny a full-blown costume: He swept around Fairbanks in a black cape and oversize Elton John glasses with a big silver star glued on the bridge of the frames. Guy in his 20s had written speeches for leading Republican politicians, including one who would later become President of the United States; Johnny in his 20s once ran for President of the United States. Johnny had his father's mania for recording the minutiae of daily life, but where Guy jotted notes on color-coded file cards stacked neatly in his left shirt pocket, Johnny had small spiral notebooks and a Harpo Marx–like entanglement of clipboards. Guy rarely talked about his feelings, but Johnny was almost compulsively confessional, broadcasting his loneliness and sexual anxieties.

But for both of them, climbing was a lifeline. Guy had nurtured his son's skill on rock and ice, top-roping the scrawny boy up his first ascents, on the Shawangunks cliffs near New Paltz, New York, and watching as the prodigy emerged and eventually outstripped him.

The mountain that loomed over both their lives was Hunter. While its giant summit plateau is more than a mile lower than the top of McKinley, eight miles to the north, Hunter has been called the hardest 14,000-foot climb on the continent. Johnny made his first attempt in May 1970, when he was 17 years old and newly emancipated from high school. His party got only 1,500 feet up the south face before bad weather forced them down.

The following year, Guy fared much worse, barely getting above his base camp. His party was defeated by bad weather and what Guy conceded were the team's "mediocre" abilities. The experience left him chastened, as if he'd flunked an important test.

It's something of a paradox that Guy, who loved bad mountain weather and went on to become one of the leading wilderness advocates of his generation, never returned to the grandest wilderness on the continent. Pressed for money, frightened of flying, and overwhelmed by the scale of Alaska, he confined himself after Hunter to what he called the dinky mountains of the Northeast and found inspiration and vicarious glory in Johnny's exploits.

As horizons were contracting for the father, they were opening for the son. In the summer of 1972, after completing his freshman year at Western Washington University, Johnny returned to Alaska, where he and four other climbers claimed the east ridge of Mount Huntington, long considered to be a deadly route. It was a resounding achievement, but while his partners celebrated, Johnny stared off at Hunter, three miles west.

The following spring he got his second crack at Hunter. He was joined by Dean Rau, from the 1970 expedition, and by two new team members, Dave Carman and Don Black. After three weeks of climbing, Waterman, Carman, and Black, who had pressed on without the more cautious Rau, reached what they believed to be Hunter's south summit. But when they returned to the town of Talkeetna, their jumping-off point, and consulted aerial photographs, Johnny was devastated to discover that the true south summit was another point farther along the ridge, 200 feet higher. Waterman burst into tears, the whole ascent suddenly a failure in his view.

Johnny moved to Fairbanks in 1974 and enrolled at the University of Alaska. The following year, heeding his father's principle of "planning all activities in detail and well in advance," he began what turned into nearly three years of preparations for his third attempt on Hunter.

The next year, halfway through the fall term, Johnny dropped out of school and found a job working on the trans-Alaska pipeline to finance the climb. He began saving money to buy equipment. He went on long runs wearing crampons on his mountaineering boots. To acclimate himself to cold temperatures, he developed the flesh-mortifying practice of bathing in an ice-filled bathtub.

In the midst of his training, Johnny returned to the East in June 1976 and spent two days visiting his father at Barra, Guy's homestead in East Corinth, Vermont, where most of the food came from the garden, the firewood was cut by hand, and the water was hauled up in buckets from a little stream. Guy was impressed with how strong his son had gotten, how much the boy had ripened into a man.

"He was building himself up for Mount Hunter," recalled his stepmother, Laura Waterman. "I could tell that Guy was proud of him, wanted him to achieve great things in the mountains. . . . Guy had talked a lot about wanting to [go] back to Alaska sometime with Johnny—just the two of them. He wanted to fly into some glaciated spot where the routes stretched up and on forever, all untouched. That was his dream. He and Johnny would do route after route, all previously untrodden. Of course, it never happened."

Father and son would stay in touch by mail over the years, but after that last summer in Vermont they never saw each other again.

It proved to be a grim year for Johnny. In August, his friend and mentor Chuck Loucks died in a fall in the Tetons. Years later, Guy dug up a letter Johnny wrote to him after learning that Loucks had been killed: "Last person in the world I expected to live longer than. . . . [Loucks's death] forever removes all legitimacy from climbing to me, but will bring us all closer together, I think."

Then, in December, Johnny's friend Lief Patterson was killed in an avalanche with his 12-year-old son. "Kind of 'hilarious,' " Johnny wrote ironically to Snyder in a letter dated January 1977, "as part of the cause of [my] falling out [with Lief] was my interpretation of climbing as . . . a desperately tragic affair. Oh well. It doesn't feel good to win that argument. Maybe he agreed with me anyway. Maybe I, or you, or anyone for that matter, will join them soon . . . I don't have a death wish, but I am trying to be realistic."

BY LATE MARCH 1978, Johnny was ready to take on what he would come to call his "nemesis": the mountain that had rebuffed his father and whose highest points had twice eluded him. The 1970 and 1973 Hunter parties had gained elevation by ascending two icefalls on the Tokositna Glacier, but the more dramatic and natural line up the south face began where the buttress rose, below and to the east of the second icefall. The route eventually rejoined the upper portion of the south ridge at around 12,700 feet, airy ground Waterman had already crossed in 1973. If he got up the buttress, he planned to traverse from the south summit across Hunter's massive summit plateau (two miles long by half a mile wide), climb the middle and north summits, and descend by way of Hunter's difficult north ridge, which fell back to the main body of the Tokositna Glacier. Suffice it to say that the route was long, audacious, and terrifyingly hard. To make the challenge supremely exacting, Waterman was going to do the whole thing solo.

"I won't be seeing you again," he told bush pilot Cliff Hudson, who dropped Waterman off on the Tokositna ice.

"You'll be back," Hudson promised.

One of the paradoxes of Waterman's solo climb and traverse is that he was noted for moving boldly and quickly in the mountains—for ascents in what is called alpine style. On Hunter, however, he used expedition-style tactics, perfected by European climbers in their assaults on 8,000-meter Himalayan peaks. Climbing the central buttress a dozen times or more, he hauled his 800-pound base camp in repeated sorties up pitches that he fixed with anchors and ropes. He would rappel down and then reascend by using mechanical devices called jumars. He had 3,600 feet of rope and 74 bags, each containing 5,000 calories of food. He eventually ate his way through much of this enormous burden, so that higher on the mountain it was not necessary to make as many repeat trips. In his journal he noted the weather, the amount of fixed rope he placed, and the number of loads carried, and he provided terse summaries of each day's highlights.

March 24: "Lost a contact lens and probably further damaged my frost-bitten fingers of a month ago."

April 12: "Read and sang verses from the Bible."

April 24: "Cried bitterly."

As the days went by, he railed at the endless wind. He wrote poems. He dug himself out from blizzards. He repaired a rip in his wind parka using dental floss. He taped his fingers to keep from biting his nails. When a snow picket pulled out during a rappel, he was lucky not to have died. To thaw out his ice-clogged jumars, he sometimes had to blow on them until he was light-headed, and when that didn't work, he flailed at the ascenders with his ice hammer, attacking the very gadgets on which his life depended. After the climb, in a letter to Brad Snyder, he wrote that when he was dragging his bags up the steeper pitches on ropes he'd fixed, "I would occasionally stop and scream for twenty minutes."

He prayed. He wept. He itched himself savagely, discovering an infestation of body lice. "It was some comfort to know I was not alone," he later noted drolly in the *American Alpine Journal*. His only connection to other people was a small AM radio and his citizens band radio, which he used to contact Hudson and other CB users who might get a message to him.

April 28: "Wrote a song 'Arbeit Macht Frei' comparing my Mt. Hunter climb to a concentration camp where inevitable death ensues. It summed up my dire thoughts."

May 7: "Noted I had the venereal condition known as crabs. Gouged myself in the leg trying to remove one of them."

May 28: "Jumars froze up on ropes today. . . . Wrote 'death' poem."

The names he chose for his camps and for the rock and snow formations confronting him on the buttress reflected the almost animate presence of the mountain in his mind and his sense of himself as the protagonist in a saga: Valhalla, First Judge, Court of the Lords, Little Prince. On his 63rd day, he reached the juncture of the buttress and the ridge. He spotted ropes he and his teammates had left in 1973. He was running out of food and would not be able to be resupplied by airdrop until he reached Hunter's summit plateau.

June 3: "Worst winds yet. . . . Dug out camp. Cried and prayed."

June 6: "Bad, windy. . . . Crabs still present. Proposition 13 passed in California."

June 7: "Led the Happy Cowboy pitch. Cornice broke resulting in forty foot fall."

By mid-June, he was past the hideous barrier known as the Happy Cowboy Pinnacle. From there on, Waterman found that the going eased a bit. The high summer nights were not dark enough for stars.

On day 81, Waterman reached the blindingly white world of Hunter's summit plateau, where he could walk without having to claw the Earth with his hands. It was, however, no paradise. Two weeks later, on June 25, six inches of snow fell, Waterman nearly stumbled into a crevasse in a whiteout, and in his log he noted: "Crampons came off boot three times, packing troubles, cried a lot." But in clear weather Hudson was able to drop a fresh supply of food, including ten pounds of potatoes and a gallon of ice cream.

At 1:50 p.m. on July 2, his 101st day on Hunter, Waterman ascended the south summit and stood atop a wrinkle of the Earth that had haunted him since his near miss five years earlier. Then, lugging his chattel into the endless winds, he moved across the plateau. He climbed the middle summit and then, on July 26, scaled Hunter's highest point, the north summit. His CB radio broadcast from there was recorded by Roy Davies in Montana, Alaska, 75 miles south: "I'm standing alone on the summit of Mount Hunter after a 124-day climb of the central buttress. I'm a mighty tired man."

Then he turned to the north ridge and his exit.

Waterman spent an incredible 145 days on the climb, traverse, and descent of Hunter. The time reflected not only the laboriousness of soloing with so much gear but also Waterman's desire to be alone on the mountain, to live amid the intensity of the place. At the beginning of the climb, he had wept for fear that he might die. But now, he noted in his log, he "cried at the thought of living." When he began to go down, the lost-in-a-masquerade sentiments of Leon Russell's song "This Masquerade" began to haunt his thoughts.

As he told Glenn Randall in an interview for *Climbing* magazine, "That song seemed to say it all to me—the dual nature of what I was experiencing, this intense desire to live, and then this song which suddenly had the influence of making me realize how sad it would be if I lived through the climb. Something far more precious would be lost if I lived through it than if I died. Living through it would mean that nature wasn't as raw as everybody wanted to believe it was, that man was far superior to the Arctic, far more capable than he had otherwise thought. Living through it would mean that Hunter wasn't the mountain I thought it was. It was a lot less."

Where Guy had found uplifting and even ennobling elements in what a "puny" human being could achieve on a mountain—puniness redeemed, as it were—Johnny found only self-abnegation and more subtle and complicated ways of perceiving the meaninglessness of his life. Where Guy had been humbled and yet somehow enlivened by the winter winds blasting over Franconia Ridge and its apex, Mount Lafayette—a ridge he considered to be sacred ground, a mountain he climbed more than 300 times—Johnny had come away from his ultimate wilderness test with the conceit that because he was still alive, nature, mountains, even the elemental lethality of the Arctic were overrated. It was not man that was puny, it was the universe. Here was his father's idealism spinning into madness: Prolonged contact with one of the most sublime mountain landscapes in the world had only deepened Johnny's disillusionment. Nature at its most savage could not compare with the wilderness of his soul, with its drunk-on-oblivion logic and self-canceling superiority: *The only mountain I can truly respect is the one that denies me the glory of its summit and punishes me for the hubris of my aspiration.*

No doubt some of the disappointment Waterman felt about leaving Hunter—"discouraged about flying out," he noted during his last day on the ice—reflected a strain of survivor's guilt as well. As Randall shrewdly observed, it didn't seem right that he had lived when "all of his close friends, those who had taught him to climb and accompanied him on his greatest adventures, had died, often in senseless accidents. . . . It seemed perverse that he should be allowed to survive a solo ascent of a climb with far more inherent danger." In a sense, Waterman found himself in the untenable position of having to apologize to a jury of dead friends for not dying.

He borrowed $20 from Hudson and returned to Fairbanks to resume a life that was in some ways much harder for him to negotiate than Hunter's icy arêtes. He got a job busing tables and washing dishes. He gave Hunter slide shows—brilliant, funny, manic performances that seared the memories of everyone who witnessed them. But the shows did not relieve his poverty or the larger estrangement of his life. He quit his job and, by the end of 1978, was living on food stamps, unemployment checks, and the generosity of friends.

TO MANY PEOPLE, Johnny wasn't the same after Hunter. Something had happened on the mountain. Dean Rau said, "After Hunter, Johnny's eccentricities became mental illness." Even Waterman himself, in his last interview with Randall, acknowledged the existence of what he termed his "Mount Hunter psychosis." He tried to explain it: "I get very upset if I think I'm going to be cold during the night I'm facing, if I think I'm going to be hungry in the next few hours. Even if I've got a lot of food and I've got a stove, if the food isn't ready to heat up and I haven't got it figured out so I can get it into my stomach real fast, I get very distraught."

The Fairbanks newspapers had not paid much attention to Johnny's 1979 campaign for a seat on the North Star Borough school board. Undeterred—or perhaps emboldened—by defeat, he formed the Feed the Starving Party and announced a bid for President of the United States, which was otherwise shaping up as a contest between Jimmy Carter, Ronald Reagan, and John Anderson. As he told Randall, "My essential campaign priority was to ensure that nobody starved to death on the Earth. I thought feeding the starving people of the world would be the most dramatic and difficult thing I could do."

Like all politicians, Johnny looked to generate unpaid media exposure, and so he hit upon the idea of returning to McKinley. As on Hunter, he would climb McKinley solo, but this time in the lethal cold of winter. He would hew to a diet of flour, sugar, margarine, and protein powder, thereby demonstrating the immoral extravagance of American eating habits. The whole plan was rigged for disaster. Having identified cold and hunger as the triggers of his Hunter psychosis, he designed a climb guaranteed to precipitate it.

Can the danger of the route he chose and the manner in which he launched himself upon it—alone and poorly equipped—be taken to indicate an ill psyche bent on suicide? Where does self-dramatization leave off and true derangement begin? How does one gauge madness in a person who speaks lucidly about crazy ideas or willingly embraces extremes of danger in pursuit of an epic vision?

He flew into the Kahiltna Glacier on December 20, 1979. The temperature was 15 below zero. On New Year's Day, his bush pilot arrived with another load of supplies. Faced with the prospect of not seeing anyone again for 135 days, Waterman capitulated. "Take me home," he said. "I don't want to die."

"I just plain cracked," he said two months later. "If I didn't make it to the top, or if I died—if I died three days, five days, or 50 days from the point my pilot flew out—nobody would know. It would be entirely a mystery. There is some kind of morbid pain involved with the fact that nobody will ever see you again." He returned to Talkeetna, planning to attempt McKinley again before the end of the winter.

In a conversation he taped in February 1980 with Joan Koponen, a Fairbanks homesteader who knew his father, Johnny said, "I'm very nervous about [the climb]. I never expect to come back from any of the climbs I go on, and I certainly don't expect to come back from this one, much as I would like to. It's kind of like a kamikaze mission."

Waterman went on to criticize his parents, arguing that parental dictatorship should be overthrown and children be allowed to solve problems like bed-wetting on their own.

"[Do] you feel that some of this feeling of antagonism against authority is because you resent your parents telling you what to do, or what not to do, when you were little?"

"I even resent it now," Johnny responded. "My mother detests my mountain climbing. She thinks it's some kind of suicidal activity, and she never supports me on it. My father is the exact opposite. He is a mountain climber himself; he thinks it is all I should do."

Two days after the interview, fire engulfed the cabin in which Waterman was staying. No one was inside at the time, but virtually everything Waterman owned was destroyed. Sleeping bags, poetry, journals, "two and a half feet" of files. A man who had compulsively documented the particulars of his existence was suddenly severed from the record of his life.

"John went berserk," Randall wrote. "He stormed into Hudson's house, seized the telephone, and called the state troopers to demand a ride to the Alaska Psychiatric Institute in Anchorage. They refused. Hudson recalled the policeman saying, 'You don't sound crazy.' Waterman shouted back, 'What do I have to do, kill a kid?' " His reaction, he later told Randall, was part of his Hunter psychosis.

The next morning, pilot Jim Okonek flew Waterman to Anchorage, and Johnny committed himself to the psychiatric institute.

"I went to visit him at API," said Carl Tobin, a climbing friend. "He was sad that he was in there. It was a self-committal—he thought he was crazy—but it was really sad. He had a song he sang for me about his McKinley climb when he was 16. From his room he could look at the window and see McKinley."

Waterman left API after two weeks, convinced the doctors were conspiring to deny him his civil rights. He returned to Fairbanks and wrote to his father, who passed on the news of Johnny's misfortune to Snyder in a letter dated April 1980: "Johnny finally wrote. After flying out from McKinley after two weeks, he was preparing to go in again for an alpine-style attempt when the cabin containing all his gear burned. He kind of hit bottom, committed himself to a psychiatric institute in Anchorage briefly, but is now back in Fairbanks, working for the Census temporarily and wondering what to do in the future."

He had less than a year to live.

IT WAS NOT ENOUGH TO WRITE SONGS ABOUT THE MOUNTAIN. On December 11, 1980, reactivating his plans to solo McKinley, Johnny applied for a permit from the National Park Service, choosing "Lone Wolf" for his expedition name. He mailed his itinerary on a difficult-to-read postcard to Robert Gerhard, the supervisor of mountaineering rangers at Denali National Park and Preserve. Johnny would be hiking in with 14 days' worth of food and 18 days' worth of white gas. He had a cache of food and gas waiting for him at 2,000 feet on the Ruth Glacier. He was hoping to reach the summit of McKinley on March 20, whereupon he would descend either to the northeast, with 70 days' worth of food and fuel waiting for him at a cache on the Traleika Glacier, or to the southwest, where a hundred pounds of food awaited at a depot on the Kahiltna Glacier.

And so, in the second week of March, Waterman left once more to meet the mountain. "I won't be seeing you again," he told Hudson when he said good-bye to the bush pilot in Talkeetna—the same melodramatic farewell he'd spoken three years earlier when he set off to solo Mount Hunter.

"You'll be back," Hudson said as he had before, but this time, as Randall noted, the bush pilot had doubts.

The Lone Wolf turned off the highway to Fairbanks at Mile 141 and shuffled toward the Ruth Glacier on snowshoes. He eventually made his way up into the Don Sheldon Amphitheater of the glacier, one of the most spectacular mountain settings in North America. Rather than follow the itinerary he had outlined, he spent two weeks fussing over his equipment and socializing with various groups of climbers camped in the vicinity of Don Sheldon's Mountain House, an octagonal hut perched at an altitude of about 6,000 feet, along a stretch of ice where pilots can land ski planes.

Waterman radioed Hudson and asked him to bring in some prepacked boxes of supplies. When Hudson delivered the cartons to the Mountain

House, Waterman returned a small CB radio he'd borrowed from his pilot. "I won't be needing this anymore."

In late March, fresh off an ascent of the north buttress of the Rooster Comb, a distinctive ridge to the west of the amphitheater, Jay Kerr and Keith Royster had skied down the West Fork of the Ruth to unwind for a few days near the Mountain House. They had camped with a couple of other climbers in their party. Around midday on March 31, sitting outside on chairs made of snow blocks and sleeping pads, they saw a skier coming up the glacier. He was wearing blue pants and a blue jacket and was hauling a red plastic sled. More notably, he was traveling unroped and alone on a course that cut a direct line through the crevasse fields close to the flanks of Mount Barrille, where the Great Gorge opens out into the amphitheater. The line was exposing the skier to hazards he could have easily circumvented by swinging more widely around the mountain.

It was Johnny Waterman.

"We had a long visit with him—about three hours," Kerr recalled. "We asked him why he liked to go through crevasse fields, and he said every time he crossed a snow bridge and it didn't fall in, he felt reborn."

Kerr was struck by Waterman's odd kit. No tent. No sleeping bag. He had a bivouac sack, a one-piece snowmobile suit, vapor-barrier boots, snowshoes, and about 20 wands for marking trail. His provisions were more bizarre—14 days' worth of sugar, powdered milk, honey, and white flour and a bag of marijuana that was mostly sticks and lint. He said he was heading for the East Buttress and a steep, ambitious route that began at 9,000 feet in the North-west Fork of the Ruth and topped out at 15,000 feet in Thayer Basin. It was unclimbed at the time and remains so to this day.

According to park ranger Roger Robinson, "It's a suicide line; a lot of big avalanches come down it. It would be like playing Russian roulette."

On April 1, a climber named Kate Bull, who was camped with a friend just north of the Mountain House, stopped by Royster's camp for a visit. They brewed a pot of tea and lolled on the snow-block chairs. It was a painfully brilliant day. Waterman came skiing up, dressed in his blue jacket and a funky wool hat. His old orange frame pack looked oddly empty to Bull.

"What are you up to, John?" she asked, struck by the fact that Waterman wasn't wearing sunglasses or sunscreen.

"I'm going to climb the East Buttress." He sat down and had a cup of tea. He took some hits on a joint that was going around.

"Jeez, John, you should really have some sunscreen on," said Bull.

"Really? Wow! OK," said Waterman.

He lingered about half an hour, answering questions the climbers put to him about his solo ascent of Mount Hunter. At one point he commented on the size of the group that morning.

"That's the way to do it, all right," he said. "It's fun to have a big camp with a bunch of people."

And then he got up, shouldered his half-filled pack, and set off up the Ruth, headed for the Northwest Fork.

Later that day, Kerr and Royster skied back up the Ruth en route to the glacier's West Fork. For a while they followed the slot of Waterman's tracks. Twice they veered off the line for a safer course. After several miles, Waterman's tracks cut away to the right and angled up into the Northwest Fork toward an area notoriously riddled with crevasses. Kerr followed the line in the snow with his eyes until he saw a dot-size figure making a beeline through white swells of ice: John Waterman in the thrall of being reborn.

He was never seen again.

ON APRIL 4, A PARTY OF CLIMBING RANGERS who knew that Waterman was traveling solo tried to pick up his tracks on the Northwest Fork, but heavy snow and wind had erased them. On April 7, mountain guide Mike Covington skied into the Northwest Fork with two clients who intended to climb the Southeast Spur of McKinley. "They noticed a single set of tracks that were either ski tracks or those left by someone pulling a sled," according to the National Park Service incident report, published in the American Alpine Club's 1982 edition of *Accidents in North American Mountaineering*. "Covington felt that the tracks only went up the glacier and did not come back down. They also seemed to be oriented more toward the East Buttress than toward the other routes on the Southeast Spur or up the Northwest Fork. Because the area was very windswept from a storm the previous week, it was very hard to distinguish the tracks and no campsite was seen. From interviews with other climbers in the area, it appears that Waterman was the only one to travel up the Northwest Fork prior to Covington's group."

Covington eventually gave up the climb he'd planned; in his judgment the avalanche danger was too great.

On April 15, the National Park Service began a small-scale search for the Lone Wolf. U.S. Army Chinook helicopters from Fort Wainwright, near Fairbanks, were practicing high-altitude landings on McKinley; Roger Robinson went along and searched the flanks of the mountain. When Kerr returned to the Talkeetna Ranger Station with his report of his encounter with Waterman, a more extensive search began.

On April 21, ranger Dave Buchanan, whose life had been changed by the week he'd spent in a White Mountains winter mountaineering course led by Guy Waterman, called the postmaster in East Corinth and requested a message be passed to Johnny's father to call the Denali park headquarters. Buchanan was there to take the call when Guy telephoned.

"Guy was very calm when I described the situation to him," Buchanan said. "It almost felt like he had been expecting a call such as this. I'm sure when he got word of a phone message from a ranger in Alaska, he knew what it was probably about and had to contemplate what was coming as he hiked into town from his homestead. It was the hardest call I ever had to make as a ranger."

On April 22, Robinson and Covington flew up the Ruth in a Bell helicopter. They spent three hours searching in the area of the East Buttress. On the Northwest Fork they picked up the single set of tracks Covington had seen earlier.

"You could vaguely make them out," Robinson said, "and if you projected the line—boom! There was the camp. It was right in the middle of a crevasse field. We could see tracks going in but none coming out."

The pilot landed near what seemed to be an old tent site. Robinson belayed Covington from the struts of the helicopter as the guide cautiously probed the ground. Within a rope length, Covington found three thinly bridged crevasses. Both men, roped together, moved carefully around the tent site and vicinity, peering in crevasses for a body or some sign of Waterman. The only evidence they turned up was some pale human feces. Robinson scooped a sample into a Ziploc bag. "We knew Waterman's diet, and we thought if we analyzed it we would be able to say conclusively we'd found Waterman's last known camp," he recalled. But in the end the proof seemed pointless, and for years the stool sample stayed in the freezer at the Talkeetna ranger station until finally somebody in government service got tired of looking at it.

HAD HIS FATE BEEN SEALED BY AVALANCHES pouring off the East Buttress? His father was inclined to think so. In a mimeographed appeal for funds, Johnny had described himself as "the man who might truly disappear into the wilderness, and come to be a part of something greater than himself." Maybe it wasn't that he wanted to die so much as he no longer cared whether he lived. Now he could stop wondering why, after all the risks he'd taken, he was alive when so many of his friends, with their caution, were dead.

It was Guy who was left to grieve and wonder. Six months later, in September, Johnny was declared legally dead. Guy wrote a letter to his nephew Dane Waterman:

"As with a climb that didn't go, I keep revolving in my mind (and heart) where things took the direction they did, how things might have gone differently, what was going on inside, what kind of father I was, etc. The special quality to all this is the utter blank impossibility of calling it back and doing it again. That Jacobean ballad which I used to think was too plain to be moving, that goes 'Will ye nae come back again?'—that now says so much. When I was first up on the Franconia Ridge this year and looked over the non-road side, at all those mountains and ridges with cloud shadows on them, I thought, Why was there not this to come back to? Was there nothing for him to come back to?"

Is there any more heartrending question a father can ask himself than "What kind of father have I been?" Or, "How might I have done things differently?" Could any romanticism be more poignant than the elder Waterman's faith in the power of a Franconia prospect to draw his son home?

Earlier in the summer, on an errand of mourning, Guy had carried Johnny's old Limmer hiking boots up on that ridge. He had dropped down off the main trail, then bushwhacked to a dramatic promontory opposite Cannon Cliff. When he arrived, a thick mist enveloped the whole ridge. For three hours he worked in the perfect privacy of a cloud, gathering rocks and piling them into a cairn. *To guard against losing their way, the son would go out from the last identified cairn as far as he could and still see it. Then the father would go out from there as far as he could without losing sight of the son . . .*

In the center he placed his son's boots, pointing them toward Alaska as best he could gauge the direction. He laid a bouquet of wildflowers on the little tower of stones. He sang some songs and recited poems. And then he hiked out the way he'd come in. Strangely, when he regained the ridge—the ridge on which he would sit down to die in the snow 19 years later—he looked back at where he'd been and saw that the mist was gone, and there was Johnny's cairn in a ring of mountains, like the last cairn before they'd lost their way.

MARCH 2003

THE MAN WHO WALKED THROUGH TIME

By Michael Shnayerson

An improbable, enlightening lunch with Sir Wilfred Thesiger, who saw Africa before the automobile and Arabia before the oil boom.

FROM A HUMDRUM SUBURB SOUTH OF LONDON, my taxi turns up a hill, and the rows of semidetached houses fall away. Horses graze in large, fenced fields. At a gate that once led to a private estate, a sign announces the Friends of the Elderly. A long, meandering drive leads to two white buildings, institutional now but with a few grace notes of lingering grandeur. Scattered across a wide, round lawn on folding chairs are a dozen or so white-thatched nursing home residents, reading, watercoloring, or just staring into space. At the front door, by contrast, an alert figure sits erect in a gray three-piece suit, his red tie neatly knotted, his silver hair swept back from his craggy countenance, his hand on a carved-wood Zulu walking stick. As he rises slowly to greet me, I feel the keenness of his gaze: proud, inquisitive, reserved but welcoming. The greatest living explorer of the 20th century has been waiting for me. Thank God I'm just a minute or two late.

At 91, Sir Wilfred Thesiger is still more active than most of his peers. With effort but determination, the explorer who once crossed unmapped desert sands leads the way up a front hall staircase. A fellow resident looks up enviously from his walker. "I don't know how he does that," he mutters. Down a winding hall, Thesiger unlocks the door to his modest, windowed room. Inside are a narrow bed, two upholstered chairs, a mahogany desk, and, on the walls, tokens from his restless, remarkable life. One framed photograph shows the 1930 coronation party of Haile Selassie in Ethiopia: There, in the fourth row, is 20-year-old Thesiger, at the start of his adventures. Near the photo hang a silver ceremonial dagger with a dazzlingly ornate case and two sheathed swords, one silver and one gold, all gifts from Arab sheikhs, given to Thesiger during his legendary Saudi Arabian desert travels of 1945 to 1950. On the bed is a striped African bedspread from his later years in Kenya. Here, too, on his old wooden desk, are page proofs of his latest, and almost certainly last, book: an album of black-and-white photos from his travels in the Middle East and Africa, all taken by Thesiger, many never before seen, titled *A Vanished World* (HarperCollins).

The book that Thesiger is best known for—the one that made him, to his own surprise, a writer and that put him in the pantheon with Mungo Park, Richard Burton, and T. E. Lawrence—is *Arabian Sands*. An instant classic when it appeared in 1959, it remains one of the most extraordinary travel chronicles ever published. (It was ranked number five in ADVENTURE's roundup of the 100 greatest adventure books, in the July/August 2001 issue.) In terse, understated prose, Thesiger describes setting out with a band of Bedouins into a region so desolate and harsh that it was known as the Empty Quarter. The *bedu,* as they were called, were its only inhabitants, crossing the sands by camel and gleefully raiding border tribes when supplies ran low. Thesiger was determined to travel with the hardiest and most daring of these tribes, the Rashid. He vowed to live up to their standards, to be as spartan as they were, and to be the first Westerner accepted as one of them. This, to him, was the gratification of travel in its highest form. Anything less was mere entertainment.

Thesiger spent most of the succeeding decades as a nomad, living among other remote tribes. Only failing eyesight and the concurrent loss of two close friends in Kenya led him to move in 1994 to a London apartment and then to a retirement home. One of his three younger brothers is still alive and occasionally visits him here. His good friend and literary executor, Alexander Maitland, visits, too. But the price of a nomadic life is all too apparent. Not very many people come, and Thesiger, private by nature, appears not to converse much with his fellow residents. Do they even know who he is? "I don't know," he says dryly. "I haven't asked them." His innate dignity makes him a hard man to read. Is he put off by my intrusion? Or is there in his gaze a glint of pleasure that a journalist has come to pay homage?

Thesiger motions me to a green-velvet-cushioned chair, which I draw close enough to his own that our knees nearly touch, for he speaks haltingly in a soft, burred voice. He fixes me with those keen eyes, which are set within a deeply sun-lined, angular face whose spatula-like nose was broken more than once in his boxing youth. After a pleasantry or two, he awaits his cue. I nod to the framed pictures of his parents that grace his bedroom dresser. They look so elegant and British Empire formal. I know that his father, also named Wilfred, was England's minister in Ādīs Ābeba (Addis Ababa), Abyssinia (now Ethiopia), when his first son and namesake was born, in June 1910. The Honorable Wilfred died of a heart attack less than a decade later. I wonder aloud, without quite spelling it out, how close the boy was to this ramrod-straight product of the Victorian age—if perhaps, to put a contemporary spin on it, the son embarked on a life of travel to connect with his lost father.

"We were very, very close," he says, somewhat affronted. "It was a tragedy that he died when I was eight. He had already begun to treat me like a companion. In Ethiopia, when he went out to hunt a lion, he took me along. He was already teaching me to shoot."

The Honorable Wilfred had come to Abyssinia as a civil servant, not as an adventurer. Nevertheless, Thesiger says, "just to get to Ethiopia in those days was an adventure. There was no railway; there were no cars. Very soon after he and my mother arrived there, I was born in a mud hut. The hut is still there, by the way. There's a notice saying I was born there."

From outside Thesiger's open window, a milk truck backs up to the kitchen to make a delivery. As its loud engine idles, Thesiger looks off in its direction with a grimace. He hates all cars and airplanes. He calls the invention of the internal combustion engine the single biggest disaster in history. In most of the places he traveled, automobiles had not yet penetrated. Yet only a few years after his peregrinations across the Arabian sands, oil exploration began in earnest. Jeeps, then roads and oil drills, soon followed; almost overnight, the Bedouin culture virtually disappeared. Thesiger was not only one of the first Westerners but among the last to see life in the Empty Quarter as it had been lived for thousands of years.

THE YOUNG THESIGER HAD BEEN SENT to the British boarding school St. Aubyn's just before his father died. He would go on to Eton, then to Oxford, but he knew where his heart still lay: "All the time I was in my schools, as soon as I got into bed, I was dreaming of Ethiopia. I remembered the names of the mountains and their shapes. I was longing, longing to go back there. I felt that that was where I belonged."

Finally a personal invitation to do just that came from a onetime ally of Thesiger's father: Ras Tafari, the regent of Abyssinia, who was about to be named Emperor Haile Selassie for uniting his country after years of tribal warfare. Thesiger journeyed to the ceremony and was met at Ādīs Ābeba on October 28, 1930, by the emperor himself. Days of great pageantry followed, the last hurrah of old-world Abyssinian splendor, marred only by the obstreperous presence of writer Evelyn Waugh, who, as a correspondent covering the scene, made his contempt for Ethiopians and English alike all too clear. Thesiger was annoyed, but he soon left the pomp and politics of the capital for a big-game hunting expedition in country inhabited by the murderous Danakil—a safari that became his first real adventure.

"We were just going on the edge of it," Thesiger says, as if there were nothing exotic in that. But that was close enough to provoke an encounter with a tribe notorious for attacking strangers, especially white ones, and castrating them. "That was the lure of it! The more dangerous it was, the more of a challenge it was. I wasn't looking for an easy trip where I could shoot a few animals and come back without risk. I wanted a serious challenge. The three previous expeditions to Danakil country had been killed. One was an army that went down to incorporate Danakil country into Ethiopia; they were completely wiped out."

Even then, Thesiger was more interested in the people of the region he was exploring than he was in the region itself. In retrospect, the canon of his writings is almost entirely about cultural customs; the landscape is merely a backdrop. He was fascinated by the way the Danakil wore leather thongs around their stomachs, one for each victim they'd castrated. "You could see by looking at a man's decorations how many he had castrated and killed," he says. "I got so accustomed to it that I found myself looking at a Danakil and thinking, Gosh, he's only killed two."

Thesiger learned early on that he preferred to travel without English companions and wanted little to do with English culture. "I found England intensely boring," he says. "Playing cricket and that sort of thing. I found it appalling." He didn't see himself as a travel writer yet or as an explorer, and he saw himself even less as an anthropologist. He just wanted the life of a big-game hunter, far from England, in one or another of the world's wild and beautiful places.

With a sterling pedigree but not much fortune, Thesiger followed his heart by joining the Sudan Political Service and serving in the British colony's unmapped interior, where he found a mentor in the district commissioner, Guy Moore. "We were the only two Europeans in this vast district. I couldn't have found a man who knew better exactly what I wanted. He encouraged me to be with the Arabs. He was viewed as an eccentric by the rest of the political service, but we understood each other perfectly."

To the shock of their colleagues, Moore and Thesiger would eat with their servants and sleep on the bare ground during their travels. In the long evenings, Moore told his protégé about the Empty Quarter and urged him to go. Unfortunately, the Second World War intervened. Thesiger declared he would join the Ethiopian Army to fight the Italians. "Don't be an ass, stay here," Moore advised. "I know you'll get your chance; just wait for it." And indeed Thesiger did, with a tour of duty that gave him the opportunity to help liberate the whole of southern Ethiopia.

"At one point, I met up with an Italian army of 2,000 men," Thesiger recounts. "They knew the war was over, so I rode up to them with a white flag, and I said, 'I want you to surrender to me. If you do, I'll be able to take you through Danakil country and hand you over properly as prisoners of war. If you don't accept this, the Ras's [Haile Selassie's] soldiers are arriving soon, and they'll massacre you, after all you've done to these people.' They said, 'We'll accept your terms.' They all had rifles, of course, so I told them to pull the bolts out of their rifles and put all the bolts in a bag, and I loaded it on a mule. They rode through the country with their guns and ammunition, but they couldn't do anything with them."

To venture into the Empty Quarter after the war, Thesiger needed a sponsor, both to pay his way and to secure permission from the sultan of Masqaṭ (Muscat) to travel into the desert from Arabia's south coast. He found one in the Desert Locust Research Organization's O. B. Lean, who hired the 35-year-old war veteran to look for locust outbreaks in the region. Though the Empty Quarter had been traversed by two previous explorers, vast regions remained unmapped. To Thesiger, these loomed as the last great challenge of desert exploration.

He started from Oman's coastal town of Salālah with a party of camels and 30 members of the Bait Kathir tribe, which lived on the Quarter's outskirts. They were the only helpers he could get at the outset, but to cross the desert, he needed the real desert Bedouins: the Rashid. When he came across a small party of them at the oasis of Mughshin, he let most of the Bait Kathir go back and forged happily into the longest stretch of his journey with companions he knew he could trust to get him through. One was bin Kabina, a proud teenage boy hardened by life in the desert. Another, whom Thesiger met soon after, was bin Ghabaisha, also young and fit. Both would accompany Thesiger on nearly all his Empty Quarter travels—devoted friends whom Thesiger came to adore and to whom he dedicated *Arabian Sands*. Now both are septuagenarians in Saudi Arabia, living near each other, with camels and cars, beneficiaries of all the cultural changes that Thesiger abhors. "They're not the same people I knew," Thesiger told Michael Asher, whose first-rate biography of the explorer was published in 1994. "They're not the same people."

As a Westerner, of course, Thesiger had to prove himself to his new companions, traveling as they did with a minimum of water and food, sleeping on the sands, and enduring daylong treks, week after week. More than once, the travelers ran out of water and had to wait until they reached the next well, which was no more than a sandy hole containing water as brackish and foul-tasting as camel urine. Thesiger was often hungry and thirsty to a degree no city dweller could comprehend, but he had no complaints. Indeed, he seemed to relish deprivation.

"I wanted to identify myself with the people I was traveling with," Thesiger says a bit testily. "This was the whole thing. I didn't want to travel with these people and sit at a table and have a European meal. I wanted to be accepted by them. So they'd cook their meals and then bring me a portion."

Thesiger looks out the window, as if seeing again the campfire of one particular day on that trip. "We were desperately hungry," he says after a pause. "We hadn't eaten meat for the better part of a month. One of us killed a hare, and bin Kabina cooked it for dinner. At one point, I called out, 'Is it ready yet?' And he said, 'Oh, not quite. Another few minutes.' A few minutes passed, and then suddenly he said, 'Oh, God.' Coming toward us, out of the desert, were three Arabs. So we sat them down and made them welcome: 'You're a thousand times welcome. . . .' Then bin Kabina picked up our dinner and he put it down in front of them. 'You are our guests,' he said.

" 'No, no, we can't do that,' they said. 'You must eat with us.'

" 'No, no, God has brought you. You're our guests.'

"So we sat there and watched them eat our dinner. That was the standard of the desert."

FOR LUNCH ON THIS BRIGHT, CLEAR DAY, Thesiger suggests the golf course restaurant, a quarter mile's walk or so up the meandering drive. He puts a hand on my arm for support, having left his stick upstairs, and we make our way together, step by careful step. I can't help but think of the 100,000 miles he estimates he's walked in his time—in the desert he traveled mostly on foot, so as not to tire the camels—and of how this walk for him now is an expedition in itself. "It's an honor to walk with you," I venture. Thesiger waves off the thought with a snort: Sentiment of this sort clearly embarrasses, or even annoys, him.

The restaurant, it turns out, is a pub attached to a vast convention-hall-like dining room on which, we are informed, 65 ladies are about to descend for lunch. Hastily we retreat to one of the outside tables and ponder our meager menus. A bit hesitantly, Thesiger orders an omelette; I do the same. The young waiter regards him with mild curiosity; in his three-piece suit and red suspenders the old adventurer looks like an Etonian from another era, which of course he is.

I mention I was struck, in reading *Arabian Sands,* by the seeming incongruities of the Rashid: As noble as they were, they also delighted in raiding any tribe they could, stealing camels, killing if necessary, demanding money for safe passage, hiring themselves out as mercenaries to one tribe to rob another, then doing the same in reverse. Once again, Thesiger reacts with some exasperation. "That was their sport!" he says. "Like football. But if they met anyone from those tribes while they were traveling, even Arabs from a hostile tribe, they'd defend them and look after them, and it would be their duty to die in their defense, because those Arabs had become their traveling companions."

On his first crossing, and on those that followed, all his companions were male. In fact, aside from his mother and a beloved housekeeper, women appear to have played no role in his life. In all those travels, I ask, did he ever feel the need for female companionship?

"No," Thesiger says shortly. "Women have never really come into my life. They've never been there."

The open admiration with which Thesiger writes of bin Kabina and bin Ghabaisha, extolling their strong good looks as much as their physical prowess and moral code, can strike readers today as almost erotic. Was there, I ask, a sort of platonic ideal at work?

"Is that what a platonic ideal is?" Thesiger asks dryly. He pauses. "Perhaps. There was no question of sex."

Our omelettes arrive overcooked on the outside and runny inside. Thesiger picks at his dispiritedly. Certainly he'd rather be in the Empty Quarter than here. For a moment or two, we eat in silence. What was it, I finally ask, that made the Empty Quarter so compelling? Wasn't it just a desert of endless dunes, like rolling ocean waves? "There was beauty in the color of the sands," Thesiger says. "To me it had an appeal. The emptiness of it. And the silence."

On one of his trips, Thesiger was nearly swallowed up by that silence, obligated to travel a distance of days without a local guide. Thesiger had told bin Kabina and bin Ghabaisha that he could guide them himself using his compass. For eight days, they headed through the silence and vastness of the desert for a village called Yabrīn, knowing that if they were one or two degrees off their course, they would miss the town, run out of water, and die.

"No, I didn't feel scared," Thesiger says when I ask. "And I thought if we missed by a bit, we'd see camel tracks from parties going to and coming from Yabrīn."

Still, I suggest, it was amazing that his companions trusted Thesiger with their lives. "I'd have trusted one of them if he'd said, 'I know the way,' " he says. "On this occasion, I said, 'I can do it with my compass,' and they believed me. I could."

In *Arabian Sands,* Thesiger describes the humble simplicity of Abū Ẓaby (Abu Dhabi), then a waterfront village on the northeast edge of the Empty Quarter. In that region, Thesiger met the sheikhs who gave him the dagger and swords that adorn his wall. One was Sheikh Shakhbut, who saw how profoundly his country might be changed by the imminent arrival of the oil companies. Fearful of the corrupting influence of wealth on his people, Sheikh Shakhbut kept all proceeds from the oil companies in a trunk under his bed. Another was Zayed, a noble sportsman with whom Thesiger went falconing. But Zayed was one of the sheikhs who encouraged the oil companies to come, a decision about which Thesiger clearly has mixed feelings. "Shakhbut was a reactionary; Zayed was the driving force. He said, 'This is where our future lies.' "

At the time, Zayed probably saved Thesiger's life by giving him a letter that enabled him to complete his circuit of the Empty Quarter through Oman, to the east. The Christian-hating imam of Oman heard about Thesiger's presence in his country and threatened to imprison him in an underground dungeon—a cell that Thesiger viewed, decades later, as a returning honored guest. Perhaps, in a sense, the imam was right to resent Thesiger. Though the Christian meant well, he did produce the first rough maps of Oman and the rest of the Empty Quarter he traveled through. Those were maps the oil companies used. "Regretfully," Thesiger allows, "in some of the areas, I knew they could go in because of my maps."

Thesiger's Empty Quarter travels stopped in 1950, because the imam and other local leaders wanted no more of the Englishman in their lands. But Thesiger had no regrets; he had accomplished his goal. And within a breathtakingly short time, he knew, oil would change everything for the Rashid. "I felt such keen resentment, anticipating how much it would change their lives. Which of course it did. It lowered their standards. Once they realized the amount of money they could make, their whole attitude changed. As did their lives. Before, honorable deeds were what defined them. Their reputations were based on generosity and loyalty and courage. The deed might happen 600 miles away, but word would get about. And the highest goal was to be spoken of with respect. Once they had cars, none of these values meant anything anymore. It was the hardness of life in the desert that had produced these standards."

After the tragic attacks of September 11—which occurred several weeks after our lunch—the cultural changes Thesiger saw beginning in Saudi Arabia would assume a new and troubling resonance. And though Thesiger's books remain a vital resource in illuminating the culture of the Muslim world, the author today declines to elaborate. "I'm not qualified to speak about that," he says. "It's not for me to say."

OVER THE YEARS, Thesiger attracted his share of critics who felt that his perspective as a traveler had a paternalistic tinge to it: Primitive tribes should stay primitive for their own good, because wealthy Westerners knew what was best for them, Westerners who went home to enjoy the fruits of capitalism they hoped to withhold from primitive peoples. Of course, Thesiger never did go home to become, by some moral measures, a hypocrite. From the Empty Quarter he went to southern Iraq to live with the Marsh Arabs in their raftlike homes and fish for his food. But the assassination of Iraq's royal family in 1958 made staying there impossible.

Only then did Thesiger sit down to write about his travels. He wrote *Arabian Sands* in longhand with pen and paper. It was a sensation when it appeared, not only for the uniqueness of his travels but for the spare beauty of his prose.

"No man can live this life and emerge unchanged," he writes in one passage. "He will carry, however faint, the imprint of the desert, the brand which marks the nomad; and he will have within him the yearning to return, weak or insistent according to his nature. For this cruel land can cast a spell which no temperate clime can match."

On a small bookshelf in the corner of his room, I notice after our return, Thesiger keeps several hardcover copies of each of his books—every author's forgivable conceit. In addition to *Arabian Sands,* I see *The Marsh Arabs* (1964), *Desert, Marsh and Mountain* (1979), *Visions of a Nomad* (1987), and his autobiography, *The Life of My Choice* (1987). His pictures and writings about Iraq's Marsh Arabs are fascinating and poignant—another lost culture, this one all but destroyed by Saddam Hussein in the wake of the Gulf

War—but ultimately not as compelling as *Arabian Sands,* because the Marsh Arabs lived a more sedentary life. "I'm convinced that the easier the life, the lower the standards," he says. "It's the meeting of challenges that produces such remarkable results."

After Iraq, Thesiger took more episodic trips: to Kenya, Sudan, Tanganyika (now Tanzania), and Morocco. In Afghanistan, he climbed mountains as the Afghans did, without ropes. "I saw no point in using ropes, because they didn't, and I was trying to insinuate myself with them." In Kenya, he was knocked down by a charging lion but managed to stick his gun in the lion's ear and fire.

Though Thesiger's time in Kenya is the least important chapter of his travel career, it is also the longest: For 26 years, off and on, he lived among the Samburu, a tribe, he says, about which he liked everything, "except that there was a good deal of raiding and counterraiding."

Even upon his arrival in Kenya, however, Thesiger had to accept that cars and planes had spoiled the region's pastoral purity. Whether he liked it or not, his first, seminal books now stood as last reports of a pre-industrial age. Today, though, Thesiger's regrets are also tinged with pride that his travels are, in retrospect, unique and unreproducible. As I prepare to go, I mention that I recently interviewed another intrepid explorer named J. Michael Fay for this magazine. Thesiger raises an eyebrow. "Yes?"

Fay, I explain, marched across nearly 2,000 miles of African jungle, dressed in shorts and sandals, with a crew of Bambendjellé Pygmies, carrying only the most basic supplies.

"How long did it take him?"

"Fifteen months."

"Hmm . . ."

One difference, I add, is that Fay had a satellite phone, so if he ran out of food, he could call to arrange a food drop by plane.

"Well, you see, that wrecks it!" Thesiger exclaims. "Then you know he's in no danger. If anything happened, he could just call and be collected. The thing about my journeys was that you knew once the telegraph lines dropped out of sight and the railway station fell away, nobody knew where you were or what you were doing. You came into Danakil country or the Empty Quarter and no one knew if they'd killed you or hadn't killed you. A telephone would have ruined the whole thing. You couldn't call and say, 'I have a headache, would you drop me some pills?' Now you can take a car or bring a phone. The challenge is gone."

Thesiger sees me downstairs, leading the way again, to my waiting taxi. At the front door of the retirement home, he takes my hand with a strong grip and, for the first time, flashes a gentle, almost shy smile. "Thank you for coming," he says with feeling. "Come back soon."

JANUARY/FEBRUARY 2002

Postscript: Thesiger died in his Surrey retirement home on August 24, 2003. He was 93.

ACKNOWLEDGMENTS

THIS ANTHOLOGY COMBINES the best work of many National Geographic ADVEN-TURE writers and editors over the last decade. An especially deep bow goes to ADVENTURE's current staff for their help in the daunting task of narrowing down the final selections, in particular John Rasmus, Stephen Byers, Michael Benoist, Mark Adams, and Cliff Ransom. Special thanks are due to ADVENTURE's art director, David McKenna, and to the indispensable Ryan Bradley, without whose tireless literary efforts this big horse would never have crossed the finish line.

Great thanks is also owed to the following contributors for permission to reprint copyrighted material previously published in *National Geographic Adventure*:

Scott Anderson: Coming of Age at Band-i-Amir (May 2007)

Jon Bowermaster: Storming the Islands of Fire and Ice (Winter 1999)

Chip Brown: The Last Cairn (March 2003)

Tim Cahill: The Moonbow Chronicles (May 2002) and The Lure of Impossible Places (October 2003)

Philip Caputo: Prisoner of Hill 52 (Winter 1999) and Among the Man-Eaters (May/June 2000)

Tom Clynes: Dangerous Medicine (May/June 2001)

Gretel Ehrlich: The Vanishing Breed (March 2008)

Michael Finkel: Thirteen Ways of Looking at a Void (September/October 2001)

Laurence Gonzales: Land of the Lost (November/December 2001)

Charles Graeber: Being the Boatman (September 2002)

Peter Heller: The Whale Warriors (May 2006)

Sebastian Junger: Colter's Way (Spring 1999) and The Lion in Winter (March/April 2001)

Paul Kvinta: Stomping Grounds (August 2004)

Peter Matthiessen: Emperors at the End of the Earth (November 2003)

Robert Young Pelton: The Legend of Heavy D & the Boys (March 2002)

David Quammen: The River Jumps Over the Mountain (January/February 2002)

David Roberts: Out of Thin Air (Fall 1999) and Finding Everett Ruess (April/May 2009)

Kira Salak: Places of Darkness (December 2003/January 2004) and Hell and Back (March 2006)

Michael Shnayerson: The Man Who Walked Through Time (January/February 2002)

Peter Lane Taylor: Off the Face of the Earth (June/July 2004)

CONTRIBUTORS

Scott Anderson is a veteran war correspondent, a contributing editor at ADVENTURE, and a contributing writer for the *New York Times Magazine*. He is the author of the critically acclaimed novels *Triage* and *Moonlight Hotel*, and the nonfiction book *The Man Who Tried to Save the World*, and, with his brother Jon Lee Anderson, *War Zones*. His work has appeared in *Vanity Fair, Esquire*, and *Harper's*. Anderson lives in upstate New York with his wife, the filmmaker Nanette Burstein.

Jon Bowermaster's OCEANS 8 project spanned a decade and took him and his teams around the world by sea kayak; six of the expeditions turned into feature stories for ADVENTURE. He is the author of ten books, his most recent being *Wildbeest in a Rainstorm*, a collection of profiles. He has received six grants from the National Geographic Expeditions Council. When on land, Bowermaster lives in Stone Ridge, New York.

Chip Brown, a former reporter for the *Washington Post,* is the author of two nonfiction books, *Afterwards, You're a Genius: Faith, Medicine and the Metaphysics of Healing* and *Good Morning Midnight: Life and Death in the Wild*. He is a contributing writer at the *New York Times Magazine* and has written articles for more than 30 national magazines including the *New Yorker, Harper's, Vanity Fair,* and *GQ*. He lives in New York City with his wife, Kate Betts, and their two children Oliver and India.

Tim Cahill's books include *Road Fever, Jaguars Ripped My Flesh,* and *A Wolverine Is Eating My Leg*. He won a National Magazine Award in 2003 for his essay "The Lure of Impossible Places" in ADVENTURE, where he is a contributing editor. The same year he received a Lowell Thomas Gold Award from the Society of American Travel Writers. His work has appeared in *Rolling Stone, Esquire,* the *New York Times Book Review,* and *Outside,* where he was a founding editor. He is also the co-author of two Academy Award-nominated IMAX documentaries. Cahill lives in Montana, in the shadow of the Crazy Mountains.

Philip Caputo is an ADVENTURE contributing editor who served in the United States Marine Corps in Vietnam from 1964 to 1967. In 1973, he shared the Pulitzer Prize for investigative reporting and was a finalist for the 1981 National Book Award for *Horn of Africa*. He is the author of 12 other books of fiction and nonfiction, including *In the Shadows of the Morning,* a collection of his travel writing, and *Acts of Faith,* a novel set in contemporary Sudan. His new novel, *Crossers,* takes place on the Mexican border and will be published by Alfred A. Knopf in October 2009.

Tom Clynes is a writer and photographer who covers environmental issues, science, and adventure travel. A contributing editor at ADVENTURE, Clynes has tracked ecomercenaries in Central Africa, retraced Edmund Hillary's climbs in New Zealand, learned to fly in the Australian outback, and chased the ghosts of outlaws and free-dom fighters in Iceland, Jamaica, and Vanuatu for the magazine. He lives in rural Vermont with his wife and two sons.

Gretel Ehrlich's writing has appeared in *The New York Times, National Geographic, Harper's, The Atlantic, Time, Life, Architectural Digest,* and *Audubon,* among other publications. Her ADVENTURE story on the Inuit of Greenland was nominated for a National Magazine Award. Her books include *The Solace of Open Spaces, A Match to the Heart, The Future of Ice,* and *This Cold Heaven.* She lives in Wyoming.

Michael Finkel has reported from more than 40 nations across six continents, cov-ering topics ranging from the elephant poachers of central Africa to the conflicts in Afghanistan and Israel to the international black market in human organs. His articles have appeared in *National Geographic, The Atlantic, Rolling Stone, Esquire, Vanity Fair, Sports Illustrated,* and the *New York Times Magazine.* He is the author of the book *True Story,* about having his identity stolen by an accused murderer. He lives with his family in Bozeman, Montana.

Laurence Gonzales won the 2001 and 2002 National Magazine Awards for stories in ADVENTURE. Since 1970, his essays have appeared in such periodicals as *Harper's* and *Rolling Stone.* He has published a dozen books, including two award-winning collections of essays, three novels, and the best-sellers *Deep Survival* and *Everyday Survival.* Alfred A. Knopf will publish his novel, *Lucy,* in the spring of 2010.

Charles Graeber is a National Magazine Award-nominated contributing editor at ADVENTURE and *Wired.* A former breakfast chef and bar columnist, he has also writ-ten for the *New Yorker, New York Magazine, The New York Times, GQ,* and *Vogue.* Born in Iowa, he now moves between a Brooklyn apartment and a retired icebreaker anchored off Nantucket. His first book will be published in the summer of 2010.

Peter Heller is a longtime contributor to NPR, a contributing editor at ADVENTURE, and the author of three books of literary nonfiction including *The Whale Warriors.* He has worked as a dishwasher, construction worker, logger, offshore fisherman, kayak instructor, river guide, and a world-class pizza deliveryman. He is currently living out of a trailer in Mexico and learning to surf.

Sebastian Junger, a contributing editor at ADVENTURE and *Vanity Fair,* is the best-selling author of *The Perfect Storm* and a National Magazine Award-winning jour-nalist, reporting on such issues as war, terrorism, and human rights from war-torn regions around the world. His next book is about Afghanistan.

Paul Kvinta's story "Stomping Grounds" was a finalist for the National Magazine Award. The piece also won the Daniel Pearl Award for Outstanding Story from the South Asian Journalists Association. A contributing editor at ADVENTURE, in 2007 Kvinta won a Knight Journalism Fellowship at Stanford University and a Templeton-Cambridge Jour-nalism Fellowship in Science and Religion at the University of Cambridge in England.

Peter Matthiessen is a naturalist, novelist, and Zen priest who, in 1974, was named to the American Academy of Arts and Letters. He has published more than 20 books over 50 years, including *Shadow Country* and *The Snow Leopard,* winners of the National Book Award for fiction and nonfiction, respectively. He is the only writer to win in both categories. He lives in Sagaponack, New York.

Robert Young Pelton has witnessed 36 wars, been kidnapped in Colombia, and survived a plane crash in Borneo. He is the author of *The World's Most Dangerous Places, Come Back Alive, The Adventurist, Three Worlds Gone Mad,* and *Licensed to Kill.* Pelton's experiences with U.S. Special Forces in Afghanistan will be detailed in his upcoming book *The Regulators, How a Down on His Luck Warlord and 12 Renegade Green Berets Won the War on Terror.*

David Quammen, a contributing editor at ADVENTURE and contributing writer for *National Geographic* magazine, is the author of 11 books, including *The Song of the Dodo* and *The Reluctant Mr. Darwin.* His most recent book, as general editor, is an illustrated edition of Charles Darwin's *On the Origin of Species.* Quammen is the recipient of three National Magazine Awards. He lives in Montana.

David Roberts first wrote about Everett Ruess in the premiere issue of ADVENTURE and since then has authored more than 40 articles for the magazine. Roberts has written 17 books on mountaineering, the outdoors, and the history of the American Southwest, most recently *The Last of His Kind.* His essays and articles have also appeared in *National Geographic, The Atlantic, Men's Journal,* and *Outside.* He lives in Cambridge, Massachusetts.

Kira Salak won the PEN award for Journalism for her story "Places of Darkness." A National Geographic Emerging Explorer and contributing editor of ADVENTURE, she was the first woman to traverse Papua New Guinea and to kayak solo 600 miles on the Niger River to Timbuktu. Salak is the author of the novel *The White Mary* and two nonfiction books, *The Cruelest Journey* and *Four Corners: A Journey Into the Heart of Papua New Guinea,* which was a *New York Times* Notable Travel Book. She holds a Ph.D. in English and lives in Montana.

Michael Shnayerson is a contributing editor at both ADVENTURE and *Vanity Fair.* He is the author of *Irwin Shaw: A Biography, The Car That Could: The Inside Story of GM's Revolutionary Electric Vehicle,* and *The Killers Within.* His latest book is *Coal River,* which tells the true story of how the residents of a West Virginia valley fought to stop mountaintop coal mining. He lives in Bridgehampton, New York.

Peter Lane Taylor is an award-winning author, photographer, and filmmaker specializing in science and adventure. His first book, *Science at the Extreme,* chronicled the work of researchers who risk their lives for scientific data. His other stories and expeditions have taken him to Antarctica, South America, Africa, and deep inside underwater caves. Taylor lives in Lansdowne, Pennsylvania, with his wife, Meggen.